# INFORMATION SEARCHING THEORY AND PRACTICE

# Information Searching
# Theory and Practice

VOLUME II OF THE SELECTED WORKS OF

## Marcia J. Bates

PROFESSOR EMERITA, DEPARTMENT OF INFORMATION STUDIES
GRADUATE SCHOOL OF EDUCATION AND INFORMATION STUDIES
UNIVERSITY OF CALIFORNIA, LOS ANGELES

Ketchikan Press
BERKELEY

Edited by Marcia J. Bates

Published by Ketchikan Press, Berkeley, CA

SERIES DESIGN & PRODUCTION
Chris Hall

ISBN 978-0-9817584-2-8

PUBLISHER CATALOGING-IN-PUBLICATION DATA
Names: Bates, Marcia J.
Title: Information searching theory and practice: volume II of the selected works of
Marcia J. Bates / edited by Marcia J. Bates.
Description: Berkeley, CA : Ketchikan Press, 2016. | Series: Selected works of Marcia J. Bates |
Includes index.
Identifiers: ISBN 978-0-9817584-2-8
Subjects: LCSH: Information science. | Online bibliographic searching. | Electronic information
resource searching. | Online library catalogs—Subject access.
Classification: LCC Z665.B316 2016 v. 2| DDC 020 -- dc23

*Text set in Calluna 9.5/12.5; heads and captions set in Calluna Sans*

*To my mentors*

*Carl Baumann*
POMONA COLLEGE

*William J. Paisley*
STANFORD UNIVERSITY

# Contents

# Acknowledgments

My heartfelt thanks go to the talented people who worked with me in preparing these volumes: Chris Hall for his book design, illustrations, and typesetting, Nicholas Carroll and Chris Hall for production management, Leonard Rosenbaum for indexing, and Doris Lechner for proofreading.

I also want to thank my parents, especially my mother, for their hard work in putting me through college. My mother made it possible for me to have the education she could only dream of.

*—Marcia J. Bates*

# Introduction to the series

The iconic image associated with Silicon Valley's new world of information technology is that of two guys in a garage tinkering with and launching new inventions that revolutionize the world. The founders of Hewlett-Packard, the founders of Apple, and, more recently, the founders of Google all fit the mold. Investors pour millions, nay, billions of dollars into these projects, with subsequent phenomenally great reward, as the products are taken up and used throughout the world. Many of these products involve information storage, transfer, and use. The average person's sense of how information can be found and utilized, sent to friends, or support study has changed drastically.

But there was a prehistory to this story. People have needed and used information since prehistoric times. They even needed it—a lot—just before the Internet exploded in people's consciousness in the 1990's. What did they do then?

It turns out that the several forms of limited information technologies available then—when investment in information retrieval research was a pittance—forced those of us who thought about these questions to become very knowledgeable about the inner workings of information seeking, the expressing of information needs, the methods of describing and indexing information, as well as the acts of searching, retrieving and utilizing information. In the field of information science, we had to understand the process at a granular level, in order to take advantage of the then-available technologies, which were usually vastly more limited than today's capabilities. We were forced to understand the process deeply, in the way that pilots used to develop a bone-deep feel for flying, before the advent of the automatic pilot and the disengagement by pilots from the core processes of keeping a plane in the air.

Many of the directions we took are now difficult to pursue, because the giant search corporations like Google and Yahoo have labeled all this intellectual territory as proprietary. In a *New Yorker* article ("When G.M. Was Google," *New Yorker,* Dec. 1, 2014), Nicholas Lemann describes a technical problem that Google's engineers "solved." But that problem was well known for decades in the information sciences, and had been addressed in a number of ways in both manual and automated systems. Google might have solved it simply by *doing a search* on the research literature of the subject.

The purpose of these volumes is to republish selected significant publications of mine, representing my work on the topics of information, the information professions, information seeking and searching, information organization, and user-centered design of information systems. The papers demonstrate the work we in my field did to understand information behavior and information system development and use, back when we had to burrow deeply into the human relationship with information in a way that is seldom done these days. There is a great deal to learn from that earlier work, and a great deal of knowledge that is being overlooked in these days of rapture with the new technologies. When the intoxication fades a bit, and people return to wanting to improve the actual ways people find and use information, then perhaps some of the approaches explored in these papers will regain prominence.

One of the "problems" of information science is that it continues to have associations with the discipline that has dealt with information storage and retrieval the longest: library science. It makes sense: There were decades of transition from all-paper information storage to various sorts of electronic storage and retrieval. The transition involved many stages of development, using various combinations of paper and electronic information processing. The computers we worked with started out with minuscule amounts of storage and processing power, and gradually managed to handle vastly more of our storage-intensive resources.

This association of information science with library science is not a problem because of the latter field's expertise and long experience with information. Rather, it is a problem only because of the astounding degree of negative stereotyping conventionally associated with the field. Could there be a greater contrast than that between the two guys in a garage, and the hermetic librarian hunched over his desk, protecting his collection from defilement by users, or the virginal spinster with the pencil stuck in the bun at the back of her head, presiding over the reference desk?

I have been astonished countless times in my life at the stubborn persistence of these stereotypes, despite all facts to the contrary. Every Christmas we are treated to a showing on television of the film *It's a Wonderful Life*, wherein, during the dream sequence, the wife of Jimmy Stewart's George Bailey, who would now have never married without him, becomes a librarian, and is shown locking the library door at night, as she comes home from her lonely work. An analysis of the social role of this librarian stereotype has yet to be written. It is a charged and deeply meaningful archetype in the popular consciousness, and deserves full analysis. In the meantime, however, this stereotype has largely doomed any chance that the new information technology world learns from what librarians know about information and people. I recall recently being in a symposium and observing a graduate student from another field, who had become interested in what we do, hastily denying—indeed, almost panicking at the thought—that her new interest had anything to do with library science.

Information science, when it launched in the 1960's, was the exciting new field that would take the old librarianship into the new world of automation. And it did do that, with great success. But information science had another "flaw" that doomed it in the thinking of many computer scientists. Not only were there more women in the field than in computer science, there was also a great deal of attention to the so-called soft side of technology, its use and integration with people's lives and work, the psychology and sociology of information.

I sat in the audience at a conference while Gerard Salton, the father of modern information retrieval, explained that it was not possible to study the human factors in information system use, because these social aspects were too squishy and unmanageable (not his exact words). It is hard to maintain a balance in a discipline between people with a social and psychological perspective and those with an engineering, technical perspective when applying their expertise to a problem. As a rule, they have fundamentally different cognitive styles, which do not necessarily mix well. Yet both these perspectives are needed where information systems are concerned. Information science has retained that balance, but consequently sometimes puts off computer scientists, many (not all) of whom literally do not see the social side of information, are not interested in it, and are happy to purge that perspective from their university departments.

For all these reasons, the extensive knowledge that has built up within information science is frequently ignored in today's research and scholarship, and in the popular consciousness. The publication of these articles of mine is my bid to draw attention to some of what has been learned in information science about information-related behavior and good information system design. In what follows, the technologies may indeed have been superseded, but pay attention to the thinking around the technologies—what we learned about people and information, what we learned about dissecting an information query and searching on it, what we learned about how people process information when approaching an information system, and what we learned about how to design an information system to support information seeking well. Much of what we learned has *still* not been implemented in information systems, despite the billions of dollars poured into the information technology world.

Finally, these papers are also of interest as a historical record of that time of transition in information research between the 1960's and the early twenty-first century. Coincidentally, the arc of my professional career happened to parallel the arc of development of modern information retrieval, and some of that history is represented in these volumes. I hope you find material of interest and value herein.

The papers reproduced here represent, in my rough estimate, about half my published work, the half I felt would be of most use today. I have always had wide interests within information science, and many of the papers could arguably fall in more than one category. I have grouped them as best I can in the categories below, arranged by volume. One popular article, on "berrypicking," appears in both Volumes II and III. Otherwise, all articles are unique.

Articles and chapters are carefully reproduced exactly as they originally appeared in print, with two exceptions: errors are corrected, and citations in reference lists that were originally listed as "in press" have been supplied with their subsequent publication information. Consequently, a few citations will be more recent than the original publication date of the article in which they appear.

**Volume I: *Information and the Information Professions***
*Information* (4 articles)
*The Information Professions* (14 articles)
*Appendix A: Author curriculum vitae*
*Appendix B: Content Lists and Index for all volumes*

**Volume II: *Information Searching Theory and Practice***
*Search Vocabulary Use* (5 articles)
*Searching Behavior* (10 articles)
*Appendix: Content Lists and Index for all volumes*

# Preface to Volume II

Searching and search techniques have been primary interests of mine throughout my career. Information searching is embedded in important social and technical contexts. Searching is a part of information seeking in general; actual active searching is the point where "the rubber meets the road" in the information seeking process, but information seeking includes much more, even passive absorption of information. The act of searching is also the central focus of information system design, which includes development of thesauri of search vocabulary, interface design, and design of underlying system search capabilities, among other features.

In the consideration of real searching by people, all these aspects need ultimately to be taken into account, or one's analysis and design process will be inadequate. In practice, however, we need to select out particular portions of these search-related activities, in order to have manageable projects to study. All the articles in this volume deal with various aspects of people's searching for information, in the first section with the interaction between searchers' vocabulary and the system-supplied indexing terms on documents, and in the second section with various aspects of searching behavior. The third volume continues with sections on *Information Seeking and Interaction* and *User-centered Design of Information Systems*.

## SECTION ONE: SEARCH VOCABULARY USE

The vocabulary used by information searchers, and whether the terms matched those used by the information system, was the focus of my Ph.D.

dissertation and of several subsequent papers. "Factors affecting subject catalog search success" and "System meets user: Problems in matching subject search terms," both 1977, were the two papers I published out of my dissertation, which was also titled "Factors affecting subject catalog search success." Matching rates were shockingly low, even with the assistance of cross-references, indicating that catalogs might not be serving the library user as well as we wanted to believe.

In 1986 I published my proposed solution to the matching problems revealed by my and other researchers' work. "Subject access in online catalogs: A design model" outlines a model for catalog subject access, with a number of example features and displays that would help the searcher have more success in catalog use and, by implication, in other textual information systems as well.

Online catalogs began to be widely used in the early 1980's, while online database searching had been developing intensively since the late 1970's. I noticed, however, that not all searching was done with a deep understanding of the powerful support that various kinds of thesauri and category sets could give to online searching. I wrote "How to use controlled vocabularies more effectively in online searching" to lay out for professional searchers the ways in which they could take advantage of these vocabulary resources.

I worked with staff at the Getty Art History Information Program (now the Getty Research Institute) in Santa Monica, California to analyze a massive body of data that they had gathered from visiting scholars' efforts at online searching, fully subsidized by the Getty while the scholars were in residence for a year. The results were published in a series of six papers appearing between 1993 and 1996. The first publication out of the study is included in this section because it addressed the unique characteristics of vocabulary used in the humanities ("An analysis of search terminology used by humanities scholars: The Getty Online Searching Project report no. 1). Typical humanities query formulations are so different from those of the sciences that entirely different kinds of vocabulary systems are needed—different in structure, not just content. I argue that searchers, librarians, and business people creating and marketing databases all need to think very differently from their conventional ways to succeed in designing and marketing information resources for the humanities.

SECTION TWO: SEARCHING BEHAVIOR

"Information search tactics" won the *Journal of the American Society for Information Science* Best Paper of the Year" Award in 1979. It represents my effort to identify various tactics that one can use to increase search success. I came up with 29 tactics in this paper, and another 17 tactics in "Idea Tactics," a companion paper not reproduced here. (The latter paper is not included because it deals with more general creativity-generating techniques, rather than ones specific to information searching.) On the strength of the interest generated by the search tactics papers, I was asked to write an *Annual Review of Information Science and Technology* article on "Search Techniques." This article traces available research on search techniques, both within and outside of information science. Early thinking was done in military efforts to find downed pilots, for example.

During the 1970's and 1980's, online database searching, and to a lesser extent, online catalog searching, dominated concerns in the field about searching methods and searching success. I taught online searching (a very time-consuming course to teach well) and soon became aware of various ways searching could be improved. I wrote about these methods in several papers, of which two are reproduced here: "Locating elusive science information: Some search techniques," and "The fallacy of the perfect thirty-item online search." The former deals with the scientific publication cycle and the ways in which one can use knowledge of the cycle to improve success in searching, and the latter addresses the error of automatically assuming that a nice-sized retrieval set indicates an optimal search. (The "How to use controlled vocabularies..." article in the prior section was another of this type of article.)

Working from the large data set of the captured searches of over two dozen visiting scholars in the humanities at the Getty Research Institute, I analyzed the search steps taken by the scholars during their year-long sabbatical leaves taken at the Getty to do research. The 1993 "A profile of end-user searching behavior by humanities scholars: The Getty Online Searching Project report no. 2" describes what we learned about both the successes and failures of humanities scholars in encountering the Boolean logic and other complexities of online database searching.

The 1989 paper, "The design of browsing and berrypicking techniques for the online search interface," came out of an effort to expand the usual thinking around database searching from a single search on a single database to a recognition that we were soon going to have the opportunity to search on many different kinds of databases, each with different access methods and search capabilities. These greater capabilities would make it possible for people to search more in the way they naturally do, in what I call "berrypicking" mode, namely, gathering a bit of information here and a bit there, modifying one's query and search techniques all along the way, as new information is gained. The paper apparently arrived at just the right time in people's thinking about online searching, and this minor paper has become the most heavily cited of all my papers. Consequently, it appears in both volumes II and III of this series, the only item presented more than once.

In 2002, I returned to this subject matter, because I had, in the meantime, come to a greater understanding of Zipf's Law and its associated types, such as Bradford's Law and Lotka's Law. Here, in "Speculations on browsing, directed searching, and linking in relation to the Bradford Distribution," I was able to link these laws to the search techniques described in the "berrypicking" paper, and therefore provide guidance, at least speculatively so, as to when and how to use the several searching techniques I had outlined in the "berrypicking" paper.

Finally, in 2007, I addressed browsing, a subject that I had been thinking about on and off for decades ("What is browsing—really? A model drawing from behavioral science research"). With the help of others' work in information science, especially that of Barbara Kwasnik, and work from psychology, I felt that I had at last penetrated to the true nature of browsing behavior. I feel that the common assumption that browsing is scanning is deeply mistaken, and that this conception works all kinds of mischief in the design of information systems to support user browsing. With my conception of the term, I believe that information system designers can at last design for the way human browsing actually happens at a physical and cognitive level.

The last two papers in this section deal with ways of structuring information to promote user understanding for searching in information sources. In teaching reference services to library students, I discovered that the existing definitions of "reference book" were, in my opinion, extremely lacking, and I set out to provide a deeper understanding of what distinguishes reference books from "regular" books in the article, "What is a reference book? A theoretical and empirical analysis." I found my definition well-substantiated by a random sample of books taken in three library types. Finally, in "Rigorous systematic bibliography," based on my understanding of Patrick Wilson's arguments in his ground-breaking 1968 theoretical work, *Two Kinds of Power: An Essay on Bibliographical Control* (Berkeley, CA: University of California Press), I developed methods of doing systematic bibliography in a rigorous way, which techniques should make it much easier for information users to take advantage of the power provided as a result of the efforts that go into creating a systematic bibliography.

# ONE

# Search vocabulary use

# Factors affecting subject catalog search success

ABSTRACT

The study examined the effects of two variables on success in searching an academic library subject catalog that uses Library of Congress subject headings. The variables were "subject familiarity," and "catalog familiarity," representing patron knowledge of a subject field and of the principles of the subject heading system, respectively. Testing was done in a laboratory setting which reproduced a real search situation. The $n$ varied with the particular test, but about 20 university students in each of the following majors participated: psychology, economics, librarianship. Success was measured as degree of match between search term and term used by the library for desired books on the subject.

Catalog familiarity was found to have a very significant beneficial effect on search matching success, and subject familiarity a slight, but not significant, detrimental effect. An interview substudy of subject experts suggested causes for the failure of subject expertise to help in catalog search term formulation.

*First published as* Bates, M. J. (1977). Factors affecting subject catalog search success. *Journal of the American Society for Information Science, 28*(3), 161–169.

Surprising results were that overall matching success was strikingly low. Since the methodology used enabled a more precise determination of match success than has been typical of catalog use studies, it appears that people may be less successful than we have thought in using subject catalogs.

## Introduction

In one sense, the catalog is the crossroads of an information facility. It is where the user starts searches of all kinds, and it represents the culmination of the library staff's efforts at organizing information for access. The catalog is where technical processes and reader services meet, where the user interfaces with the information store. This paper describes a study (Bates, 1972) that deals with that moment of truth when user meets catalog.

Many studies on catalog use report user satisfaction as a criterion of performance for the catalog—and this is indeed one valuable measure. But it has its dangers. Users, even highly educated ones, are notoriously ignorant of library resources and organization. If the catalog has little by way of feedback mechanisms, then the users may report satisfaction because they do not know what they are missing and do not *expect* more. The study described here used a different methodology from that of many catalog use studies, one that made it possible to determine objectively what is in the catalog on a given subject request and whether the users got to it—self-reported satisfaction aside.

## Previous research on catalog use

Many catalog use studies have been produced, but the cumulative knowledge resulting from them is not great. Much of the work appears in library master's theses wherein the same or similar questions are tested over and over again. Some of the work in this area (not just in the master's theses) uses poor or suspicious research methodology. Furthermore, while some questions are asked repeatedly, often the next logical question that follows from one research study is never asked by any subsequent studies. There have, however, been some excellent recent large-scale studies in this area. Here, just the principal research results of interest for this study will be reviewed. Other research results of relevance will be mentioned where appropriate in the discussion in later sections.

*1. Absolute amount of use of the catalog.* Little is available on this, but in a huge study, Lipetz (1970) did find that there were about 320,000 instances of people using the catalog (for all types of use, not just subject access) of the main library at Yale University in a year (1970, p. 33), or about 100 per hour of opening (1970, p. 34).

*2. Author/title catalog vs subject catalog search.* These are also known as "known-item" versus subject searches, which is almost the same distinction (it is possible, but not common, to make a known-item search in a subject catalog). Whichever way they are described, the range on relative use of the two types of search is the same—between about 20% and 50% of all catalog searches are for subject, the remainder for author/title or known item. At least fifteen studies have yielded data on this question. Montague (1967) summarized a number of them; see also ALA (1958), Lipetz (1970), and Tagliacozzo and Kochen (1970).

*3. Relation of subject catalog use to subject expertise.* There is considerable evidence that as users go up the academic ladder, they tend to use the subject catalog less and less relative to the author-title catalog. Frarey (1953) and Montague (1967) discuss a number of studies relating to this question. No studies were found that investigated why this trend exists. Do advanced students and scholars simply need to use the author-title catalog more relative to the subject catalog, or do they find the subject catalog less and less useful in and of itself?

*4. Purposes for using subject catalog.* Three early studies which need to be replicated under modern conditions [Irwin (1949), Markley (1950), and Miller (1942), discussed in Frarey (1953)] found that use of the subject catalog is divided about equally between (a) selecting books on a subject, and (b) finding the shelf location of books in order to make book selection in the stacks. Thus, a large number of users find this two-step process of subject-catalog-then-stack searching easier or more satisfactory in some way than they do searching in the subject catalog alone.

*5. Number of one-place searches in subject catalog.* Three major studies of catalog users provided data on the percentages of one-place (one look-up) searches, as distinct from multiplace searches in the subject catalog in academic and research libraries. Between 66% and 77% of the searches were one-place searches [Knapp (1944), ALA (1958), Tagliacozzo and Kochen (1970)]. Thus, this study, which concerns only the first term used by searchers, deals with the *entire* search in two-thirds to three-quarters of the cases.

*6. Effectiveness rating of the subject catalog.* Ratings of effectiveness of the subject catalog vary greatly, probably because they are based on varying criteria. In summarizing several studies, Frarey (1953) estimates effectiveness at about 70% (1953, p. 162). See also ALA (1958) and Lipetz (1970); success figures in these studies went up to 86%. A more specific effectiveness rating is the proportion of catalog users who find the material sought on the first try. Reports are fairly consistent here at about half [e.g., Knapp (1944), Malcolm (1950), Quigley (1944)].

## Research design

The main purpose of the study was to test the effects of familiarity with (1) the subject area of search and (2) the principles of catalog organization, on subject catalog search success. The study produced, as a byproduct, interesting and suggestive figures on absolute success rates in matching one's terms with the catalog's terms. In addition to the basic laboratory test with students on subject search terms, subject experts were interviewed in order to get greater understanding of their motivations and interests with regard to the selection of subject terms. These results and their significance will be explored below. Additional results on patterns of match between student-generated and library-assigned terms will be published in another paper.

The study was done in a laboratory setting, with university students in an academic library context (University of California at Berkeley). The subject cataloging approach used was that embodied in the Library of Congress' list of subject headings, 7th ed. (Quattlebaum, 1966), and in David Haykin's book *Subject Headings* (1951), the official statement of principles underlying the list. (Library of Congress subject headings are used in most large libraries in the United States.)

*Subject familiarity* was defined as knowledge of a specified academic field. *Catalog familiarity* was defined as knowledge of the structure of the system of Library of Congress (LC) subject headings (subject terms). The basic method chosen to test the effects of these variables was to contrast experimentally groups of university students who differed on the variables. Rates of match between the student-generated and library-assigned subject headings for a topic were computed, and then the equality of means hypothesis tested in order to determine if there were significant differences in student performance which could be associated with the two variables.

The test means used was to present the students with a hypothetical situation in which they must state the term they would use to look up given subjects. Specifically, they were asked to imagine themselves in a situation where they were unable to find a book in the library (described by means of its title and abstract, but no author) which had been recommended to them by a professor as useful for a paper they were writing. They were, therefore, to have turned to the subject catalog to try to find another book on the very same subject. What term would they use in their search?

They were thus being asked to generate a subject heading for a subject area of search that happened to coincide with the contents of a particular book. The test of search success was whether the subject search term generated by a student was the same as that applied to the book by the library. The device in the instructions of having the students find another book just like the one described was used in order that they would generate headings from a searcher's, rather than a cataloger's standpoint. If they had been instructed to create headings for the books directly, they would then be playing cataloger. The consequences of the latter mind set for nonlibrarians are unpredictable.

Let us now look at the design in more detail, considering the students, the books/headings, and the matching process respectively.

## Students

To achieve contrast on subject familiarity, student specialists were selected in each of two fields, psychology and economics. Specifically, senior undergraduates and graduate students majoring in the two fields (minimum 20 quarter units in major field) were recruited. As an additional check, they were questioned, after the experimental test, on various kinds of exposure that they might have had to their own and the contrasting fields, to ensure that they knew a lot about their own field and little about the other. The use of 2 groups of subject majors, tested on their own and the other field, not only enabled the contrast of subject knowledge versus lack of knowledge in a field, but also controlled for any peculiarities that might be associated with any single subject field.

It was originally hoped that psychology and economics students could be arrayed by their subject knowledge and catalog familiarity into a six-celled research design that contrasted high and low subject familiarity against three levels of catalog familiarity. A catalog familiarity questionnaire was devised which was intended to test working, effective knowledge of the catalog and familiarity with typical forms of subject headings, not the technical vocabulary of the library field.

Pretests showed that there was almost no difference in catalog familiarity among even these advanced college students—performance by all was uniformly low. Hence a third group of students, library master's students who had studied cataloging, was introduced to provide contrast on catalog familiarity.

Students were volunteers, recruited in their classes, and paid a modest amount for participation. The field of the study was not revealed to the psychology and economics students during recruitment so as to keep self-selection to a minimum. The entire test took about one hour. The $n$ varied slightly for reasons of experimental detail, but in every case results are based on at least 22 psychology students, 22 economics students, and 17 library students.

### Books and headings

The research design called for students to be presented with the titles and abstracts of books, to which they would respond by stating the subject term they would use in finding books just like the test ones. Books and abstracts were selected by a somewhat involved, but carefully random, process in the two fields, in psychology from *Psychological Abstracts* (1927), and in economics from *Economics Library Selections (Series I)* (Johns Hopkins, 1965). Fifteen were selected in each subject. In the experimental test, the abstracts from both fields were randomly intermixed in presentation order.

There were two major constraints on selection: (1) The book had to have a publication date between 1954 and 1962, in order to control for vocabulary change and to accommodate peculiarities of the abstracting services. (2) The most important criterion was that the book had to have been indexed with only one subject heading. In this way the student term could be matched unambiguously with the library's term.

This is not as constricting a requirement as it may at first appear. Avram et al. (1967) found, in a study conducted at the Library of Congress, that among books cataloged by LC in the "regular" series between 1950 and 1964, there was only one subject heading assigned in 53.6% of the cases. Library of Congress indexing is used by the University of California at Berkeley where both students and books/headings were drawn.

One may still wonder whether students would get higher match rates with books having several headings assigned to them. To test this possibility, an additional group of 14 library students was given a set of 30 abstracts for books that had been selected on the same basis, but which all had two or more headings assigned to them. The student performance scores, based on the closest match among the several headings for each book, were distinctly *worse* on multiple headings. One may speculate that multiple-heading items are perhaps more complicated subjects, hence harder to define in subject terms.

## Matching process

Subject term responses of the students were compared with the single subject heading actually applied by the library to the book, and a score ranging from 0 to 4 points was assigned to the response. These scores were assigned according to the following criteria of match:

> Disregarding differences between student term and library term with respect to punctuation, capitalization, hyphenation, abbreviation, spelling (unless it is not clear what the intended word is), and the presence or absence of initial articles, assign, on a left-to-right basis, 4 points for perfect match with library-assigned heading; 3 points for match on two or more words; 2 points for match on one word; 1 point for match on root of one word; 0 points for no match; and 3 points for perfect match with a see reference given in the LC list of subject headings 7th ed. (Quattlebaum, 1966), which leads to the library-assigned heading. Exception: On the one heading which was for a person, full credit was given if the last name alone appeared in the student response.

Students were given points for partial matches on the assumption that partial matches in real life would leave the searcher in alphabetical proximity to desired headings in many cases. Hence, a partial match might in fact be an adequate lead-in to the desired area of the catalog at least some of the time. The graduated point sequence was not based on any empirical evidence of actual success with partial matches.

Performance scores were computed by adding the total of each student's point scores on all response items for each of the two subjects. Maximum score was thus $4 \times 15 = 60$ for each subject, for each student. The equality of means test was done on this figure.

## Interviews with subject experts

In an effort to understand better the responses of the subject majors, all student responses to headings in their own fields were collected on a list. These lists were then taken to subject experts, overwhelmingly faculty, in the two fields for reactions in individual recorded interviews. Specifi-cally, they were asked: "Are there any reasons related to the thinking and organization, or terminological preferences in your field, which lead you to prefer one or more of the terms used by the students to the one used by the library?" Interviewees responded on items that interested them or that represented areas of expertise, all of their own choosing. Often they added preferred terms of their own in their responses. Nine psychologists and five economists were involved altogether; each of the 30 items was responded to by four to seven people.

## Results

Tables 1 and 2 display the results of the tests on the variables of subject and catalog familiarity. For catalog familiarity, in Table 1 the library student scores are contrasted against the nonmajor-field scores of the psychology and economics majors. For subject familiarity, in Table 2 the combined scores of psychology and economics majors are contrasted on own field version opposite (nonmajor) field.

A balance between the number of psychology and economics scores *within each cell* was maintained throughout the two tables in order to cut out possible effects due to characteristics of subject field or headings for subject field. For example, the *n* of 44 in Tables 1 and 2 consists of 22 economics students, and 22 psychology students. To make the results com-parable to those of the other students and to avoid dependency problems in data analysis, library student responses in only one subject field were used. The field was selected randomly for each student within the quota constraint of equal numbers of students for each subject field. Library students were also questioned on subject background and included in Table 1 only if non-experts.

In Table 1 it is evident that familiarity with the principles and forms of subject headings makes for a significant off-scale improvement in match-ing performance. In Table 2, the performance difference associated with subject expertise is not significant, but it approaches significance in the opposite direction from what we might expect. We would expect subject expertise to improve search success. Instead, these results suggest that subject expertise *may* (since the score does not reach significance) have a slightly detrimental effect on one's performance with a subject catalog.

More light was shed on the effect of subject expertise on search success through the interviews with subject experts. Interviews were recorded and reactions carefully scored. Through a complicated assessment that cannot

TABLE 1. *Catalog familiarity: Library vs non-library students on non-expert responses*

| LIBRARY STUDENTS | NON-LIBRARY STUDENTS |
|---|---|
| $m = 22.2$ | $m = 13.5$ |
| $n = 26$ | $n = 44$ |
| $s^2 = 24.0$ | $s^2 = 38.6$ |

*Legend:* m = mean matching score of students falling in the cell (maximum score possible: 4 points x 15 responses = 60.0); n = number of students in sample; $s^2$ = sample variance.

*Test used:* $z = \dfrac{(\bar{x} - \bar{y})}{\sqrt{\sigma_x^2/n_x + \sigma_y^2/n_y}}$

(Difference of means, normal distribution)

NOTE: *Difference of means test significant off scale (z = 6.7).*

TABLE 2. *Subject familiarity: Non-library students on own and opposite (non-expert) fields*

| OWN FIELD | OPPOSITE FIELD |
|---|---|
| $m = 12.0$ | $m = 13.5$ |
| $n = 44$ | $n = 44$ |
| $s^2 = 48.0$ | $s^2 = 38.6$ |

NOTE: *Difference of means test not significant (z = 1.1), but note that direction of difference is toward greater success* outside *one's field. (Tests and symbols are same as those cited in Table 1.)*

be described here for reasons of space, the results of the interviews also suggest a slightly detrimental effect on search success associated with subject expertise.

Table 3 summarizes some interesting results of the interview study. The table contains only those cases where the library-assigned heading was clearly consensually *disliked,* and some *one* other specific heading was simultaneously clearly *preferred* by the respondents. The preferred headings were ones suggested by the student majors or solely by the professors.

It is immediately noticeable that the professors' preferred headings are both more specific and more precise. They tended to want subjects more specifically delineated, and they also found some of the LC headings to

TABLE 3. *Headings consensually preferred by experts over the library-assigned headings*

| | LIBRARY HEADING | EXPERTS' PREFERRED HEADING |
|---|---|---|
| 7. | Personality | Personality, cultural determinants |
| 8. | Human behavior | Comparative psychology |
| 10. | Psychology—Hist. | Psychology—Soviet Union or USSR |
| 15. | Psychology | Developmental psychology |
| 20. | Commonwealth of Nations—Econ. condit. | British Commonwealth—Econ. policy |
| 26. | Economics—Hist. | Economics, history of thought |
| 29. | China (People's Republic of China, 1949-    )—Econ. condit. | China—Econ. statistics |
| 30. | Southwest, New—Econ. condit. | (—)—Econ. geography (did not agree on first section) |

NOTE: *Numbers of headings refer to book titles in the Appendix.*

be so imprecise as to be misleading. The subdivision (subheading), "Econ. condit.," that appears in numbers 20, 29, and 30 is illustrative. Evidently, LC assigns this phrase to documents with any sort of economic approach to a topic. As the experts pointed out, the first item was really on economic policy, the second on economic statistics, and the third on economic geography. As another example, the terms "Human behavior," "Psychology," and "Personality" were all too broad for the psychology professors—though notice that the preferred headings were not any longer or more specific than many headings in the LC list. A number of other criticisms were offered by both groups of professors (see Bates, 1972, Chap. 6).

Let us now consider one more measure on the data. Heretofore in this paper, the measure that has been used for search success is based on the degree of match between the student's term and the actual library-assigned term for the book. This we call the "basic" score. We might, instead, have looked at whether the student-generated heading matched with *any existing* heading in the LC system. In other words, if the student had looked that term up in the catalog, would (s)he have found anything? Scores with this latter approach we call "existence" scores. For comparison purposes, student responses were also scored, using the same four-point algorithm, for existence matches.

Before citing the results, however, it will be helpful to look more closely at just what those two types of scores mean. We may start with this question: Why should we be concerned with finding just the one term that indexes the book representing the topic of interest? If the student thinks up a term based on the abstract, then surely the term will be "in the ballpark" most of the time. Is not the existence score then a good enough measure? Is the basic score perhaps too stringent?

It may well be that a measure based on the *one best* term is too stringent since there may be other books of interest in the catalog under related terms, and that a measure based on *any* matching term is too loose since not all responses will in fact be "in the ballpark." We wish to argue here, however, that the basic score is a better, truer, indicator of search success. The reasons behind this position have to do with the particular characteristics of searching with Library of Congress subject headings.

Searching in library catalogs based on the LC system is not like Boolean searching where any given book may be drawn by numerous terms. If there is only one heading assigned to a book—which, as has already been noted, is the case over half the time with LC—then a subject search *must* use that heading if that book is to be retrieved. Furthermore, in the LC system, synonyms are supposed to be controlled. It can be argued that this does not always happen, but to the extent that it does, other terms are going to be on *different* subjects, related subjects perhaps, but not the same—desired—subject. Thus, to truly home in on one's topic of interest, it is necessary to show perfect subject term choice.

In addition to term choice, hierarchical level plays a special role in determining search success with an LC-based catalog. The LC system uses the rule of specific entry, which holds that a book is to be entered under the most specific term that describes its entire contents. Thus, a subject heading applied to a book should have the same scope of coverage as the contents of the book and may be neither broader nor narrower. (Mismatches in book/term specificity nonetheless necessarily occur when a term of proper specificity is not available in the LC list.) It is thus expressly forbidden, for example, to apply the terms "Mental tests" or "Psychology" to a book on the Rorschach test, either alone or in conjunction with the term "Rorschach test." By the rule of specific entry, the only term that may be applied to such a book is "Rorschach test."

So the searcher looking under either of the broader terms will not find listed there any monographs on the Rorschach test. In addition, if the library has eliminated "see-also" references to save money—as the University of California at Berkeley Library had done at the time of the study—then the user will find no references to the more specific term, "Rorschach test," in the catalog. Incidentally, see-also references that go upward hierarchically, i.e., superordinate references, are forbidden altogether in LC. So searches going in at too specific a level get no help, whether the library uses see-also references available in the list or not.

But suppose the user looks up a term at the wrong specificity level. Will (s)he not be dissatisfied and think up a new term, such as "Rorschach test," to use in the catalog search? The answer is maybe not, because if the user looks under "Mental tests," for example, (s)he will probably find books that deal partly with the Rorschach test and will go away thinking that (s)he has gotten all there is to get from the catalog on the subject—while missing all of the monographs specifically and wholly devoted to the topic.

It seems reasonable to assume that the average user does not appreciate the subtle problems of synonymy, subject term choice, and hierarchical level.[1] Thus if a look-up produces little or only marginal material, the searcher's assumption may be not that there is something wrong with the term choice, but rather that the library just does not have any better material. The difficulties noted here in finding the right subject term on the one hand, and the statistics cited earlier in the paper that as many as 77% of subject searches are one-place searches on the other hand, suggest that something of this sort does happen.

Existence-matching scores do not reveal how well the searcher is doing on either subject choice or hierarchical level selection. In using the LC system—low in redundancy, with limited see-also references, and requiring the use of the rule of specific entry—the user must home in precisely on the "best" subject heading to get at the material of real interest. We conclude, therefore, that basic matching scores are a better (though doubtless not ideal) measure.

The existence-matching scores computed in this study nonetheless provide results that can be used productively. In Table 4 are contrasted the results of the three groups of students on basic and existence scores.

Let us examine Table 4.[2] Both the basic and existence scores were based on the same four-point scale. We do not know what the likelihood is, in real catalog searches, of matching either the most central heading in the case of basic scores, or a presumably related heading in the case of existence scores. Implicitly, in our laboratory approach, a score of 1 out of 4 assumes a 25% chance of coming upon the right heading in the same general section of the catalog, 2 out of 4 a 50% chance, etc. If we accept these proportions

---

1 Once when this research was described to a Ph.D. astronomer, he exclaimed: "What's all the fuss about? If you're interested in a subject, you just go look it up in the catalog under its name!"

2 Tagliacozzo and Kochen (1970) scored their existence matches differently and got different results. A subsample from the Bates study was scored, as best could be determined, by the same algorithm as used in the Tagliacozzo and Kochen study for comparison purposes. Readers interested in the methodological differences in these two studies, and their consequent results, should see the discussion in Bates (1972, pp. 125–133).

TABLE 4. *Basic and existence mean matching scores of all students on all headings*

| | BASIC MATCHING | EXISTENCE MATCHING |
|---|---|---|
| Economics Students $n = 22$ | 12.6 (21%) | 37.1 (62%) |
| Psychology Students $n = 23$ | 13.1 (22%) | 36.0 (60%) |
| Library Students $n = 17$ | 20.9 (35%) | 38.2 (64%) |

NOTE: *Means are based on results from all thirty headings for each student, but are presented as per fifteen headings in order to be comparable with results presented in earlier tables. Score percentages of maximum score of 60.0 are in parentheses. A slight bias may exist in the scores due to the fact that the library students are experts in neither field, while non-library students are experts in one field.*

as rough estimates of likely absolute success in catalog searching on any one heading,[3] then the percent of success relative to the total possible score that is reported in Table 4 may be taken as a rough estimate of likely overall absolute success rate in searching. Viewed in this light, student success on the first catalog look up—which as we have already noted, is usually the only look-up—is very low. Non-library students are getting the best material in a subject search (basic matching rate) only a little over a fifth of the time (~ 20%), whereas students with library training succeed over a third of the time (35%). It would appear, however, that everyone *feels* successful most of the time, about three-fifths (existence matching rate), because the heading they look up in the catalog is all or partly matched, and will, of course, have some books listed under it. To put this another way, we may surmise that *non-library students actually find the best material on a subject about a third of the time that they think they have found the best material* (~ 20%/60%). Even library students find the best material only a little over half the time that they think they have on the first try. Training searchers to look more than one place in the catalog, and giving them feedback in the form of see-also references can thus be seen to be essential to effective catalog use.

Petrof's (1962) study of catalog use is worthy of note at this point. She found that graduate and undergraduate students looked more places in the catalog when searching outside their field of expertise than within. She concluded that it is easier to locate material within the field of specialization on the first try than outside the field of specialization (1962, p. 19). Since this

---

3 Note that this assumption was not necessary to the earlier considerations of subject and catalog familiarity because scores were *comparative* there; no assumptions were being made about absolute search success.

study found that subject expertise did not improve matching success rates, one wonders if instead a confidence factor was involved. Perhaps students assumed they were looking in the right place when they used a term familiar to themselves from their own field, but when they had to go outside their own field they wanted to make sure they got all the relevant material by looking under several terms. It would be ironic if these presumptions led to better catalog use outside than inside one's expert field.

## Summary and conclusions

We have learned that one's search success can be markedly improved through knowledge of and familiarity with the subject heading approach used in LC-based catalogs. We have suspicions, based both on the main study results and the interview substudy, that subject expertise may actually be a slight hindrance to effective subject catalog use. The interviewed subject experts found that the subject headings applied in their fields were not specific or precise enough. And finally, in comparing basic versus existence matching scores, we found that subject majors (in total combined scores of perfect and partial matches of headings) found *the one* heading describing their subject of interest about one-third of the time they matched with *some* heading. This suggested to us that users might think they have found what the catalog (and hence, the library) has to offer a lot more often than they in fact have.

There are two fundamental interrelated questions raised here about academic library catalogs—questions barely explored in the research literature: (1) What is the ideal role for scholar users of the academic library catalog in their information searching; (2) from an overall within-library bibliographic control and information access standpoint, how best should the academic library catalog be organized?

From the results of this study we can suspect that we are not serving the subject expert well—and "subject expert" here includes even undergraduate students who have only twenty quarter units in their majors. Perhaps we should turn this around and say that the LC-based academic library catalog, to judge by user performance, is so designed as to treat every user as a general user. One fares as well as one can fare with an LC catalog with a modicum of knowledge of the subject of search interest.

Now it may be that this is what we want from academic library catalogs. Specialists may prefer to start from bibliographies which list relevant materials in a subject area, regardless of whether they are present in a given library (see Swank [1945] for a discussion of this issue).

Advanced scholars (graduate and above), particularly, may frequently not want to restrict their searches to what is contained in a particular library, and a library catalog subject search is necessarily so restricted. But we may still question whether a subject access system that does not take advantage of subject experts' knowledge—particularly in an environment aswarm with experts—is optimal.

Additionally, other data in this study suggest that while users, other than library students, at several academic levels perform at about the same level, that one level is disturbingly low. How many college graduates, indeed, how many Ph.D.'s, have heard of the rule of specific entry?! Yet knowledge of this rule and general familiarity with typical term patterns make a very marked difference in search success. Have we in the library/information services field perhaps not thought through the consequences of our own rules? That, for example, users (not just catalogers) must understand the rule of specific entry for effective catalog use? To help users cope with existing catalogs, library use instruction should include an explanation of specific entry and some consciousness raising on the complexity of subject description.

But what about use of the LC system over the long term? To find the (often just one) place where the monographs on a subject are to be found in the catalog, one must come into the catalog with both the right subject term selection and phrasing, *and* the precisely correct level of specificity. In addition there may be few see-also references and there will be no superordinate see-also references.

Is it reasonable to use such a low-redundancy subject access system? On the basis of the results in Table 4, we must consider the possibility that the typical academic library catalog may be a major contributor to under-utilization of library collections. By suggesting a few, often marginally relevant, sources to the user, who has usually failed to look up the most central term, the catalog provides *some* help, and allows the naive user to go away satisfied that the library has yielded its treasures.

The current academic library subject catalogs were developed under conditions of severe resource limitations. With more than one or two subject entries per book, card catalogs would have become cumbrously large—hard to use, hard to file in, hard to find room for. In the early days, catalog entries often had to be handwritten. The current subject heading system, therefore, was deliberately developed to be minimally redundant.

But with automation, we have the opportunity to introduce many access points to a given book. We can now use a subject approach—not necessarily coordinate indexing—that allows the naive user, unconscious of and uninterested in the complexities of synonymy and vocabulary control, to blunder on to desired subjects, to be guided, without realizing it, by a redundant but carefully controlled subject access system.

And now is the time to change—indeed, with MARC already so highly developed, past time. If we simply transfer the austerity-based LC subject heading approach to expensive computer systems, then we have used our computers merely to embalm the constraints that were imposed on library systems back before typewriters came into use!

In this necessarily brief discussion we have only scratched the surface in considering the two questions raised a few paragraphs ago. Both more research, to delve more deeply into these questions, and more solid thinking need to take place before we can hope to develop a truly rational and rationalized system of subject access for library users. But it is about time—if we call our field a science, whether library or information—that we did just that.

APPENDIX

## Books and Subject Headings Used in Study
*(Numbers by headings are used for reference in the text of article.)*

PSYCHOLOGY

1. Bachrach, Arthur J. *Psychological research: An introduction.* 1962.
   Psychological research.
2. Estabrooks, George H. *Hypnosis: Current problems.* 1962.
   Hypnotism.
3. Evans, Jean. *Three men: an experiment in the biography of emotion.* 1954.
   Psychology, Pathological.
4. Freud, Sigmund. *On creativity and the unconscious.* 1958.
   Psychoanalysis.
5. Gesell, Arnold et al. *Youth: the years from ten to sixteen.* 1956.
   Adolescence.
6. Ghiselli, Edwin E.; Brown, Clarence, W. *Personnel and industrial psychology.* 1955.
   Psychology, Industrial.
7. Honigman, John J. *Culture and personality.* 1954.
   Personality.
8. Russell, Chaire; Russell, W.M.S. *Human behavior.* 1961.
   Human behavior.
9. Schoenwald, Richard L. *Freud: the man and his mind. 1856–1956.* 1956.
   Freud, Sigmund, 1856–1939.
10. Simon, Brian (ed.) *Psychology in the Soviet Union.* 1957.
    Psychology—Hist.
11. Skinner, B.F. *Verbal behavior.* 1957.
    Language and languages.

12. Small, Leonard. *Rorschach location and scoring manual.* 1956.
    Rorschach test.

13. Smedslund, Jan. *Multiple-probability learning: an inquiry into the origins of perception.* 1955.
    Perception.

14. Stacey, Chalmers L.; De Martino, Manfred F. (eds.) *Understanding human motivation.* 1958.
    Motivation (Psychology).

15. Zubek, John P.; Solberg, Patricia Anne. *Human development.* 1954.
    Psychology.

## ECONOMICS

16. Abbott, Lawrence. *Quality and competition: An essay in economic theory.* 1955.
    Competition.

17. Beal, Edwin George, Jr. *The origin of likin.* 1958.
    Taxation—China.

18. Berkowitz, Monroe. *Workmen's compensation: The New Jersey experience.* 1960.
    Workmen's compensation—New Jersey.

19. Cartter, Allan M. *Theory of wages and employment.* 1959.
    Wages.

20. Hoover, Calvin B. (ed.) *Economic systems of the Commonwealth.* 1962.
    Commonwealth of Nations—Econ. condit.

21. Kaysen, Carl. *United States vs United Shoe Machinery Corporation: An economic analysis of an antitrust case.* 1956.
    United Shoe Machinery Corporation.

22. Keiper, Joseph S., *et al. Theory and measurement of rent.* 1961.
    Rent (Economic theory).

23. Minchinton, W.E. *The British tinplate industry: A history.* 1957.
    Tin plate.

24. Morgenstern, Oskar. *The validity of international gold movement statistics.* 1955.
    Gold—Stat.

25. Roberts, Benjamin C. *Trade union government and administration in Great Britain.* 1956.
    Trade-unions—Gt. Brit.

26. Schumpeter, Joseph A. *History of economic analysis.* 1954.
    Economics—Hist.

27. Sigafoos, Robert A. *The municipal income tax: Its history and problems.* 1955.
    Income tax, Municipal—U.S.

28. Woods, (J.D.) and Gordon, Limited. *The Canadian agricultural machinery industry.* 1956.
    Agricultural machinery—Trade and manufacture—Canada.

29. Yin, Helen, and Yin, Yi-chang (comps.) *Economic statistics of mainland China 1949-1957.* 1960.
    China (People's Republic of China, 1949- )—Econ. condit.

30. Zierer, Clifford M. (ed.) *California and the Southwest.* 1956.
    Southwest, New—Econ. condit.

## REFERENCES

American Library Association. (1958). *Catalog use study, director's report by Sidney L. Jackson.* Chicago, IL: ALA.

Avram, H.D.; Guiles, K.D.; Meade, G.T. (1967). Fields of information on Library of Congress catalog cards: Analysis of a random sample, 1950–1964. *The Library Quarterly, 37*(2), 180–192.

Bates, M.J. (1972). *Factors affecting subject catalog search success.* (Unpublished doctoral dissertation). University of California, Berkeley.

Frarey, C.J. (1953). Studies of use of the subject catalog: Summary and evaluation. In M.F. Tauber (Ed.), *The subject analysis of library materials* (pp. 147–166). New York: Columbia University, School of Library Service.

Haykin, D.J. (1951). *Subject headings: A practical guide.* Washington, DC: U.S. Government Printing Office.

Irwin, R.A. (1949). *Use of the card catalog in the public library.* (Master's thesis). Chicago, IL: University of Chicago.

Johns Hopkins University, Dept. of Political Economy, & University of Pittsburgh, Dept. of Economics. (1965). *Economics Library Selections. Series I, New Books in Economics.* Pittsburgh: Department of Economics, University of Pittsburgh, [1954]–1965.

Knapp, P.B. (1944). The subject catalog in the college library: An investigation of terminology. *The Library Quarterly, 14*(3), 214–228.

Lipetz, B.A. (1970). *User requirements in identifying desired works in a large library.* (ED 042 479). New Haven, CT: Yale University Library.

Malcolm, R.S. (1950). The student's approach to the card catalog: A study based on a survey of student use at the library of the University of Pittsburgh. (Master's thesis). Pittsburgh: Carnegie Library School, Carnegie Institute of Technology.

Markley, A.E. (1950). The University of California subject catalog inquiry: A study of the subject catalog based on interviews with users. *Journal of Cataloging and Classification, 6*(4), 88–95.

Miller, R.A. (1942). On the use of the card catalog. *The Library Quarterly, 12*(3), 629–637.

Montague, E.A. (1967). *Card catalog use studies: 1949–1965.* (Master's thesis). Chicago, IL: University of Chicago.

Petrof, B.J.G. (1962). *A Study of the use made of the subject approach to library materials of the Trevor Arnett Library.* (Master's thesis). Atlanta University, Georgia.

*Psychological Abstracts.* (1927–). Lancaster, PA: American Psychological Association.

Quattlebaum, M.V. (Ed.). (1966). *Subject headings used in the dictionary catalogs of the Library of Congress* (7th ed.). Washington, DC: Library of Congress Subject Cataloging Division.

Quigley, H. (1944). An investigation of the possible relationship of interbranch loan to cataloging. *The Library Quarterly, 14*(4), 333–338.

Swank, R. (1945). The organization of library materials for research in English literature. *The Library Quarterly, 15*(1), 49–74.

Tagliacozzo, R., & Kochen, M. (1970). Information-seeking behavior of catalog users. *Information Storage and Retrieval, 6*(5), 363–381.

# 2

# System meets user: Problems in matching subject search terms

ABSTRACT

Sixty-one undergraduate and graduate students in psychology, economics, and librarianship provided the subject terms they would use to search an academic library catalog in 30 hypothetical search instances. The subject indexing tested was that of the Library of Congress, which is used in most large libraries in the United States. The large number of responses on each search instance enabled an unusually detailed, systematic evaluation of various aspects of the LC approach. Results (including evidence of many inadequacies) were produced on see references, subject/place order, noun/ adjective order, specific entry, direct entry, and *a priori* probability of subject term matching. It was found to be very difficult to develop a good strategy for searching a catalog using LC subject headings. The overriding conclusion was that the LC subject cataloging approach is badly in need of rationalization.

## Introduction

The catalog is the principal information access device in most libraries and information centers. In order to use this device successfully, the user, whether librarian or general user, must, when approaching the catalog, generate a term which matches with some term in the catalog. Ideally, that matched term is not just any term in the catalog, but rather the best one,

*First published as* Bates, M. J. (1977). System meets user: Problems in matching subject search terms. *Information Processing & Management, 13*(6), 367–375.

the term where the largest number of items of interest to the searcher is to be found. Looking under the best term right away is particularly important with library catalog searches, as opposed to, say, on-line bibliographic searches, because research reveals that between two-thirds to three-quarters of catalog subject searches involve only one lookup (Tagliacozzo & Kochen, 1970; ALA, 1958; Knapp, 1944). Evidently, most library catalog users do not revise their original search and try again.

There are problems, to be sure, but on the whole the matching process is fairly straightforward with author/title, or "known-item" searches. It is with subject searches that matching becomes much more problematic. Research reported in this and a companion paper (Bates, 1977), based on an earlier, unpublished dissertation (Bates, 1972), deals with subject term matching.

The subject term structure used in the research was that embodied in the Library of Congress' list of subject headings, 7th edition (Quattlebaum, 1966), and in David Haykin's book, *Subject Headings* (Haykin, 1951), the official statement of principles underlying the list. The catalogs in most large libraries in the United States, especially academic libraries, use the LC approach and subject headings list.

The particular methodology used in the study enabled a more detailed analysis of search matching success than has been possible with most subject catalog studies. That analysis revealed some serious problems with the LC subject heading approach, which will be discussed below.

## Method

The study was designed to test the effects of the variables of subject familiarity (in-depth knowledge of the subject field of search) and catalog familiarity (in-depth knowledge of the organizing principles of the subject term structure in the catalog) on user search success with a catalog. In order to control for the peculiarities of a particular subject field, student undergraduate and graduate majors in *two* subject fields were selected, psychology and economics. Their performances within and outside of their own subject majors were contrasted for the effect of subject familiarity. Their performances in their non-major field, for example, psychology student results in the field of economics, were then compared with those of library students to test the effect of catalog familiarity.

Results on this basic test are reported in Bates (1972). But a very interesting by-product of the test on the variables was a body of results on searcher-term/library-term matches. Because sample *groups* of people were used in each of thirty search instances, it is possible to say something about trends and patterns in search term responses and search matching success.

Specifically, this was a laboratory study, done with university students in an academic library context (University of California at Berkeley). The test means used was to present the students with hypothetical situations in which they must state the term they would use to look up given subjects. They were asked to imagine themselves in a situation where they were unable to find a book in the library (described by means of its title and abstract, but no author) that had been recommended to them by a professor as useful for a paper they were writing. They were, therefore, to have turned to the subject catalog to try to find another book on the very same subject. What term would they use in their search?

They were essentially being asked to generate the book's subject heading, i.e., the term that would, in reality, lead them as searcher to the book in question in the subject catalog. The device in the instructions of having them find another book just like the one described was used in order that they would generate headings from a searcher's, rather than a cataloger's standpoint. If they had been instructed to create headings for the books directly, they would then be playing cataloger. The consequences of the latter mind set for non-librarians are unpredictable. By using a book abstract to describe the topic that the students were to search on, an objective means was provided for determining search success, viz., degree of student term match with the library-assigned heading for the book.

The LC system is low in redundancy. Vocabulary is controlled and books have very few terms assigned to them, generally just one. Hence, to get a strong test of search success, the study was designed so that it was possible to determine what *one* term the student's term "should" match with, not just whether the search term matched with *any* term in the catalog.

Students were senior undergraduate and graduate volunteers, recruited in their classes, and paid a modest amount for their participation. The field of the study was not revealed to the psychology and economics students during recruitment in order to keep self-selection to a minimum. The *n* varied slightly, depending upon experimental details, but results reported in the following are all based on the responses of at least 22 economics students, 22 psychology students and 17 library students.

Books and associated abstracts were selected by a somewhat involved, but carefully random, process, in psychology from *Psychological Abstracts* (1927– ), and in economics from *Economics Library Selections (Series 1)* (Johns Hopkins, 1962). Both psychology and economics books were restricted to the date range 1954–62. In order that student-generated terms could be matched unambiguously with library-assigned terms, another constraint on book selection was that the book had to have been assigned only one subject heading by LC. According to a study done by Avram et al. (1967), this is a condition that held for 53.6% of books cataloged at LC in the "regular" series between 1950 and 1964. Fifteen books were selected in each subject and randomly mixed in presentation order on the test. Students spent about an hour altogether on the test.

## Results

The study design made possible a wealth of different sorts of analyses of patterns of student response and of match with library-assigned headings. Results of the most important analyses performed will be described in this section. For reasons of space, the detailed scoring algorithms involved in these analyses will not be presented here; the reader is referred to the original study for them (Bates, 1972).

When considering student production of headings, one question that arises is: What influence does previous library experience have on the kinds of headings students tend to produce? Do they make matching errors of a certain type because they have previously been exposed to a different subject heading system? We might expect such effects to have been attenuated by the time the student reaches the senior level in college, but on the other hand, library use is generally low enough among college students (Lane, 1966; Barkey, 1965), that they may not have had enough exposure to the University of California's system to change habits.

As it happens, the picture is less complicated than might be expected. The LC subject heading approach is used in most of the larger libraries in the United States. Most school and other small libraries use the *Sears List of Subject Headings* (Westby, 1972), a list deliberately patterned on the same principles as are used in the LC list. The only difference is that the Sears headings tend to be shorter (broader), and there are fewer of them than in the LC list.

Research has shown a remarkable overlap in the two lists, as many as 40% of the book-indexing assignments in a comparison study being *identical,* and most of the rest being cases of the Sears heading being more general than the LC heading (Jackson, 1962, also described in Jackson, 1961; see also Harris, 1969). So, if previous experience may be expected to influence student responses, it may be expected only in the direction of providing headings broader than the ones applied by the University of California Library, not ones different in any in-principle sense.

*See references* The sample-sized groups responding on the same items enabled a determination of the value of see references. If no one out of over sixty people ever used a see reference term that led to the library-assigned heading for a book, then we may suspect that the reference would be of little value for many catalog searchers in real life who are interested in that subject. (See Appendix for a list of the headings used in this study; see Bates, 1972, for associated books and abstracts.)

In fact, a distinct pattern appeared in the types of see reference terms used by students. The great majority of see references suggested in the LC list for the headings used in this study were not used at all by the students. Out of 31 references for 12 of the headings—the other headings did not have any see references associated with them—only six references appeared even once in the responses. These were quite popular, however, there being a total of 64 uses of just these six terms.

An examination of the used and unused terms leads to the following conclusion: The see reference lists contain a number of obscure and outdated terms that would probably be used, if at all, only by persons researching the history of a subject. Examples from this study are "Braidism," see "Hypnotism"; or "Psychotechnics," see "Psychology, Industrial." The sorts of references that were much more popular are (1) those from terms more popular than those preferred by LC, e.g., "Psychology, Abnormal," see "Psychology, Pathological," or (2) from one reasonable term for the subject to another, e.g., "Psychology—Research," see "Psychological Research." It would appear to be relatively easy to cut down the number of the more outdated forms and increase the number of popular, likely, variants of the terms actually selected as valid headings.

*Subject/place order* One of the continuing problems with LC subject headings centers around the precedence to be given to subject and place in the heading. In some subject fields it seems better to have the main headings be by countries or other place names, and to subdivide, i.e. attach subheadings to, those countries by subject aspects. Certainly, geography is such a field. In other instances, place may seem to be secondary and the desirable ordering in the catalog to be by subject, with the place names scattered about under the various subjects. The simultaneous application to a book of the same terms in the two orders is not permitted in the LC approach; one or the other order must be used, as suggested by the subject heading list.

In a study of the LC subject heading list, Bartol Brinkler (1962) found that actual practices by LC for subject/place ordering were quite confused. The most recent public statement that he was able to find of LC policy on which subject areas were to be given which subject/place ordering was dated 1924—several subject heading list editions ago. As it happened, all the subject/place headings used in the Bates study were from economics; Brinkler found the current state of subject/place ordering in economics headings particularly confused: "In spite of some areas of consistency, there would seem to be no overall pattern for the treatment of economics" (Brinkler, 1962, p. 54).

Knapp (1944), in her study, surmised that "in general, students look for local or national material under the subject and for material about a foreign country or nonlocal city under the place name" (1944, p. 226). Using the eight economics headings that involved subject and place, in different orders, in this study (see Appendix), student responses were scored to see if Knapp's suggested pattern was confirmed. There was no confirmation of the hypothesized pattern; in fact, there was no discernible pattern of subject/place ordering in the student responses.

*Noun/adjective order* Another persistent problem with the alphabetico-specific approach, of which the LC list is an example, concerns the proper order to be given to nouns and adjectives in headings where both appear. In the list of headings used in this study, "Human behavior" and "Psychology, Pathological," are examples of two different solutions, and arguments can and have been made for using both orderings. In this study, the interest was solely in determining what the students tended to prefer. Student responses were tallied for the ten headings in this study, in both orders, that each contained one noun and one adjective in the main heading (see Appendix for headings used). The responses were found overwhelmingly to favor the natural noun/adjective ordering, e.g., "Human behavior," not "Behavior, Human."

*Specific entry* Extensive analysis was done on the student responses in terms of "specific entry." The rule of specific entry, dating from Charles Cutter's *Rules for a Dictionary Catalog* (1904), is the most important single rule or principle associated with American subject catalogs. (Also see Haykin, 1951, p. 103) The rule holds that a book is to be entered under the most specific term that describes its entire contents. Thus, a subject heading applied to a book should have the same scope of coverage as the contents of the book, and should be neither broader nor narrower. (Mismatches in book/term specificity nonetheless necessarily occur when a term of proper specificity is not available in the LC list.)

It follows, in addition, that the cataloger is not to index a given document simultaneously under a specific term and any other term that is either broader or narrower. For example, a book on psychological tests will be

TABLE 1. *Mean number of student responses per specificity level*

| STUDENT TERM RELATIVE TO LIBRARY TERM: | LIBRARY STUDENTS N=26 | NON-LIBRARY STUDENTS N=44 |
|---|---|---|
| high (too general) | 2.8 | 5.3 |
| same specificity | 8.1 | 6.5 |
| low (too specific) | 4.1 | 2.9 |
| no response or non-assignable | 0.0 | 0.3 |
| TOTAL | 15.0 | 15.0 |

assigned the term "Mental tests," but may not, by the rule of specific entry, be assigned, in addition, a more specific term, such as "Rorschach test," or a less specific term, such as "Psychology." This principle is what creates the so-called "dictionary catalog," in which the user can look up any subject (or author, or title) of interest, and find books entered there whose entire scope is the same as the scope of the term looked up.

Thus, in order for the user to get to the central place in the catalog where the monographs on a subject may be found, s/he must apply the rule of specific entry in searching—not only catalogers need to understand it. It is therefore of considerable interest to see how well the students did in homing in on the same specificity level in their responses as in the terms used by the library.

There are no generally agreed on principles for comparing or judging specificity levels. An extensive, pragmatic algorithm was developed to use in comparing all student responses to library headings. To test the consistency of scoring under the algorithm, a retest several weeks later showed a 92% rate of identical scores assigned.

Despite the fact that borderline cases were conservatively assigned to the "same level of specificity" category, it turned out that all students failed quite frequently on this dimension of catalog search, going too broad or too narrow about half the time. Average numbers of headings in each category for library and non-library students (in their non-major fields) are listed in Table 1 above.

Ninety-five per cent confidence intervals (based on Student's $t$ distribution) showed only a tiny overlap between the entries of one row and none in the other rows. Hence differences between library and non-library students are almost certainly solid and not due to sample variation.

Let us look closely at the table. Library students, who knew the rule of specific entry, did do better on getting headings in the "same" category—but not as much better as we might expect. What went wrong? Though the library students tended to be more specific than the non-library students, who were very fond of broad terms, they also were too specific much more often than the non-library students, and they thereby lost some of the benefit of their knowledge of the rule.

Two causes for the relatively poor showing of the library students were surmised. First, there is simply the matter of differences in judgment. If the library students tended to be more specific than the non-library students, they would likely be *too* specific more often than the non-library students as well. But the second cause is more interesting. It turns out that the Library of Congress (and hence the libraries using LC cataloging) does not consistently apply the rule of specific entry. Haykin (1951, p. 10) states:

> There are limits to the principle of specificity, however, beyond
> which its application does not appear to serve the best interests
> of the reader. For example, to provide for material on raw silk,
> in any but a textile library, under *Raw silk* would separate it
> from very closely related material on other forms of silk. . . .

So all users are bound to fail some of the time, even where they consistently apply the rule of specific entry—because the library does not follow the rule all of the time. To the extent that the library does not follow the rule of specific entry, search term generation becomes almost a random guessing game for the user.

How many of the failures may be attributed to these two causes? For the library students, a rough guess is that 2.8 of the headings in the "low" row are there due to judgmental differences, i.e. the same number of headings that are found at the upper "high" end. If that is the case, the remaining average 1.3 heading failures could be said to be due to the second factor, viz., LC's failure to apply the rule of specific entry.

A study by Harris (1969) confirmed in another way the failure of LC to follow the rule of specific entry consistently. She found a "correlation of 0.675 between the number of subdivisions (excluding form and geographical subdivisions) and the number of entries in the LC official catalog under a 5% random sample of headings drawn from the LC subject heading list" (1969, p. 60). In other words, it would appear that in many cases subdivisions are added to main headings in order to shorten the length of file behind a heading. Thus, the rule of specific entry is not consistently applied in yet another sense, because in the case of short files, applicable subdivisions are not added, and in the case of long files, they are.

*Direct entry*  The rule of direct entry is often confused with specific entry, but it is actually a distinct principle essential to the alphabetico-specific catalog. This rule states that books are to be entered under the most specific term, without any intervening broader terms (see Haykin, 1951, pp. 3–4, 103). A book on the Rorschach test should be entered under the specific and direct term "Rorschach test," not under, say, "Psychology—Rorschach test." The latter heading is fully specific, but not direct. "Psychology—Rorschach test" is an example of so-called topic subdivision and, according to Haykin (1951, pp. 35–36), is discouraged from use in LC. Other kinds of subdivisions are allowed, however: form, e.g., "Economics—Bibliography"; geographical, e.g., "Taxation—China"; and period, e.g., "United States—History—1817–1825."

Persistent use by student respondents of topic subdivisions would imply that they assumed that the catalog was structured along so-called alphabetico-classed principles (Coates, 1960), wherein, say, as one example of several possible alphabetico-classed patterns, broad main headings are alphabetized in relation to each other, but then subdivided further in a classified manner, so that narrower subjects show up only as subdivisions of broader subjects. This would be the case, for example, if "Rorschach test" appeared only as a subdivision of "Psychology."

Students' responses were searched for instances of *indirect* entry, i.e. topic subdivision. Only clear-cut cases of topic subdivision were tallied. A total of ten non-library students (and no library students) were found who each made four or more, up to sixteen, such errors out of thirty headings. Such a misapprehension of the structure of the catalog should be easy to correct in library use courses and should lead to improved search success.

Unfortunately, the LC list itself may be incorporating more and more indirect, topic subdivision terms, in violation of its own alphabetico-specific principles. The editors of the new 8th edition, published in 1975, while still avowing adherence to the principles for subject heading formation stated in Haykin's book (Library of Congress, 1975, p. viii), wherein topic subdivision is largely forbidden, now explicitly acknowledge "Topical Subdivisions" in the introduction, and note that "many of these subdivisions occur with great frequency. . ." (1975, p. xii). Yet as Haykin (1951, pp. 35–36) says:

> . . . the use of topics comprehended within a subject as
> subdivisions under it is to be avoided. It is contrary to
> the principle of specific entry, since it would, in practice,
> result in an alphabetico-classed catalog. . . . That subject

catalogs, as a matter of fact, contain headings subdivided
by topics is evidence of a lack of a clear understanding
of the purpose of the alphabetical subject catalog. . . .

We have already noted the problems made for the user trying to do an intelligent search, when the rule of specific entry is not consistently followed. The same goes for violations of the rule of direct entry. How can we hope to train users in good searching practice if we cannot tell them whether to expect a broader term to precede their specific term of interest?

There is further the more general point that if a catalog is not to be completely chaotic, any shift to an alphabetico-classed pattern must be done in a consistent manner, based on across-the-board decisions. Alphabetico-classed catalogs should start from a mutually exclusive, jointly exhaustive set of several hundred major subject terms, each to be subdivided by a consistent classified pattern. Selective introduction of classified subdivisions here and there, without an overarching organizational base, can only lead to chaos. It is very unlikely that, in fact, LC has any overall intention of moving to an alphabetico-classed pattern, but, by their own admission, some such elements are creeping in.

The 8th edition of the LC subject heading list reflects a great deal of effort to improve access to LC subject cataloging practices for the local library cataloger. The introduction is considerably expanded and a great many more subdivisions are provided, along with extensive scope notes, so that catalogers may better merge the product of their local efforts with the LC printed cards bought for some (or most) new acquisitions. Unfortunately, development and refinement of theoretical principles behind the selection and organization of terms appears to have fallen before the practical exigencies of coping with particular needs for new subject terms. Now that the list is growing to near-astronomical size (2026 three-column 9 x 12 in. pages), lacks in theoretical development and inconsistencies in application—which in earlier, simpler times, would have been of little moment—are now becoming very evident. As noted in many ways in this paper, these lacks and inconsistencies are making it difficult for the user to do an intelligent search in the product of this subject cataloging approach.

***A priori probability of term matching*** The discussion so far has been based on an experimental design in which success was measured by match between student term and the term actually assigned to a test book/abstract by the library. But in real life searchers in fact often match with *some*, presumably related, heading in the catalog, if not the one most central to the topic of interest. It is thus possible to provide a weaker measure of success by determining the match rate with any, i.e., the most closely matching, legitimate heading in the system.

For comparison purposes, student responses were scored on both bases in the study, the degree of match with the one library-assigned heading being called the "basic" score, and the degree of match with the closest legitimate existing heading being called the "existence" score. These results were discussed in detail in Bates (1972, 1977), but one aspect is of interest for our consideration of response patterns in this paper. It was found that library students did much better than non-library students on the basic score. Summing exact and partial matches, library students scored 35% of the maximum score possible, vs 22 and 21% for the psychology and economics students respectively, a very marked difference. This difference in performance can be ascribed to the library students' familiarity with typical patterns of LC headings and with the specific entry and direct entry rules.

But on the existence score we note a curious thing: all students did about the same. The student groups received the following percentages of the maximum possible score: psychology, 60%; economics, 62%; library, 64%. Why do library students not do better? An exploration of this question leads to an additional interesting element in considering the user's relationship to the catalog as an information access device.

We noted earlier that the whole response set of the library students was shifted downward in terms of specificity. They apparently acted on the rule of specific entry, while the non-library students, not being aware of specific entry, frequently gave terms that were too broad to index the books. We must be careful here to distinguish specificity from breadth and narrowness in the general sense. A specific term is not always a narrow term. For example, the specific term to describe a book on the whole field of psychology is "Psychology." Nonetheless, if the non-library students fail on specificity by going broad much more often than the library students do, then it is reasonable to assume that the average term suggested by that group is broader in the general sense than the average term suggested by the library students.

Let us take this a step further. It could be expected that on an *a priori* basis, broader suggested terms would be easier to match with existing library terms than narrower ones. Broader terms are usually shorter, simpler, and more generally agreed upon in phrasing. This supposition was tested empirically with the data and verified. Each of the subject major groups was divided into two groups based on the number of "high" specificity scores (response too broad) they received. The average existence scores of these groups were then computed. The half of the psychology students with the most "high" scores on the specificity measure averaged over six percentage points higher in existence matching scores than the half of the psychology students with few "high" scores. The difference between the corresponding groups of economics students was even greater: exactly nine percentage points. So we may assume that the relative advantage enjoyed by the library students through their greater knowledge of the cataloging approach is lost on existence matching because they use more specific and therefore harder-to-match search terms.

It is no fault of the LC list that broad terms are easier to match *a priori* than narrow terms. But within the existing structure of rules and practices with LC subject headings, this fact makes for difficulties for the user in devising a subject search strategy.

**Search strategy** Let us draw together this information on *a priori* matching success with the other findings in the paper and consider the factors involved in developing a general search strategy. We will not distinguish between exhaustive searches and the "a few items on" sort. The considerations below should apply to most searches except those in which the requirements are so loose that almost any indexing system and any search strategy would suffice, for example, the need: "I've got to do a book report on *something* in economics by Friday."

So here, based on this research, are what we see to be the factors involved in devising a general search strategy for use with an LC-based subject catalog: Use of the rule of specific entry means that the most thorough coverage of a subject of interest can be found only by using specific terms. In the example used earlier, the searcher interested in the Rorschach test will find no whole books on the Rorschach test in the catalog under "Mental tests" or "Psychology." These latter terms are to be applied by catalogers only to books on those whole subjects. Thus, the searcher interested in the Rorschach test who uses broader terms instead, should find, at best, only book chapters or sections on the test in books of broader scope.

So, it seems good, indeed, almost essential, to use a specific heading. But, the rule of specific entry is not always followed and the searcher may fail for going in at a level more specific than that used by the catalog. How can the user guess whether "Rorschach test" will or will not be too specific for the catalog? In addition, a point not mentioned earlier: see also references that go upward hierarchically, i.e. superordinate references, are forbidden with LC, so the user going in at too specific a level will get no helpful feedback from the catalog. Also, the rule of direct entry may be violated, and a broader term used as entry point after all. Finally, the searcher's *a priori* chance of matching with any narrower heading is smaller than that with broader headings. So it seems good to use a broad heading. . . .

As the sequence of these two paragraphs shows, the person who attempts to optimize search strategy may be forced into an endless circle. There is no clearly preferable strategy for searches in general in an LC-based subject catalog. The only way, really, to tell the user to search such a catalog is to make *many* tries, to enter the catalog at many specificity levels and under many different terms and to stop the search only when the headings are not producing any more materials of interest.

## Summary and conclusions

See references in 30 hypothetical search instances were found to be of some use, that is, some see references were heavily used while many were not used by any of the more than 60 students. No discernible pattern in subject/place order was found in the student responses. Students did, however, overwhelmingly favor the natural order of nouns and adjectives, i.e. adjective first, in subject headings.

Knowledge of the rule of specific entry was presumed to be responsible for the fact that library students did better than non-library students in suggesting terms at the same specificity level as the library-assigned terms. It was suggested that library students were also hurt, however, by the fact that the rule of specific entry is followed by LC only some of the time. Non-library students failed frequently on the rule of direct entry, that is, a number of them frequently provided indirect subject headings. It was noted, however, that indirect headings may become increasingly common in the LC list, thus confusing efforts to instruct users to avoid indirect entry. Finally, it was found that the *a priori* probability of matching broad terms was greater than that of matching narrow terms.

Drawing all these results together, it was suggested that the LC approach to subject indexing is so designed that the user has no clearly preferable strategy for searches in general. For both of two major likely strategies, use of broad terms and use of specific terms, disadvantages weigh heavily against advantages.

In a more general sense, these results point to one major conclusion. The subject access approach used in most of the larger libraries in the United States badly needs to be rationalized. What rules there are, are not consistently followed, and the system, even at its best, does not permit the development of rational, high-yield search rules.

The LC subject heading approach was developed in other, and simpler times. (The first edition was published in 1910.) As a straightforward compendium of simple, specific topics, it served through many years. But information is more complex, subjects more interdisciplinary, libraries far larger these days. With a smaller collection and fewer headings it may not have made much difference what all the consequences were of the rule of specific entry, for example. But now it does.

Through automation, extensive changes, which once would have been prohibitively expensive with manual card catalogs, are now much more feasible. At the least, *future* cataloging can be done differently, even if conversion is impractical.

This research, and an examination of the LC subject heading list, convince this observer that the costs in search inefficiency and retrieval failure that can be presumed to arise from such an outdated and overburdened system are too high. Professional responsibility for the organization and management of our resources requires that we clean up and transform the muddled system of subject access that now exists in major American research libraries.

## The 30 test subject headings

o = heading with *see reference* leading to it.

x = heading with *see reference* leading to it that was used by one of the students.

s = heading used in subject/place-order test.

n = heading used in noun/adjective order test.

| O | X | S | N | TEST SUBJECT HEADINGS |
|---|---|---|---|---|
| o | x |  | n | 1. Psychological research |
| o |  |  |  | 2. Hypnotism |
| o | x |  | n | 3. Psychology, Pathological |
|  |  |  |  | 4. Psychoanalysis |
| o |  |  |  | 5. Adolescence |
| o | x |  | n | 6. Psychology, Industrial |
| o |  |  |  | 7. Personality |
| o |  |  | n | 8. Human behavior |
|  |  |  |  | 9. Freud, Sigmund, 1856–1939 |
|  |  |  |  | 10. Psychology—Hist. |
| o | x |  |  | 11. Language and languages |
|  |  |  | n | 12. Rorschach test |
| o |  |  |  | 13. Perception |
|  |  |  |  | 14. Motivation (Psychology) |
| o |  |  |  | 15. Psychology |
|  |  |  |  | 16. Competition |
|  |  | s |  | 17. Taxation—China |
|  |  | s | n | 18. Workmen's compensation—New Jersey |
| o |  |  |  | 19. Wages |
|  |  | s |  | 20. Commonwealth of Nations—Econ. condit. |
|  |  |  |  | 21. United Shoe Machinery Corporation |
| o |  |  |  | 22. Rent (Economic theory) |
|  |  |  | n | 23. Tin plate |
|  |  |  |  | 24. Gold—Stat. |
|  |  | s | n | 25. Trade-unions—Gt. Brit. |
|  |  |  |  | 26. Economics—Hist. |
|  |  | s |  | 27. Income tax, Municipal—U.S. |
|  |  | s | n | 28. Agricultural machinery—Trade and manufacture—Canada |
|  |  | s |  | 29. China (People's Republic of China, 1949– )—Econ. condit. |
|  |  | s | n | 30. Southwest, New—Econ. condit. |

# REFERENCES

American Library Association. (1958). *Catalog use study, director's report by Sidney L. Jackson.* Chicago, IL: ALA.

Avram, H.D., Guiles, K.D., & Meade, G.T. (1967). Fields of information on Library of Congress catalog cards: Analysis of a random sample, 1950–1964. *The Library Quarterly, 37*(2), 180–192.

Barkey, P. (1965). Patterns of student use of a college library. *College & Research Libraries, 26*(2), 115–118.

Bates, M.J. (1972). *Factors affecting subject catalog search success.* (Unpublished doctoral dissertation). University of California, Berkeley.

Bates, M.J. (1977). Factors affecting subject catalog search success. *Journal of the American Society for Information Science, 28*(3), 161–169.

Brinkler, B. (1962). The geographical approach to materials in the Library of Congress subject headings. *Library Resources & Technical Services, 6,* 49–64.

Coates, E.J. (1960). *Subject catalogues: Headings and structure.* London: Library Association.

Cutter, C.A. (1904). *Rules for a dictionary catalog* (4th ed.) Washington, DC: U.S. Government Printing Office.

Harris, J.L. (1969). *Subject headings: Factors influencing formation and choice: With special reference to Library of Congress and H.W. Wilson practice.* (Doctoral dissertation). Columbia University, New York.

Haykin, D.J. (1951). *Subject headings: A practical guide.* Washington, DC: U.S. Government Printing Office.

Jackson, S.L. (1961). Sears and LC subject headings: A sample comparison. *Library Journal, 86,* 755.

Jackson, S.L. (1962). The Sears and Library of Congress lists of subject headings, report of a sample comparison. *Illinois Libraries, 44,* 608.

Johns Hopkins University, Dept. of Political Economy, & University of Pittsburgh, Dept. of Economics. (1965). *Economics Library Selections. Series I, New Books in Economics.* Pittsburgh: Department of Economics, University of Pittsburgh, [1954]–1965.

Knapp, P.B. (1944). The subject catalog in the college library: An investigation of terminology. *The Library Quarterly, 14*(3), 214–228.

Lane, G. (1966). Assessing the undergraduates' use of the university library. *College & Research Libraries, 27*(4), 277–282.

Library of Congress (1975). *Library of Congress Subject Headings* (8th ed., 2 Vol.). Washington, DC: Library of Congress.

*Psychological Abstracts* (1927– ). Lancaster, PA: American Psychological Association.

Quattlebaum, M.V. (Ed.). (1966). *Subject headings used in the dictionary catalogs of the Library of Congress* (7th ed.). Washington, DC: Library of Congress Subject Cataloging Division.

Tagliacozzo, R., & Kochen, M. (1970). Information-seeking behavior of catalog users. *Information Storage and Retrieval, 6*(5), 363–381.

Westby, B.M. (Ed.). (1972). *Sears list of subject headings* (10th ed.). New York: H.W. Wilson.

# 3

# Subject access in online catalogs: A design model

ABSTRACT

A model based on strikingly different philosophical assumptions from those currently popular is proposed for the design of online subject catalog access. Three design principles are presented and discussed: *uncertainty* (subject indexing is indeterminate and probabilistic beyond a certain point), *variety* (by Ashby's law of requisite variety, variety of searcher query must equal variety of document indexing), and *complexity* (the search process, particularly during the entry and orientation phases, is subtler and more complex, on several grounds, than current models assume). Design features presented are an *access* phase, including *entry* and *orientation*, a *hunting* phase, and a *selection* phase. An end-user thesaurus and a front-end system mind are presented as examples of online catalog system components to improve searcher success during entry and orientation.

The proposed model is "wrapped around" existing Library of Congress subject-heading indexing in such a way as to enhance access greatly without requiring reindexing. It is argued that both for cost reasons and in principle this is a superior approach to other design philosophies.

*First published as* Bates, M. J. (1986). Subject access in online catalogs: A design model. *Journal of the American Society for Information Science, 37*(6), 357–376.

## Introduction

These are times of great excitement in information systems design. With the advent of online catalogs, the nature of catalogs and access to library materials has changed more in a handful of years than it has in all the rest of the twentieth century. But the changes have been more technological than conceptual. Online catalogs to date have added powerful capabilities to the traditional catalog, yet system designs, generally, have still not gone beyond implementing the card catalog in online form, with some established online search features tacked on. As valuable and as difficult as these accomplishments have been, they have only scratched the surface of what is possible with online systems (cf. Hildreth, 1984).

We might compare the current situation to that of the automobile in the earlier part of this century. At first, cars were designed like "horseless carriages," i.e., identical in shape and aerodynamics to carriages; only later did designers sort out what features should be altered to better suit the requirements of a vehicle that could move vastly faster than carriages had. So far, many of the features of the online catalog resemble the features of that horse and buggy known as the card catalog. We are just beginning to see features being designed for online catalogs which take fuller advantage of the capabilities of online systems. Designs by Doszkocs (1983), natural-language search queries and automatic term stemming and weighting; Morehead et al. (1984), weighted computations of relatedness between query and fiction records; Cochrane and Markey (1985), and Markey and Demeyer (1985), novel uses of book classifications to improve subject access; Hjerppe (1985), application of the "hypertext" concept to catalogs, i.e., breaking the linearity of the traditional file and providing links in a variety of directions from displayed records; and Noerr and Bivins-Noerr (1985), linkages between many different fields in different records, among others, are early indicators of the shift to the design of catalogs truly suited to online use.

In this article the question of subject access in online catalogs is considered anew from its philosophical underpinnings. Design principles are proposed and example system components are described which express those principles. The sequence of topics of discussion is as follows: After this introduction, a literature review is presented, asking the question: Is improvement in online catalog subject access really needed? In the next section, design principles differing radically in some respects from the traditional model are proposed and discussed under the rubrics of "uncertainty," "variety," and "complexity" (See Fig. 1). Implications of these principles for the design of subject access in online catalogs are drawn in the subsequent section. The design features are described in the next section, and some example system components are described in section that follows. Many system components might be possible based on the suggested design philosophy; the proposed components, an "end-user thesaurus" and a "front-end system mind" are presented to illustrate and substantiate the recommended approach. A summary completes the article.

While the suggested approach to subject access is significantly different from the conventional one, a design is recommended which uses existing Library of Congress subject cataloging, i.e., which wraps that cataloging into a new, sophisticated system. Not only does this approach save the vast amounts of money that would be necessary to recatalog existing records, but it also turns out to be philosophically preferable, costs aside, for reasons to be argued. The proposed system features should provide more sophisticated intellectual access to library materials in the context of equally enhanced sophistication in the use of online capabilities.

## Background: Is improvement in online catalog subject access really needed?

As Cochrane (1983) has recently noted, a shift is taking place in our assumptions about the relative importance of descriptive and subject access to materials in catalogs. Traditionally, the weight of effort and attention was given to descriptive cataloging. For example, in 1950 the University of California at Berkeley needed to reduce cataloging arrears and undertook some studies to see if the subject cataloging could be cut back to save time. Descriptive cataloging cutbacks were not examined because it was felt that no time could be saved in that area (Markley, 1950, p. 88). After a study in which it was found that students averaged slightly over two subject catalog uses per year (i.e., 40,000+ student subject catalog uses per year, if there were 20,000 students in the university), it was concluded that "this use is insufficient in quantity to justify the continuance of the subject catalog in its present form" (Markley, 1950, p. 91). In the article, the possibilities that the subject approach might be important to students and that the relatively low use might be due to inadequate design of the subject access were never considered.

Actually, subject access has constituted between 10% and 62% of card catalog use all along, with an average of about 40% (Markey, 1984, pp. 76–77)—hardly trivial. Rather, it appears that there has been something of a bias against library subject access; it has been seen as a nice extra, rather than as something essential.

The great popularity of subject access among online catalog users has restored the subject approach in the thinking of the field to its rightful place as a major form of access to library materials. Recent articles have closely

**Uncertainty:** Document description and query development are indeterminate and probabilistic beyond a certain point.

**Variety:** Variety of query formulation must be as great as variety of document description for successful search.

**Complexity:** Entry to and use of an information system is a complex and subtle process.

## FEATURES

**Access Component:** Emphasizes natural language semantics.
    **Entry:** Searcher need only "hit side of the barn" to get into network of terms.
    *Example element facilitating entry:* **End-user thesaurus.**

    **Orientation:** System assists searcher in orientation, exploration, and in generating necessary variety in search formulation.
    *Example element facilitating orientation:* **Front-end system mind.**

**Hunting Component:** Emphasizes command language syntax.
    Keyword, post-coordinate, and "docking" match permitted.

**Selection Component:** Emphasizes natural language syntax.
    Significant additional information from document provided to assist selection.

FIG. 1. *Design model: A variety enhancement model for online subject access.*

examined the strengths and weaknesses of Library of Congress subject headings, the major type of subject headings used in large libraries in the U.S. (Boll, 1982; Kirtland & Cochrane, 1982; Mischo, 1982). The Council on Library Resources study found that subject uses constituted 59% of all online catalog uses across many types of libraries and online systems (Matthews et al., 1983, p. 144). Even though the keyword matching capability of many online catalogs constitutes a great improvement over traditional card catalog subject access (and is probably responsible for much of the interest in subject searches), additional subject-related search capabilities were at the top of the list of desired further improvements named by users (Matthews et al., 1983, p. 134). In separate studies, Kaske and Sanders (1980) and Larson and Graham (1983) found similar enthusiasm for subject assistance. Additional subject-related catalog capabilities have also been recommended by a number of authors and study groups (Markey, 1984; Brownrigg & Lynch, 1983; Holley & Killheffer, 1982; Jones, 1983; Lawrence, 1985; Mandel, 1981, 1985; Mandel & Herschman, 1983; McCarn, 1983; Russell, 1982).

    If we accept that subject access in library catalogs is coming to be valued now and much attention is shifting to it, the question still remains of how much of our resources should go into it. The question might be turned around to say, with all the power of online subject searching of catalogs—Boolean logic, keyword match, truncation, etc.—have we, perhaps, already given the user all the search capability that is practically necessary?

Reviews of card catalog use studies have found average satisfaction rates in subject searching of around 70% or slightly better (Frarey, 1953, p. 162; Hafter, 1979, p. 217). These results have generally been taken as indicating satisfactory performance on the part of catalogs. As Hafter said, in the context of reporting this figure: "Users have a very high success rate at the catalog" (Hafter, 1979, p. 217). Yet in a review of studies evaluating reference services, Rothstein found rates of satisfaction on the part of the public of around 90% (Rothstein, 1964, pp. 464–465). Reviewers might as easily have looked with dismay upon this 70% figure and noted how much below reference services catalogs are rated by their users.

How have online catalogs done? In the Council on Library Resources survey across 29 libraries (academic, public, and state/federal) 46% of users found their search "very satisfactory," and another 34% found it "somewhat satisfactory." In terms of specific retrieval performance, 17% found more than they were looking for, 28% found all or most of what they were looking for, 40% found some, and 16% found nothing (sum of 101% due to rounding error) (Matthews et al., 1983, p. 151). Summing the first three gives 85%, a definite improvement over the card catalog results.

Still, even these figures could stand some improvement. To put them differently, 56% of the searchers found only some or none of what they were looking for, and an unknown additional number found only most of what they were looking for (part of the 28% figure). When we consider that most of these libraries were very large, and that in the academic libraries 60% of the users were undergraduate students (Matthews et al., 1983, p. 89) whose needs would rarely fall outside the scope of a good academic collection, then we must assume that a fair number of failures, on the part of students or catalog, led to suboptimal retrieval.

There is a crucial weakness, furthermore, in all subject catalog use studies that ask users for expressions of satisfaction. The user can decide whether the materials found were satisfactory or not, but *has no way of knowing what was missed.* We find the same problem with the above-mentioned studies of satisfaction with reference service. A few years after Rothstein's survey found that average 90% satisfaction rate, several studies came out showing that the actual number of correct answers given by public library reference services was on the order of 50% [e.g., Crowley & Childers 1971; Childers, 1980]. The users were satisfied, all right, but in many cases only because they did not know what they were missing.

My research provided a comparable result for catalog use. In an experimental setting, students were asked to state what word or phrase they would use to search in the subject catalog for a book just like the one described in the title and abstract of a real book. The degree of match was then computed between the students' terms and the headings actually used by the University of California at Berkeley library to index the books in question. This approach tested whether people would actually hit upon specific relevant material in a search rather than just whether their term would match with any heading in the catalog, whether or not that heading indexed material relevant to their query. As with the studies on the correctness of reference questions, the results were much less positive. Matching scores for student terms on the first lookup were just over 20% of the maximum possible, even when credit was given for partial term and partial word matches (Bates, 1977, p. 166). Requiring match with the index terms for a series of specific relevant books is a stringent test, but one providing a truer measure of recall success than the searcher's own guess about whether or not good material was found.

For all these reasons, it appears that we may still find much improvement possible in library catalogs. Now, while we are in the midst of designing online systems, and both our attitudes and the systems are open and flexible, is the time to investigate ways of bringing about those improvements.


## Design principles

### Indexing and access according to "uncertainty principle"

In 1974, in an article entitled "The Scientific Premises of Information Science," Rosenberg argued that "Most of the research done to date in information science has been ... in what we can broadly call the tradition of Newtonian mechanics" (Rosenberg, 1974, p. 264). According to Zukav, "Classical [Newtonian] physics is based on the assumption that our reality, independently of us, runs its course in space and time according to strict causal laws. Not only can we observe it, unnoticed, as it unfolds, we can predict its future by applying causal laws to initial conditions" (Zukav, 1979, p. 134). Rosenberg again: "The method [in Newtonian physics] for discovering the mechanism or cause is to reduce all phenomena to their basic component parts, to dissect, to simplify. Also essential to the methodology is the notion of objectivity—the removal of the observer from that which is observed" (Rosenberg, 1974, p. 264).

But in the modern physics of quantum mechanics and Einstein's relativity, unsettling discoveries were made that had ramifications beyond the physical laws being discovered. In studying the subatomic world of quantum mechanics, Heisenberg demonstrated that it is impossible to measure both the position and the momentum of a particle at a given instant. This was not a conclusion based on the inadequacy of measuring instruments. Rather, the physical nature of the subatomic world is such that the very act of measuring changes the thing measured. The most that physics could do was state probabilities, but it could never state with certainty the position and momentum of a particular particle at a particular moment. This discovery of Heisenberg's is known as the "uncertainty principle" (Zukav, 1979, pp. 132–136).

In recent years other scientific fields, particularly the social sciences, have been recognizing that the ideal of the perfectly objective observer is simplistic and naive, and that the observer and the observed may interact in extremely complex ways that are very difficult to sort out. Further, it has been observed that human social systems may operate according to certain common patterns with certain probabilities, but may be indeterminate at the level of specific behaviors at specific moments. Here I wish to argue that an uncertainty principle is similarly appropriate for study of some of the behavioral aspects of information science.

Our Newtonian/mechanistic assumption has been that somewhere there is an ideal indexing system or language that will enable us to produce the one perfect description or set of descriptions for each document. These ideal descriptions will, in turn, produce the best possible match with users' needs as expressed in queries. Each improvement in human or machine indexing is to take us closer to that ideal.

But suppose instead that that ideal is impossible in principle, because both indexing behavior and information searching behavior are at least in part indeterminate and probabilistic? Wilson argued persuasively a number of years ago that it is practically impossible to define what "subject of a document" means, that is, to define what it is that a person looks for in identifying the subject of a document (Wilson, 1978, pp. 69–92). By implication, therefore, it is practically impossible to instruct indexers or catalogers how to find subjects when they examine documents. Indeed, we cataloging instructors usually deal with this essential feature of the skill being taught by saying such vague and inadequate things as "Look for the main topic of the document."

There is more to this issue than arguments in principle, however. We also have an extensive body of empirical data that suggests the impossibility of the Newtonian ideal, viz., indexer consistency studies. A great number of these studies were conducted in the 1960's, and no matter what measure of consistency was used, rates of inconsistency in indexing were found to be very high (Stevens, 1965; Cooper, 1969). Two indexers well trained in an indexing system (interindexer consistency) would frequently index a given document differently, and even the same indexer (intraindexer consistency) would use different terms at different times on the same document. For example, a typical result is found in a study by Jacoby and Slamecka (Jacoby & Slamecka, 1962), reported in Stevens (1965): The interindexer consistency was found to be 20% and the intraindexer consistency 50% (Stevens, 1965, p. 159). These results were puzzling and disturbing, but have been largely ignored in subsequent years, perhaps because our mechanistic view of information retrieval has no explanation for these results.

To demonstrate this point further, let us note the results of extensive association studies done in psychological research. The patterns of association in the human mind are extraordinarily complex and multifarious. In these studies people are given a term and asked to state the next term that comes to mind. The research shows that even the simplest terms like "river" or "whistle" evoke a variety of responses in people. In repeat studies many of the same terms will come up, with similar frequencies as in earlier studies, so probabilities can be stated for common associations. For example, among men the term "whistle" evokes the words "train," "blow," "girl," and "noise" with frequencies, respectively, of 14%, 13%, 11% and 6% (Bilodeau & Howell, 1965, p. 19). But there is no way to say which of these common terms (or the occasional "far-out" term) a particular individual will name in a specific instance. Furthermore, the effort to examine the thought processes to determine what was behind the mentioned term are so intrusive (the observer disturbing the observed processes) that we are unlikely ever to know what was involved. It may even be that at times these human thought processes are in some part random in that the potential to associate to two given terms from "whistle" may be virtually identical and only some random chemical process in the mind trips the association in one direction or another. Whatever the mechanism, we as observers must note that associations are various and many to even the simplest of stimuli.

Similar results have been found closer to home. Furnas et al. were interested in identifying the best names to use for text-editing operations so that these names could be used in the design of automated text-editing systems. So they conducted several related experiments on this question. For example, in one, 48 secretarial and high-school students were given a sample manuscript with author's corrections and asked to "prepare a typed list of instructions for someone else who was actually going to make the changes but did not have the author's marks" (Furnas et al., 1982, p. 251). Here one might expect the range of terms used to be much smaller, since each individual is asked to describe a specific operation, rather than free associate. Yet the authors note: "The most striking result from the verbal production data was the great diversity in people's descriptions . . . The average likelihood of any *two people* using the same main content word in their descriptions of the same object ranged from about .07 to .18 for the variety of stimulus domains studied [including the above mentioned experiment]" (Furnas et al., 1982, p. 252).

It seems quite likely, then, that indexer consistency studies reflect the same variability in associations that have been found in these psychological and office automation studies. In other words, these are fundamental human traits, and show up wherever human beings have the opportunity to make mental associations. In one reading of a document certain features are noted, in the next reading other features are. The associations indexers will make to the words of the document differ and so the weight the indexer attaches to different topics or aspects of the document's contents will also differ. Hence the terms chosen will differ. We must live with the fact that while certain patterns may recur, we usually cannot predict indexing behavior in a specific instance.

It is appropriate at this point to recall that Bush's dream of a "memex," written up in what is generally considered to be the founding article of information science (Bush, 1945), contained features closer in spirit to the approach being discussed here than to that of the traditional information retrieval system. Bush's dream was of a system that had the rich and sometimes random connections found in the human mind. He envisioned a system in which the user could set up connections between any two thoughts or entries he or she wished. He accepted without dismay that these connections might be irrational, illogical, or inconsistent. He accepted that the associations people make in their minds between one thought and another or one word and another go along an extraordinary variety of lines. Bush's memex, in effect, mimicked the dense interconnectivity of human thought processes. (In what follows, the searcher will not be able to set up connections, but may follow up any of a huge variety of connections provided by the system.)

Now, if, in given instances, indexers are inconsistent from one to another or from one time to another, and we accept that this is characteristic of human beings, might we not also assume that search terms and phrases put to an information retrieval system will also show the same variety and unpredictability? That is, if a group of 50 searchers all had the same problem to search, would they not also show the same inconsistency in terms used as found among the indexers?

In general, it is harder to answer this question, because there have not been searcher consistency studies in the way that indexer consistency studies were performed, although recent research by Fidel on trained, experienced online intermediaries suggests that on questions of any complexity, the agreement between searchers on search terms is low (Fidel, 1985). Lilley and I, in separate card catalog studies, found similarly low overlap in terminology used in searching the same queries in card catalogs. Lilley asked 340 students to give subject headings that they might search on to find six books. An average of 62 different headings were suggested for each book (Lilley, 1954, p. 42). In my study (Bates, 1977), students were asked to state the search term they would use to find a book just like the one described in an abstract. The study was not designed to examine intersearcher consistency, but a scan of the responses of undergraduate and graduate students reveals the same enormous variety found by Lilley. For example, 71 students responded to the first of the books in my study; they produced 46 different headings (some varying by singular/plural only), no one of which was suggested by more than six people.

Let us assume, then, that there is a certain indeterminacy associated with information description and retrieval that is rooted in the nature of the human mind. Given a document, it is impossible (and is likely to remain so) to predict exactly what description a trained indexer will give to it. Given a topic of interest to a searcher, it is impossible to predict what specific aspect of the topic a searcher will pursue and which specific terms or phrasings of terms the searcher will use. Rather than viewing this human characteristic as an obstacle to overcome, let us instead work with this complexity and variety, and design information systems that accept and use this trait.

Having said that, then what do we do to meet this situation? An answer is to stop trying to design systems that will *target* the desired information through perfect pinpoint match on the one best term; rather, design systems to *encompass* the answer by displaying and making it easy to explore a variety of descriptive terms.

Show searchers a wide range of descriptive terms and thereby implicitly educate them on the need to produce variety. Do not worry about whether any one term is the best to search with; rather, get the searcher in the habit of using a number of terms (for recall searches), or at least exploring various terms until the most descriptive ones are found (for precision searches).

Incidentally, in this discussion the literature drawn from psychology on association patterns is dated from the 1960's because once psychologists exhausted the limits of the research model of tallying associations, they went on to try to develop models for the internal mental processes that lead to these association patterns and other manifestations of thought (Schank & Colby, 1973; Johnson-Laird et al., 1984). In what follows, however, it is not being proposed that we mimic human thought within the system in an artificial intelligence manner; rather it is proposed that we make available the means in the information system to facilitate the searcher's own rich associative tendencies.

## High variety, redundancy.

It is appropriate at this point to introduce Ashby's law of requisite variety, which he described in his book *An Introduction to Cybernetics* (Ashby, 1973). The law of requisite variety holds that for a system (whether machine or organism) to function successfully, it must generate as much variety in its responses to the environment as the environment generates as input to the system (Ashby, 1973, pp. 202–212) (with the exception of the cases where the same response can be used for more than one disturbance). Variety may come in the form of a physical disturbance or of information. Any time the homeostatic stability of a system is threatened by some environmental input, whether a rise in temperature detected by a thermostat or news that a relative has died (or, alternatively, received the Nobel Prize), the system must produce some response which restores stability and enables it to continue functioning normally. In the case of the thermostat, its response may be to kick on the air conditioner. In the case of the human being, the appropriate response may be to mourn (or celebrate) until the emotional stress of the news has been discharged and stability returns. If the human being responds with inadequate variety, then impairment in functioning may appear. For example, in the case of the loss of a loved one, suppose the individual denies the loss and the associated grief, and tries to go on as normal, with the usual set of responses, instead of generating a new, appropriate, response. The grief then "goes underground," may ultimately cause disruptions in other relationships, and can even lead to depression and death.

We can see countless instances in our own and others' lives where people have responded with inadequate variety to environmental variety. For example, a worker in an industrial city may provide successfully for his family for many years—meeting a great variety of challenges, but when a major new one comes along, like the closure of the main manufacturing plant in town, may be unable to produce an adequate response—such as looking for work in another city or industry—to cope successfully with it. Then, too, there is no law that says that there even exists a possible response to certain challenges. Ashby's law only says that to function successfully, a system's variety must match the variety of environmental inputs, that is all.

Now let us take the law of requisite variety and apply it to information retrieval (IR) systems. With information systems the situation is the reverse from those described above: We want the variety (information) and we initiate the interaction by producing the "response" (search formulation) in order to provoke the variety (information).[1] We cannot get the full, desired information unless the variety of our search formulation is as great as the variety in the information. If, as I have argued in the previous section, indexers produce great variety in their indexing, then in order to cope successfully the searcher must produce an equal variety in formulating a search on any given topic.

There are two logical strategies in the design of IR systems that have been used to promote a good match in the variety of these two systems, the IR system and the human searcher. The strategies are *(1) reduce the variety of the IR system (specifically, document description)*, and *(2) increase the variety of the searcher (specifically, searcher's query)*. Both of these strategies are used currently in the design of index languages. Strategy 1 is accomplished by vocabulary control. The principal purpose behind controlling vocabularies is to reduce the variety in natural language expressions that would otherwise appear in the indexing, particularly, the variety in word forms (e.g., singular/plural, verb conjugations, etc.), syntactical variations (e.g., different word orders), and synonymy.

This strategy has had considerable success in improving information retrieval performance—but it has its limits. The variety that is wreaking havoc in indexer consistency studies is not the variety mentioned above in word forms, synonyms, etc., because those are controlled in the indexing languages used by the indexers. Rather, indexer inconsistency must be due to selecting different topics or features to emphasize, or to making a different decision in a close judgment call where the document's topic might fall within two areas. We cannot reduce that sort of variety, because that is not variety of expression, but rather variety of meaning. We do not want to merge conceptually distinct topics in an indexing language; to do so would be to impoverish the language's ability to describe the distinct topics we want to be able to retrieve on. Operationally, such merging of distinct topics would be disastrous for precision. To put it differently, we can reduce the variety in the language used to describe information, but we cannot reduce the variety in the information itself without defeating the point of an IR system. Thus the strategy of reducing the variety in the information system has been pushed to its limit.

---

1   This approach nonetheless falls within the Ashby model on the grounds that in order to generate new responses to meet new challenges the system must sometimes permit some variety, in the form of non-life-threatening information, to come in. Homeostasis is then restored when the new information makes it possible for the system to generate a new, effective response to some disturbance which is more life threatening than the information is. (See Ashby, 1973, p. 212.)

The second strategy, of increasing the variety of the searcher's query, is used also in controlled vocabularies, but to a much smaller extent. The principal mechanism is the provision of cross references. See references refer from unused to used terms for a topic, and see also references refer from one topic to related topics. Note that increasing the searcher's variety through the use of cross references does not cancel out the first strategy; the variety provided the searcher upon entry is then channelled to the more limited set of accepted terminology.

Despite the enormous variety in expression in the phrases for a topic that people bring to an information system, index languages seldom have more "see from" (unused) terms in them than used terms. In other words, the index language provides a little variety of expression for the searcher, but not much. Variety in topics as provided by see also references is generally viewed by practitioners as the least important part of an index language. Some or all of the see also reference terms may not be added to catalogs in times of staff shortage. In online systems, cross references are the last to be added to online catalogs, and only a few online databases contain the cross references used in thesauri.

It is a fundamental premise of this article that the second strategy, that of increasing the searcher's variety, has been underutilized and contains great potential for improving information retrieval. Many of the approaches proposed in this article deal with various ways of implementing the second strategy. Online capabilities make it much easier to implement these than was formerly the case, and we are only just beginning to see the potential. Most searchers do not realize the great variety that exists in the target information. They use a reasonable term for the topic and stop there. The system must not only help the searcher generate the variety, but also first show the searcher that the variety is there.

Another closely related way to look at this matter is through the concept of redundancy. In Shannon's information theory, redundancy can be described, loosely, as the difference between the maximum efficiency possible in coding a message and the actual efficiency (Shannon & Weaver, 1949, p. 13). For example, in English, the phrase, "I am tired," contains some redundancy because the word "am" is the first person singular, and only that, for the verb to be. Thus "I" really tells us nothing here that we do not already know from the word "am"; it constitutes redundancy in the coding of the message. Of course, English grammar requires that we use the word "I"; that is simply one of the many ways grammar builds redundancy into language.

Despite its popular connotation of waste, redundancy is very valuable in communication, which is no doubt one of the reasons why redundancy is so common in language. Shannon pointed out that noise is very common in communication channels, from the static of radio broadcasts to the background chatter of a cocktail party to the typographical errors of a computer printout. Redundancy in speaking or writing provides insurance that the message gets through. For example, if either the 1 or the am of the above message were missing, the receiver could still guess the meaning intended.

A subject catalog is a communication channel as well. The receiver (searcher) needs information about books, which is conveyed by catalog entries. This communication channel functions in a particular way, however. The messages (catalog entries) are labeled by subject headings, and the message is not transferred until and unless there is a match between subject heading and term used by the searcher. To increase the chances of matching, there should be a number of these labels for each book.

Another way to state this variety/richness desideratum is to say that information systems should be generous. (See also Hildreth's recommendations for the user interface [Hildreth, 1982, p. 59].) An information system is the gateway into the realms of learning and knowledge. The gate currently provided by typical catalogs is tight and narrow. Most people with an ounce of intelligence and curiosity enjoy exploring through books and other carriers of information. I will even go so far as to suggest that catalogs and other information retrieval systems should be fun. Whoever talks about catalogs being fun? But why should they not be? People enjoy exploring knowledge, particularly if they can pursue mental associations in the same way they do in their minds. People of all ages enjoy computer games, some of them quite intellectually demanding. Should that not also carry over into enjoying exploring an apparatus that reflects knowledge, that suggests paths not thought of, and that shows relationships between topics that are surprising? We might turn it around and say that any indexing/ access apparatus that does not stimulate, intrigue, and give pleasure in the hunt is defective.

It is appropriate now to look at the Library of Congress subject heading (LCSH) approach (Chan, 1978) in the context of the terminology being used in this section. In traditional cataloging practice, economy has been an overwhelming consideration. In a library with a million books in it, to add just one additional card per book to the catalog would enlarge the catalog by one million cards, a formidable addition to catalog bulk. So the pattern has been to purge redundancy in every way possible. The average number of subject headings assigned per document by the Library of Congress and large academic libraries is very low: 1.3 in a study at LC for the years 1950–64 (Avram et al., 1967, p. 189), and 1.4 in a 1979 study of

OCLC records (O'Neill & Aluri, 1981, p. 78). Such minimal redundancy is accomplished by the following means.

*Precoordinate, whole document indexing* The cataloger working according to Library of Congress principles (at LC or elsewhere) is trained to index the whole document, not parts or concepts within it. This practice leads to the assigning of a single, sometimes long, subject heading—often with attached subheadings called subdivisions—which is, in fact, a good reflection of the contents of the entire document. Closely linked to this practice is the concept of precoordination. Indexing systems designed for coordination (or combination) of descriptive terms by the searcher are called "postcoordinate," and those designed for combination by the indexer/cataloger are called "precoordinate" (see Foskett, 1982 pp. 433-434). Library of Congress practice is precoordinate, so the subject concepts appear in that single long heading instead of in separate entries. Additional headings are assigned only if there is no one heading available which reflects the contents of the entire document. Thus, in a card catalog there is typically only one subject access point per document. Precoordinated, whole document indexing contrasts with concept indexing systems (as used in many abstracting and indexing services), which may use ten, fifteen, or more terms per document, each constituting a different entry and reflecting a distinct concept. The practical value of this approach for keeping down the bulk of card catalogs is evident. Unfortunately, however, in a card catalog the content words of this long heading can be accessed only through the first word in the main heading, which is the word by which the entry is filed in the subject catalog. The searcher must use that one word or a cross reference to it or fail utterly to find books indexed there. In an online catalog with keyword matching, the searcher can get access to other words buried in the heading behind the initial word.

*Uniform heading* The principle of uniform heading holds that for any particular description there is to be one and only one heading reflecting that description. For example, "hypnosis" should not also be expressed by the synonymous term "hypnotism." One or the other of these terms must be chosen to be the one uniform heading for the topic, with a cross reference from the other term.

An even more interesting implication of this rule is that the same description may not be expressed in different word orders. So apart from a few exceptional cases where this sort of thing is allowed, if, say, the heading "Capitalism—United States" is approved, then by the rule of uniform heading, the cataloger is expressly forbidden from applying the heading "United States—Capitalism" to any document. It can be seen that keyword matching capabilities in an online catalog will overcome some of the limitations of the uniform heading practices of LC. However, keyword matching will not help with the next feature of LC heading practice:

*Specific entry* The rule of specific entry is the single most important rule of LCSH subject cataloging and dates to Cutter's writings (Cutter, 1904). (See also Chan, 1978; Dunkin, 1969; Miksa, 1983.) It holds that each book is to be entered under a heading which is specific to the content of the book, that is, which is neither broader nor narrower in scope than the scope of the book's contents. These headings are, in turn, alphabetically arranged, thus producing what is known as an "alphabetico-specific catalog." The resulting catalog was to enable the searcher to find books on exactly the topic in mind, without having to worry about whether the topic was part of some broader category.

This approach contrasted with that of classified catalogs popular in the nineteenth century, which were arranged by classified hierarchies. The searcher interested in memory, for example, might have to look under "Psychology—Cognition—Memory" in a classified catalog. None of these terms would be alphabetically arranged; the entire catalog would be arranged in a classified sequence, so Psychology would be next to Social psychology, then Sociology, etc. Consequently, the searcher would usually have to use an alphabetical index to the catalog.

Cutter's direct alphabetical approach sounds much preferable, but there were some unanticipated consequences from it (at least the way it was developed by LC). By the rule of specific entry, a book on all of psychology should be given a heading like "Psychology," one on all of cognition the heading "Cognition," and one on memory, the heading "Memory." LC interpreted the rule of specific entry to mean that there could be no posting upward. That is (but for a few exceptions—see Boll, 1982), the cataloger is expressly forbidden from entering the memory book under cognition or psychology. Thus the searcher who looks up "Cognition," thinking to find a book on memory, will instead find only books that are on the whole topic of cognition. A book on just one aspect of cognition, such as memory, will be indexed only under "Memory" and not under "Cognition."

The problem with this, of course, is that material of interest to the searcher may be found in books at all levels of specificity. Both the broader and narrower terms are, in an alphabetical file, distributed all over the file. All the different subtopics within cognition besides memory will be spread all over the catalog, as will all the subtopics within psychology besides cognition, and so on. Cross references were intended to make up for this alphabetical splitting apart of conceptually related hierarchies, but in LC practice see also references upward to broader terms are forbidden.

Thus the searcher is only directed to terms at the same or more specific levels. Usually, there are not very many of even these latter references anyway.

It is the rare user who has ever heard of the rule of specific entry, let alone thought out the implications of it. My research showed that end users frequently entered the catalog under terms that were broader than the subject they were actually interested in (Bates, 1977, pp. 370, 371). So it is likely that the average user expects to find books on memory under "Psychology" or "Cognition;" when no such books are found, or only books on all of cognition with some mention of memory, the searcher assumes the library has no other more relevant books and thus misses all the books wholly devoted to memory. But by limiting entries for each book to only the level of specificity found in that book, the LC system eliminates the redundancy that would be introduced by posting a book to other levels of specificity as well. This is one major area where LC's low-redundancy practices must be compensated for by system assistance in online catalogs. The searcher interested in memory who uses "Cognition" will not be helped by current online catalog search capabilities such as keyword matching, Boolean logic, or truncation.

*Limited syndetic structure* The "syndetic structure" of a catalog is its cross-reference structure, usually consisting of see and see also references. Though the study was on a limited number of cases, my research found LCSH see references frequently outdated and limited to just a few of the likely search terms used by searchers (Bates, 1977, p. 369). Likewise, in a study of online catalog use, Markey found that 5% of online accesses were exact matches with LCSH cross references (Markey, 1984, p. 66). Further, as noted above, see also references to broader terms are excluded from LCSH catalogs (though they appear in coded form in the LC subject heading list).

*Access vocabulary interfiled with catalog entries* The tradition in American libraries is that the apparatus for finding good terms and moving from illegitimate to legitimate terms is built into the catalog, that is, interfiled with the catalog entries. The searcher goes directly to the catalog and looks up a term; it either matches with a subject heading actually indexing book(s) or with a cross reference—or nothing. Generally, no separate access guide is provided to the user. In such a system, then, each additional cross reference added to help the searcher find the legitimate terms adds to the bulk of the catalog. It is not surprising, then, that cross references, like the rest of LC indexing, were kept to a minimum. (This tradition might be questioned; after all, might it not be easier for the searcher to follow cross references and check term relationships in the pages of a book, rather than having to walk twenty feet to another part of the catalog for each cross reference? But to my knowledge, the provision of thesauri or other user aids specifically designed for the end user of a catalog has never received serious consideration until recently. Some libraries make the LCSH list available to patrons, but that list is designed for indexers and is hard for end users to follow.)

All of these various devices in the design of Library of Congress subject heading practice add up to an indexing system with extremely low redundancy—just over the one heading per book that would be the lowest possible redundancy in such an environment. What happens to this low-redundancy system in an online environment and how access in LC-based catalogs might be improved will be discussed later.

*Complexity: Access to and interaction with system complex and subtle.*

We have seen from the argument heretofore that the user, rather than being possessed of a simple straightforward need requiring an equally straightforward match with documents in the system, may instead be a wonderfully complicated creature with associations firing in all directions and information interests to match. To do right by this user we will have to design a system that helps the user take advantage of these powerful associative propensities.

But rich associations are not all. There are at least three other senses in which interaction with an information system, especially at the beginning of a search, may be complicated. A well-designed system should help with these needs too.

**Getting in in the first place** In both manual and online catalogs the user must launch the search with a subject term. For the search to be successful, the term must not only match with some term in the system, but must match, either directly or through cross references, with a term describing *relevant* material. As I have argued earlier, LCSH uses so few terms for indexing each document and provides so little assistance to the searcher that the latter is hard to do. In an online catalog with keyword matching, matching with some term is not hard to do, but then the searcher is often stalled if the term is a poor one for the information need. The cross-reference network is quite small (if it has even been built into the online catalog) and scope notes or other explanations or suggestions are sparse or nonexistent. I therefore propose the Side-of-the-Barn Principle: In a properly designed system, to get into the system and to get going searching effectively, the searcher need only hit the side of a barn, i.e., any reasonable English language word or phrase should get the searcher started and linked to explanatory, guiding information to assist in the search.

*Formulating and articulating the query* Belkin has argued persuasively that we are demanding too much when we expect a client to approach an information system with a reasonably well-articulated query. To state their needs, people have to describe what they do not know. In effect, people do not naturally have "queries"; rather, they have what he calls an "anomalous state of knowledge" (Belkin, 1982, p. 62).

In addition "A document, after all, is supposed to be a statement of what its author knows about a topic, and is thus assumed to be a coherent statement . . . " (Belkin, 1982, p. 64). He goes on to argue: "Thus, the document is a representation of a coherent state of knowledge, while a query or other text related to an information need will be a representation of an anomalous, or somehow inadequate or incoherent state of knowledge" (Belkin, 1982, p. 64). So traditional systems which require a match between systematic information (a coherent document) and a query representing ignorance and incoherence may be requiring a match between two fundamentally dissimilar sorts of text.

Earlier, Taylor had demonstrated that even with the traditional understanding of "query," users frequently go through four stages of developing and articulating their query (Q1–Q4): all the way from a visceral, felt need (Q1), through a conscious need (Q2), to an expressed, formalized need (Q3), and finally to a need compromised to meet the user's assumptions about the requirements of the information system being used (Q4) (Taylor, 1968, p. 182). He was dealing with people approaching reference librarians. If a client arrives when still in one of the earlier stages, librarians can adapt and assist people to articulate their need. Similarly, if the client has already over-adapted the query to meet mistaken assumptions about the nature of the information system (Q4), the information specialist can help the end user work back to the true need. There is no built-in human intermediary for people when they use an online catalog, however—unless we find a way to design in that assistance.

*Docking* Any time a person approaches an information retrieval system, whether that system is another human being or a machine, an initial phase of orientation or "getting a feel for" must be gone through before settling down to do searching proper. Awareness of this need has developed slowly over the years in the writing on the reference interview and negotiation. Reference librarians have long sighed with frustration over the propensity of patrons to make very general requests of librarians at the desk, rather than stating their specific need directly and immediately. Schiller argued that the reason patrons so often do this is not perversity but a real need to establish a connection with the librarian, to get a feel for the rules of the game and to begin the interaction in some common topic area (Schiller, 1965, p. 58). The user, after all, does not know if a question on "metatarsals" will make any sense to the librarian. If the librarian does not understand this query, embarrassment could ensue. So, according to her argument, the patron first makes a request at a broad level of generality that the librarian is sure to know: "Can you tell me where the medical books are?," then if the librarian shows willingness to help further, goes into the detailed question.

Eichman took this argument further. Using the linguist Leech's writings on functions of language use, he identified a "phatic" function that generally takes place initially between two individuals (Eichman, 1978, pp. 217–218). The purpose of phatic speech is to open channels of communication. Such speech occurs frequently in various contexts in human communication, and Eichman argued that it is common to the initial phase of the reference interview. Eichman's analysis thus provides a theoretical basis for the anecdotal argument made by Schiller.

Research on card catalogs suggests that people make the initial approach there on a general level as well. I found search terms generated by end users to be more commonly too broad than too narrow (Bates, 1977, p. 370). This use of broad entry terms is a good strategy, statistically, for the searcher. Comparing the half of the subjects in my study who tended to use broad terms against the half who tended to use narrow terms, I found a substantially higher percentage of matches with some term in the catalog for the former than for the latter (Bates, 1977, pp. 372, 373). In short, those who take the same approach to the inert system as they might to another human being, i.e., using broad, general terms, have a better chance of finding common ground and entering the system. In LCSH catalogs, unfortunately, the rule of specific entry guarantees that while they may match with some term, it is often not the best term for the information need because it is at the wrong level of specificity (see discussion under "variety" principle).

There are other senses in which finding common ground might be necessary for the searcher entering an information system. When a human being is the respondent, rapid adaptations can be made on both sides. The librarian who receives the halting request of the seven-year-old can immediately adapt in a way different from what she or he does when approached by the busy physician wanting the latest research data. Questions can be asked which immediately pinpoint vital parameters of the query so the entire transaction can be relatively brief. But even the best online systems lack most of the adaptive features of human respondents. Almost all of the adaptability therefore necessarily resides in the human searcher in a searcher-machine interaction. What the machine must do is provide the information to enable the human being to make the best adaptation to and use of the system.

Let us call this process of adaptation "docking." Just as the skipper of a boat cannot pilot the boat at 40 miles an hour straight toward the slip, then suddenly slam on the brakes and come to a complete halt just an inch from the dock, but must instead slow down well in advance and maneuver into the slip, so also must the information system user do some initial maneuvering before hitting the ideal selection of information.

There are at least two senses of docking in the discussion above. One is the maneuvering based on an understanding of how the system works, not necessarily its inner workings, but how to interact as an end user (cf. Borgman, 1986). The second sense is that based on an understanding of the conceptual and linguistic world of the subject retrieval system in use in the system.

## Implications of principles for design of subject access in online catalogs

The thrust of the section on the uncertainty principle is that we cannot predict the term an indexer will use to describe a document or a searcher will use to describe a query topic. The selection will not be totally random; both will probably draw from a fairly small cluster of terms (though even that cannot be guaranteed), but we have no way of knowing which of these terms will be selected in a given case. So we must assume that even with a carefully controlled indexing language, a book can be described by many terms and both indexers and searchers are likely, collectively, to use a variety of these terms.

The individual searcher, however, is usually unaware of the many terms that might be used and certainly does not appreciate the complexity of information description and retrieval. In the section on the variety principle this point was reinforced in the discussion of the law of requisite variety: In order to succeed in information retrieval the searcher needs to generate as much variety in a search formulation as there is variety in the indexing of the topic of interest. Current systems do little to help the searcher generate the necessary variety.

In the section on the complexity principle it was argued that entering an information system, getting a feel for it, and figuring out which terms to search on are complex and subtle processes. Every system has implicit assumptions and patterns of operating which the searcher can pick up on only when exposed to the "thinking" of the system. Searchers must go through an orientation phase where they get a feel for how the system handles problems of document access, a feel for the index language, and a deeper sense of the meaning of given terms by seeing them in the context of a semantic network.

All of these points underline the difficulty of entering and matching with terms in the system and argue for much more powerful means of assisting the searcher, particularly in the early phases of the search process. In the next section some specific recommendations will be made for helping the searcher.

But, first, we need to consider how to relate the current system, i.e., Library of Congress subject headings in manual and online catalogs, to the proposed approach. It would certainly be highly desirable to make use of existing indexing, rather than reindexing, while still improving access. It turns out that there is indeed a way to utilize current indexing in the context of the recommended changes—a way which may be the best approach anyway, cost considerations aside.

Earlier it was noted that the design of Library of Congress subject headings stringently purged redundancy from the subject description of books. On the face of it then, the current Library of Congress subject indexing would seem to be a poor candidate to be a part of an improved system relying on variety and redundancy to help searchers enter the system and find desired materials. This turns out not to be so, however, for several reasons.

(1) The problems that have been emphasized in the discussion have to do with getting into the system (i.e., matching one's initial term with some term in the catalog), getting oriented, and finding good terms for one's topic of interest. All of these things are fairly independent of document indexing. It is possible, for example, to have a huge entry vocabulary—much larger than is found in the set of cross references in the current Library of Congress subject headings list—with references to used terms without increasing the size or character of the legitimate vocabulary. As we shall see, much can be done to aid access that is independent of the indexing of individual documents.

(2) Though Library of Congress indexing is done with few headings— usually only one—those headings often contain several, even numerous, content-bearing words. In a card catalog the searcher can get at the heading only through the first word, which is the basis for the sort in the linear card file. But in an online catalog with keyword matching capability, the user can search on any of the significant words contained in the heading. Such keyword matching thus opens up Library of Congress subject heading indexing to much richer retrieval possibilities. Clever use of the Library

of Congress Classification and Dewey Decimal Classification numbers (Cochrane & Markey, 1985; Markey & Demeyer, 1985) opens up even more possibilities for controlled vocabulary access. Additional free text access on titles and other subject information bearing elements of the record completes the picture. The typical catalog record has now become a rich source of subject information in the online environment. Of course, many of these features are already being used; the question now is how to use these features in a unified and powerful approach to subject access.

(3) Recent research by Schabas (1982) sheds light on the question of whether better indexing would make a difference in retrieval performance. She compared the retrieval performance of Library of Congress subject headings and PRECIS in a Canadian selective dissemination of information system. PRECIS, a system developed by Austin (Austin, 1974; Richmond, 1981; Mahapatra & Biswas, 1983), has many advantages in principle over LCSH. It follows more consistent principles than LCSH, is better founded on linguistic principles, and by its design it is capable of having more up-to-date vocabulary than LCSH. It was surprising, therefore, that Schabas's results showed the two systems' retrieval performance to be similar, with PRECIS being somewhat superior to LCSH only in the area of social science terms.

There was another striking statistic in her study as well. While the performance differences were minimal between these dramatically different indexing systems, performance was very significantly improved by adding title terms to either LCSH or PRECIS. Specifically, recall was significantly improved with very minimal decline in precision. So the addition of the simple mechanism of free text searching on title terms made a vastly greater improvement in retrieval performance than all the subtle, complex, changes in indexing techniques to be found in PRECIS as over against LCSH.

The answer to these puzzling results lies in the interaction of the online retrieval system and the original indexing. The small difference between PRECIS and LCSH indexing performance can probably be explained by the fact that the very characteristics which most distinguish these two indexing systems are ignored by the retrieval system. In Schabas's study retrieval was done by matching SDI profile terms against the PRECIS indexing, LCSH indexing, and title. Yet PRECIS and LCSH are both whole-document indexing systems. The effort in each case is to come up with a single well-formed descriptive phrase describing the whole book. The ingenuity of PRECIS lies in the well-developed grammar for creating several multiword entries, each featuring a different entry word, out of that one descriptive phrase. In a manual system, each of these created entries would be found at a different point in an alphabetical index. Since the online system matches on individual words in the descriptive phrase anyway, much of that ingenuity is wasted. On the other hand, LCSH lacks this grammar for multiple entries; in fact, as discussed earlier, the rule of uniform heading precludes the creation of alternate entries out of the same descriptive phrase in most cases. However, since the online system matches with individual words in the heading, multiple entries are created de facto by online systems anyway. Thus, the strengths of PRECIS are ignored, and the weaknesses of LCSH vis-a-vis PRECIS are largely overcome when these indexing systems are used in conjunction with typical online search system capabilities—hence the similarity of outcome in Schabas's study.

It is for these reasons that I would argue that designing a sophisticated up-front system and wrapping its new features around an old indexing system with well-documented weaknesses (LCSH) may nonetheless be a very powerful approach to take to online catalog retrieval. PRECIS is, to my knowledge, the most powerful whole-document indexing system available today, the best candidate to replace LCSH. Yet even if the enormous effort were made to convert Library of Congress practices to PRECIS, the improvement in retrieval performance would, if Schabas's study is any guide, be minimal. Instead, retrieval improvement must be gained in a different way—through something like the front-end system mind to be described later.

So, to summarize the implications of the arguments in the first part of this article for the design of online subject catalog access:

- There will invariably be variety in the indexing of any given topic.

- To cope successfully with an information system, the searcher must generate as much variety in search formulation as the system produces in description of a given topic.

- Searchers need help getting into and getting oriented to information systems.

- Searchers are likely to be unaware of the need for variety in searching and have difficulty generating variety even when they do become aware of the need.

- Therefore, the system should help the searcher enter the system, get oriented, and generate the necessary variety.

## Design features

The proposed model has three conceptual components: access, hunting, and selection (see Fig. 1). Within access there are two subelements: entry and orientation. These components reflect the major stages of the user's search. The dividing line between these stages is not always clear cut, and the searcher may move back and forth between stages or cycle through them in a regular pattern—perhaps without awareness that the system design contains these elements. It is argued, however, that our thinking for design purposes will be clarified if we identify and work with these distinct components. In the following discussion emphasis is placed on the access phase as the area needing the most change from current systems. Changes in access will in turn have implications for hunting and selection which cannot be developed in this article.

## Access

The searcher has first the problem of getting into the system, getting a feel for how the system works and what the options are, and exploring among the possible subject terms. The access stage most emphasizes natural language semantics, i.e., the meaning and conceptual relationships among words and index terms.

*Entry* The first job of the user is to get into the system in the first place. Though this is a very brief phase of the search, it is a crucial one, because if too many difficulties (sometimes any difficulties) are encountered, the user will not persist. Here we exercise the Side-of-the-Barn Principle and make it possible for the searcher to get into the system with any reasonable English language word or phrase. An "end-user thesaurus" is proposed to help the user with entry and, to a lesser extent, with the later stages of the search as well.

*Orientation* Of all the stages this is the one most ignored in current online catalogs; hence it will be strongly emphasized here. (Such attention as has been given tends to be more in online bibliographic system research, particularly in gateway systems and the like, e.g., Meadow et al., 1977; Marcus, 1983; Williams & Preece, 1980.)

The system should be designed to assist users to articulate queries and formulate them in good terms—including helping them generate the variety necessary to cover the many ways indexers and authors have talked about topics of interest. The system helps searchers get a feel both for how to interact with the system and for the intellectual world of the system through exploration of vocabulary and relationships between terms. Finally, the system provides searchers with links and associations between terms that may be surprising and stimulating of further thought and information seeking.

It is proposed that both entry and orientation be facilitated by a system component known as a "front-end system mind," or FSM. The FSM, to be described below, contains the end-user thesaurus (mentioned under "Entry") as well as a variety of linkages among terms and document indexing of a sort that encourages awareness of other search terms, exploration of unanticipated possibilities, the making of mental associations, and the development of a "feel" for the system.

## Hunting

Hunting features are the best developed aspects of current systems. Many of the current features such as keyword match, implicit Boolean AND, and searching on various bibliographic fields may remain in the new model—though it will be a while before the full impact of the availability of an FSM on the hunting phase can be worked out. Some features would need to be rethought, given the availability of a powerful access component. Linguistically, the emphasis in the hunting phase is on command language syntax, i.e., most of the power of the system at this stage is in system capabilities exercised through command language syntax.

## Selection

At this stage the searcher is assisted in selecting documents (i.e., document citations) to take away. Here the emphasis is on natural language syntax. That is, definitions of terms do not matter so much as their use in the operational context of document texts. While a searcher initially pursues a topic in general, it is usually particular aspects, attitudes, or approaches to the topic that finally interest the searcher and help him or her decide to select a particular document. This subtle information can usually only be found in the text of the document itself, so it is valuable at this stage to provide portions of the documents—contents lists, introductions, or other sections of text.

# Some suggested system components

## Access

Throughout this article a number of needs have been identified that the access apparatus should help the searcher meet: (1) getting into the system in the first place, (2) following up a wide variety of mental associations, (3) generating as much variety in search terms as exist in the indexing of a topic, (4) articulating and formulating a query, (5) "docking" with the system in both the operational and conceptual/linguistic senses. I propose to meet these needs with a front-end system mind, or FSM. The FSM is a dense semantic network. The network relationships may be of almost indefinitely many types, only some of which will be suggested here. It is called front-end because it is the part of the system the searcher encounters first, and while the FSM can and will be used throughout the search, its heaviest use is expected to come at the beginning and early stages of the search. It is called a system mind because it reflects the thinking and organization imposed on the data by systems designers and catalogers. By working with the FSM the searcher is implicitly shown how to deal effectively with the main product of that thinking, the book cataloging in the subject catalog proper. This FSM facilitates entry with an end-user thesaurus and supports orientation efforts with an even more powerful cluster of capabilities to be described below.

*Entry assisted with an end-user thesaurus* First, let us distinguish an end-user thesaurus (ET) from an indexer thesaurus (IT). "Thesaurus" is defined for our purposes here as a controlled vocabulary used for document description. An indexer thesaurus is a thesaurus designed for use by indexers. The product of thesaurus use, the indexing, is of course intended for the end user, but the thesaurus itself is designed primarily for indexer use and only secondarily or not at all for the searcher, whether intermediary or end user. Most thesauri in use today are indexer thesauri, although some are beginning to show some features intended to help the searcher or end user (Piternick, 1984). The following lists of features of indexer and end-user thesauri are not exhaustive; rather, they highlight contrasting features.

An indexer thesaurus:

1. Excludes many terms that would actually be used by indexers in indexing. Examples are those terms that are to be established according to some set pattern, such as personal names as subjects, or terms that are constructed out of standard parts. Many of the headings produced by Library of Congress subject heading rules are of both of these types. For example, the so-called "floating subdivisions," i.e., standardized subdivisions, may be added to main headings at cataloger discretion, and do not appear in the main body of the LCSH list where the user might seek them.

2. On the other hand, an IT includes some terms not used in a particular library or database, if the library or database does not yet have any documents on the topic.

3. Gives scope notes for only those terms indexers are likely to have trouble with, not end users. Scope notes also often only elucidate problem areas of the term's usage, and do not describe all aspects of its application, a point which may be lost on the end user.

4. Often uses terms or codes ("xx," "BT," etc.) known only to indexers.

5. Provides cross references within the grammar of the thesaurus, that is, it gives terms which are phrased in typical index term fashion, viz., noun and noun adjective phrases predominantly, rather than the looser grammar of the end user. Also, an IT does not provide cross references from highly colloquial terms and terms that indexers would not be likely to look up. On the whole, size of cross-reference set is limited.

An end-user thesaurus (See also Piternick [1984]):

1. Lists all terms in use in catalog or database at any given time.

2. Carefully distinguishes terms actually used in a given catalog or database from those not used in it.

3. Gives scope notes for problems likely to be encountered by end users and even provides some definitions.

4. Uses self-explanatory names for terms or relationships.

5. Provides a vast entry vocabulary, geared to end-user propensities. This fifth feature is particularly important and marks the most noticeable difference between end-user and indexer thesauri. The entry vocabulary should be several times as large as the set of legitimate terms. This entry vocabulary is then linked through see references to legitimate terms. Very colloquial terms are included, and the grammar of entry terms may be loose. Note that the looseness of the *entry* terms does not prevent having *legitimate* terms that meet high standards of coherence and good indexing grammar. In an online ET word-form variations can also be included. It might be possible to replace certain common variations with carefully designed automatic truncation routines to reduce bulk. Extensive see also references are also provided.

In manual systems the propensity of ITs to give all legitimate terms, not just the ones used in a particular library, can be confusing for the searcher who looks in vain in the catalog for a listed word. Thus an ET for a manual catalog should clearly designate which terms have actually been used in the catalog. In online systems, however, there is more flexibility in handling this problem. For example, if a user inputs a legitimate, but as yet unused term, a match may be made against title terms.

The use of an ET should lead to a greatly increased hit rate upon first entering a term on a topic, i.e., should thus constitute the implementation of the Side-of-the-Barn Principle. Such an improvement would in itself constitute a major contribution to catalog success rates. In my research on card catalogs, I found matching scores of only about 60% of the total possible score with any term in the catalog (whether or not it was a good match with the topic of interest or at the right level of specificity), even when partial credit was given for partial matches (Bates, 1977, p. 166).

Further, in a study of the Syracuse University online catalog, SULIRS, Markey categorized 859 accesses made by searchers during the course of 188 online searches. Known item access points and errors constituted 27% of the accesses, various forms of exact and partial matches with Library of Congress subject headings and cross references 37%, and a category she called "whatever popped into the searcher's mind," 36% (Markey, 1984 p. 66). The accesses in this last category consisted overwhelmingly of words containing subject content, but which did not resemble LC headings, for instance, "Painter Goya," and "Development projects in Uganda" (Markey, 1984, p. 70).

The second category, the exact and close LCSH matches, had a 21% "no retrievals" rate (output sets of size zero), i.e., a 79% match rate with something, while the third ("whatever") category had a 65% no retrievals rate, or only a 35% positive match rate. (The combined average positive match rate across both categories is 57%.) (Markey, 1984, p. 66) With a failure rate of over three times that of the second category, the third category, at 65%, is clearly ripe for improvement. Yet it is just these colloquial, non-index-language terms that are missing from the entry vocabulary of current thesauri. If the searcher could get a match with these more colloquial phrases which would then lead to a display of various controlled vocabulary terms better expressing the searcher's interests, then great improvements in searcher success rates can be expected. Furthermore, if the searcher can thus hit *some* term virtually every time upon first entry to the system, rather than 57% of the time, we will have nearly doubled the frequency with which the searcher has a positive experience right off with the system. The searcher will be involved in an interactive exchange with the system, rather than emotionally thrown off by a zero response, and hooked into a network of terms after the first word input nearly every time.

*Orientation assisted through additional powerful features of the FSM* As discussed above, the FSM contains the vast entry vocabulary of an end-user thesaurus. Once the entry vocabulary has helped the searcher match with a term, the searcher is then connected to a dense semantic network. That network contains the end-user thesaurus, i.e., the entry vocabulary and the legitimate terms, plus a network of associations between terms and concepts that is much richer and more varied than that found in the typical thesaurus or authority file. The kinds of relationships that are possible are almost unlimited; only some of them will be suggested here.

Before describing those relationships, however, it is important to make clear the relationship between the FSM and the document indexing. The FSM is independent of but linked with the document indexing. All the goals of the FSM—to help people get into the system, explore, make their own mental associations, discover the many topics related to their interests and the many terms under which material might be found—can be met by the searcher without having to plunge directly into searching of documents. Once we have freed ourselves from the traditional assumption that access vocabulary has to be interfiled with the indexing as it was in a card catalog, then we can develop an enormously rich and complex FSM, and not have to load all that depth and complexity onto the indexing of individual documents. At the same time, the FSM can be different, and more than, an online subject authority file, which is a kind of indexer thesaurus.

It has been assumed throughout this discussion that there are many links among the terms in the FSM. As long as (1) every term in the FSM is linked to some document index term(s), in many cases by being linked to some other FSM term which is the one actually connected to the document indexing, and (2) every document has some term or terms which is linked to terms in the FSM, then much of the FSM can be independent of document indexing, while the user can still search documents at any time.

For example, suppose we have an FSM linked to existing LCSH book records. The many variant terms made available in the FSM can be linked to one or more appropriate LCSH headings or directly matched with title terms. At any time during the process of the search, the searcher may ask to have specific documents listed out for any particular term. A very high percentage of the terms the searcher might use would not be actual LCSH headings (though a number of them might be title terms). But LCSH headings could be linked on a one-to-many basis to colloquial and other variant terms in the FSM. Where the natural language term is ambiguous or multi-meaning the searcher could be shown the two or more LCSH terms which might stand for that term and be asked which is meant. The searcher responds with the term number and document records are brought up on the screen.

It can be seen that, in principle, an FSM can be linked to any document indexing, that is, indexing done by any thesaurus. The FSM may itself be very sophisticated, and change through time, while the original document indexing stays the same. While the FSM is conceptually distinct from the book indexing, the internal file structure of the FSM should be designed so that the searcher may ask at any time to see individual documents indexed by search terms (or ones linked to them by cross references), i.e., the searcher should not have to withdraw from one file, the FSM, and enter another, documents file, to see document indexing.

Now to the types of relationships possible: Alphabetical lists of terms, legitimate and not, and including word-form variations, may be displayed, as well as all the conventional thesaurus relationships—narrower, related, and broader terms (the Library of Congress subject headings list does not currently distinguish between these types of relationships). If the FSM is properly designed, the searcher should be able to follow chains of association indefinitely far in the FSM by following references to parents/children and related terms.

These relationships would be much more clearly understandable if displayed on the screen as trees, with the search term in boldface at the heart of the tree. Not infrequently, a given term is a part of several different trees. For example, the term "bond" may be a part of trees in finance, law enforcement, anthropology, chemistry, and adhesives. If all of these were to be shown at once or in short succession on a screen, the searcher may be helped in at least two ways: (1) if exploration or browsing is of interest, the searcher would be stimulated by the prospect of a number of quite different lines of search, and (2) if a more directed search is wanted, the searcher will realize that the one meaning the searcher had originally in mind may be confounded with other meanings in searching unless something is done.

But conventional thesaurus relationships are only the start. The nice thing about the FSM is that many relationships can be shown, some of them in parallel, overlapping, or, as mentioned above, in multiple hierarchies. Redundancy in access is good; it encourages exploration and orientation. Redundancy in access does not imply redundancy in indexing. Providing greatly enhanced and sometimes redundant access does not mean that we are improving recall at the expense of precision. We are insuring that the searcher finds the best terms up front, so both recall and precision should be improved.

All sorts of relationships can be developed using the Library of Congress Classification (LCC) and Dewey Decimal Classification (DDC). I will not review them all here; they have been well described by others (Cochrane & Markey, 1985; Markey & Demeyer, 1985; Svenonius, 1983). For example, trees expressing the well-organized hierarchies of the DDC can be displayed, or see also references can be made up out of the relationships in the DDC hierarchies. Alternatively, the hierarchical layers above and below the entry term can be shown in outline form for those who prefer that sort of display.

Another kind of linkage perhaps most closely approximates some of the strange associations we make normally in thought. Upon entering a term, the searcher may receive a sampling of other terms, both subject and bibliographic, which co-index documents indexed under the entered term. In an online catalog, that means that when a term matches one or more words in one of the subject headings (or possibly also title) of a book, the user is then shown the other tracings (added entries), plus perhaps the main entry, in the record. Some of the added entries will be closely related, as with a conceptually close subject term, or an author who is a frequent writer in the chosen subject field; other entries will be puzzling and stimulating to further thought, as with a subject heading indexing a totally different aspect of the book. Such a technique might be particularly valuable for the searcher in the humanities or history, because mental associations in these fields often move back and forth among topics, important individuals, and writers on certain topics.

A very similar co-indexing capability has already been developed in the ESA/RECON system. Called "Zoom," the feature rank orders by frequency all descriptors (or terms in other designated fields) in all records (up to 200) in a retrieved set. The resulting output is a list of the entry term and all co-indexed terms in the document set, with the added benefit that these terms are rank ordered by frequency in the set. As Ingwersen notes, the Zoom feature may help the searcher identify preferred (high frequency) search terms, new terminology, appropriate natural language terms, synonyms, serendipitous associations, and different spellings, among other things (Ingwersen, 1984, p. 482).

Closely related to the idea of co-indexing is a proposal by Mischo that title terms of book records be linked as see references to the first topical subject heading appearing in those records. Searchers using a title term will then be referred to applicable subject headings. Mischo notes that such cross references would be particularly valuable in cases where the most current terminology has not yet been converted into a subject heading (Mischo, 1981, pp. 11, 12).

So the searcher, upon entering a single word or phrase initially, may be shown by the FSM an extensive network of related terms in a single or successive screensful. See Figure 2 as an example of the system's response to the input term of "Hysteria." Terms in the figure represent only some of the possibilities in the design of an FSM—ones easily accessible to this author.

To keep down the FSM vocabulary size a little, sometimes this matching may be accomplished by keyword match on significant words in the entry phrase, or sophisticated stemming algorithms on individual words. Any such word or phrase the searcher uses will in turn always be linked to some other part of the network. Selective definitions and scope notes will be available. Relationships between terms will be explained in lay language, and extensive help screens will be available.

After seeing the initial screen(s), the searcher may follow up these associations by using "action codes" in association with terms or document numbers. (Where many terms are displayed on the screen at once, they may be automatically numbered so the searcher need only input the action code number plus term number or numbers.) Some possible action codes might be the following:

ACTION CODES

1. Show me other words for the same subject [i.e., synonyms]

2. Show me other related topics [i.e., related terms]

3. Show me the subject classification for this topic area [i.e., trees]

4. Show me broader topics in this subject area

5. Show me narrower topics in this subject area

6. Show me other terms indexing this (these) books [i.e., co-indexing]

7. Show me the definition of this term

8. Show me how this term is used to index books [i.e., scope notes]

9. Show me some book titles on this subject

10. Show me other books like this one

The tenth code may be used for any of a variety of interesting algorithms in which relatedness is measured and top-ranked books printed out on screen. For example, the algorithm might be that among the set of books which have a subject heading that matches a subject heading in the

## Library of Congress Headings [selected]

Hysteria *see also*
  Demoniac possession
  Ecstasy
  Paralysis, Hysterical
  Trance
  Witchcraft
Hysteria, Epidemic *see also*
  Chorea, Epidemic
Hysteria (Social psychology) use for
  Mass hysteria
  National hysteria

## ORION (UCLA online catalog) [selected]

Hysteria—Etiology
Hysteria—Infancy & childhood—Congresses
Hysteria—Diagnosis—Case studies

## Co-Indexed terms [selected]

Psychoanalysis—Methodology—Addresses,
  essays, lectures
Neuroses
Psychophysiologic disorders
Mass behavior
Anti-communist movements—United States
Industrial psychology
Epilepsy
Pseudopregnancy
Hysteria (Social psychology)—Case studies
Malaysia—Race relations
Medicine—Philosophy
Breuer, Josef 1842–1925 Studien über Hysterie—
  Addresses, essays, lectures. [Subject]
Personality
Nervous system—Diseases
Obsessive-compulsive neuroses

## Trees derived from Dewey Decimal Classification

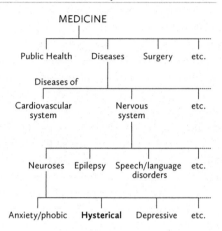

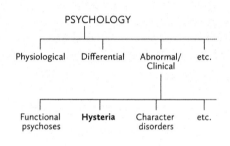

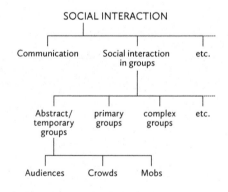

---

Sample Documents [selected]:

Bivin, G. D. (1937). *Pseudocyesis*. Bloomington, IN: The Principia Press.

Kerckhoff, A. C. (1968). *The June bug: A study of hysterical contagion*. New York: Appleton-Century-Crofts.

Krohn, A. (1978). *Hysteria: The elusive neurosis*. New York: International Universities Press.

Lee, R. L.-M. (1980). *The social meaning of mass hysteria in West Malaysia and Singapore* (Doctoral thesis). Ann Arbor, MI: University Microfilms International.

FIG. 2. *Example FSM response to input term "Hysteria."*

indicated book record, the most recent twenty titles will be printed out which have the most non-trivial words in common with the initial book, i.e., a quorum match.

Many of the relationships suggested in these action codes have already been developed and would not require the great labor of developing classification schemes and thesauri from scratch—though the work to transform these source materials into FSM use would still be extensive. I am proposing that a cluster of these techniques be brought together in the FSM so that the searcher sees a great variety of relationships.

As long as appropriate linkages are made between terms, the FSM can be updated with the latest terminology without updating the LCSH indexing (or not as frequently)—an important money-saving feature. Library of Congress Classification and Dewey Decimal Classification numbers already appear in almost every entry. Thesaurus terms for the FSM could be drawn from many sources—already existing technical thesauri from many fields, the relative index to the Dewey Decimal Classification (DDC), or the subject terms in the schedules of the DDC or the Library of Congress Classification. As online searchers are discovering, one can use all sorts of thesauri, not just the one for the database being searched, to generate search terms for free text (as opposed to controlled vocabulary) searching. Online catalog users would have a similar freedom in using the FSM for access.

## Hunting

Now we may consider the hunting component of the system. With the availability of an FSM, the hunting component will need to be rethought. I can explore only a few of the possibilities here. The searcher will have the option of jumping over the FSM entirely and going straight into term matching as in current systems (probably not a good idea in most cases), doing FSM exploration only (i.e., technically, no hunting at all), or, most commonly, some mix of the two. The searcher can pull up example documents the way online searchers do now to see whether they have found terms that index relevant materials.

Alternatively, the searcher may do what are in effect a number of minisearches, each trial with particular terms producing more or fewer relevant documents. Currently, with searches in online bibliographic systems, we have a tendency to think of the search as a matter of successive iterations in modifying the search formulation until we find, finally, the one best formulation of the query—then we have those results printed out offline. But with an FSM, it is easy for the searcher to follow up a number of variant but closely related lines of thought. The search that started on

Canadian Parliamentary politics might spread into relations between the federal and province levels, relations with language minorities, and so on. Each step of the way the searcher selects a few items and, in an ideal future catalog, has them printed out at that moment. No one of these minisearches is a better, more refined search formulation than the others; rather they represent different stages or parts of a multifaceted search.

In Figure 1 the new model is said to permit "docking" match. By that is meant that the searcher does not have to produce immediately the one (and usually only one) subject heading used by the library in a perfect, "pinpoint" match. Instead, the searcher may explore a variety of terms at various levels of specificity, look at sample document records, and, like the sailor coming up to the dock, gradually dock into the best heading(s) or title terms for the search in question.

## Selection

Evidence from many studies over the years has shown that the average catalog user makes little use of some of the more obscure elements of standard book description such as size of book and many of the notes (Markey, 1980, p. 19). At the same time, there have been recommendations from catalog studies that more subject information be added to records to improve search success (Atherton, 1980, p. 109). Cochrane has picked up on this result to suggest that subject information be added to the catalog record from contents lists, index, introduction, etc. She has experimented to check for costs and retrieval effectiveness (Settel & Cochrane, 1982; Atherton, 1978). As discussed earlier, added subject information about individual books would be most useful at the selection stage of catalog searching, though ability to search on an expanded record may be valuable earlier in the search too. In a system such as that proposed in which the old cataloging information would be retained, additional subject information could be added in documents indexed from the present time on. With growth, records with added subject information would soon constitute a substantial part of the file.

*Problems and potential with the new model* A catalog designed according to the new model should enable searchers to get into the system easily, i.e., get help immediately for pursuing their search almost no matter what initial term they use, enable them to "dock," i.e., get a feel for the system in several senses, help them to generate as much variety in their search formulations as exists in the desired information, enable them to explore the knowledge represented in the catalog, and, finally, provide them extensive information about candidate documents to help them decide which to select. All this would be done with the help of an end-user thesaurus, a front-end system mind linked to existing Library of Congress subject heading indexing, powerful system search capabilities, and additional information in the document records to help in selection.

*Cost* A system which does not require reindexing of existing documents, coupled with an up-front system which can be altered while individual book indexing remains the same, is likely to be far cheaper than a number of other alternatives that would produce a comparable degree of improvement in the existing setup. There are many different kinds of network relationships possible, and they need not all be put up at the same time. Staged development would permit immediate benefit to be gained from each segment of development work on the FSM. Furthermore, the FSM can be essentially universal. Once developed, it can be used with fairly minor modification by all libraries using Library of Congress headings.

*But will searchers use it?* Traditional card catalog studies found that users often did not look in more than one place, even when they found nothing under the first term. Three studies found percentages of one-place searches ranging from 66% to 77% (Knapp, 1944; American Library Association, 1958; Tagliacozzo & Kochen, 1970). If people will not do simple follow-up, how can we expect them to use a powerful system such as the one proposed here? First, early evidence is that people do persevere more in online catalogs: Markey found that just 26% of the searchers in the Syracuse online catalog study made one-place (single access) searches (Markey, 1984, p. 66). In a card catalog one must walk elsewhere to try another drawer, whereas in an online catalog one can make another try with just a few keystrokes.

Matthews and Lawrence contrasted online catalog systems that automatically display headings as the first result of a search with systems that display only records as the result of a search request. They found that "systems displaying headings are particularly effective in improving user satisfaction with subject-searching features and in *reducing causes of user impatience* with the system" (Matthews & Lawrence, 1984, p. 366 [italics added]). So browsing first for headings, though it might appear to cause delay, actually appears to be preferred by users. It appears that once it is a little easier to explore variant terms, people are willing to do it. We also know from information-seeking research, however, that people have a powerful preference for information easily acquired and will bypass information sources that are known to have good information if they are perceived as the least bit difficult to use (Allen & Gerstberger, 1967; Rosenberg, 1967).

What all these results suggest is that on the one hand, the user is not aware of the complexity and variety necessary in subject searching and the system should therefore show the user other possibilities through display of terms related in the many ways suggested for the FSM. On the other hand, the searcher does not want to have to do any extra work. The way to reconcile these two trends is to show the searcher FSM relationships *automatically* upon searcher entry of terms, and give them simple one- or two-character codes to use to explore further. If the searcher does not want to use this information or follow up in any way, the searcher need only *ignore* the contents of the screen and input the next term or command—no action whatever need be taken on the displayed information.

In sum, *if an FSM is going to be used, it must feel very easy to use.* Searchers do not have to be aware of the mechanics of searching; the system makes it completely clear and simple. Searchers should be able to concentrate on the content of the search topic and the system responses. Those responses in turn should be generous and the exploration in the system mind should feel fun. Then they will use it.

## Summary

It has been argued that indexing is fundamentally indeterminate beyond a certain point, that searcher variety must equal indexing variety, and searching is complex and subtle. For all these reasons, the subject searcher must be assisted in ways that have conventionally not been available in catalogs. Now that online capabilities have been added to catalogs, various new forms of assistance to the searcher can be provided, vastly improving searcher success. An end-user thesaurus and a front-end system mind have been described as example system components to help the searcher.

There are many other ways of helping the searcher in the design of online catalogs but, it has been argued, whatever else they do, those methods must incorporate some means of enabling the searcher to enter the catalog more easily with a matching term, get oriented readily to the "thinking" of the system, explore terminology, ideas, and book records with pleasure, generate variety in the search formulation, hunt in powerful ways, and have more information available about each book to enable more effective selection. A system expressing these features will more fully realize the possibilities inherent in online systems, and will, above all, enable the searcher to perform truly powerful, pleasurable, and easy searches.

# REFERENCES

Allen, T.J., & Gerstberger, P.G. (1967). *Criteria for selection of an information source. Alfred P. Sloan School of Management, working paper No. 284-267.* Cambridge, MA: MIT Press.

American Library Association. (1958). *Catalog use study, Director's Report by Sidney L. Jackson.* Chicago, IL: ALA.

Ashby, W.R. (1973). *An introduction to cybernetics.* London: Methuen.

Atherton, P. (1978). *Books are for use: Final report of the Subject Access Project to the Council on Library Resources* (ED 156 131). Syracuse, NY: Syracuse University School of Information Studies.

Atherton, P. (1980). Catalog users' access from the researcher's viewpoint: Past and present research which could affect library catalog design. In D.K. Gapen & B. Juergens (Eds.), *Closing the Catalog: Proceedings of the 1978 and 1979 Library and Information Technology Association Institutes* (pp. 105-122). Phoenix, AZ: Oryx Press.

Austin, D. (1974). The development of PRECIS: A theoretical and technical history. *Journal of Documentation, 30*(1), 47-102.

Avram, H.D., Guiles, K.D., & Meade, G.T. (1967). Fields of information on Library of Congress catalog cards: Analysis of a random sample, 1950-1964. *The Library Quarterly, 37*(2), 180-192.

Bates, M.J. (1977a). Factors affecting subject catalog search success. *Journal of the American Society for Information Science, 28*(3), 161-169.

Bates, M.J. (1977b). System meets user: Problems in matching subject search terms. *Information Processing & Management, 13*(6), 367-375.

Belkin, N.J., Oddy, R.N., & Brooks, H.M. (1982). ASK for information retrieval: Part I: Background and theory. *Journal of Documentation, 38*(2) 61-71.

Bilodeau, E.A., & Howell, D.C. (1965). *Free association norms by discrete and continued methods.* New Orleans: Tulane University, Department of Psychology.

Boll, J.J. (1982). From subject headings to descriptors: The hidden trend in Library of Congress subject headings. *Cataloging & Classification Quarterly, 1*(2/3), 3-28.

Borgman, C.L. (1986). The user's mental model of an information retrieval system: An experiment on a prototype online catalog. *International Journal of Man-Machine Studies, 24*(1), 47-64.

Brownrigg, E.B., & Lynch, C.A. (1983). Online catalogs: Through a glass darkly. *Information Technology and Libraries, 2*(1), 104-115.

Bush, V. (1945). As we may think. *Atlantic Monthly, 176*(1), 101-108.

Chan, L.M. (1978). *Library of Congress subject headings: Principles and application.* Littleton, CO: Libraries Unlimited.

Childers, T. (1980). The test of reference. *Library Journal.* 105(8), 924-928.

Cochrane, P.A. (1983). A paradigm shift in library science. *Information Technology and Libraries, 2*(1), 3-4.

Cochrane, P.A., & Markey, K. (1985). Preparing for the use of classification in online cataloging systems and in online catalogs. *Information Technology and Libraries, 4*(2), 91-111.

Cooper, W.S. (1969). Is interindexer consistency a hobgoblin? *American Documentation 20*(3), 268-278.

Crowley, T., & Childers, T. (1971). *Information service in public libraries: Two studies.* Metuchen, NJ: Scarecrow Press.

Cutter, C.A. (1904). A. *Rules for a dictionary catalog* (4th ed.) Washington, DC: U.S. Government Printing Office.

Doszkocs, T.E. (1983). CITE NLM: Natural-language searching in an online catalog. *Information Technology and Libraries, 2*(4), 364-380.

Dunkin, P.S. (1969). *Cataloging U.S.A.* Chicago, IL: American Library Association.

Eichman, T.L. (1978). The complex nature of opening reference questions. *RQ, 17*(3), 212–222.

Fidel, R. (1985). Individual variability in online searching behavior. *Proceedings of the American Society for Information Science 48*[th] *Annual Meeting, 22*, 69–72.

Foskett, A.C. (1982). *The subject approach to information* (4th ed.) London: Clive Bingley.

Frarey, C.J. (1953). Studies of use of the subject catalog: Summary and evaluation. In M.F. Tauber (Ed.), *The subject analysis of library materials* (pp. 147–166). New York: Columbia University, School of Library Service.

Furnas, G.W., et al. (1982). Statistical semantics: How can a computer use what people name things to guess what things people mean when they name things? *Proceedings of the Human Factors in Computer Systems Conference* (pp. 251–253), Gaithersburg, MD. New York: Association for Computing Machinery.

Hafter, R. (1979). The performance of card catalogs: A review of research. *Library Research, 1*(3), 199–222.

Hildreth, C.R. (1982). *Online public access catalogs: The user interface*. Dublin, OH: OCLC.

Hildreth, C.R. (1983). Pursuing the ideal: Generations of online catalogs. In B. Aveney & B. Butler (Eds.), *Online Catalogs, Online Reference: Converging Trends* (pp. 31–56). Proceedings of a Library and Information Technology Association Preconference Institute, Los Angeles. Chicago, IL: American Library Association.

Hjerppe, R. (1985). *Project HYPERCATalog: Visions and preliminary conceptions of an extended and enhanced catalog.* Paper presented at IRFIS, 6th, Frascati, Italy.

Holley, R.P., & Killheffer, R.E. (1982). Is there an answer to the subject access crisis? *Cataloging & Classification Quarterly, 1*(2/3), 125–133.

Ingwersen, P. (1984). A cognitive view of three selected online search facilities. *Online Review, 8*(5), 465–492.

Jacoby, J., & Slamecka, V. (1962). *Indexer consistency under minimal conditions.* Bethesda, MD: Documentation, Inc.

Johnson-Laird, P.N., et al. (1984). Only connections: A critique of semantic networks. *Psychological Bulletin, 96*(2), 292–315.

Jones, C.L. (1983). Summary recommendations from subject access meeting. *Information Technology and Libraries, 2*(1), 116–119.

Kaske, N.K., & Sanders, N.P. (1980). On-line subject access: The human side of the problem. *RQ, 20*(1), 52–58.

Kirtland, M., & Cochrane, P. (1982). Critical views of LCSH—Library of Congress subject headings: A bibliographic and bibliometric essay. *Cataloging & Classification Quarterly, 1*(2/3), 71–94.

Knapp, P.B. (1944). The subject catalog in the college library: An investigation of terminology. *The Library Quarterly, 14*(3), 214–228.

Larson, R.R., & Graham, V. (1983). Monitoring and evaluating MELVYL. *Information Technology and Libraries, 2*(1), 93–104.

Lawrence, G.S. (1985). System features for subject access in the online catalog. *Library Resources & Technical Services, 29*(1), 16–33.

Lilley, O.L. (1954). Evaluation of the subject catalog. *American Documentation, 5*(2), 41–60.

Mahapatra, M., & Biswas, S.C. (1983). PRECIS: Its theory and application—An extended state-of-the-art review from the beginning up to 1982. *Libri, 33*(4), 316–330.

Mandel, C.A. (1981). *Subject access in the online catalog.* Report, Council on Library Resources. Washington, DC: Council on Library Resources.

Mandel, C.A. (1985). Enriching the library catalog record for subject access. *Library Resources & Technical Services, 29*(1), 5–15.

Mandel, C.A., & Herschman, J. (1983). Online subject access—Enhancing the library catalog. *Journal of Academic Librarianship, 9*(3), 148–155.

Marcus, R.S. (1983). An experimental comparison of the effectiveness of computers and humans as search intermediaries. *Journal of the American Society for Information Science, 34*(6), 381-404.

Markey, K. (1980). Research report on analytical review of catalog use studies. (OCLC/OPR/RR-80/2, ED 186 041). Columbus, OH: Research Department, Office of Planning and Research.

Markey, K. (1984). *Subject searching in library catalogs: Before and after the introduction of online catalogs.* Dublin, OH: OCLC Online Computer Library Center.

Markey, K., & Demeyer, A. (1985). *Dewey Decimal Classification online project.* Paper presented at International Federation of Library Associations and Institutions, 51st, Chicago, IL.

Markley, A.E. (1950). The University of California subject catalog inquiry: A study of the subject catalog based on interviews with users. *Journal of Cataloging and Classification, 6,* 88-95.

Matthews, J.R., et al. (Eds.). (1983). *Using online catalogs: A nationwide survey.* New York: Neal-Schuman.

Matthews, J.R., & Lawrence, G.S. (1984). Further analysis of the CLR online catalog project. *Information Technology and Libraries, 3*(4), 354-376.

McCarn, D.B. (1983). *Online catalogs: Requirements, characteristics and costs.* Report of a conference sponsored by the Council on Library Resources, Queenstown, Maryland, 1982. Washington, DC: Council on Library Resources.

Meadow, C.T., et al. (1977). *Individualized instruction for data access (IIDA) final design report.* [ERIC: ED 145 826]. Philadelphia, PA: Drexel University Graduate School of Library Science.

Miksa, F. (1983). *The subject in the dictionary catalog from Cutter to the present.* Chicago, IL: American Library Association.

Mischo, W.H. (1981). *Technical report on a subject retrieval function for the online union catalog.* (OCLC/DD/TR-81/4). Dublin, OH: OCLC Development Division, Library Systems Analysis and Design Department.

Mischo, W. (1982). Library of Congress subject headings: A review of the problems and prospects for improved subject access. *Cataloging & Classification Quarterly, 1*(2/3), 105-124.

Morehead, D.R., Pejtersen, A.M., & Rouse, W.B. (1984). The value of information and computer-aided information seeking: Problem formulation and application to fiction retrieval. *Information Processing & Management, 20*(5/6), 583-601.

Noerr, P.L., & Bivins-Noerr, K.T. (1985). Browse and navigate: An advance in database access methods. *Information Processing & Management, 21*(3), 205-213.

O'Neill, E.T., & Aluri, R. (1981). Library of Congress subject heading patterns in OCLC monographic records. *Library Resources & Technical Services, 25*(1), 63-80.

Piternick, A.B. (1984). Searching vocabularies: A developing category of online search tools. *Online Review, 8*(5), 441-449.

Richmond, P.A. (1981). *Introduction to PRECIS for North American usage.* Littleton, CO: Libraries Unlimited.

Rosenberg, V. (1967). Factors affecting the preferences of industrial personnel for information gathering methods. *Information Storage and Retrieval, 3*(3), 119-127.

Rosenberg, V. (1974). The scientific premises of information science. *Journal of the American Society for Information Science, 25*(4), 263-269.

Rothstein, S. (1964). The measurement and evaluation of reference service. *Library Trends, 12*(3), 456-472.

Russell, K.W. (Ed.). (1982). *Subject access.* Report of a meeting sponsored by the Council on Library Resources, Dublin, Ohio, 1982. Washington, DC: Council on Library Resources.

Schabas, A.H. (1982). Postcoordinate retrieval: A comparison of two indexing languages. *Journal of the American Society for Information Science, 33*(1), 32–37.

Schank, R.C., & Colby, K.M. (Eds.). (1973). *Computer models of thought and language.* San Francisco, CA: W.H. Freeman.

Schiller, A.R. (1965). Reference service: Instruction or information. *The Library Quarterly, 35*(1), 52–60.

Settel, B., & Cochrane, P.A. (1982). Augmenting subject descriptions for books in online catalogs. *Database, 5*(4), 29–37.

Shannon, C.E., & Weaver, W. (1949). *The mathematical theory of communication.* Urbana, IL: University of Illinois Press.

Stevens, M.E. (1965). *Automatic indexing: A state-of-the-art report* (NBS monograph no. 91). Washington, DC: United States G.P.O.

Svenonius, E. (1983). Use of classification in online retrieval. *Library Resources & Technical Services, 27*(1), 76–80.

Tagliacozzo, R., & Kochen, M. (1970). Information-seeking behavior of catalog users. *Information Storage and Retrieval, 6*(5), 363–381.

Taylor, R.S. (1968). Question-negotiation and information seeking in libraries. *College & Research Libraries, 29*(3), 178–194.

Williams, M.E., & Preece, S.E. (1980). Elements of a distributed transparent information retrieval system. *Proceedings of the American Society for Information Science 43rd Annual Meeting, 17*, 401–402.

Wilson, P. (1968). *Two kinds of power: An essay on bibliographical control.* Berkeley, CA: University of California Press.

Zukav, G. (1979). *The dancing Wu Li masters: An overview of the new physics.* New York: William Morrow.

# 4

# How to use controlled vocabularies more effectively in online searching

## Introduction

We have long recognized that powerful retrieval in online searching can be gained through the combined use of natural language and controlled vocabularies. The idea of a "controlled vocabulary," however, does not represent a single theory or approach to indexing or classification. There are actually many types of controlled vocabularies in databases. Often a single database will contain several types. Effective use of these vocabularies requires a strategic understanding of which types of classification and indexing are involved, and taking advantage of the particular mix of vocabularies in a given database to achieve optimum retrieval.

Most database controlled vocabularies date from the days when the databases were print products only, and represent a variety of theories on indexing and classification. In this article I will first describe and explain seven common types of subject vocabularies in databases. Secondly, I will describe some specific search techniques for taking advantage of the strengths of particular types of vocabularies. Finally, I will suggest an overall strategy for identifying and using vocabulary types when approaching a new database.

*First published as* Bates, M. J. (1988). How to use controlled vocabularies more effectively in online searching. *Online, 12*(6), 45–56.

# Spectrum of approaches to subject description

## *Seven types of subject description*

Figure 1 lists seven major types of subject description that can be found in online and CD-ROM databases today. For convenience of discussion, these types are arrayed from broad to specific, that is, typical terms or categories in types that appear higher in the list are broader, more general, than typical terms or categories in types that are lower in the list. For example, a typical category in the NTIS classification, a hierarchical classification, may be an entire academic discipline, such as geography or civil engineering, while a typical descriptor in a science thesaurus might be a particular metal alloy or a chemical compound.

Note that there exists a very large number of types of controlled vocabularies: in fact, almost every specific vocabulary has some unique features. With some particular vocabularies, therefore, the order of types in Figure 1 would be different. I am grouping and generalizing types for the sake of simplifying our discussion of what is, in fact, a very complex topic. Furthermore, some people would be uncomfortable with the idea of calling classification categories "vocabulary." We will use that term here to promote our understanding of the full array of subject approaches to information in databases.

## *Controlled vocabulary and natural language*

The top six types of vocabulary in the list can all be considered forms of controlled vocabulary, while the last, natural language, is uncontrolled. For our purposes here, "natural language" refers to the text in the record as prepared by the original writer of the document or abstract. Such text

SEVEN TYPES OF SUBJECT DESCRIPTION

Hierarchical classification
Category codes
Subject headings
Descriptors
Faceted classification
Post-controlled vocabulary
Natural language

FIG. 1. *Array of subject description from general to specific*

follows the rules only of ordinary, "natural," speaking and writing; it is not an artificial language designed just for information retrieval.

"Controlled vocabulary" refers to index terms or classification codes that have been created to provide consistent and orderly description of the contents of documents or records. Such vocabulary may be "controlled" in one or more of several ways:

- by limiting many of the normal linguistic variations in natural language (regulating whether terms appear in singular or plural, permitting only certain verb endings, etc.)

- by regulating the word order and structure of phrases, and

- by cutting down the number of synonyms or near-synonyms so that only one way of describing a given topic is allowed in the vocabulary.

In addition, aids to indexers and searchers may be provided in the form of cross-references between terms and scope notes defining terms closely. (Still other features, to be described below, can be found in classifications.) Typically, with a controlled vocabulary, a list or thesaurus of allowable terms or categories is developed, and both indexers and searchers consult that list when using controlled vocabulary.

## Post-controlled vocabulary

A disadvantage of typical controlled vocabulary lists, however, is that they are rather inflexible with respect to new terms and topic areas when they appear in a rapidly changing discipline. New vocabulary cannot be included until it has been evaluated and integrated into a new edition of the thesaurus.

A post-controlled vocabulary, on the other hand, has some of the advantages of natural language and some of those of controlled vocabulary. Typically, with a post-controlled vocabulary, indexing is not limited to an established list. Rather, natural language terminology is permitted as it appears in new incoming documents, but indexers then do something to that vocabulary to assist searchers. For example, they may create lists of closely related terms, or "hedges," so that the searcher may see at once and enter easily a whole list of ORed terms on a topic. In this way the searcher covers a topic well without having to think up a dozen other related terms to ensure coverage.

| SUBJECT HEADINGS | DESCRIPTORS |
|---|---|
| Pre-coordinate | Post-coordinate |
| Whole-document indexing | Concept indexing |
| Designed for alphabetical index | Designed for Boolean searching |
| Average 1–5 headings per document | Average 5–25 descriptors per document |
| *Example databases:* | *Example databases:* |
| Library of Congress databases | ERIC |
| WILSONLINE databases | INSPEC |
| COMPENDEX | NTIS |
| | PsycINFO . . . plus many more |

FIG. 2. *Differences between subject headings and descriptors*

The BIOSIS "Keywords" are an excellent example of a post-controlled vocabulary. These terms are drawn from the natural language of the titles of documents indexed in BIOSIS. Frequently appearing terms are listed as "Keywords" in the Master Index of the *Search Guide—BIOSIS Previews Edition*. The presence of these terms in this index will give the searcher ideas, but any natural language term, whether appearing in the Master Index or not, may appear in document titles and consequently constitute a searchable keyword. Controlled terms for a given topic ("Concept Codes" and "Biosystematic Codes") as well as term frequencies are listed next to the keywords so that the searcher may decide which is best to use in particular instances. In addition, BIOSIS indexers add some "controlled keywords" to ensure complete coverage. (See the "Content Guide" of the *Search Guide* for information on these supplemental terms.) Because the post-control done by the indexers adds some consistency, subject searching on this vocabulary can be expected to be more effective, as a rule, than pure natural language searching.

### Index terms: Subject headings vs. descriptors

We shall next examine subject headings and descriptors, which are two of the most important classes of controlled vocabulary. Differences between these two forms of index term are summarized in Figure 2. Subject headings date back to the nineteenth century and have been the traditional form of subject description used by the Library of Congress (e.g., LC MARC and REMARC databases), and by academic libraries for books. Wilson Indexes

(*Readers' Guide, Applied Science and Technology Index,* etc., available through WILSONLINE), as well as *Engineering Index* (COMPENDEX online), use this approach as well.

Subject headings often contain a main heading followed by one or more subdivisions, as in "United Nations—Armed Forces—Juvenile literature" (from *Library of Congress Subject Headings*). Subject headings are "pre-coordinate," that is, all the subject elements are combined into a single long heading by the indexer. The idea is to describe the whole document in that one heading, or at most, in a handful of such headings.

Descriptors, on the other hand, got their big boost after World War II, when science information specialists realized that subject headings were insufficiently detailed to describe highly specific scientific articles and reports. They experimented with a variety of different forms of manual access, with names like "peek-a-boo cards" and "edge-notched cards." Quite a number of indexing theories were involved, and some descriptors were quite broad, while others were very specific. However, the principal heritage, for our interests here, of that stage of development of subject description is that in many indexing languages individual descriptors were intended to describe *a single concept used within a document,* rather than the whole document—hence the phrase "concept indexing." Descriptors are generally short, one to three words usually.

Along with this concept indexing approach went the idea of Boolean searching. It is sometimes forgotten that Boolean searching originated with manual information retrieval systems, and predated online searching by decades. Since any one index term did not describe the whole document, retrieval was designed so that searchers would use Boolean logic to combine whatever set of specific concepts they wanted for their query at the time of search, and then see which documents contained that particular combination of concepts. This type of indexing was called "post-coordinate," because the searcher, rather than the indexer, combined the elements of the subject description. Concept indexing is usually more specific, with 5–25 terms assigned to individual documents.

To illustrate the differences between these two broad classes of index terms, examples are given in Figure 3 of subject headings and descriptors used in the same topic area of sports as a part of education. The WILSONLINE *Education Index* and the ERIC *Thesaurus of ERIC Descriptors* are used as sources.

In this example, the ERIC descriptors may seem quite broad compared to the subject headings, thus contradicting my statement above that descriptors are usually quite specific. There are a couple of reasons for

| Sports subject headings in<br>WILSONLINE's *Education Index* | Sports descriptors in ERIC's *Thesaurus* |
|---|---|
| Athletes | Athletes |
| Athletes—Health and hygiene | Athletic Coaches |
| Athletes—Nutrition | Athletic Equipment |
| Athletes—Physical examinations | Athletic Fields |
| Athletes—Psychology | Athletics |
| Athletes—Scholastic achievements | . . . |
| Athletes—Training | Sport psychology |
| Athletes—Wounds and injuries | Sportsmanship |
| Athletic associations | |
| Athletics | |
| Athletics—Administration | |
| Athletics—Equipment—Catalogs | |
| Athletics, Intercollegiate | |
| Athletics, Intercollegiate—Finance | |
| . . . | |
| Sports—Accidents and injuries | |
| Sports—Accidents and injuries—Prevention | |
| Sports—Accidents and injuries—Statistics | |

FIG. 3. *Subject headings and descriptors*

this apparent contradiction. First, note that the headings in the *Education Index* example are pre-combined (pre-coordinate), so more than one subject element appears in most headings. ERIC descriptors, on the other hand, are not combined until the time of search. Compare the ERIC search described later in this article to see an example of a more specific query.

Secondly, the topic of a whole document may be broad or specific, and individual concepts within a document may be broad or specific. Therefore, reflecting this range, *individual* subject headings and descriptors will vary in specificity. The difference in breadth between subject headings and descriptors shows up in the overall pattern of indexing. Descriptor systems apply far more terms as a rule than subject heading systems do, identifying numerous individual concepts, rather than describing the whole document in one or two headings.

## Classifications vs. indexing vocabularies

What distinguishes a classification scheme from an index term vocabulary? There are many practical distinctions, but there is a more theoretical distinction that is actually the most important for understanding such systems for online searching. Index terms are fundamentally *linguistic,* while classification schemes organize *conceptual categories.* The intent with indexing vocabularies is to find good, compact words or phrases to use to describe documents. Language has many phrases and words that overlap in meaning, however, even when synonyms and near-synonyms have been purged through vocabulary control. For instance, "Emotional Adjustment" and "Emotional Problems," both legitimate terms in ERIC, have some overlap in meaning and some distinctive aspects of meaning.

With classification schemes, on the other hand, the goal—not always achieved but always sought—is to have completely distinct conceptual categories that are mutually exclusive and jointly exhaustive. That is, there should ideally be no overlap in meaning between categories of a classification (i.e., mutually exclusive categories), and no gaps, that is, no areas left uncovered by categories of the scheme (i.e., jointly exhaustive). As a part of making these rigorous categorical distinctions, classifications are generally further organized in a structured manner not seen in index vocabularies. Two such types of structures are described below as "hierarchical" and "faceted" classifications.

In order to define categories this rigorously, and to be sure to exclude overlap in meaning, it is sometimes necessary to label categories with lengthy and awkward names. For example, the BIOSIS Concept Code "Tropical and Semitropical Fruits and Nuts; Plantation Crops" is not the sort of phrase that would ordinarily be used in an index language, but rather defines a carefully demarcated conceptual category. Since the terminology describing categories in classification schemes can be awkward, it is desirable to have some compact notation, such as classification codes, to stand for the categories.

The more highly developed classification schemes used in online databases generally have such codes assigned to the categories. Note, however, that the presence of codes does not necessarily indicate a classification. In the PsycINFO thesaurus (*Thesaurus of Psychological Index Terms*), for example, codes have been assigned to index terms in order to abbreviate search term input time, but the thesaurus contains a true index vocabulary, not a classification.

## Category codes

"Category code" is the label I have given to descriptive systems that have some classificatory features and some index term features and can therefore

## CC54512 NONPARASITIC DISEASES

*CODE FREQUENCIES* **Major (7760) Minor (2040)**

*CODE APPLICATIONS* This code retrieves studies on plant diseases caused by non-biological factors, such as weather conditions and pollution.

*EXAMPLES—STUDIES ON* • Pollution • weather • plant nutrient deficiencies or toxicities • toxic effects of pesticides on plants • soil waterlogging • genetic and developmental disorders

*STRATEGY RECOMMENDATIONS*

- For studies on genetic disorders of plants, use this code with appropriate keywords and the *Plant Genetics* code CC03504.

- For studies of the adverse effects of radiation on plants, use this code with appropriate keywords and the *Plant Physiology, Biochemistry and Biophysics Radiation Effects* code CC51516.

- For studies on plant diseases caused by climatic factors, use this code with appropriate keywords and the *Bioclimatology and Biometeorology* code CC07504.

- For studies of physiological factors relevant to plant disease development, use this code with appropriate keywords and relevant *Plant Physiology, Biochemistry and Biophysics* codes. See Directory, page B-15.

- For studies on the effects of environmental pollutants on plants, use relevant *Phytopathology* codes and the *Air, Water and Soil Pollution* code CC37015.

## CC54514 PARASITISM AND RESISTANCE

*CODE FREQUENCIES* **Major (7950) Minor (570)**

*CODE APPLICATIONS* This code retrieves studies on plant host susceptibility and resistance to diseases.

*EXAMPLES—STUDIES ON* • Breeding for resistance • genetic, physiological and morphological factors relating to plant resistance

*STRATEGY RECOMMENDATIONS*

- For studies relating plant genetics to disease resistance, use this code with appropriate keywords and the *Plant Genetics and Cytogenetics* code CC03504.

- For studies on plant resistance to entomological pests, use this code with appropriate keywords and relevant *Economic Entomology* codes. See Directory, page B-7.

- For studies on plant resistance to fungi, algae, bacteria, and other agents, use this code with appropriate keywords and relevant *Phytopathology* codes. See Directory, page B-14.

FIG. 4. *Concept codes from BIOSIS. These are two of the ten codes within the broader area of phytopathology, or plant disease. Note the extensive scope notes and carefully worked out strategy recommendations. Though these "concepts" are formed like index terms, they also have classificatory features in that their coverage is made rigorously mutually exclusive and jointly exhaustive.*

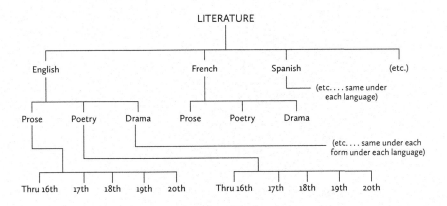

FIG. 5. *Hierarchical classification. (Based on Needham, C.D. [1971].* Organizing Knowledge In Libraries *[2nd Rev. ed., p. 120]. London: Seminar Press).*

be considered a mixed type. BIOSIS "Concept Codes" are an example of this type. Sample Concept Codes are reproduced in Figure 4.

BIOSIS Concept Codes are a mixed type, because, on the one hand, the concepts are very carefully and rigorously defined and given code numbers, rather in the manner of classification categories, but on the other hand, while grouped logically, the concepts are not embedded in a highly defined structure in the manner of most classification schemes. See the discussion of classification types below.

## Hierarchical and faceted classifications

A hierarchical classification is the traditional, "family-tree" type classification in which each category is successively broken down into smaller and smaller subdivisions. A simplified example, made up for illustration purposes, appears in Figure 5. Each level of the hierarchy is divided out by what is called a characteristic of division. For example, in Figure 5, categories on the first level are distinguished by language (French literature, English literature, etc.), the second level by form (prose, poetry, drama, etc.), and the third level by historical period (sixteenth century, seventeenth century, etc.). So the characteristic of division of the first level is language, of the second level, form, etc.

In using such a scheme for classifying materials, a distinctive notation is assigned to each possible category created by the hierarchy. In Figure 6, examples of such categories and notations are provided for the literature classification.

**LITERATURE**

100 English Literature
  110 English Prose
      111 English Prose thru 16th Century
      112 English 17th-Century Prose
      113 English 18th-Century Prose
      114 English 19th-Century Prose
      115 English 20th-Century Prose
  120 English Poetry
      121 English Poetry thru 16th Century
      122 English 17th-Century Poetry
      (etc.)
  130 English Drama
      131 English Drama thru 16th Century
      (etc.)
200 French Literature
  210 French Prose
      211 French Prose thru 16th Century
      (etc.)
  220 French Poetry
      221 French Poetry thru 16th Century
      (etc.)
  230 French Drama
      (etc.)
300 Spanish Literature
  310 Spanish Prose
      (etc.)

FIG. 6. *Labelled categories for hierarchical classification*

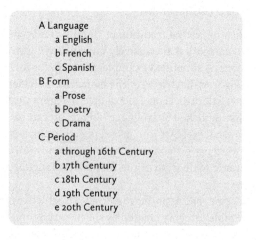

A Language
  a English
  b French
  c Spanish
B Form
  a Prose
  b Poetry
  c Drama
C Period
  a through 16th Century
  b 17th Century
  c 18th Century
  d 19th Century
  e 20th Century

FIG. 7. *Faceted classification*

| Aa | English Literature |
|---|---|
| AaBa | English Prose |
| AaBaCa | English 16th-Century Prose |
| AbBbCe | French 20th-Century Poetry |
| AcBaBb | Spanish Prose and Poetry |
| AcBaBbCb | Spanish Prose and Poetry of the 17th Century |
| BcCd | 19th-Century Drama |
| Ce | Literature of the 20th Century |

FIG. 8. *Labelled categories for faceted classification*

A faceted classification, on the other hand, creates a separate, free-standing list for each characteristic of division. In Figure 7 the components of the hierarchical classification in Figure 5 have been converted into a faceted classification. This imaginary faceted classification of literature contains one facet list for language, another for form, and another for date. In a manual faceted system, a classifier would create a class number for a document by selecting a piece of notation from each facet, as needed, and stringing them together to represent a document. Example notation is included in Figure 7, and some example topics and their associated combined notation are shown in Figure 8.

Faceted classification has been little used in the United States for manual information systems, but it is coming to be used a lot in online databases. In online databases, indexers usually assign the facet elements independently, and do not combine them into a single notation. This approach leaves the searcher the freedom to combine the elements with Boolean logic as he or she wishes at the time of search, and makes for the same flexibility found with concept indexing described above.

In Predicasts, for example, shown in Figure 9, a searcher can choose one code from a facet list for industry ("Product Code"), another from a facet list for form of activity ("Event Code"), and another for geographical region ("Geographic Code"). One then ANDs them all together to produce a very specific, detailed search formulation.

It is easier to create very specific categories with faceted classifications than with hierarchical classifications. We can see why when we consider what it would take to represent the Predicasts categories in a hierarchical classification. Currently, with the faceted approach in Predicasts, any element in any facet can be combined with any element in any other facet.

Imagine how many tens or even hundreds of thousands of possible combinations there are. Each product code can be combined with every

## EVENT CODES

**12 Organizational History**
Formation
Private to Public Co
Reorganization
Bankruptcy
Liquidation
Expropriation
Headquarters Data
Public to Private Co
Organizatnl Change NEC

**13 Subsidiary-to-Parent Data**
Parent owns 100%
Parent owns 80–99%
Parent owns 50–79%
Affiliate-to-Parent Data
Division-to-Parent Data
Joint Venture-to-Parent Data
Parent Information NEC

**22 Planning & Information**
Planning
Management Policy & Goals
Operations Research
Venture Analysis
Management Consulting
Model Building
Information Gathering
Information Dissemination
Planning NEC

**23 Production Management**
Supervisory Management
Production Planning & Control
Plant Engineering
Safety Management
Materials Handling
Environmental Management
Energy Management

**33 Product Design & Development**
Product Development
Prototype Built
Product Testing
Market Testing
Product Introduction
Product Applications
Product Discontinued
Products NEC

**34 Product Specifications**
Mechanical Properties
Chemical Properties
Electrical Properties
Structural Properties
Functional Properties
Energy per Unit (Properties)
Process Health Hazards
Price/Performance Data

## PRODUCT CODES

| | |
|---|---|
| 28664 | **Aromatic Hydrocarbons** |
| 286641 | Cumene |
| 286642 | Divinylbenzene |
| 286644 | A-Methylstyrene |
| 286645 | Alkylbenzenes |
| 2866451 | Dodecylbenzenes |
| 2866452 | Methylbenzene |
| 2866453 | Ethylbenzene |
| 286647 | Styrene Monomer |
| 286648 | Polymethylbenzenes |
| 2866481 | Mesitylene |
| 2866482 | Durene |
| 2866483 | Pseudocumene |
| 286649 | Aromatic Hydrocarbons NEC |
| 2866491 | Stilbene |
| 2866492 | Methyinaphthalene |
| 2866493 | Anthracine |
| 2866494 | Coumarone |
| 2866495 | Methyl Styrenes NEC |
| 2866499 | Misc Aromatic Hydrocarbons |
| **28665** | **Cyclic Amines** |
| 286651 | Aniline |
| 286652 | Aniline Derivatives |
| 2866521 | Dimethylaniline |
| 2866526 | Oxydianiline |
| 286653 | Heterocyclic Amines |
| 2866537 | Aminopyridines |
| 286655 | Diphenylamine |
| 286656 | Benzidines & Toluidines |
| 2866561 | Benzidine |
| 2866562 | Dimethylbenzidine |
| 2866563 | Dichlorobenzidine |
| 2866565 | Dianisidine |
| 2866566 | Dimethyl-p-Toluidine |
| 2866567 | Toluenediamine |
| 2866568 | Toluidine |
| 2866569 | Benzidines & Toluidines NEC |
| 286657 | Cyclohexylamine |
| 286658 | Xylidines |
| 2866585 | Xylenediamines |

## GEOGRAPHIC CODES

### EUROPE

| | |
|---|---|
| 4 | All codes beginning with 4 |
| 4 E | Europe |
| 4 F | Europe ex USSR |
| 4 G | Central Europe |
| 4 L | Southern Europe |
| 4 M | Mediterranean |
| 4 N | Northern Europe |
| 4 T | OECD Europe |
| 4 W | West Europe |
| 4 CO | COCOM |
| 4 EC | European Community |
| 4 NA | N Atlantic Treaty Org |
| 4BEJ | Benelux |
| 4BEK | Belg-Lux Econ Union |
| 4BEL | Belgium |
| 4DEN | Denmark |
| 4FRA | France |
| 4GRE | Greece |
| 4IRE | Ireland |
| 4ITA | Italy |
| 4LUX | Luxembourg |
| 4NET | Netherlands |
| 4UK | United Kingdom |
| 4WGE | West Germany |
| 4ZEC | Other EC |

### WEST EUROPE EX EC

| | |
|---|---|
| 5 | All codes beginning with 5 |
| 5 W | West Europe ex EC |
| 5 EF | European Free Trd Assn |
| 5 SC | Scandinavia |
| 5AND | Andorra |
| 5AUT | Austria |
| 5FAE | Faeroe Islands |
| 5FIN | Finland |
| 5GIB | Gibraltar |
| 5GRL | Greenland |
| 5ICE | Iceland |
| 5LIZ | Liechtenstein |
| 5MAT | Malta |
| 5MON | Monaco |
| 5NOR | Norway |

FIG. 9. *Sections of Predicasts facets*

single geographic code and/or event code. Anywhere from zero to several elements can be drawn from a single facet and ORed together. And so on. The number of possible highly specific descriptions of the information needed that the searcher can create explodes almost astronomically.

In a hierarchical scheme, on the other hand, each allowable combination is specified in advance, and given distinctive notation. If that were done with Predicasts, the search manual would be many hundreds of pages longer than it is now.

We can better see the difference between these two approaches to classification by comparing a Chinese menu to the more conventional type of menu. The Chinese menu tells you to select one item from each of several lists. The total possible number of meal combinations that results from this approach is quite large, even though the lists may be fairly short. In a more conventional menu, all the possible meal combinations are specified in advance (often with the statement "No substitutions, please") and the customer is consequently actually limited to fewer possible meal combinations, even though the menu may be quite long. While it is in principle possible to create just as many categories as one wants in a hierarchical scheme, and list them out in a lengthy list, in practice it is so tedious and expensive that it is usually not done. Thus, most hierarchical classifications contain far fewer total possible categories than is the case with faceted classifications.

### Array from broad to specific

To review, common types of subject description in databases have been arrayed from broad to specific, that is, typically, categories or terms in the types near the top of the list in Figure 1 are broader than is the case for those toward the bottom of the list. Natural language, at the bottom of the list, is the most specific of all subject description, because it allows the full range of variation in vocabulary, orthography, and syntax that is found in written language. Post-control adds just a little control, being much more permissive of terminology than descriptors and subject headings. Subject heading systems describe the whole document in one or more headings, while descriptor systems apply a large number of terms reflecting individual concepts, so the overall pattern of indexing in the latter systems tends to be more specific. Because relatively short lists of facet elements can be combined in many different ways, faceted classifications can more easily be highly specific than hierarchical classifications, in which combinations of elements are specified in advance.

## Optimal use of controlled vocabularies in searching

In this section we will discuss ways of using these various types of subject description to good effect in searching online.

### Hierarchical classification codes and category codes

Broad to medium-broad hierarchical classification codes can seldom be used by themselves. Examples of these are the codes in NTIS, COMPENDEX, and RILM Abstracts. Such codes usually retrieve hundreds or thousands of documents, because they are so broad. However, they may be used effectively in combination with other more specific terms. Classification codes of medium breadth, such as those used in INSPEC and MathSci, and the category codes (BIOSIS "Concept codes") can sometimes be used by themselves, or, more often, used in ANDed sets with other codes, or used in conjunction with other more specific types of search vocabulary.

In addition, there are three particular circumstances where broad to medium subject categories may be very useful:

1) *Current awareness* Researchers like to keep up to date by scanning a wide range of journals and other literature, representing both their specific research specialty, as well as closely related research areas. The online equivalent of this can be done by entering a broad to medium classification code for the general research area and ANDing it with the code for the latest update in the database. This combination achieves the researcher's goal by producing a list of citations that covers just the most recently entered materials in a broad subject area. At the same time the list is normally not too lengthy, because the retrieval is limited to the very most current items. For example, searching INSPEC in DIALOG, one can input the code for "Information storage and retrieval" and AND it with the code for "latest update" as follows:

SS CC = 7250 AND UD = 9999

2) *Unsettled vocabulary in a new research area* This approach is also good on those occasions where a research topic is so new that there are no generally agreed-upon descriptors in use for it yet. Providing that the new research topic is generally understood to fall within a given broad area of research, one can enter the code for that broad area, ANDed with codes for recent updates in the database, and scan for relevant articles. In this manner the classification serves as a backup for handling the limitations of descriptor vocabulary.

There are at least two other options for dealing with this situation. First, one may do free-text searching on a hedge of ORed natural language words and phrases that have been used for the new topic. This approach is frequently to be preferred as the most straightforward. However, it is in the very nature of new research areas to contain some confusion; in such a case it is not as obvious as usual which articles are relevant. Preselecting citations by searching only on recognized terms in use to date may limit retrieval more than one wants. In some cases, giving the researcher a chance to scan through a list of the most recent items in the broader topic area may be a surer way for him or her to identify all the relevant items.

Secondly, one may search on a key reference in a citation database such as SciSearch or Social SciSearch. In those cases where one or more key references are frequently cited, use of a citation database can enable one to leapfrog the vocabulary problem entirely.

*3) Distinguishing different word meanings* Any given term may be used in a variety of different ways in a database, particularly in the case of databases covering many areas, such as NTIS. "Bond" can be used in materials science, chemistry, anthropology, and finance, for example. By ANDing the specific term (whether controlled vocabulary or natural language) with the classification category of interest to the searcher, any other meaning of the term can be automatically ruled out. In NTIS, 71 is the code for Materials Science, and the subsection B within that category is "Adhesives and sealants." The following search statement will restrict the retrievals on truncated "Bond" to the field of adhesives and sealants:

SS SH = 71B AND Bond?

I have chosen an extreme example, in that NTIS covers a very wide range of disciplines. This procedure is useful in databases with narrower coverage too, however. Even within a single field, terms are often used in several subtly, but significantly, different ways. These multiple meanings can be eliminated through clever use of classification codes.

## Subject headings

Subject headings were not originally designed to be used with Boolean searching—the searcher was supposed to hunt in alphabetical catalogs or indexes for the complete heading. Many systems of descriptors, on the other hand, were intended from the beginning to be used with Boolean logic, and were designed accordingly. The question of whether subject headings work as well for online searching as descriptors do has never really been resolved in research.

Sometimes, with subject heading systems, the searcher has no way of knowing which subdivisions may be used with which main headings.

This problem is particularly acute with Library of Congress subject headings. The *Library of Congress Subject Headings* list is quite confusing for the uninitiated on this matter; only trained catalogers can make this determination in some cases. Consequently, an attempt to make a controlled vocabulary search on a main heading plus subdivision can be a gamble. Is that combination in fact in use? The use of free-text proximity searching may be both simpler and surer in such cases. On the other hand, where heading and subdivision can be identified, or only a main heading is needed, one can enjoy the same benefits that generally accrue with controlled vocabulary. Searches on main headings alone may prove to be quite broad in coverage; one may wish to AND in more specific free-text terms as well. On the whole, subject headings are more useful when somewhat broader topics are wanted.

There is another very important fact to keep in mind about subject headings: Since far fewer headings are assigned as a rule to each item than is the case with descriptors, combining several subject headings in a search formulation (specifically, one that is limited to controlled vocabulary) is more likely to produce a null set than is the case with descriptors. This, again, is more likely with Library of Congress databases wherein very limited numbers of headings are assigned, than with the other systems described earlier.

Since subject headings often contain several subdivisions, the databank may mount a database, e.g., DIALOG's versions of COMPENDEX and LC MARC, so that the searcher can search on individual sections of the heading, or the sections in combination. For example, in COMPENDEX, the heading "Light—Brillouin scattering" is treated as two headings in DIALOG, to enable searchers interested in either topic to find documents indexed under either term. The (L) operator in DIALOG enables the searcher to require that the two elements appear together *in the same heading,* so that one does not retrieve documents with "Light" as a part of one heading and "Brillouin scattering" as a part of another heading.

WILSONLINE calls the entire heading, that is, main heading plus subdivisions, a "Descriptor String," and calls each element of the string, whether main heading or subdivision, a "Subject Heading." Thus, in WILSONLINE, as with the DIALOG-mounted databases mentioned above, one has the option of searching on the whole heading or its component parts. WILSONLINE examples:

find mathematicians/soviet union/biography (ds)
find mathematicians (sh)

*Descriptors*

Recall that the fundamental idea of concept indexing is that no one descriptor describes the content of the entire document—the numerous descriptors applied to the document do so only *jointly*. This contrasts with subject heading systems, where a single heading is supposed to describe the whole document. From the beginning, even before online searching was available, it was assumed with descriptor systems that the searcher would identify the key concepts in the search query and search on a Boolean combination of the concepts. Though one does sometimes find a single descriptor that exactly describes the desired topic, it is more often the case that descriptors must be *assembled together* in a Boolean statement using ORs, ANDs, and NOTs to create a whole that represents the information need.

Beginning searchers sometimes believe that their job is to find a single topic label and input just that one concept in a simple one-word or one-phrase search formulation. This apparently reasonable approach runs counter to the way descriptor-based systems are in fact designed. Rather, the task is to find the several concepts which jointly represent the topic. Research has shown this misconception to be common among ERIC searchers, for example. Both poor recall and poor precision are the result.

When searching a descriptor-based database, one's prospective search formulations that contain only one or two terms should be reviewed with these questions in mind: "Are all the important concepts ANDed in? Are there significant term variations that could be ORed in?" One's strategy in dealing with a descriptor system may contrast sharply, therefore, with the strategy used for a subject heading system.

ERIC and PsycINFO are typical of controlled vocabularies designed as concept indexing terms. ERIC, for example, provides in many cases several terms that may be relevant to a given topic area. These terms sometimes overlap partially but not completely. In a thorough search, clusters of these terms should be ORed together. Furthermore, auxiliary information is indexed, such as grade level of students involved or type of document, so that it is possible to AND terms for the central topic of interest with other terms representing the auxiliary information and gain much more precision in the output set. For example, for a query on the problems high school student athletes have with meeting required academic performance levels, the following search formulation may be designed:

Athletes AND (Academic Achievement OR Student Improvement OR Academic Standards) AND (High School OR Secondary Education)

## Faceted classification

As discussed earlier, great specificity in description of information need is possible with faceted classifications by combining elements from each of several facets. Such power is not restricted to bibliographic databases.

In Figure 10 we see an example from the DIALOG bluesheet for American Men and Women of Science, a biographical directory.

Each Additional Index represents a facet of information about the biographees. Combining elements from each facet makes it possible not only to home in on a highly specific subset of the file, but also to produce information not explicitly available in the file. For example, drawing on the Additional Indexes listed in Figure 10, we may search for that set which is all Nobel Prize winners in the state of California:

S HA = Nobel AND ST = CA

In the example, we not only locate profiles of all Nobel Prize winners in California very quickly, we also find out how many such winners there are (assuming the file is complete), a piece of information that may be nowhere directly mentioned in the directory. As more and more directories and other traditional reference books are brought up online, it will be possible to do this powerful faceted searching in many ways with these additional indexes.

## Post-controlled vocabulary and natural language

Some benefits of post-controlled vocabulary in searching have already been discussed above. Since this article is concerned with use of controlled vocabularies, nothing more will be said here about the use of natural language in searching.

# Identifying and using vocabulary types in a new database

## Identification

To take advantage of controlled vocabularies in a database, it is first necessary to identify what types of subject description are available in it. To do so, it is important to examine the *producer* documentation, i.e., the information put out by the creators or publishers of the database, as well as that provided by the databank. In order to provide a common format across various databases, online services such as DIALOG and BRS generally provide common labels for subject elements, such as "Descriptor," or

## ADDITIONAL INDEXES

| PREFIX | FIELD NAME | EXAMPLES | |
|--------|-----------|----------|---|
| AD= | Institution and Street | E AD=SMITHSONIAN | S AD=CARNEGIE(W)AD=INST |
| BS= | Birth Statistics | E BS=FRANCE | S BS=CINCINNATI(F)BS=OHIO |
| CD= | Children Statistics | E CD=2 | S CD=3 |
| CN= | Country Name | E CN=MEXICO | S CN=UNITED KINGDOM<br>S CN=WEST(W)CN=GERMANY |
| CP= | Concurrent Positions | E CP=CONSULT | S CP=PROF(W)CP=JOHNS(W)CP=HOPKINS |
| CY= | City | E CY=BALTIMORE | S CY=LOS ANGELES<br>S CY=RAPID(W)CY= CITY |
| DC= | Discipline Code | E DC=03002007 | S DC=02002000 |
| EC= | Employment Classification | E EC=ACADEMIC | S EC=CONSULTING |
| ED= | Education | E ED=PHD | S ED=UNIV(W)ED=CHICAGO |
| EX= | Professional Experience | E EX=INTERN | S EX=PASTEUR(W)EX=INST |
| HA= | Honors and Awards | E HA=NOBEL | S HA=BORIS(W)HA=PREGEL(W)HA=AWARD |
| HD= | Honorary Degrees | E HD=PURDUE | S HD=UNIV(W) ED=CHICAGO |
| LP= | Language Proficiency | E LP=SPANISH | S LP=CHINESE |
| ME= | Memberships | E ME=CHEM | S ME=NAT(W)ME=ACAD(W)ME=SCI |
| MS= | Marriage Statistics | E MS=80 | S MS=57 |
| NA= | Biographee Name* | E NA=ACKEMAN | S NA=BROWN, DONALD D |
| ST= | State/Province | E ST=BC | S ST=MD |
| SX= | Sex | E SX=F | S SX=M |
| YB= | Year of Birth | E YB=19 | S YB=31 |
| ZP= | Zip Code | E ZP=60601 | S ZP=21210 |

*Also searchable in the Basic Index

FIG. 10. *Additional indexes of American men and women of science*

"Classification code," regardless of the type of vocabulary involved. Thus, if only the *databank* documentation (database chapters, newsletters, etc.) is examined, it is difficult to tell what type of vocabularies are being used.

The publishers of databases, on the other hand, generally describe the unique features of the indexing provided in their databases, and often publish thesauri and other term lists as well. Failure to buy available producer documentation for a frequently used database can be a classic example of being "penny wise and pound foolish." The online time saved through proper use of available subject vocabularies can quickly make up for the cost of a $50 or $100 set of producer database documentation. The better developed the database vocabulary is, the more this holds true.

So when first working with a new database, one should examine both databank and producer documentation regarding the database to identify unique features, as well as to discover the variety of forms of subject access provided by the database. It is quite common, particularly in the sciences, for databases to have both an index vocabulary of some kind and a classification. Figure 11 displays the types of subject description available in several major databases.

BIOSIS, for example, has a hierarchical classification in its Biosystematic Codes, Category codes in its Concept Codes, Post-controlled vocabulary in its Keywords, and, of course, natural language. COMPENDEX, with its CAL Codes, has a medium broad hierarchical classification, subject headings, and natural language. For subject searching, the citation indexes, SciSearch and Social SciSearch, are limited to natural language, but have the advantage of covering several disciplines at once.

### Use in searching

In using these types of vocabularies in searching, the basic principle to keep in mind is first to identify what type of controlled vocabulary a database uses, and then use each type in a way that corresponds with the needs of the query. Specifically, one goes through the following steps:

- Determine which types of vocabulary are available in the database

- Identify each distinct search concept in the query

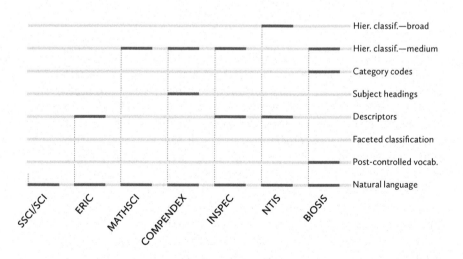

FIG. 11. *Forms of subject access in various databases*

- Assess how broad or specific each concept is

- Use the type of vocabulary for each concept that corresponds with its breadth

- Combine in normal Boolean fashion in the search formulation.

This series of steps is similar to the steps recommended for the preparation of BIOSIS profiles. This approach can be used with all databases, however, once one knows how to recognize the controlled vocabulary types.

Once one has identified the sorts of controlled vocabulary a database contains, as in Figure II, one can use the level of breadth of controlled vocabulary that is appropriate to each concept in the query. Suppose, for example, one is searching INSPEC and is interested in applications of general systems theory to the design of information retrieval systems. INSPEC has a classification code for the first term, a descriptor for the last term, and the middle term can be entered free-text. In this way, the searcher uses search terms from the database producer's vocabulary that more or less match the specificity of the concepts in the query. ("Design," the middle term, is not very specific in this case.) The results can then be manipulated to increase or decrease output, and to eliminate false drops. Use of vocabulary in this way—that is, vocabulary appropriate to the nature of the query terms in the first place—will increase the quality of searches overall.

5

# An analysis of search terminology used by humanities scholars: The Getty Online Searching Project report no. 1

ABSTRACT

The Getty Art History Information Program carried out a two-year project to study how humanities scholars operate as end users of online databases. Visiting Scholars at the Getty Center for the History of Art and the Humanities in Santa Monica, California, were offered the opportunity to do unlimited subsidized searching of DIALOG® databases. This first report from the project analyzes the vocabulary terms twenty-two scholars used in their natural language descriptions of their information needs and in their online searches. The data were extracted from 165 natural language statements and 1,068 search terms. Vocabulary categories used by humanities scholars were found to differ markedly from those used in the sciences, a fact that imposes distinctive demands on thesaurus development and the design of online information systems. Humanities scholars searched for far more named individuals, geographical terms, chronological terms, and discipline terms than was the case in a comparative science sample.

*First published as* Bates,[1] M. J., Wilde,[2] D. N., & Siegfried,[2] S. (1993). An analysis of search terminology used by humanities scholars: The Getty Online Searching Project report no. 1. *The Library Quarterly, 63*(1), 1–39.

1  Graduate School of Library and Information Science, University of California, Los Angeles.

2  The Getty Art History Information Program.

The analysis provides substantial support for the growing perception that information needs of humanities scholars are distinct from those of scholars in other fields, and that the design of information-providing systems for these scholars must take their unique qualities into account.

## Introduction

Stimulated by scholars' increased access to online databases such as those offered by Dialog Information Services, the Getty Art History Information Program launched a two-year program in 1989 to study how humanities scholars, engaging in their characteristic modes of research, use online databases when they are given the chance to do unlimited searching, unconstrained by cost. The study was intended to probe a number of aspects of the scholars' experiences with online searching, including their reactions to the use of the online databases, the role the searching had in their research work, their search techniques and learning curve, their queries, and the search terms they used. The results of the study are to be reported in a series of articles, of which this is the first.[3]

The data analyzed for this article are the natural language statements the scholars gave describing or commenting on their queries, and the search terms used by the scholars in their online searches. The analyses reported here were prompted by the observation that the wording the scholars used in their natural language statements contradicted some prevailing assumptions in information science about subject terminology in online searching. This article identifies, quantifies, and discusses the principal categories of search terms the scholars used in both their natural language statements and their online search statements to DIALOG.

## Background

Empirical research into information-seeking behavior among members of various academic and research communities focused almost exclusively on engineering and the sciences during the 1960s, and on the social sciences in

3  Marilyn Schmitt conceived the Getty Online Searching Project; she designed the study together with Susan Siegfried and Deborah N. Wilde. Siegfried and Wilde carried out the collaborative project plan and oversaw the gathering of data throughout the project. Marcia Bates analyzed the data, formulated conclusions, and contributed insights from the discipline of information science. Research assistant Vanessa Birdsey coded the data into categories developed by Bates. Jeanette Clough and Katherine Smith transcribed the DIALOG search statements for subsequent analysis.

the 1970s. Although Sue Stone reviews a number of studies done before 1980, she points to the "relative neglect" of the humanities until the late 1970s. Her review (Stone, 1982) and the work begun in the late 1970s by the Centre for Research on User Studies (for example, Corkill & Mann, 1978) mark the beginning of a modern era of interest in humanities scholars' information seeking on the part of researchers in library and information science.

During these decades, reviews, research projects, and commentaries drew attention to the unique characteristics of the information-seeking behavior of humanities scholars (Broadbent, 1986; Case, 1991; Corkill & Mann, 1978; Gould, 1988; Guest, 1987; Lowry & Stuveras, 1987; Rahtz, 1987; Schmitt, 1988, 1990; Stam, 1984; Stam & Giral, 1988; Stielow & Tibbo, 1988; Stone, 1982; Tibbo, 1989; Wiberley, 1991; Wiberley & Jones, 1989). While many of these studies dealt with the research behavior of scholars in general, few paid attention to these scholars' use of online databases. However, during the last few years this lack has begun to be remedied. Serious attention is now being given to online searching in the humanities: its particular requirements, problems with databases and their vendors, and specific search techniques (Boyles, 1987, 1988; Crawford, 1986; Everett & Pilachowski, 1986; Katzen, 1986; Lehmann & Renfro, 1991; Loughridge, 1989; Mackesy, 1982; Ross, 1987; Ruiz & Meyer, 1990; Stern, 1988; Walker, 1988, 1990; Walker & Atkinson, 1991).

A few empirical studies have examined actual uses of online databases by or for scholars in the humanities. Janice Woo (1998) studied how three graduate students at Columbia University made online use of the *Avery Index to Architectural Periodicals*. Sylvia Krausse and John Etchingham elicited the reactions of scholars to database searching when a grant subsidized the cost of their searches (Krausse & Etchingham, 1986). Jan Horner and David Thirlwall tested several hypotheses regarding uses of online searching by social science and humanities scholars (Horner & Thirlwall, 1988), and Jitka Hurych (1986) analyzed formal online search requests to compare the use of online search services across disciplines (sciences, social sciences, and humanities).

Of particular relevance to this article are studies of humanities vocabulary and indexing. Stephen Wiberley, who has conducted two large research projects on indexing vocabulary in the humanities, studied the vocabulary of encyclopedias and dictionaries (Wiberley, 1983) and of abstracting and indexing services (Wiberley, 1988) in the humanities to test the truth of the cliché that the vocabulary of the humanities is vague and imprecise. He found, on the contrary, that much of the vocabulary in the humanities, which consists largely of names of individuals and works, is in fact very precise.

Geraldene Walker studied how certain trial subject terms were distributed across nine databases available on DIALOG (Walker, 1990; Walker & Atkinson, 1991). Bella Weinberg (1988) argues that the scholar is ill served by indexing systems that deal only with the topic, or "aboutness," of materials. She states that scholars need, in addition to topic, "comment" information that describes point of view and/or the specific argument or theory presented. Some of this literature will be examined in more detail later.

## Project methodology

### Population

All Visiting Scholars during 1988–89 and 1989–90 at the Getty Center for the History of Art and the Humanities in Santa Monica, California, were invited to participate in the project, but not all chose to do so.[4] Eleven of the fifteen scholars visiting the center during 1988–89 agreed to participate in the project, and two spouses (scholars in their own right) also participated. Twelve of the eighteen scholars during 1989–90 agreed to participate, along with three spouses. Though the numbers of participants for the two years add to twenty-eight, one individual in the 1989 group stayed for the second year, for a total of twenty-seven different people.

For purposes of this study, "participation" was defined as taking the DIALOG training. Some scholars did no searching, however, or searched only with help from an experienced searcher. We were interested only in those individuals who searched on their own at some time during their stay at the Getty: that is, those who produced natural language statements and search statements while acting as true end users. Eleven participants conducted such unassisted searches in 1989, and twelve did so in 1990. Since one person stayed the second year, twenty-two different people produced the data analyzed here. From now on, discussion of the scholars producing data for this study will refer to this smaller group. One of this group did just one unassisted search but made no natural language statement, for a final total of twenty-one individuals producing natural language statements and twenty-two producing online search statements.

In the second year of the experiment, one individual spent more than five times as many hours searching as any of the other scholars—in

---

4   The J. Paul Getty Trust is a private operating foundation. Two of its programs are the Getty Art History Information Program and the Getty Center for the History of Art and the Humanities. These two entities collaborated on this project.

fact, more time than all the others put together. Since the vast majority of participants did relatively little searching, the various analyses in the study were based on the early hours of the scholars' experience as searchers. We decided to end the analysis of the prolific scholar's searching at a point beyond the amount done by everyone else but well before the end of his total searching time—on the grounds that analyzing later stages of searching with a sample of one would be of little use. Thus, total numbers of natural language statements and search terms for this individual in the analyses in this article are based on the subset of material actually analyzed, not the entire record.

The thirteen male and nine female scholars came from France, Germany, Great Britain, Hungary, Italy, and the United States. Eight were native English speakers; the nonnative speakers' command of English ranged from adequate to excellent. The scholars' research interests included the history of art and architecture, film history, social history, philosophy, comparative literature, classics, the history of music, and social and cultural anthropology. The group comprised university professors, independent scholars, a curator, an architect, postdoctoral scholars, and doctoral candidates.

### Training, setting, and other arrangements

Participants were given one day's training by Amy Greenwood, a DIALOG staff trainer, in late January and early February for the 1989 group, and in November of the second project year for the 1990 group.[5] The scholars then had twenty-four-hour-a-day access to a workstation in the Getty Center Library near their offices until they left in the summer. Next to the workstation were placed documentation for DIALOG, as well as thesauri and word lists for several arts and humanities databases. The latter included *RILA (International Repertory of the Literature of Art) Subject Headings, Architectural Keywords,* and *Historical Abstracts Index.*

In preparation for this project, a program was written to capture a complete transaction log of the DIALOG searches done by the scholars at the workstation. These data were captured for the study with the permission of both Dialog Information Services and the study participants. Scholars were instructed to print out all desired search results at the terminal, rather than having them sent from DIALOG. Consequently, we have a complete record of their entire searches—both search statements and results.

---

5   One scholar arrived at the Getty Center after the training had ended and so was trained individually by Jeanette Clough of the Getty Center, rather than with the group.

The Art History Information Program arranged for a limited DIALOG account, which gave the scholars access to a large subset of about sixty of the DIALOG databases. Databases in the package, drawn from the social sciences, arts, and humanities, included all those thought to be of interest to arts and humanities scholars, such as *Art Literature International (RILA), The Architecture Database (RIBA),* and *Historical Abstracts.* (Although *RILA* has since been superseded by the bilingual *Bibliography of the History of Art [BHA]*, the database is still accessed through DIALOG as *Art Literature International.*) Bibliographic databases covered journal articles, books, and dissertations. Some directories, for example, *Marquis Who's Who,* and some full-text databases, for example, *Academic American Encyclopedia* (no longer available on DIALOG), were also included. DIALINDEX®, the database of DIALOG databases, was included, as were citation databases, for example, *Arts & Humanities Search®.*

Participants were encouraged to make an appointment for an "assisted search" at some time during the months after the training. In other words, an experienced online searcher would answer questions and help in any way desired while the scholar searched. During the first year, six scholars requested an assisted search during the spring of 1989, and one of these had a second one as well. In 1990 one scholar had three assisted searches, three had two, five had one, and six had none.

Some scholars were also offered the opportunity to have an experienced searcher do a "comparative search." Essentially, the expert searcher redid one of the searches the scholar had already done. The scholar first submitted a written search request to the expert, who then conducted the search (without discussing with the scholar what he or she had done). The results of the comparative searches were discussed in an interview with the scholar. In 1989 seven scholars requested comparative searches (performed by Kathleen Salomon of the Getty Center Library). These comparative searches took place after the scholars had done most of their searching for the year; none occurred earlier than May 4, 1989. They were discontinued in the second year.

Two group review sessions were offered during the second year. Three people attended the first one in January 1990, and five people (including one who also attended the first session) attended the second one in March. (In both years help with assisted searches was provided by Jeanette Clough of the Getty Center Library, who also conducted the two group review sessions.) Overall, the project was designed to encourage scholars to do their own searching; generally, assistance was made available only through the DIALOG help line, not locally.

# Analysis of natural language statements

## Methodology

*Introduction* As a part of their participation in the study, the scholars were asked to type in a description of their query at the beginning of each search they performed. As these descriptions were not preceded by a DIALOG command, they were meaningless to DIALOG and had no effect on the online search itself. However, this text was captured by the program that recorded a complete transaction log of the search. Thus both natural language statements and the entire online search were recorded at the moment of search and made available for later analysis. The natural language statements analyzed in this study consisted of all the descriptions of queries and other comments that the scholars input during their unassisted searches. No natural language statements associated with assisted searches were analyzed; the analysis was restricted to comments searchers made as they worked on their own.

Because the scholars were searching on their own without experimenter prompting, their natural language statements did not always correspond perfectly to their online searches. On occasion scholars entered searches for which they failed to provide a natural language statement. In other cases, they made several comments on a single search or searched the same or a similar query in another search session. Sometimes these repetitions seem to represent a shift from one way of thinking about a search to another approach, and sometimes they entailed the incorporation of new terms.

*Categories* Several sets of terminological categories were developed and experimented with in order to find those that best revealed the special characteristics of the vocabulary used by humanities researchers in online information seeking. The intent was to discover what was unique about humanities online terminology.

The following categories were selected. They consist of three broad classes divided into subcategories:

1. Type of search need
   a. A specific work or publication
   b. Works or publications by an author—specific item not stated
   c. Works on a subject—all senses of subject, including material about a work or an author

2. Bibliographic features
   a. Bibliographic form of desired materials
   b. Publication date or date range of desired materials

3. Types of subjects
    a. Works or publications as subject
    b. Individuals—all sorts of people, including authors, as well as fictional, mythical, or religious characters
    c. Geographical name
        i. Noun form
        ii. Adjective form
    d. Date or period
        i. Date or date range
        ii. Period
        iii. Time modifier
    e. Discipline
    f. Other proper term
    g. Other common term

***Comments on the categories*** "Type of search need" included three broad types of search likely to be conducted: for a specific work, for any works by an author, and for works on a subject, which may include searches on works and authors *as subjects*. The phrase "work or publication" is used because a searcher may seek either a specific publication or a work of an author that may appear in any number of different editions, translations, and so forth.

An additional category concerned certain bibliographical features—specifically, bibliographic form and publication date or range of publication dates. Bibliographic form means the common forms of publication, such as books, articles, dissertations, and so forth. Publication date refers to the date of any bibliographic entities to be retrieved, not the time period covered in the text of the items.

Finally, the largest set of categories contained types of subject searches. The category of works as subjects may include works of any of the kinds studied in the humanities—literary, artistic, musical, and so forth. Individuals include any real, fictional, or mythical characters. Geographical names include political or historical entities with geographical boundaries, for example, "United States" or "Weimar Republic." "Adjective form" refers to adjectives such as "Dutch."

Date may refer either to specific dates or to date ranges, for example, 1812 or eighteenth century. Period refers to verbal labels for historical periods, such as "Renaissance." While the actual time spans that such terms encompass may be a matter of debate, the terms were included because they are widely and productively used. Time modifier refers to terms such as "early" in "early nineteenth century," which further specify the stated date range or period.

Discipline refers to broad areas of study, such as history, music, or the humanities. The relatively frequent appearance of terms of this sort was one of the surprising results of this study, and a detailed analysis of this category of terms is included below. Since many subjects can be considered "areas of study," this category was coded conservatively: only very broad terms were counted, such as "humanities," down to and including university department-sized areas, such as "art history." "Film," for example, as an area of study, is large enough to merit an entire department on some campuses, but not on others, and so was not categorized as a discipline term.

"Other proper terms" included all proper subject terms not included in any of the above categories of subject, and "other common terms" included all common subject terms not included above. A term was considered proper if it was normally written with uppercase initial letters and common if normally written with lowercase initial letters. Some examples of other proper terms encountered in the study are the following: the "Annunciation," the "Hanging Gardens," and the French title of an individual being researched: "Surintendant des Batiments." Examples of other common terms are "synaesthesia" and "intuition."

A final note is in order on the distinction between the first and third group of categories listed above: type of search need and type of subjects. There is an important distinction between a search for a work *itself* and a search for a work *as subject*. It is one thing to search for Brecht's *Threepenny Opera* itself and quite another to search for books or articles discussing it. Similarly, there is a great difference between searching for works *by* Brecht (author search) and works *about* him (subject search).

This distinction between the work itself and materials about the work has an implication for category definition that might not be immediately evident. In the humanities, scholars may be interested in works of all kinds—paintings, dance and musical compositions, literary works, and so forth. Works of all these types were therefore categorized under works as subjects. On the other hand, when a scholar searches for the work itself in a bibliographic database, that work must be bibliographic in nature: that is, it must be some sort of recorded work of the kind typically contained in library catalogs and databases. Such databases might contain a record for a novel, but not for a painting. So the types of works actually included within the categories of work as type of search need and work as type of subject were necessarily different.

*Identification and coding of terms* Each of the three broad categories listed above—type of search need, bibliographic features, and type of subject—was coded separately for each natural language statement (NLS). The third category, type of subject, was coded for an NLS only if subject had been identified as a type of search need for that NLS.

One of the complications of an analysis such as this is the question of what constitutes a subject term. Is it a single concept expressed in one or more words, or is it strictly a single word? In library and information science the word "term" normally has the former meaning. If we accept that interpretation, then how do we decide whether a phrase contains one or more concepts? With these data, it was very difficult to isolate what the user considered a unitary concept. As noted earlier, searchers were given great flexibility in making comments and describing searches. They wrote in ordinary narrative style, sometimes quite colloquially, sometimes cryptically. And such difficulties are certainly not limited to this study. Even when experts identify concepts as a part of thesaurus development, rules for different thesauri and term lists can vary in this regard. Furthermore, even the application of a given set of rules, such as those in a thesaurus standard, can be complex and difficult. As one standard notes, "The establishment of procedures for dealing consistently with compound terms introduces one of the most difficult areas in the field of subject indexing" (International Organization for Standardization, 1986, p. 9). Finally, in online searching, various searchers—or even one searcher under different circumstances—may treat single words and multiword phrases very differently.

This problem is well illustrated by phrases that appeared in three successive natural language statements: "funerary masks," "funerary representation," "representation of Christ." The searcher might or might not have thought of each of these three as unitary concepts. Thesauri also might handle them variously. Would "Christ representations" be a distinct term, like "funerary mask," or would "Christ" and "representation" be treated as distinct concepts?

Similarly, when recording these natural language statements, the scholars were about to do an online search. Would the wise searcher treat each of these three phrases (1) as a descriptor, that is, as a unitary concept, (2) as composed of distinct words that must be combined with Boolean logic, or (3) as a natural language phrase, which must be expressed with proximity operators? The last case represents an in-between situation, in which the searcher finds the phrase meaningful as a phrase, and thus wants the words to be in proximity, but may not expect to find the phrase as a descriptor—that is, recognized as a unitary concept by the database's thesaurus.

This is not to suggest that the scholars, who were inexperienced in online searching, would have considered any or all of these issues but, rather, that even if they had, the matter would remain difficult to interpret. Thus, counting the individual terms in the thesaurus sense in these natural language statements appeared to be problematic, to say the least. More important, the attempt to impose our interpretation on the scholar's terminology could have biased the analysis and reduced the validity of the results.

Thus, we took a different approach. Our fundamental unit of analysis in the natural language statements became the "appearance" of a category in the statement. That is, if some language representing a category appeared anywhere in a natural language statement, whether in one or several words, or in one or several instances, that event, called an "appearance," would be counted as one in the tally. For example, we did not attempt to decide whether "funerary representation" was one or two concepts. Both of these words, "funerary" and "representation," fit the other common category. Therefore, this statement was coded as having one or more instances of the other common category, that is, as one appearance of that category. In like manner, "Greek and Roman libraries" would be counted as one appearance of the geographical (adjective form) category and one appearance of the other common category.

A terminological problem still remains. If "some language" regarding a geographical location appears in a scholar's natural language statement, and we call that event an "appearance" in the tally, we still need to be able to refer to that "some language" in some compact way. Hence in the following discussion of the analysis of the natural language statements, we will use the word "term" with the special understanding that it refers to the "some language" in the definition of "appearance." For example, when we say that a geographical term appeared in an NLS, we mean that some language, in one or more words and in one or more instances, which had some geographical meaning, appeared in the NLS. "Term" and "appearance" are used in these defined senses in tables 2, 3, 4, and 9, and in the accompanying text. "Search term" will have a distinct definition in the later discussion of the analysis of terms used by the scholars in their online search formulations.

Finally, when a specific title of a work was named either as the item being sought or as the subject of interest, the title of the work was coded as a title only; the words in the title were not coded into categories.

*Details of wording* Scholars were encouraged both to describe their search topics and to make any comments they wished on the search itself. It was felt that anything the searchers chose to say about the search while it was going on might help us understand their use of the online searching capability.

Consequently, wording of the comments is varied in completeness and detail. In each case, the terms of the natural language statements were coded as fully as possible given the information available. Elements of the statements that were comments of one sort or another, not descriptions of current or projected searches, were not coded. A small percentage of the statements contain no codable terms of any kind, as in "I'm continuing," and "I need some info to complete a book review." The second statement failed to make clear what kind of information was needed, so this item was not coded.

In other cases, the information given makes coding possible in some categories, but not others. For example, "Now a broader subject search." Here, the type of search can be coded, but no specific subject terms.

In some cases, a natural language statement is partly a query statement and partly a comment. In these cases the former was coded and the latter ignored, as in the following example: "I will search in the philosopher's index any articles or book written about the problem and the history of imagination, as discussed in the late eighteenth century. I just discovered a book which I did not know of, and now I would like to get to know at least other secondary literature in order to trace further 18$^{th}$-century material in the libraries." The second sentence was treated as a comment.

*Relation of natural language statements to information needs* Two final, subtle, but important issues of methodology arise in the coding of the natural language statements. The first has to do with the relationship of information need to online search formulation. Many years ago Robert Taylor (1968) noted that users of information services frequently compromise their real needs when they come to use information services or resources: that is, they formulate their queries according to what they think the system can offer, so the query as presented may differ significantly from the real need.

More generally, in all online searching the information need as it arises in the researcher's mind must be transformed into the query, which is then formulated in search statements understandable to the system. After their day of DIALOG training, the scholars were aware that an information need must be converted into search statements using a rigid syntax and various other rules that differ greatly from common discourse.

Both meaning and syntax are thus liable to change during this process of transformation from need to query to search formulation. What point along this continuum do the scholars' natural language statements represent? Are they closer to the conversational mode the researcher might use with a friend or fellow scholar, or to the rigid syntax required by the online system?

The answer is that the statements appear to be closer to the former than to the latter. The scholars' tone is generally conversational and natural, if somewhat abbreviated. The searchers are probably talking more to those of us conducting the study than to DIALOG, although their wording may already contain some of the compromises needed to communicate with DIALOG. It seems reasonable to assume that the scholars' queries as stated are fairly close to their true needs. Thus in studying the natural language statements we learn of the terminology (and, more generally, the categories of terminology) that humanities scholars use when they discuss the information needs they bring to an online system.

The second issue concerns another aspect of the conversational context. If in their natural language statements the searchers are speaking to those of us conducting the study, they may provide information that they would not normally feel a need to provide in searching queries that were not being observed. In particular, one feature that appeared in some of the statements aroused such a suspicion. Searchers sometimes provided explanatory tags for the personal names they listed in their descriptions of information needs, as in the following examples (tag lines are italicized): "I am looking for articles and books recently written about Victor Cousin, Samuel Taylor Coleridge, and Hegel, *three philosophers of the early 19th century*" and "Henry van de Velde, *Belgian architect and designer.*"

Nine percent of the natural language statements studied contained a personal tag line of this sort. Are these tag lines elements that scholars would normally have in mind as their query, or are they added to their usual expression of information need as explanatory elements for the researchers? Whatever the answer to this question, another possibility must be considered as well. Perhaps the searchers are using these tag lines in anticipation of needing such information in their search formulations. In that case, the statements with personal tags would be somewhat closer to search formulations than is the case with other natural language statements.

The current structure of most databases makes it impossible to use the information in the tag lines effectively in a search formulation, at least not in this form. Often the name alone is not only sufficient but in fact is the best way to search on the person of interest. However, one database of central importance in art, *Art Literature International* (previously *RILA*, now superseded by *Bibliography of the History of Art*), uses lengthy tag lines in the descriptors for individuals, for example, "Tissot, James Joseph Jacques, French painter, 1836–1902." So searchers may have added these tag lines in their statements as a result of exposure to this pattern in studying the *RILA* database, either in training or as they began to search.

TABLE 1. *Types of search*

| TYPE OF SEARCH | FREQUENCY | % |
|---|---|---|
| Work or publication itself | 10 | 6 |
| Materials by an author (specific items not designated) | 5 | 3 |
| Material on a subject | 147 | 89 |
| Both work or publication and subject | 1 | 1 |
| Both author and subject | 2 | 1 |
| TOTAL | 165 | 100 |

It is difficult to guess after the fact the source(s) of this tendency and whether these tag lines represent integral elements of the query or supplemental conversational information for the benefit of those conducting the study. Because of this uncertainty, the data on natural language statements were analyzed both with and without the tag lines to see whether similar or different patterns in category frequencies emerged.

## Results

*Statements* Searchers made a total of 188 natural language statements. Subtracting from this number those that did not contain even partial descriptions of information needs or planned searches, we were left with 165 natural language statements, which form the basis of the analysis below.

*Distribution of natural language statements by individual* The distribution of the number of NLSs across searchers varies widely, with some being quite prolific and others saying, and searching, little. The number of statements per individual ranged from one to thirty-nine, with a median of four. The five most prolific searchers, all with thirteen or more statements, jointly account for 61 percent of all natural language statements. The searcher who carried over from 1989 to 1990 contributed two statements during 1989 and thirteen in 1990. The scholar with thirty-nine statements was the most prolific overall in amount of searching and amount of time spent searching.

*Type of search* Listed in table 1 are figures for types of search. Since 150, or 91 percent, of the natural language statements indicated a subject search of some kind, it appears that the scholars used these databases primarily

TABLE 2. *Frequencies of subject categories in natural language statements*

| SUBJECT CATEGORY | FREQUENCY | PERCENTAGE OF ALL NLSs[a] | PERCENTAGE OF SUBJECT NLSs[b] |
|---|---|---|---|
| Works or publications as subject | 8 | 5 | 5 |
| Individual as subject | 74 | 45 | 49 |
| GEOGRAPHICAL NAME: | | | |
|   Noun form | 16 | 10 | 11 |
|   Adjective form | 22 | 13 | 15 |
|     TOTAL GEOGRAPHICAL TERMS | 37 | 22 | 25 |
| CHRONOLOGICAL TERMS: | | | |
|   Date or date range | 18 | 11 | 12 |
|   Period | 9 | 5 | 6 |
|   Time modifier | 8 | 5 | 5 |
|     TOTAL CHRONOLOGICAL TERMS | 26 | 16 | 17 |
| Discipline | 35 | 21 | 23 |
| Other proper | 11 | 7 | 7 |
| Other common | 85 | 52 | 57 |

NOTE: *Percentages may add to more than 100 percent because an NLS may contain more than one type of term. Since it may also contain more than one type of geographical or chronological term, individual figures within those categories need not sum to the "total" figures for them either.*

[a]*Total of 165.*    [b]*Total of 150.*

as subject search resources, not for bibliographic verification or as a means of seeking out specific items. They also had access to UCLA's ORION online catalog, and interviews show clearly that they understood that the catalog would work better as a finding device for known citations than would online databases.

*Subject categories* All figures in table 2 are for appearances in natural language statements of the designated subject category. The first figure is the number of statements containing the designated category; the second figure is that number converted to a percentage of all natural language statements; and the third figure is the percentage of subject search NLSs that the raw number represents. Since natural language statements frequently contain many different kinds of terms, figures can add to far more than 100 percent—but note that all figures are for percentages or numbers of NLSs containing the category, not total mentions of that category. Frequencies for works and individuals are for these *as subjects*, not for the work itself or for the works of an author.

More than one type of date term can appear in the same natural language statement, so the percentage of total NLSs containing date terms is smaller than the sum of the percentages for the subcategories within date, as is also true for subcategories within geographical terms.

Summarizing from table 2, of all subject natural language statements made by these scholars, about half mention one or more individuals or characters, a quarter mention some geographical entity, a sixth mention some date or period, and a quarter mention an intellectual or academic discipline. At the same time, nearly three out of five mention other common subject terms.

These figures begin to highlight some of the differences between the vocabularies of the humanities and of other disciplines. Subject terms falling in our "other common" category predominate in many fields in science and engineering, and in the thesauri for those fields as well. Yet if we turn our figures around, we can say that in the Getty study fully 43 percent of all subject NLSs (100 percent minus 57 percent) make no mention whatever of the kind of subject terms that are the very heart of science and engineering search queries. On the other hand, the humanities queries contain significant percentages of subject categories that are seldom seen in the sciences.

***Contrast with science queries*** To substantiate the point that science queries differ from those in the humanities, we compare the statistics for these natural language statements with those for the search queries used in a major research project performed for the National Science Foundation (NSF) by Tefko Saracevic and Paul Kantor, who reported the results of their research in a series of 1988 articles in the *Journal of the American Society for Information Science*.

One of Saracevic and Kantor's articles includes an appendix reporting the questions used in their NSF study (Saracevic & Kantor, 1988, pp. 195–96). Elsewhere, the authors described these statements as containing "a summary of the text for each question" used in the study (Saracevic & Kantor, 1988, p. 179). The questions were from forty different users, who posed one written question each. The texts of the questions reported are in standard English; they have not yet been converted into search statements and so are roughly equivalent to the statements by users in the present study: that is, they represent a midpoint between original information need and search formulation presented to the system. The NSF statements are more consistent, however, in that all have been converted into a standard format, as in the following examples: "the relationship and communication processes between middle aged children and their parents" (Saracevic & Kantor, 1988, p. 195) and "occurrences, causes, treatment, and prevention of retrolental fibroplasia" (Saracevic & Kantor, 1988,a p. 195).

The forty queries in the NSF study came from many subject fields. (All of the NSF questions would be classified as subject queries according to the definition used in this study.) For comparison with the results in this study, we grouped the NSF queries into three broad classes: (1) arts and humanities; (2) social and behavioral sciences, including management, social work, and other applied social science fields; and (3) natural sciences, engineering, and other applied science fields, including medicine. The number of NSF queries falling into each of the three broad subject areas were two, twenty-two, and sixteen, respectively.

Table 3 displays the frequencies of the major subject categories in this study and in the social and natural science queries of Saracevic and Kantor's NSF study. The two arts and humanities queries were excluded from the latter. The method of counting appearances of term categories that was used in this study was also used in calculating figures for the NSF study.

Though the frequencies in the NSF study are based on fewer statements, the contrast in distribution of subject categories between the studies is so dramatic that we can state with confidence that, as represented in these data, the arts and humanities differ from the sciences in fundamental ways. Other common terms were used in all sixteen natural science queries; only once was a category besides "other common" used. By contrast, fewer than three out of five Getty statements mentioned such other common terms. None of the NSF queries mentioned individuals or characters as subjects, while half of the Getty statements did. None of the NSF queries mentioned discipline, while a quarter of the Getty statements did. Many other contrasts could be drawn.

In fact, after seeing the results in table 3, we returned to the data and made another tabulation. Combining all other types of terms besides other common, that is, all non–other-common terms, only 18 percent of the Saracevic social and natural science queries used one or more non–other-common terms, while 84 percent of the Getty natural language statements did.

So other common terms are only moderately important for humanities queries, while they are the essence of science queries. On the other hand, proper names of individuals and other proper terms, works as subjects, and geographical, chronological, and discipline terms are vital to humanities queries, but much less important in the sciences.

Table 3. *Frequencies of subject categories in NSF and Getty studies*

| CATEGORY | NSF SOCIAL SCIENCE | | NSF NATURAL SCIENCE | | NSF TOTAL | | GETTY TOTAL | |
|---|---|---|---|---|---|---|---|---|
| | N | % | N | % | N | % | N | % |
| Total subject queries | 22 | 58 | 16 | 42 | 38 | 100 | 150 | 100 |
| Works or publications as subject | 1 | 5 | 0 | 0 | 1 | 3 | 8 | 5 |
| Individuals as subject | 0 | 0 | 0 | 0 | 0 | 0 | 74 | 49 |
| Geographical name | 3 | 14 | 0 | 0 | 3 | 8 | 37 | 25 |
| Chronological term | 1 | 5 | 0 | 0 | 1 | 3 | 26 | 17 |
| Discipline term | 0 | 0 | 0 | 0 | 0 | 0 | 35 | 23 |
| Other proper term | 3 | 14 | 1 | 6 | 4 | 11 | 11 | 7 |
| Other common term | 22 | 100 | 16 | 100 | 38 | 100 | 85 | 57 |

NOTE: *Percentages are the percentage of total query statements in each sample in which one or more terms of a given category appeared.*

These extremely marked contrasts suggest that humanities online information seeking differs in fundamental ways from that of the subject domains that research into online searching has hitherto studied in greatest detail. If we are inclined to suspect that the differences in results might be due to some difference in design of the two studies rather than the subject matter, we are reassured by contemplating the two NSF queries in the humanities. Although two queries are too few for proper comparison, it is interesting to note that the pattern exhibited by the two NSF humanities queries is very similar to that of the statements in this study.

While both of the NSF humanities queries mention other common terms, one also mentions geographical and chronological terms, and the other mentions geographical, chronological, discipline, and other proper terms as well. So just two humanities queries contain six appearances of categories other than other common, while all the remaining thirty-eight NSF queries put together contain a total of only nine such instances. Clearly, information queries of the sciences and the humanities differ in fundamental ways.

In fact, we can identify a standard type of arts and humanities query, as exemplified by one each from the NSF and Getty studies: NSF, "meaning of the cat in Italian renaissance (1450–1600) religious paintings" (Saracevic

& Kantor, 1988, p. 196); Getty, "image of the tree in literature, art, science, of medieval and renaissance Europe."

*Further analysis of the Getty/NSF contrast* Let us look more closely at the contrast between the Getty and NSF studies to see whether we can discern causes or alternative explanations. One immediate possibility is that the difference may be due chiefly to humanities scholars' strong interest in research on individuals. Because half of the subject natural language statements in the Getty study concerned individuals and nearly that many contain no other common terms, perhaps these two facts are related and account for most of the differences.

We therefore extracted all the statements that contained no other common terms and analyzed them separately as a group. Of the total group of 165 Getty natural language statements, eighty (or 48 percent) contained no other common terms whatsoever. Seventeen percent of the eighty NLSs without other common terms represented searches for works or authors rather than subjects. Another 64 percent of the eighty were searches for individuals as subjects, and another 10 percent were searches for works or publications as subjects.

So, for a grand total of 91 percent of the cases in which no other common terms were present, the scholar was searching for particular works, for works by an author, or for works or individuals as subjects. We can see from this fact that the large number of natural language statements with no other common terms correlates strongly with the tendency of humanities scholars to study particular works and individuals.

Keep in mind, however, that although this set of statements excludes other common terms, the scholars mentioned types of subject terms other than works and individuals in these statements as well. Five percent used geographical terms, 4 percent chronological terms, 11 percent discipline terms, and 5 percent other proper terms.

On the other hand, often when other common terms do appear, many of the other types of terms that are distinctive to humanities statements appear as well. For example, in twenty-three natural language statements (the seventy-four NLSs on individuals as subject in the entire sample minus the fifty-one on individuals in the "no other common terms" sample), other common terms appear in conjunction with searches for individuals. Similarly, the great majority of geographical, chronological, discipline, and other proper terms also appear in statements in which other common terms appear. In other words, even in those humanities subject searches that more closely resemble science queries because they contain other

TABLE 4. *Frequencies of natural language statement categories with and without personal tags*

| CATEGORY | ALL NLSs[a] | | NLSs WITHOUT TAGS[b] | |
|---|---|---|---|---|
| | N | % | N | % |
| *Type of search need:* | | | | |
| Work or publication itself | 10 | 6 | 10 | 7 |
| Works or publications by author | 5 | 3 | 3 | 2 |
| Subject | 147 | 89 | 134 | 89 |
| Both work or publication + subject | 1 | 1 | 1 | 1 |
| Both author and subject | 2 | 1 | 2 | 1 |
| TOTAL | 165 | 100 | 150 | 100 |
| *Types of subjects (as percentage of total sets):* | | | | |
| Works or publications as subject | 8 | 5 | 8 | 5 |
| Individuals as subjects | 74 | 45 | 60 | 40 |
| Geographical name | 37 | 22 | 28 | 19 |
| Chronological term | 26 | 16 | 20 | 13 |
| Discipline term | 35 | 21 | 30 | 20 |
| Other proper term | 11 | 7 | 10 | 7 |
| Other common term | 85 | 52 | 71 | 47 |

[a]*Total of 165.*
[b]*Total of 150.*

common terms, the queries nonetheless also contain many of the category types that are distinctive to the humanities.

*Personal tags* We mentioned earlier that the presence of personal tags in the descriptions of individuals might be responsible for some of the distinctive features of the natural language statements. To test this hypothesis, the fifteen NLSs (9 percent of the total of 165) that contained personal tags were removed from the set of NLSs and the figures recomputed for the master set of categories. Table 4 presents the two computations in one. The figures in the two left-hand columns are for the entire set of 165 NLSs, and those in the right-hand columns are for the set of 150 NLSs without personal tags. (The fact that there are 150 NLSs dealing with searches for subjects, and the same number for NLSs without personal tags, is purely coincidental; the two sets are different.)

As the table shows, removing the natural language statements with personal tags changes the overall pattern very little. Differences between science and humanities statements do not appear to be due to the presence of personal tags.

*Discipline terms* As noted earlier, one of the surprises of this analysis was the large number of discipline-related terms that appeared in the natural language statements. The following discipline terms were mentioned once or more: architecture, art, art history, education, engineering, history, humanities, literature, music, philosophy, rhetoric, and science. These terms were generally not used as references to the fields as academic disciplines; rather, they most commonly referred to the artistic activity or the products of that activity that the scholar was studying, as in the following examples: "checking for articles on Nietzsche and music," "image of the tree in literature, art, science, of medieval and renaissance Europe," and "metropolitanism in American architecture." Another subset was represented by the common phrase, "history of": "any articles or book written about the problem and the history of imagination."

Others were part of longer, more specific phrases, such as "ephemeral art." Of the thirty-five discipline terms, eleven (or 31 percent) were of this type: part of a longer phrase that would make it a more specific term. The other twenty-four instances were freestanding.

These discipline terms are of particular interest for online searching, because one of the cardinal sins in online searching is considered to be the use of the name of an entire subject field in one's search. It is thought of as pointless to enter a term representing the subject of an entire database; one does not ask for "architecture" in an architecture database or "aluminum" in an aluminum database.

Even when the discipline and the database differ, as, for example, in indexing or searching for architecture in a literature database, search terms of this sort are assumed to be so broad as to be useless. Indexers seldom apply terms of such breadth. Consequently, requiring the presence of such terms in a search formulation will guarantee that all those relevant records that contain the other terms wanted by the searcher but lack discipline term indexing (the usual case) will fail to be retrieved. Free text matches might be made, but success with these is unpredictably dependent on the author's usage of discipline terms in title or abstract. Yet 23 percent of all the subject queries in this study contained a discipline term of some sort. (Problems would be less severe with the portion of discipline terms that are used in a longer, more specific phrase. As noted earlier, about a third of the discipline terms were of this type.) The results with respect to discipline terms raise questions about whether the design of online databases and their indexing schemes match humanities scholars' information needs as well as they might. The variety of types of discipline terms should be studied in greater depth.

*Bibliographic features* The third broad area of terms coded was bibliographic features. Two categories were coded: (1) preferences for bibliographic format (book, article, etc.) and (2) publication date or date ranges.

Only three natural language statements (or 2 percent) specified publication date or date range. Either this factor is unimportant for the scholars, or they specify such date ranges only later in their thinking during the search, perhaps when they are actually formulating the search statements.

Of the 165 natural language statements, forty-two (or 25 percent) mentioned some desired bibliographic form. On this bibliographic feature all forms mentioned in an NLS were also counted individually in order to identify frequencies of particular forms. Most of the forty-two NLSs mentioned articles: 20 percent (thirty-three NLSs) of the total 165 NLSs, with 9 percent of the total (fifteen NLSs) mentioning other forms, such as books and dissertations. (Figures add to more than forty-two NLSs because some statements mentioned more than one form.)

Often when "articles" were specified, the term seemed to have been used simply as the most convenient way to express the information need. At times, "articles" appeared to be used interchangeably with phrases like "literature on," "material on," and so forth. Since most of the databases the scholars searched include primarily citations to articles, the specification of "articles" was nearly meaningless. (Incidentally, when scholars used the word "literature" in the same way—that is, to indicate materials wanted—it was not counted as a discipline term.) All in all, specification of bibliographic features appears to be of only modest importance in the natural language statements.

*Categories used infrequently* During the several transformations of category sets, we experimented with other categories as well but dropped them because they applied to too few natural language statements in the sample to be of significance. However, a larger sample, or a different one, might find these categories worthwhile. Since all of the categories used in this study were developed with respect to a single sample, their validity should be tested and revised with other samples. In any case, there is some value in reporting that the candidate categories were not as productive as expected.

The study of movements is sometimes important in the humanities—movements among either the people studied ("nationalism") or those doing the studying ("the New Criticism"). In this study only four natural language statements contained such terms. Classes of works ("symphonies") and classes of creators ("painters") were considered as well but also produced few examples. The latter appeared primarily in personal tag lines. Finally, a very specific form of place is the name of a building or institution, and a very specific form of time is a named event. These, too, produced a smattering of occurrences. In later tabulations, when these trial categories were eliminated, the terms were tallied under the broader category to which they belonged.

## Analysis of online search terms

### Methodology

**Introduction** Because the analysis of scholars' natural language statements revealed an interesting array of subject categories that researchers into online searching discuss only infrequently, it seemed appropriate to analyze the actual search terms the scholars used in their DIALOG searches to see whether they also showed the same pattern of subject category assignments. Thus the approach taken here was to identify the scholars' search terms and assign them to the categories used in the analysis of natural language statements. Nonsubject categories of search, which proved in the first study to be a small part of the scholars' searching, were not analyzed. Otherwise, study conditions were the same.

The seemingly straightforward task of assigning subject search terms to categories proved surprisingly difficult. This task, which produced interesting results, also raised a number of methodological issues. The subsections below represent each of the major decisions made about how to analyze these data. Because we used a technical distinction between "type" and "token" (explained below), we will reserve the term "type" for that technical meaning and avoid other senses of the term in this section. Specifically, when referring to the categorization of terms, we will refer to categories of subject search terms rather than their types.

**Definition of search term** In our study of natural language statements it was easy to identify the natural language statement and difficult to distinguish terms within the statement. In this substudy, we encountered the opposite difficulty; the search term was easy to identify, but the query was not.

Let us define an online search statement as the searcher's input to the search system that begins immediately after a system prompt and ends with a carriage return or enter. In looking at any series of such search statements, it is difficult to identify with confidence the search formulation that a searcher intended to represent a search query. What the searcher thinks of as a single query may be expressed in one or several online search statements. For example, suppose a searcher combines two terms with a Boolean OR in one statement, then in the next statement uses a Boolean AND to combine the results of the previous statement with another term. Did the searcher have all three terms in mind all along and intend to create the final result through the two-step process, or did he or she originally intend to search only with the first statement, then revised it into another query after seeing the results of the first? In a study of the transaction logs recording the search statements it is impossible after the fact to be confident of what really constitutes a complete query as the searcher intended it.

On the other hand, it is easy to identify distinct terms within the formal, artificial syntax of the DIALOG command language. A search term is defined here as the string of characters bounded by the beginning or end of the search statement and by Boolean operators. This simple definition provided a basis for identifying and categorizing search terms. So in our analysis of online search terms the unit of analysis is the individual search term.

The search statement "Select Kandinsky AND German literature" contains two search terms: "Kandinsky" and "German literature." Thus, a search term may contain more than one word. It may also contain proximity operators, truncation, and prefix and suffix codes. For example, the entire phrase "urban (w) experience?/de" was considered a single term. Boolean operators within a proximity phrase or suffix-coded phrase were considered a part of the phrase and did not mark a separate term. For example, "urban(w)(experience OR milieu)" was treated as a single proximity phrase, and "(film? OR cinema? OR kino?)/ti" was treated as a single suffix-coded phrase. "Urban AND (experience OR milieu)," on the other hand, contains three distinct search terms.

*Categories of subject terms* Search terms were assigned to the same set of categories as in the analysis of natural language statements, with two exceptions. First, in categorizing geographical search terms it was often difficult to determine whether a term was used as an adjective or noun. Frequently, both categories were implied in truncated search terms such as "German?" which can refer to either "German" or "Germany." Thus all geographical name search terms were grouped into a single category. Second, in a few cases it was impossible to determine the proper classification of a search term or assign it to a single category. Those cases were placed in an "uncertain classification" category.

*Types and tokens* Linguistic analysis makes a fundamental distinction between a type count—a count of each distinctive term—and a token count—a count of each use of a term. Here is an invented example: If the total set of terms input by a scholar consisted of "Schoenberg," "Schoenberg," "Schoenberg," and "Europe," then this set of terms contains two types ("Schoenberg" and "Europe") and four tokens (all four terms listed above). The task of translating the type/token distinction into the online search environment proved to entail some subtle problems.

We decided to count types rather than tokens in order to eliminate repetitions and focus on distinct search terms. This study contained a number of repetitions of the sort shown in the example above. Users frequently revised search formulations, repeated a query during a later search session, or made errors of one sort or another and had to repeat the search formulation.

Our underlying interest was in identifying, categorizing, and counting the number of distinct search term types used by the searchers. Since our focus was on search terms (as defined in an earlier subsection), not just terms in general, it was desirable to identify and count search term types, not just general term types. It is necessary to understand the implications of this choice to interpret the resulting data.

Two kinds of grammar were operative for the terms studied here: that of standard English and that of the artificial DIALOG command language. To illustrate the consequences of this situation, consider the truncated and untruncated search terms "art?" and "art." In DIALOG's command language, the presence of the question mark produces a search that matches on a very different set of terms in the database indexes than would be the case without the question mark. "Art" can match only with "art," while "art?" can match with "artist," "article," and the like. To search using one and then the other version of the term would be a perfectly rational act for a searcher. In standard English, however, "art" and "art?" might be considered two tokens of the same type. To reflect the online searching environment, our count treated the two terms as distinct search term types rather than as two tokens of one type.

Many of DIALOG's grammatical features produce similar results. With proximity operators, for example, the "(w)" operator requires that words in matching terms be adjacent and in the same order as in the proximity phrase, while the "(n)" operator requires that they be adjacent but in either order. The addition of numbers within these operators, such as "(2w)," allows the search words to be matched even if that number of words, or fewer, intervene. Just as with truncation, the difference between "history

(1w) philosophy" and "history (1n) philosophy" allows for different possible matches with the database in the actual search, even though the words themselves are the same. In the case of the "(n)" operator, the above example will match with history of philosophy as well as philosophy of history, whereas the "(w)" version will match only with the former. Since the family of matching phrases allowed by each proximity operator combination is different, the two phrases were defined as distinct types.

Similarly, the presence or absence of suffix codes was considered to mark distinct types rather than merely tokens. For example, "architecture," "architecture/de," and "architecture/de,ti" were considered to be three search term types. Suffix codes, by definition, stand for fields that DIALOG has determined are subject related and are therefore contained within the "Basic Index." As a variant in search technique, a searcher may specify that a term be searched on only some of the several subject-related fields (generally, descriptor, title, abstract, and one or two others, depending on the database). In that case, the searcher enters a suffix code for the desired subject field(s).

Another kind of DIALOG code, the prefix code, such as "AU =" for author, almost always refers to fields other than subject. Since in this study the use of subject-related prefix codes was very small, all uses of prefix codes were excluded.

**Combination terms** "Search term" has been operationally defined as the string of characters bounded by Boolean operators and the beginning or end of a search statement. However, many scholars combined into one phrase—sometimes using correct DIALOG syntax and sometimes not—search terms containing distinct categories as defined in this study. Here are three examples: "Beethoven (n) pastorale," "ferrarese (w) painters (w) fifteenth century," and "sex? germ? (lit? OR cult?) mod?" Interpreting these phrases for online searching is problematic. The first two phrases are technically correct in their use of the DIALOG syntax, while the third phrase uses incorrect syntax. For a variety of reasons, the first two phrases would fail in a search in many databases, but not necessarily all. In particular, *Art Literature International* (that is, *RILA*) uses long, compound headings of this sort, which might match if the search terms were worded correctly.

As a practical matter, and whether the search formulation is correct or incorrect, it is impossible to classify these long phrases in one or the other of the categories used here. "Beethoven (w) pastorale" is made up of a person and a work, two elements that need to be classified independently. Unlike our analysis of natural language statements, in which distinct concepts

TABLE 5. *Search term tokens and types*

| | NUMBER |
|---|---|
| Search term tokens | 2,467 |
| Search term types: | |
|    Single formal | 931 |
|    Combination formal | 137 |
| TOTAL FORMAL SEARCH TERMS | 1,068 |

NOTE: *All figures (both tokens and types) include search terms without affixes and with suffixes. Prefix-coded terms are excluded.*

were difficult to identify with confidence, we found that once the search term as a whole was demarcated by the DIALOG syntax, it was generally not difficult to identify such distinct concepts within the larger term. We therefore decided to identify distinct terms *within* search terms when we believed that the searcher clearly intended distinct concepts.

In the analysis these are called "combination terms." They were tallied independently of the single search terms, as well as combined with them in a total figure. To distinguish the two senses of "search term," we called one the "formal" sense (bounded by Boolean operators, etc.), and the other the "informal" sense (distinct concepts identified by the study analysts).

It was usually relatively easy to distinguish between the separate informal search terms in a combination term because different categories of terms, such as composer (individual) and symphony (work) were stated. Sometimes, however, terms of the same category occurred together in the same phrase. An example is "form gestalt," which represents both the English and German words for the same term. We decided to categorize the phrase "form gestalt" as a combination term, with both terms categorized as "other common" terms. "Weimar? (2n) america?" is another example of combining two concepts of the same category, by using two distinct geographical names in the same phrase. In such cases, these were also considered "combination terms" and were given their own categories: "other common + other common" and "geographical + geographical," respectively.

## Results

As noted earlier, a distinction was made in the tally between (1) the "formal" definition of search term as the string of characters bounded by Boolean

TABLE 6. *Single search terms input by scholars*

| SUBJECT SEARCH TERM CATEGORIES | N | % |
|---|---|---|
| Works or publications as subject | 44 | 4.7 |
| Individuals | 351 | 37.7 |
| Geographical name | 59 | 6.3 |
| Date or date range | 11 | 1.2 |
| Period | 16 | 1.7 |
| Time modifier | 0 | 0 |
| Discipline term | 23 | 2.5 |
| Other proper term | 50 | 5.4 |
| Other common term | 362 | 38.9 |
| Uncertain classification | 15 | 1.6 |
| TOTAL | 931 | 100.0 |

operators and the beginning or ending of the search statement and (2) the "informal" definition of search term as a conceptually distinct term that fell within a term as demarcated by the formal definition. Where only one conceptually distinct (informal) term was identified within the formal term, formal and informal term were by definition identical. We considered a "single term" to be a formal term that contains just one informal term, and a "combination term" to be a formal term that contains two or more informal terms. Therefore, by definition, the sum of all single and combination terms (the whole combination, not its constituent terms) is equal to the sum of all formal terms.

Looking first at the results for formal terms, table 5 provides figures for actual search terms input by scholars (tokens), as well as total single and combination formal terms (types) input by the scholars. The ratio of types to tokens is 43 percent.

Table 6 presents totals for categories of all single formal terms, and table 7 presents totals for categories of all combination formal terms. Here are some examples of the search terms included in the count in table 6: "portrait painting" is an other common term; "alexandria" is a geographical name; "newton? (w) isaac" is the name of an individual; "renaissance" is the name of a period. Here are examples of combination terms included in the count for table 7: "unesco, bibliotheca" (other proper + other common); "mantegna (w) miniature" (individual + other common); "humanities (w) (method? OR methodology)(w)(comparison usa europe)" (discipline + three other common + two geographical name).

TABLE 7. *Combination search terms input by scholars*

| SUBJECT SEARCH TERM CATEGORIES | N | % |
|---|---|---|
| Other common + other common | 20 | 14.6 |
| Other common + date | 2 | 1.5 |
| Other common + discipline | 15 | 10.9 |
| Other common + geographical | 28 | 20.4 |
| Other common + individual | 12 | 8.6 |
| Other common + period | 5 | 3.6 |
| Other common + other proper | 3 | 2.2 |
| Discipline + discipline | 7 | 5.1 |
| Discipline + geographical | 7 | 5.1 |
| Discipline + period | 2 | 1.5 |
| Geographical + geographical | 2 | 1.5 |
| Geographical + period | 2 | 1.5 |
| Geographical + other proper | 3 | 2.2 |
| Individual + individual | 6 | 4.4 |
| Individual + period | 1 | .7 |
| Individual + other proper | 1 | .7 |
| Individual + work | 7 | 5.1 |
| Period + other proper | 2 | 1.5 |
| Other proper + other proper | 1 | .7 |
| Other common + date + discipline | 2 | 1.5 |
| Other common + date + geographical | 2 | 1.5 |
| Other common + discipline + geographical | 2 | 1.5 |
| Discipline + geographical + period | 3 | 2.2 |
| Date + discipline + geographical | 1 | .7 |
| Other common + discipline + geographical + period | 1 | .7 |
| TOTAL | 137 | 99.9 |

NOTE: *Percentages add to less than 100 because of rounding error.*

In table 7, for simplicity's sake, combinations containing more than two instances of the same category, of which there were few, were grouped with the dual category. For example, the term "(film OR cinema? OR kino?)/ti" was grouped in the "other common + other common" category.

TABLE 8. *Total informal search terms (both single and combination) input by scholars*

| SUBJECT SEARCH TERM CATEGORIES | N | % |
|---|---|---|
| Works or publications as subject | 51 | 4.1 |
| Individuals | 384 | 30.8 |
| Geographical name | 114 | 9.1 |
| Date or date range | 18 | 1.4 |
| Period | 32 | 2.6 |
| Time modifier | 0 | 0 |
| Discipline | 70 | 5.6 |
| Other proper term | 62 | 5.0 |
| Other common term | 500 | 40.1 |
| Uncertain classification | 15 | 1.2 |
| TOTAL | 1,246 | 99.9[a] |

[a]*Adds to less than 100 percent because of rounding error.*

As noted earlier, the formal definition of search term sometimes did not match with what the scholars clearly intended as search terms. All the combination terms counted in table 7 occurred because the scholars grouped several (informal) search terms together within a single (formal) search term as normally defined. Many, if not most, of these combinations were ineffectual, since they represented incorrect use of DIALOG's search features.

Since the informal terms often appeared to represent the distinct concepts the searchers originally intended, it is valuable to see how many distinct informal terms of each subject category they used, whether in single or in combination search terms. Table 8 presents these data.

We may illustrate the coding for table 8 using the last example listed above for table 7 ("humanities (w) method? . . . ," etc.). That single formal combination term contained the following informal search terms: one discipline, three other common, and two geographical name. So for that term, a total of six term counts will be added to the tally in table 8: one discipline, three other common, and two geographical.

All terms in table 8 are types, rather than tokens, as in tables 6 and 7, with one exception: while multiple uses, that is, tokens, of formal combination search terms as a whole were purged and reduced to types, individual informal terms within combinations were not checked for duplication with single terms or terms in other combinations.

TABLE 9. *Percentages of NLS appearances and informal search terms in each category*

| TYPE OF SUBJECT SEARCH TERM | PERCENTAGE OF ALL NLS "APPEARANCES"[a] | PERCENTAGE OF ALL INFORMAL SEARCH TERMS[b] |
|---|---|---|
| Works or publications as subject | 3 | 4 |
| Individuals as subject | 27 | 31 |
| Geographical name | 13 | 9 |
| Chronological term | 9 | 4 |
| Discipline term | 13 | 6 |
| Other proper term | 4 | 5 |
| Other common term | 31 | 40 |
| Uncertain classification | 0 | 1 |
| TOTAL | 100 | 100 |

NOTE: *Data in column 1 are extracted from column 1 of table 2; data in column 2 are extracted from table 8.*

[a]*Total of 276.*

[b]*Total of 1,246.*

All three tables reveal roughly the same pattern as found in our analysis of natural language statements. Humanities scholars use a wide variety of categories of terms in their searches, just as in their natural language statements. In table 8, 1 percent of the terms fall into the "uncertain" classification, 40 percent into "other common," the most common category by far in Saracevic's science queries, and all the rest (59 percent) fall into some other category.

At this point it would be desirable to compare the two sets of results more closely. Do the scholars' natural language statements contain the same percentages of the various categories as their search terms? The results of these two substudies cannot, in fact, be properly compared, for reasons discussed earlier. The unit of analysis in the first substudy was the entire natural language statement; figures are for numbers of statements containing one or more instances of a category, that is, "appearances." The unit of analysis in the second substudy was the individual search term. Thus no comparison between the two substudies can be exact, and no comparative statistical analyses have been done.

However, while keeping the above caveats in mind, it is possible to get an approximate sense of the relationship between the data in the two substudies. Table 8 presents the percentage of all informal search terms in each category. By reanalyzing the data in table 2, we produced a unit of analysis closer to that used in table 8.

If we add the total appearances listed in the first column of table 2 (rather than the total NLSs), we may compare percentages of total appearances for each category in the first substudy against percentages of total informal search terms in the second substudy. These figures are only roughly equivalent, but nonetheless revealing.

Table 9 compares percentages of each category in the two substudies. (The sum from col. 1 in table 2, or 276, is based on total geographical and total chronological terms, not on individual categories, such as "date or date range," within these broad categories. In table 9, all kinds of geographical and all kinds of chronological terms are combined.)

If we again keep in mind how approximate this comparison is, the two kinds of units—natural language statement appearances and informal search terms—exhibit a similar pattern. However, some of the term categories that are most distinctive to humanities researchers' work—geographical, chronological, and discipline terms—show up less frequently in informal search terms than in natural language statements. Is this because researchers do not need these terms for an effective search, or because they cannot find ways to express these aspects of their information needs effectively in the online environment?

On the other hand, searches on individual names, another category of term more common for humanities searchers, increased when researchers turned their natural language statements into search terms. Did our method of counting terms in NLSs ("appearances" of one or more terms in a category) undercount the number of distinct instances of the "individual" category in the NLSs? Or are individual names easier to express in searching than other subject categories needed by these scholars? In the interviews, to be detailed in a later report, one scholar mentioned that he had resorted to more searching on individual names because he had difficulty formulating searches for other kinds of subject terms. Was his experience typical? These questions will be discussed in the next section.

## Discussion and conclusions

Twenty-two Getty Visiting Scholars produced the data that are analyzed in this first report of the Getty Online Searching Project. Most of the total of 165 natural language statements (NLSs) describing projected online searches constituted searches for subjects, as opposed to searches for works or authors. Searches on individuals as subjects were very popular; 45 percent of the NLSs mentioned them. Geographical names, terms referring to dates and historical periods, and discipline terms were popular as well.

Categories of terms used were compared to those of a major study conducted by Saracevic and Kantor and funded by the National Science Foundation (Saracevic & Kantor, 1988). The NSF study analyzed the results of online searching done largely on social and natural science queries. Virtually no terms for works as subjects, individuals as subjects, or geographical, chronological, or discipline terms appeared in that study; the terms that overwhelmingly predominated were what our study identified as "other common" terms: 100 percent of the science statements contained these terms, while only 57 percent of the subject natural language statements in this study contained them. On the other hand, combining all term categories besides other common, only 18 percent of the science queries used these other terms categories, while 84 percent of the Getty subject natural language statements did. The contrasts between the kinds of terms found in the two studies were very marked overall.

The second part of the study, which categorized scholars' online search terms, produced roughly similar results. Of all the distinct informal term types the scholars used in their searches, 59 percent were other than other common.

Owing to various factors operating in the data analysis, results of the two substudies were not easily compared. Means were found, however, to produce a rough comparison between the percentages of subject categories appearing in searchers' natural language statements and search terms, respectively. It was found that search terms referred to relatively more individuals and other common terms than natural language statements did, and to relatively fewer geographical, chronological, and discipline terms.

The fact that both substudies showed a pattern of frequent use of terms besides other common complements the work of Stephen Wiberley (1983, 1988), who studied the access points in encyclopedias, dictionaries, and abstracting and indexing services in the humanities. Although he used different categories, which makes direct comparison impossible, Wiberley also found a high incidence of personal names and other proper nouns. In the studies described in this article, natural language statements of information needs and online search terms also contained many such terms. Thus, the information needs of scholars (analyzed here) and the design of the resources intended to meet them (analyzed in Wiberley's articles) appear to match in a general way.

However, Wiberley also found that the percentages of proper terms varied widely from one humanities field to another. The percentage of what he called "singular proper" terms, that is, terms that name "a person or creative work whose existence in space and time has been ascertained" (Wiberley, 1988, p. 26), ranged from 24 percent in a philosophy index to 93 percent in an English literature index. If we combine our categories of "works" and "individuals," the result should be fairly close to Wiberley's singular proper. Individuals, as defined here, can include mythical and fictional characters, but otherwise the term is similar to Wiberley's.

A combined total of 50 percent of the natural language statements referred to both works and individuals as subjects. Thirty-five percent of the informal search terms constituted the same combination of categories. The humanities abstracting and indexing service that most closely reflected the interests of the Getty scholars was *RILA* (*International Repertory of the Literature of Art*). In Wiberley's count, 48 percent of the terms in *RILA* were singular proper, a figure that fits well with the figures in the substudies here. (Note that logically there is no reason that the figures should necessarily be close. We would expect that a hypothetical perfect arts and humanities information database would have many of both kinds of terms, but, to meet researchers' information needs perfectly, it might be necessary, for example, for it to contain a proportionally larger set of singular proper names than would appear in scholars' queries.)

In her dissertation, Helen Tibbo (1989) asked a sample of historians what kinds of information they would like to have in abstracts of historical materials. The four highest-ranked categories of information they mentioned, and the percentages of respondents requesting that category, were as follows: (1) specific dates and time span indicators (100 percent), (2) names of geopolitical units (100 percent), (3) names of individuals and/or groups (96 percent), (4) main topic or subject of work (92 percent) (Tibbo, 1989, p. 540).

The equivalent of other common does not appear on this list until fourth place. Elsewhere Tibbo concludes that "the facets of time, place, and specific topic" are used by historians "to delimit their research, classify their literature, and organize college curricula" (Tibbo, 1989, p. 591). Historians, too, want many of the kinds of terms our group of scholars wanted. Thus, three large empirical studies—Wiberley's, Tibbo's, and ours—all point to the importance of terms besides other common to humanities researchers.

This contrast between other common and all other term categories is an important one, for several reasons. The other common terms that overwhelmingly predominated in the science queries of Saracevic and Kantor's NSF study in fact constitute the heart of what are considered "subject" terms in much writing on thesauri and search vocabulary. Modern principles of thesaurus development received their chief impetus after

World War ll, when science and technology libraries and indexing services needed more detailed and technically accurate indexing than previous systems had made possible. Apparently, however, the predominance of science and engineering in the early days of thesaurus theory development led to a heavy emphasis on other common terms and a corresponding underemphasis of non–other-common terms.

The problems are not limited to thesauri. Even the *Library of Congress Subject Headings*, which predates the development of modern thesaurus principles, and which makes detailed provision for geographical, period, and form subdivisions, uses some period subdivisions only to subdivide extra-large files. Where there are many entries under a main geographical heading the subdivisions are used; where there are few, they are not. With such unpredictable application—that is, unpredictable for the searcher—it is impossible to make reliable use of these non–other-common subdivisions in online searching. Yet, clearly, for the humanities scholar, meaningful online searches can generally be carried out only through use of both non–other-common and other common terms, with the emphasis on the former.

We suspect—although it would take another study of a different kind to determine this—that the relative underemphasis of non–other-common terms in thesauri and database indexing makes the use of such terms more difficult for online searchers. This may explain why scholars in the study made relatively less frequent use of several categories of non–other-common terms in search terms, in comparison to their use in natural language statements.

The Getty Art History Information Program (AHIP), now the sponsor of the bilingual *Bibliography of the History of Art (BHA)*, the successor to *RILA*, is also currently conducting several projects relating to non–other-common terms. The results of these projects should contribute to solving some of the humanities scholar's problems highlighted by our research. Some facets in the *Art and Architecture Thesaurus*, such as the "Styles and Periods" facet, codify certain kinds of non–other-common terms that are relatively neglected in thesauri. *The Getty Union List of Artist Names*, scheduled for release in 1992, is a database of several hundred thousand artists' names, drawn from nine Getty projects, that clusters together the often voluminous name variations referring to a single artist, both during the artist's lifetime and afterward.

Geographical names are problematic because geographical jurisdictions and names change through time. Coverage of geographical names is frequently limited in thesauri and, consequently, in indexing. The Getty's *Thesaurus of Art-Historical Place Names (TAP)*, a hierarchical database of place names now in preparation, should make possible complete and consistent retrieval of geographical materials. Ultimately, we hope to see catalogers and information users able to draw upon these various resources in a linked "virtual" database of descriptive terms, all developed to a uniform standard accepted throughout the world of scholarship.

The results have other implications for online searching as well. Research, practical searching advice, and the teaching of online searching all give relatively short shrift to the non–other-common terms identified here. Searching on names is discussed relatively little (for example, Everett & Pilachowski, 1986). As noted earlier, one scholar commented that he often searched on names because he found searching on other kinds of terms more difficult. The question of whether other scholars do the same merits more research.

These results concerning the use of chronological and discipline terms have particularly interesting implications for online searching. Dates and date ranges need to be represented in certain ways in bibliographic records to permit effective online retrieval. *Historical Abstracts*, a database in which dates are of obvious critical importance, experimented for several years before finding ways of coding dates that allowed flexible retrieval, that is, that allowed searches to be made using both stringent and loose requirements ("high-precision" and "high-recall" searches, respectively). Proper handling of dates for effective online retrieval is not obvious and is not yet widely understood. (See also discussion in Bates, 1992.) Dates should be considered another category of term used in thesauri, and thesauri should instruct indexers in how to represent chronological terms effectively. Only in that way will good date indexing make effective online retrieval possible.

The frequent use of discipline terms, in the natural language statements in particular, creates a paradox for the indexing and searching of online databases. Because these terms are very broad, they are normally seen as poor candidates for use in either indexing or retrieval. Yet these terms are often meaningful for humanities scholars. The scholars in the Getty project used them in nearly a quarter of their natural language statements. Only 6 percent of their search terms were discipline terms, however. Had they "learned their lesson" and discovered how ineffectual such terms are for online retrieval, given current indexing practice?

The sample of discipline terms used in this study was too small for confident identification of all the senses in which they are used, but scholars in various fields clearly use them in a variety of ways. Perhaps it would be possible to introduce these discipline terms into database indexing and retrieval by providing a special classification that indicated the various special senses in which humanities scholars use them. Discipline terms would thus have more specific meanings and provide more precise retrieval for humanities searchers. This question merits additional study.

Finally, our results point to another online searching issue in the humanities. Table 7 provides statistics on 137 search terms that were combinations of (informal) terms within single (formal) terms. In other words, within a single phrase bounded by the beginning or end of the statement and by Boolean operators, the scholars combined terms in all the different ways displayed in the table—twenty-five ways in all.

Many of these combinations would not be effective in a search; they are examples of the novice searcher still trying to master a not-so-simple formal command language syntax. But the large number and complex variety of these combinations shows how often humanities scholars need to combine the various term categories identified in the study. And the combinations could be fruitful: combining several broad terms (for example, discipline + date/period + geography) could lead to a narrow search. The point we have been trying to make here has no bearing on whether the scholars in the Getty study were expert online searchers: we are arguing that if the necessary indexing terms have been omitted from the databases through ignorance of their potential usefulness to the scholarly process, even expert searchers will be hampered in their searching efforts.

In the NSF study data for the natural sciences (table 3), on the other hand, every statement contained other common terms and only one statement contained one or more other proper terms. Thus, in the NSF natural science data, only two of the combinations listed in table 7 of this report were possible even in principle: other common + other common and other proper + other common.

The need, therefore, of humanities scholars to combine terms from a wide variety of distinct categories suggests that searching in the humanities may be inherently more complex than in the sciences. Yet there are many problems associated with developing good search formulations even in the sciences. Thus, the particular problems associated with effective searching in the humanities merit far more attention than they have been given to date.

This study has revealed the distinctive characteristics and needs of humanities scholars with respect to both thesaurus features and online searching. Thesauri developed for the humanities need to give attention to the non–other-common categories of terms identified here (works and individuals as subjects, geographical, chronological, discipline, and other proper terms), in addition to the other common terms. Indexers and searchers alike need to be able to draw upon the controlled vocabulary of each category consistently and easily.

Because of the very large number of terms needed for good coverage of individuals, works, and geographical names, it is probably unrealistic to include terms from all these categories, as well as others, in a single thesaurus for a given humanities discipline. However, term development in these various categories should be coordinated within a common framework or philosophy, and the results made available to indexers and searchers in a convenient form.

Likewise, training for searchers and help screens and other online aids for searchers, as well as search capabilities in online systems, need to be designed to take full cognizance of the unique characteristics of online searching in the humanities. Geographical, chronological, and discipline terms in the online environment hold particular promise for improvement.

To summarize, this study and other recent studies demonstrate that information seeking, vocabulary, and online searching in the humanities have many unique features that have been given relatively short shrift in theory and practice in library and information science. It is understandable that library and information science research has attempted to follow standard scientific practice by trying to generalize principles of thesaurus development and online searching across all disciplines. It may be, however, that in doing so some critical distinctions between disciplines have been overlooked, which has meant that certain groups of users have been underserved. The next stage of development in the theory of the field may therefore be to give closer attention to the unique features that differentiate subject literatures and disciplines—an intriguing prospect.

## REFERENCES

Bates, M.J. (1992). Implications of the subject subdivisions conference: The shift in online catalog design. In M.O. Conway (Ed.), *The future of subdivisions in the Library of Congress Subject Headings system* (pp. 92–98). Report from the 1991 Subject Subdivisions Conference sponsored by the Library of Congress. Washington, DC: Library of Congress Cataloging Distribution Service.

Boyles, J.C. (1987). Bibliographic databases for the art researcher: Developments, problems and proposals. *Art Documentation, 6*(1), 9–12.

Boyles, J.C. (1988). The end user and the art librarian. *Art Libraries Journal, 13,* 27–31.

Broadbent, E. (1986). A study of humanities faculty library information seeking behavior. *Cataloging & Classification Quarterly, 6*(3), 23–36.

Case, D.O. (1991). The collection and use of information by some American historians: A study of motives and methods. *The Library Quarterly 61*(1), 61–82.

Corkill, C., & Mann, M. (1978). *Information needs in the humanities: Two postal surveys. CRUS Occasional Paper No. 2.* (BLR & DD Report No. 5455). Sheffield, England: Centre for Research on User Studies.

Crawford, D. (1986). Meeting scholarly information needs in an automated environment: A humanist's perspective. *College & Research Libraries, 47*(6), 569–574.

Everett, D., & Pilachowski, D.M. (1986). What's in a name? Looking for people online—humanities. *Datebase, 9*(5), 26–34.

Gould, C.C. (1988). *Information needs in the humanities: An assessment.* Stanford, CA: Research Libraries Group.

Guest, S.S. (1987). The use of bibliographical tools by humanities faculty at the State University of New York at Albany. *Reference Librarian, 7*(18), 157–172.

Horner, J., & Thirlwall, D. (1988). Online searching and the university researcher. *Journal of Academic Librarianship, 14*(4), 225–230.

Hurych, J. (1986). After Bath: Scientists, social scientists, and humanists in the context of online searching. *Journal of Academic Librarianship, 12*(3), 158–165.

International Organization for Standardization. (1986). *Documentation, guidelines for the establishment and development of monolingual thesauri* (2nd ed.). (International Standard ISO 2788). Geneva: International Organization for Standardization.

Katzen, M. (1986). The application of computers in the humanities: A view from Britain. *Information Processing & Management, 22*(3), 259–267.

Krausse, S.C., & Etchingham, J.B., Jr. (1986). The humanist and computer-assisted library research. *Computers and the humanities, 20*(2), 87–96.

Lehmann, S., & Renfro, P. (1991). Humanists and electronic information services: Acceptance and resistance. *College & Research Libraries, 52*(5), 409–413.

Loughridge, B. (1989). Information technology, the humanities and the library. *Journal of Information Science, 15*(45), 277–286.

Lowry, A., & Stuveras, J. (1987). *Scholarship in the electronic age: A selected bibliography on research and communication in the humanities and social sciences.* Washington, DC: Council on Library Resources.

Mackesy, E.M. (1982). A perspective on secondary access services in the humanities. *Journal of the American Society for Information Science, 33*(3), 146–151.

Rahtz, S. (Ed.). (1987). *Information technology in the humanities: Tools, techniques and applications.* Chichester, England: Ellis Horwood/John Wiley.

Ross, J.E. (1987). Artists and poets online: Issues in cataloging and retrieval. *Cataloging & Classification Quarterly , 7*(3), 91–104.

Ruiz, D., & Meyer, D.E. (1990). End-user selection of databases—part III: Social science/arts & humanities. *Database, 13*(5), 59–64.

Saracevic, T., & Kantor, P. (1988). A study of information seeking and retrieving: II. Users, questions, and effectiveness. *Journal of the American Society for Information Science, 39*(3), 177–196.

Schmitt, M. (Ed.). (1988). *Object, image, and inquiry: The art historian at work.* Santa Monica, CA: The Getty Art History Information Program.

Schmitt, M. (1990). Alas, the failure to communicate: Thoughts on the symbiosis of scholars, information managers and systems experts. *Art Documentation, 9*(3), 137–138.

Stam, D.C. (1984). How art historians look for information. *Art Documentation, 3*(4), 117–119.

Stam, D.C., & Giral, A. (Eds.). (1988). Linking art objects and art information. *Library Trends, 37*(2), 117–264.

Stern, P. (1988). Online in the humanities: Problems and possibilities. *Journal of Academic Librarianship, 14*(3), 161–164.

Stielow, F., & Tibbo, H. (1988). The negative search, online reference and the humanities: A critical essay in library literature. *RQ, 27*(3), 358–365.

Stone, S. (1982). Humanities scholars: Information needs and uses. *Journal of Documentation, 38*(4), 292–312.

Taylor, R.S. (1968). Question-negotiation and information seeking in libraries. *College & Research Libraries, 29*(3), 178–194.

Tibbo, H.R. (1989). *Abstracts, online searching, and the humanities: An analysis of the structure and content of abstracts of historical discourse.* (Doctoral dissertation). University of Maryland, College Park, MD.

Walker, G. (1988). Online searching in the humanities: Implications for end-users and intermediaries. *Proceedings of the 12th International Online Information Meeting* (pp. 401–412). Oxford, England: Learned Information.

Walker, G. (1990). Searching the humanities: Subject overlap and search vocabulary. *Database, 13*(5), 35–46.

Walker, G., & Atkinson, S.D. (1991). Information access in the humanities: Perils and pitfalls. *Library Hi Tech, 9*(1), 23–34.

Weinberg, B.H. (1988). Why indexing fails the researcher. *The Indexer, 16*(1), 3–6.

Wiberley, S.E., Jr. (1983). Subject access in the humanities and the precision of the humanist's vocabulary. *The Library Quarterly, 53*(4), 420–433.

Wiberley, S.E., Jr. (1988). Names in space and time: The indexing vocabulary of the humanities. *The Library Quarterly, 58*(1), 1–28.

Wiberley, S.E., Jr. (1991). Habits of humanists: Scholarly behavior and new information technologies. *Library Hi Tech, 9*(1), 17–21.

Wiberley, S.E., Jr., & Jones, W.G. (1989). Patterns of information seeking in the humanities. *College & Research Libraries, 50*(6), 638–645.

Woo, J. (1988). The Online Avery Index End-User Pilot Project: Final report. *Information Technology and Libraries, 7,* 223–229.

# TWO

# Searching behavior

# Information search tactics |

ABSTRACT

As part of the study of human information search strategy, the concept of the search tactic, or move made to further a search, is introduced. Twenty-nine tactics are named, defined, and discussed in four categories: monitoring, file structure, search formulation, and term. Implications of the search tactics for research in search strategy are considered. The search tactics are intended to be practically useful in information searching. This approach to searching is designed to be general, yet nontrivial; it is applicable to both bibliographic and reference searches and in both manual and on-line systems.

## Introduction

For all the developments in automated and semiautomated information retrieval, nothing yet matches the ability of experienced human searchers—whether known as "information specialists" or "reference librarians"—who move skillfully among an enormous range of resources, both manual and on-line, to develop bibliographies or answer questions. We know discouragingly little about just what those skills are and how they develop; we cannot yet define what it is that an experienced searcher knows that a beginner does not.

First published as Bates, M.J. (1979 ). Information search tactics. *Journal of the American Society for information Science, 30*(4), 205–214.

In this article, the concept of the information search tactic is introduced and various particular tactics are named and described. These tactics are designed to be of assistance to the searcher while in the process of searching, and secondarily in teaching fledgling searchers their work. They may also suggest various lines of research on search strategy, including, ultimately, efforts to describe and distinguish the skills of the experienced searcher.

The plan of this article is first to give a brief literature review of human information search strategy; second, to discuss the concept of the tactic; third, describe the 29 tactics to be used in information searching; and finally, show some implications of tactics for research in search strategy.

The orientation of this article is toward professional, as opposed to lay, information searching. The tactics, intended to be practically useful in information searching, are applicable to both bibliographic and references searches[1] in both manual and on-line systems, and to all types of questions and subject fields.

Much of the searching done by the professional information specialist requires very little in the way of strategy. Simpler, so-called "ready reference" questions are usually answered by mentally retrieving in a second or two the name of a suitable source, going to the source, and getting the answer. In such cases, the tactics proposed below are seldom needed. The tactics are primarily designed to help in more complex searches—those involving many stages, or those that resist the automatic mental retrieval of satisfactory answering sources.

A few of the tactics described are well known and discussed—though often unnamed—in the library/information science literature; others may be used but are not consciously articulated, let alone named; and still others may be unknown in every respect to most searchers, instructors, or researchers in the field. Even with those tactics that a searcher already uses and recognizes, there may be benefit to be gained by reading about them nonetheless. It is a basic premise of this article that to *articulate* and *name* a tactic makes it more available in the searcher's mind; it makes it more easily and readily applied.

A major orientation of the article is to focus on and use the strengths and flexibility of human thinking processes. It is suggested that search theory and practice may be advanced through a greater attention to the specifically *human, psychological processes* involved in searching, as distinct from the logical, or formal, properties of the process. In addition, we turn

---

1 A bibliographic search is a search to find bibliographic citations to material that will contain the information of interest. A reference search is a search to find information to answer a question directly.

from a focus on the machinery, the information technology, to the brain that is running it.

## Information search strategy literature

There is relatively little literature dealing with information search strategy—especially by that name. We must look several places to find all that might be relevant to the subject. The phrase "search strategy" is probably found most often in the literature of computer on-line searching.

Stevens (1974) reviews a number of these articles (also see issues of *Online Review*, founded in 1977). Typically, in these articles search strategy is viewed as specific to on-line searching. The on-line search is not seen as a part of a broader search process. To put it another way, the unifying factor is the computer on-line system, not the human being running the terminal.

Some literature deals with whether computers can assist the searcher or be used for any of the steps normally performed by humans (see, e.g., Carlson, 1964; Meredith, 1971; Jahoda, 1974; Paisley & Butler, 1977). Interesting insights about human searching are sometimes provided by these human-machine comparisons, and receive later mention in this article where relevant.

While the phrase "search strategy" is less commonly used in traditional librarianship, the field has had a longstanding interest in the "reference process," which sometimes includes searching procedures. Though reference work has been recognized as a library function since before the turn of the century, traditional texts in reference work said little or nothing about searching (Wyer, 1930; Shores, 1954; Cheney, 1971). Hutchins (1944) was exceptional in her attention to how to answer questions. As for theory of search strategy, there has been essentially none until quite recently; in fact, up to the 1970s, there was ongoing debate about whether there was theory of any kind in Wynar (1967). Since Wynar's article noting the lack of theory in the field, a number of articles have appeared positing reference theories (Vavrek, 1968; Emery, 1970; Rugh, 1975; Holler, 1975; Whittaker, 1977), but these are fairly brief and general and say little about searching.

However, some articles have appeared that deal more specifically with information searching. Neill (1975) applies the psychologist Guilford's "Structure of Intellect" model to the reference process, and Benson and Maloney (1975), in their analysis of the search process, focus on building a "bibliographic bridge" between system and query.

A number of attempts have been made to analyze the reference process or, more specifically, the search process, in flow chart form. Katz (1974), in a modern reference text that deals much more extensively with searching than earlier texts, reviews no less than eight such models. (Incidentally, Katz's chapters on searching in the recent editions of his text [1974, 1978] constitute excellent reviews of this literature.) These models vary in specificity. Stych's model (Katz, 1974, pp. 134–135), for example, goes into great detail, down to the type of reference book and even specific sources, to try for answers at various decision points. On the other hand, the Rees and Saracevic model (Katz, 1974, p. 137) gives "selection of search strategy" as a single step in a ten-step model of the reference process.

Nothing was found in this literature on search tactics, or dealing with search strategy from the standpoint of tactics. Josel's article, "Ten Reference Commandments" (Josel, 1971), with hints for reference work, comes closest.

Finally, one other body of literature may be expected to be of use: that on the psychology of problem solving. Nothing was found in that literature directly related to information searching, but Adams (1976, p. 66) lists a number of verbs as general problem-solving "strategies," an approach which resembles that used here for tactics. Where appropriate, other references are made below to the problem-solving literature.

## The concept of the search tactic

In order to elucidate the role of the tactic in human information searching, it is first useful to distinguish various types of models that may be developed in studying this area. At least four different sorts of models of search strategy can be distinguished, models for *idealizing* searching, *representing* searching, *teaching* searching, and *facilitating* searching.[2] An ideal model specifies ideal search patterns on the basis of mathematical, system analytic, or other formal criteria of optimality. Representation models exist for the scientific purpose of describing, and ultimately predicting and explaining, the human behavior known as information searching; these models represent what people actually do or think in searching. A good teaching model is one that makes it easy for people to learn to search. A model for facilitating searching is one that searchers can use while in the process of searching, one that helps them search more efficiently or effectively.

These different functions impose different requirements for what constitutes good models in each case. Conceivably, a very good single model could be found that would be optimal for all these purposes in one. But it

---

2   These four types of models may also be useful in conceptualizing research on human behavior in other areas of information science, e.g., classification/indexing and relevance assessment.

is more likely that different models will have to be found for each function. For example, system analytic or mathematical theories of optimal searches, while good descriptions of ideal searching, may be predicted to be of little interest for the practice of searching to the typical information specialist, whose mathematical background is limited.

Good models that join the teaching and practice functions are more likely to be found than ones that join other pairs of these functions. But even here differences can be found. The best way to learn something when first encountering it may be different from the best way to think about that same thing once familiar with the ideas.

The model presented here is intended primarily as a facilitation model and secondarily as a teaching model. It is assumed at this point that the model will function well in both capacities; later testing will determine whether it is, in fact, useful in neither, one, or both of these capacities. Students of search behavior who are attempting to develop representation models may find this an interesting starting place as well. The concept of the tactic, as well as particular tactics, may be found to be useful and appropriate for describing the behavior of skilled searchers. (Different results may be found for those who have and for those who have not been exposed to the concepts in this article.)

"Strategy" and "tactics" are terms best known for their military uses. *Webster's New Collegiate Dictionary* (1956) defines them as follows:

> *Strategy:* The science and art of employing the armed strength of a belligerent to secure the objects of a war, esp. the large-scale planning and directing of operations in adjustment to combat area, possible enemy action, political alignments, etc.; also, an instance of it.

> *Tactics:* 1. (usually construed as sing.) The science and art of disposing and maneuvering troops or ships in action or in the presence of the enemy. 2. (usually construed as pl.) Hence, any method of procedure; esp., adroit devices for accomplishing an end.

Strategy deals with overall planning; tactics deals with short-term goals and maneuvers.

Let us now adapt these terms for use in information searching. The definitions below are general and simple, and may be refined in later theoretical development.

*Search tactic*  A move made to further a search.

*Search strategy (in searching)*  A plan for the whole search.

*Search strategy (as an area of study)*  The study of the theory, principles, and practice of making and using search strategies and tactics.

*Search behavior*  What people do and/or, as far as can be determined, what they think when they search.

Every move a person makes toward the goal of finding desired information is seen as a tactic. Hence, there can be good, or effective, tactics and bad ones. The purpose of this model is to suggest tactics that are thought likely to improve the effectiveness or efficiency of a search. The word "likely" is important, however. These tactics are heuristic; they may help, but not necessarily. Furthermore, a tactic may be good in one situation and not in another. Further development of the model may make it possible to state the circumstances under which certain tactics are most likely to be useful. (See also the section "Implications of Search Tactics for Research in Search Strategy.")

The tactics described here are concerned with the search proper: threading one's way through the file structure of the information facility to find desired sources, fitting the search as conceptualized to the vocabulary of the system/resources, and monitoring the search, that is, keeping it on track. Another aspect of searching, getting ideas to overcome a stymied search, will be dealt within a future article, "Idea Tactics." Other areas of the overall search process which may lend themselves to the development of search tactics are the reference interview, the initial analysis of question and search design, consultation with the patron during and after the search (which may be considered a part of the reference interview, broadly conceived), and determination of the relevance of information found.

Four types of tactics are distinguished here:

1. *Monitoring tactics* are tactics to keep the search on track and efficient.

2. *File structure tactics* are techniques for threading one's way through the file structure of the information facility to desired file, source, or information within source.

3. *Search formulation tactics* are tactics to aid in the process of designing or redesigning the search formulation. (These tactics are not restricted to computer search formulations.)

4. *Term tactics* are tactics to aid in the selection and revision of specific terms within the search formulation.

A note on "file structure," since the phrase is used here in a somewhat unconventional way—All the information in a typical information facility can be seen as organized into a structure. Typically, there are a number of different types of file, each ordered according to different principles, and these files are interrelated through common access in a central file such as a catalog. (The concept of "file" as used here includes not only those things conventionally called by that name, but also any ordered set of information individuals. The "book" is a typical such individual; thus, for example, the ordered set of books contained in the A/Z call number range of a library's main stack collection is also a file.) The closest traditional librarianship comes to a name for this structure of files is "bibliographic control," a phrase used in so many different ways as to be almost meaningless. In information science, "file organization" is generally restricted to computer usage. So, "file structure" is used here to refer to the overall pattern, or structure, of organization of information in an information facility.

This concept is not to be confused with particular classification or indexing systems. The point here is that there is a more general way of viewing information organization than through particular systems. All indexing and classification systems provide a structure; the interest here is in the fact of the structure, not in the specific character of that structure. It is seen that the tactics, though they deal with threading one's way through the file structure, do so independently of particular systems of information organization.

With regard to the whole set of tactics, some overlapping will be noticed, as well as some hierarchical relationships. VARY, for example, will be seen to be the general case, against several specific forms of variation that follow it in the term tactics. These relationships have been retained for two reasons.

First, if we view the identification and understanding of tactics as our problem to solve as researchers, then the following point on research strategy needs to be made: While our goal over the long term may be a parsimonious few, highly effective tactics, our goal in the short term should be to uncover as many as we can, as being of potential assistance. Then we can test the tactics and select the good ones. If we go for closure too soon, i.e., seek that parsimonious few prematurely, then we may miss some valuable tactics.

Second, it may prove that a larger set of tactics, including even overlapping ones, makes a better facilitation model anyway, for psychological reasons. I suggest that this is likely the case. The use of these tactics is a form of creative problem solving. In such cases the mind may not work in logical, regular patterns. It may come at a problem from many different levels and angles. It may use one tactic on a particular type of problem one time and a different one on the same sort of problem the next time. In other words, we may find that the requirements of a good facilitation model of searching include some redundancy, and that an across-the-board application of parsimony (economy of logical formulation and expression) is more appropriate to ideal and representation models. (Even if this is so, it nonetheless does not preclude the possibility that parsimony is desirable in some respects in a facilitation model. For example, while using a large, nonparsimonious set of tactics, it may still be desirable to have *definitions* of the tactics that are as concise as possible.)

## Search tactics

In Table 1 are listed and defined all of the (presumably useful) tactics for the search proper that I have been able to discover to date. The 29 tactics are adapted from my own experience and thinking, from the literature, and from the comments of colleagues and students.

Since tactics are moves, they are presented in verb form. One may think of them either as commands (CUT!) or as infinitives (TO CUT). Names of tactics have been selected to be brief and striking.

### Discussion of tactics

Definitions of tactics are given below in the context of a broader discussion and explanation. Where no discussion is deemed necessary, definitions are stated alone.

MONITORING TACTICS
Tactics to keep the search on track and efficient.

■ M1. CHECK  To review the original request and compare it to the current search topic to see that it is the same.

■ M2. WEIGH  To make a cost-benefit assessment, at one or more points of the search, of current or anticipated actions. Among other things, the searcher might consider whether any other approach would be more productive for the effort.

■ M3. PATTERN  Frequent experience with a type of question may lead to an habitual pattern of search (see also Katz, 1978, p. 87ff). If, for example, a common request in an academic library is for addresses of

TABLE 1. *Summary of information search tactics and definitions.*

## MONITORING TACTICS:

*Tactics to keep the search on track and efficient.*

| | |
|---|---|
| M1. CHECK | To review the original request and compare it to the current search topic to see that it is the same. |
| M2. WEIGH | To make a cost-benefit assessment, at one or more points of the search, of current or anticipated actions. |
| M3. PATTERN | To make oneself aware of a search pattern, examine it, and redesign it if not maximally efficient or if out of date. |
| M4. CORRECT | To watch for and correct spelling and factual errors in one's search topic. |
| M5. RECORD | To keep track of trails one has followed and of desirable trails not followed up or not completed. |

## FILE STRUCTURE TACTICS:

*Techniques for threading one's way through the file structure of the information facility to desired file, source, or information within source.*

| | |
|---|---|
| F1. BIBBLE | To look for a bibliography already prepared, before launching oneself into the effect of preparing one; more generally, to check to see if the search work one plans has already been done in a usable form by someone else. |
| F2. SELECT | To break complex search queries down into subproblems and work on one problem at a time. |
| F3. SURVEY | To review, at each decision point of the search, the available options before selecting. |
| F4. CUT | When selecting among several ways to search a given query, to choose the option that cuts out, eliminates, the largest part of the search domain at once. |
| F5. STRETCH | To use a source for other than its intended purposes. |
| F6. SCAFFOLD | To design an auxiliary, indirect route through the information files and resources to reach the desired information. |
| F7. CLEAVE | To employ binary searching in locating an item in an ordered file. |

## SEARCH FORMULATION TACTICS:

*Tactics to aid in the process of designing or redesigning the search formulation.*

| | |
|---|---|
| S1. SPECIFY | To search on terms that are as specific as the information desired. |
| S2. EXHAUST | To include most or all elements of the query in the initial search formulation; to add one or more of the query elements to an already-prepared search formulation. |
| S3. REDUCE | To minimize the number of elements of the query in the initial search formulation; to subtract one or more of the query elements from an already-prepared search formulation. |
| S4. PARALLEL | To make the search formulation broad (or broader) by including synonyms or otherwise conceptually parallel terms. |
| S5. PINPOINT | To make the search formulation precise by minimizing (or reducing) the number of parallel terms, retaining the more perfectly descriptive terms. |
| S6. BLOCK | To reject, in the search formulation, items containing or indexed by certain term(s), even if it means losing some document sections of relevance. |

## TERM TACTICS:

*Tactics to aid in the selection and revision of specific terms within the search formulation.*

| | |
|---|---|
| T1. SUPER | To move upward hierarchically to a broader (superordinate) term. |
| T2. SUB | To move downward hierarchically to a more specific (subordinate) term. |
| T3. RELATE | To move sideways hierarchically to a coordinate term. |
| T4. NEIGHBOR | To seek additional search terms by looking at neighboring terms, whether proximate alphabetically, by subject similarity, or otherwise. |
| T5. TRACE | To examine information already found in the search in order to find additional terms to be used in furthering the search. |
| T6. VARY | To alter or substitute one's search terms in any of several ways. |
| T7. FIX | To try alternate affixes, whether prefixes, suffixes, or infixes. |
| T8. REARRANGE | To reverse or rearrange the words in search terms in any or all reasonable orders. |
| T9. CONTRARY | To search for the term logically opposite from that describing the desired information. |
| T10. RESPELL | To search under a different spelling. |
| T11. RESPACE | To try spacing variants. |

researchers, then the librarian may soon develop a sequence of sources to search, arranged by their likely productivity. To PATTERN is to make oneself aware of a search pattern, examine it, and redesign it if not maximally efficient or if out of date.

■ M4. CORRECT To watch for and correct spelling and factual errors in one's search topic. These may exist in the topic as presented originally by the user (cf. Josel's first "reference commandment" [Josel, 1971, p. 146]), or may slip into the searcher's thinking in translating a verbal request, or in remembering (without having in hand) a written request. In observing bibliographic searching done by several librarians, Carlson noted that the searchers would allow inaccuracies, particularly spelling errors, to slip into their search formulation. One librarian, for example, had a request on "neuroglia," and searched instead on "neuralgia," a very different concept. He noted several cases where a difficult technical term was not written down and the librarians "would search for the *remembered* spelling, usually not find it, and then stop the search for that term" (Carlson, 1964, p. 29).

A clue to errors in the request as stated may be provided by suspicious coincidences. Josel's fourth "reference commandment" is "Coincidence is no coincidence." As he says: "When a patron wants to have a biography of Saint Edmund Hall, born 1226, and you find the same name listed as a college of Oxford University, and 1226 as its date of construction, do not doubt the patron needs further talking to" (Josel, 1971, p. 146).

▨M5. RECORD To keep track of trails one has followed and of desirable trails not followed up or not completed. In complex searches it is sometimes necessary to return to the source of information or citations recorded earlier in the search. For example, after recording a number of citations from a periodical index, the searcher may then attempt to retrieve the articles cited and find a blind lead. The citation needs to be checked again in the original source. But unless the source, volume date, and subject term searched under were recorded, the searcher may have to go through the entries under a dozen terms or in several volumes to locate the desired citation. Similarly, if productive on-line and manual bibliographic search formulations are retained, later repeat effort may be saved.

As for trails not followed up or not completed, Carlson noted the following in his observations of librarians:

> They are not consistent in recording what they find or what they intend to check later. In many cases, the human will find cross references and state that they will check these cross references later. Unless they make some written note, they never seem to check them. Each librarian studied, at some

time during the search, noticed some discrepancy either in an item being scanned, or in an item recorded as acceptable, and made the verbal comment that he would check this later. Once again they almost never made a written note about this and when they did *not* write a note, they never did check the item. The discrepancies which arose during the search were thus not clarified. (Carlson, 1964, pp. 29–30)

The searcher may *choose* not to follow up some side trail or problem, but it appears that such choices are often made by default, rather than deliberately.

### FILE STRUCTURE TACTICS
Techniques for threading one's way through the file structure of the information facility to the desired file, source, or information within source.

■ **F1. BIBBLE**  One way to cope with the file structure is to find a way to do without it altogether. The only neologism among the set of tactic names, BIBBLE is based on the abbreviation "bibl." for "bibliography." To BIBBLE is to look for a bibliography already prepared, before launching oneself into the effort of preparing one. More generally, to BIBBLE is to check to see if the search work one plans has already been done in a usable form by someone else.

■ **F2. SELECT**  To break complex search queries down into subproblems and work on one problem at a time. This tactic is a well-established and productive technique in general problem solving. As each subproblem is solved, the parts can then be knit into a solution to the whole, larger problem.

■ **F3. SURVEY**  To review at each decision point of the search the available options before selecting. In Carlson's description of human searching behavior, he noted the following problem: "There is almost no look-ahead in the human search procedures. All of the librarians studied exhibited to some extent this lack of look-ahead. They would often scan each entry as they came to it and then encounter a heading which would alter the search procedure." He concludes: "Here the lesson is very clear: humans should scan over a reference document before making any detailed searches through it" (Carlson, 1964, p. 35). Psychologically, this is a problem of "going for closure" too soon, that is, settling on a source or approach prematurely. In employing SURVEY, one resists that temptation and presumably achieves a more effective search.

For example, in a bibliographic search, instead of selecting the first index that comes to mind, one thinks of all the major indexes in the subject and then selects the one best suited to the particular query. Then, instead of moving immediately to a subject entry term within the index, one first scans through the thesaurus to find the best term or terms for the subject.

■ F4. CUT   When selecting among several ways to search a given query, to CUT is to choose the option that cuts out, eliminates, the largest part of the search domain at once. In my opinion, this tactic is of fundamental significance in our field, and is relatively little known or discussed. Here are some examples: When looking up a book written by Smith and Brzustowicz, the search will be much briefer if one looks under Brzustowicz (assuming the file has entries under co-authors). In most files, there will be far fewer entries to scan under the latter name. Thus, in choosing to search under the latter name, with its few entries, one has cut out a larger part of the search domain than would be the case when searching under Smith, and has shortened the search accordingly.

Similarly, in a subject search, other things being equal, one should look up the most specific elements of the topic first. For example, in using a KWIC (rotated title term) index, the searcher will find desired material on the topic "Research in Retinopathy" much faster by looking under the more specific term "retinopathy," because there will be fewer entries.

The concept of CUT has received the most explicit use in information science in manual coordinate indexing searching. If one pulls three subject-term cards for an ANDed search on terms A, B, and C, then makes comparisons among term cards to find the documents indexed under all three terms, the smart tactic is to start with the card with the fewest document numbers posted on it (cf. Foskett, 1969, p. 232). Since all acceptable documents must have all three terms assigned to them, the card with the fewest documents posted exercises the most control and eliminates the largest part of the search domain.

■ F5. STRETCH   Naturally enough, one tends to think about information resources in terms of the uses for which they are intended. However, almost all reference sources can be used productively for some other purpose than intended. The internal organization of a file or reference book is designed around certain uses. Thus, access via certain record elements is provided, and access via other elements is not. But even though formal access is not provided, that other information is there in the source nonetheless. Introductions, which are outside the formal internal file organization of an information source, may also be informative in unexpected ways.

In general, it may be assumed that the most efficient searching involves using sources for their intended purposes. But when such approaches fail, answers may still be found by putting in the harder work to ferret out information incidentally provided. Thus, to STRETCH is to use a source for other than its intended purposes. However, it should be kept in mind that to STRETCH effectively the searcher must first *think* differently, he/she must think about all the information that is in a source, not just about the ordinary uses of it.

For example, after searching unsuccessfully through many directories for the address of an engineer, the searcher may recall that patents contain the name of the inventor and also the business affiliation, since the patent is usually owned by the company she/he works for. If the engineer has patented anything, then the address should be available in the nearest patent file.

■ F6. SCAFFOLD Hodnett discusses the use of what he calls "auxiliaries" (Hodnett, 1955, p. 94ff.), which are aids in problem solving which may or may not themselves be a part of the solution, but which make the solution possible. The technique of using auxiliaries is often employed in mathematics, where a seemingly irrelevant theorem is introduced, a theorem with little intrinsic interest, but one that enables the main theorem to be proved.

The use of scaffolding in construction is another such example. When the building is finished, the scaffolding is torn down, but the building could not have been built without it. In information searching, it is sometimes the case that the shortest route through the file structure is a dead end. In that case one may build a roundabout path to the answer by going through files or sources that themselves may seem to have nothing to do with the question. One may acquire an additional piece of information that in no way contributes directly to the answer but which makes it possible to search for the answer in some other source. Thus, to scaffold is to design an auxiliary, indirect route through the information files and resources to reach the desired information. For example, after unsuccessfully seeking information on an obscure poet, the searcher may find out who the poet's contemporaries were and research them in hopes of finding mention of the poet.

■ F7. CLEAVE To employ binary searching in locating an item in an ordered file. (For those unfamiliar with this principle: In binary searching one first looks at a record in the middle of an ordered, e.g., alphabetized, file. One then determines the half of the file in which the desired record must lie. Then the middle record in that half of the file is looked at, and the quarter of the file in which the record must lie is determined. Then one looks at the middle record in the quarter section of the file, and so on until the desired record is discovered. In each case, the file is split in two, hence the term "binary" [see also Meadow, 1973].)

Formally, binary searching is a more efficient approach than serial or random searching. Yet a rigid adherence to this principle would probably be wasteful, since human beings have additional contextual knowledge about many files. For example, a searcher looking for the telephone number of the Ajax Corporation will not start the search in the middle of the white pages. On the other hand, a general awareness of binary searching may enable searchers to improve efficiency, particularly when confronting large and unfamiliar files. The use of CLEAVE, as well as means of testing its usefulness, are discussed in more detail in Bates (1978).

## SEARCH FORMULATION TACTICS
Tactics to aid in the process of designing or redesigning the search formulation.

■ S1. SPECIFY  To search on terms that are as specific as the information desired. Specificity is one of the crucial concepts in systems of information access. Almost all systems of classification and indexing require that descriptions assigned to materials be as specific as the content of the materials and as the indexing system itself allows. Sears and Library of Congress subject headings use the "rule of specific entry" which requires entry of materials under the most specific terms that still encompass the content of the item; coordinate indexing, with its focus on "concept" indexing, brings about highly specific description, and so on.

Thus, specificity at the time of indexing requires specificity at the time of retrieval. An indexing system may or may not allow entry under broader terms as well, but it will almost always require specific entry. Thus, it is probably the case that starting with specific terms in all kinds of searches (including both bibliographic and reference) will be the most productive approach (for further discussion see Bates, 1978).

■ S2. EXHAUST  To include most or all elements of the query in the initial search formulation, or to add one or more of the query elements to an already-prepared search formulation. Both this and the next tactic, REDUCE, are related to Lancaster's use of "exhaustivity" (Lancaster, 1968, p. 71 ff.). In searching, the more exhaustive a search is, the more of the elements of a complex request have been included in the search formulation. For example, the searcher interested in the "training of teachers of mathematics for the elementary grades" has a four-element problem. An exhaustive search would include all four elements in its formulation. Both EXHAUST and REDUCE deal implicitly with the number of elements in the query that are to be ANDed together in the search formulation. The more exhaustive the search statement, the more stringent the requirements, and thus the fewer the documents likely to be returned on a search.

While this tactic is probably most useful for Boolean searching, it is also meaningful for other kinds of searches. For example, in a catalog using Library of Congress subject headings, one can decide between searching under the main heading only or more exhaustively under the main heading plus geographical, bibliographical form, or other nontopical subdivisions.

■ S3. REDUCE To minimize the number of elements of the query in the initial search formulation, or to subtract one or more of the query elements from an already-prepared search formulation. REDUCE is the opposite of EXHAUST. This tactic reduces the number of ANDed elements in the search formulation, making the search specification less stringent, and thus increases the number of documents likely to be returned on a search.

■ S4. PARALLEL To make the search formulation broad (or broader) by including synonyms or otherwise conceptually parallel terms. PARALLEL and PINPOINT deal implicitly with elements in a query that are to be ORed together. Though these tactics are most readily applied in on-line Boolean searching, they may also be used in manual searching. For example, in the process of manually compiling a bibliography, one may look over catalog subject headings and terms in periodical indexes and expand the number of similar terms searched under (PARALLEL), either at the beginning of the search or after getting some experience with the type and quantity of materials under each term.

■ S5. PINPOINT To make the search formulation precise by minimizing (or reducing) the number of parallel terms, retaining the more perfectly descriptive terms. PINPOINT is the opposite of PARALLEL.

■ S6. BLOCK To reject, in the search formulation, items containing or indexed by certain term(s), even if it means losing some document sections of relevance. This tactic deals implicitly with the Boolean AND NOT. The term NOT was not used, however, because the concept extends beyond the usual applications of Boolean searching. For example, in doing a manual literature search, one may choose to reject all items containing a certain word in the title. BLOCK was selected as the name of this tactic to draw attention to the tricky side of NOT—to the fact that in eliminating a document that contains an undesired term, one may also block out desirable material that happens to be found in the same document.

## TERM TACTICS

Tactics to aid in the selection and revision of specific terms within the search formulation.

■ T1. SUPER To move upward hierarchically to a broader (superordinate) term. Searchers may be assisted by pointers in a thesaurus or may have to rely on their own knowledge to devise the term.

■ T2. SUB To move downward hierarchically to a more specific (subordinate) term.

■ T3. RELATE  To move sideways hierarchically to a coordinate term.

■ T4. NEIGHBOR  To seek additional search terms by looking at neighboring terms, whether proximate alphabetically, by subject similarity, or otherwise. Coates pointed out many years ago that all manual (and we should add today, most automated) information organization systems do two fundamental things: locate and collocate (Coates, 1960, Chap. 3). The primary function of such systems is, of course, to enable the searcher to find, or locate, desired materials. However, such systems also necessarily *collocate* entries. In any ordered file everything must be next to something else. Many of the historical arguments over the relative merits of classification and indexing systems were as much about collocation as location. Consider, for example, the old debate over whether to have classified or alphabetico-specific subject catalog access. A classified catalog collocates entries by their conceptual relationship; an alphabetico-specific catalog collocates entries only by their alphabetical order. These two approaches have different strengths and weaknesses and different consequences for search strategy (Coates, 1960, Chap. 3).

To use this tactic is to expand the search by examining the proximate entries, whatever they are. In on-line searching, one examines whatever proximate entries are made available by the on-line program one is using. (NEIGHBOR happens to be the current term for the appropriate command in the SDC ORBIT® search language.)

Incidentally, the use of NEIGHBOR may be extended beyond term selection to resource selection as well. Since classification systems collocate books, it is easy to extend a search by examining related sources collocated on the shelves of the reference stacks.

■ T5. TRACE  To examine information already found in the search in order to find additional terms to be used in furthering the search. Two of the most common ways of doing this are to scan descriptor term lists in citations retrieved in on-line searching, and to scan on a catalog card the list of other headings that have been given to the document in question. These other headings on the catalog card are called the "tracings," hence the name for this tactic (cf. Josel's seventh "reference commandment" [Josel, 1971, p. 147]).

■ T6. VARY  To alter or substitute one's search terms in any of several ways. See remaining term tactics for some specific variations.

■ T7. FIX  To try alternative affixes, whether prefixes, suffixes, or infixes. Several may be done at once through truncation routines.

■ T8. REARRANGE  In any system where terms may contain more than one word, word order may make a difference in retrieval success.

To REARRANGE is to reverse or rearrange the words in search terms in any or all reasonable orders.

■ T9. CONTRARY To search for the term logically opposite from that describing the desired information. For example, one may want information on "cooperation" and, after an unsuccessful search, change the term to "competition."

■ T10. RESPELL To search under a different spelling. CORRECT dealt with maintaining correct spelling, among other things. But with RESPELL the concern is not with correctness, but with effectiveness. Particularly in current on-line search systems, there are a great many spelling variations that show up in the citations. One must expand the spelling variations to insure good recall. RESPELL is occasionally needed in manual systems too, where, for example, one needs to change from U.S. to British spelling to search successfully in a source.

■ T11. RESPACE Spacing, particularly in hyphenated words, or words that appear with various spacings, can be critical in search success. To RESPACE is to try spacing variants. While spacing problems are most glaring in some automated search files, such problems can also be serious with manual files. The two fundamental variants in filing rules—word-by-word filing and letter-by-letter filing—differ on how the blank space is to be treated in filing (American Library Association, 1968; Needham, 1971, p. 339). Both of these rules are in wide use. The searcher who is thinking in terms of one filing rule and enters a source that uses the other may miss the desired material.

## Implications of search tactics for research in search strategy

As experience is gained with these tactics, leads for the development of ideas and research in other areas of human information search strategy should emerge. Some possible directions that have already come to mind follow.

(1) Various tactics form clusters as responses to situations where a search produces too many or too few documents. For example, where too few documents are produced, the searcher might try SUPER, RELATE, REDUCE, PARALLEL, NEIGHBOR, TRACE, and VARY, among others. Too many documents, on the other hand, might lead to the use of SUB, EXHAUST, PINPOINT, and BLOCK.

A few steps may be taken in moving from a facilitation model of *tactics* to a facilitation model of *strategy* (i.e., to a model that suggests helpful search strategies or techniques for developing strategies) by distinguishing typical stages of searches and then looking for useful patterns in tactics use at those stages. If the searcher is aware that a small cluster of tactics is most likely to be useful at a given stage, then she/he can concentrate on just those few at that stage.

(2) It was stated earlier that the tactics presented in this article are restricted to those dealing with the search proper: monitoring the search, threading through the file structure, and fitting search query to system/ resource vocabulary. With experience, other tactics in the aforementioned categories should emerge. For example, in a system as complex as an information facility, there are surely more useful file structure tactics than have been noted here. Tactics can also be developed for the other elements of the reference process that have been left out here. (As noted earlier, I will present "idea tactics," ways of getting ideas to help with stymied searches, in a future article.) Tactics can also be developed for moves in the reference interview. The complexity of the interview process has been recognized in recent years, and a considerable literature is developing in that area (see, e.g., Lynch, 1978). In many cases, the reference interview, in effect, continues into the search process itself, as the searcher returns with partial material to show the requester. User feedback during the search adds another dimension of complexity to the search, and feedback-related tactics should ultimately be included in any comprehensive view of search tactics.

Another aspect of the reference process with tactical potential is the stage in which the search query is analyzed. It is at this point that search strategy is developed. It might be possible to enrich or advance upon the flow-chart models of search strategy already developed by devising specific tactics suitable for this initial analysis phase. For example, Jahoda recommends as one step in the reference process: "select sequence of specific titles to search" (Jahoda & Olson, 1972, p. 155). Thus, "SORT," to mean, for example, sorting the sources responsive to a query from most to least likely to be of help, might be seen as one tactic to be used in this phase. Finally, tactics to aid in the evaluation of relevance of retrieved materials would represent yet another element of the reference process.

After these various sets of tactics have been developed, an ultimate goal of creating a single, comprehensive set of tactics can be envisioned. The set would incorporate all elements of the reference process, from initial interview with patron all the way to final determination of relevance and final negotiation with patron. It would provide a unifying mode for viewing the reference process and could constitute the core of a course in reference/information searching.

(3) WEIGH suggests a whole small subarea of investigation. WEIGH is a capsule name for an on-the-spot cost-benefit assessment. Cost-benefit analysis in library/information science generally involves extensive studies and mathematical models. WEIGH, on the other hand, deals with what people can evaluate *in their minds in a few seconds*. What is needed is a class of rules-of-thumb that the searcher can use while searching. Such rules would be concerned with, among other things, how to choose among several sequences of actions or among several sources. For the latter, the rules might take into account likely productivity of source, likely effort in use, and characteristics of query requirements, such as exhaustivity desired or "importance" of query.

These rules might look simple but they would be based on sophisticated testing to discover them in the first place. The point here is that while there is a well-developed science of cost-benefit analysis for systems researchers to use, there is no such science for information searchers to draw on while they are in the process. What is needed, in short, are searching decisions rules that minimize cognitive strain (cf. Bruner, Goodnow, & Austin, 1956, p. 82ff.). Since staff costs are usually the largest part of an information facility's budget, anything that can be done to enable searchers to work faster should be a valuable improvement in information facility system performance.

(4) One of the fundamental issues in search strategy is when to stop. Two example stopping questions: How does one judge when enough information or citations have been gathered? How does one decide to give up an unsuccessful search? At least two of the tactics in the set proposed here suggest testable areas for stopping. SURVEY was recommended as a way of making sure one has found a good source, or best term, for searching. Use of SURVEY can not only aid in effectiveness, but also in efficiency. If the searcher does not use this tactic and searches under the first term that comes to mind, time may be wasted with that term in reading and recording (or having printed out) citations, before the realization that there are better terms to use. Thus, SURVEY may be presumed to aid both efficiency and effectiveness of the search. But there must be a limit. In surveying, one could review every source in a library or every term in a thesaurus. Such thoroughness would waste time. Usefulness of this tactic probably follows a curve in which additional SURVEYing beyond a certain point produces diminishing returns. Testing may demonstrate where that point is.

WEIGH also includes some stopping questions. If, for example, one has mentally sorted relevant sources from most to least likely to produce information on the query, then when is the optimal time to stop searching in one source and move to the next one? That point may well come before one has exhausted every conceivable possibility in a given source.

## Summary

After reviewing briefly the literature of human information search strategy, four types of models of information search strategy were defined: models for idealizing searching, representing searching, teaching searching, and facilitating searching. The model in this article was presented as being primarily a facilitation model and secondarily a teaching model.

The concept of the search tactic was defined, as well as four categories of tactics for the search proper: monitoring tactics, file structure tactics, search formulation tactics, and term tactics.

Twenty-nine tactics were named, defined, and discussed, and various implications of search tactics for research in search strategy were discussed.

### ACKNOWLEDGMENT

This work was supported in part by a grant from the University of Washington Graduate School Research Fund.

### REFERENCES

Adams, J.L. (1976). *Conceptual blockbusting.* San Francisco, CA: San Francisco Book.

American Library Association. (1968). *ALA rules for filing catalog cards* (2nd ed., abridged). Chicago, IL: ALA.

Bates, M.J. (1978). The testing of information search tactics. *Proceedings of the American Society for Information Science Annual Meeting, 15,* 25-27.

Benson, J., & Maloney, R.K. (1975). Principles of searching. *RQ, 14*(4), 316-320.

Bruner, J.S., Goodnow, J.J., & Austin, G.A. (1956). *A study of thinking.* New York: Science Editions.

Carlson, G. (1964). *Search strategy by reference librarians: Part 3 of the final report on the organization of large files.* Sherman Oaks, CA: Hughes Dynamics, Advanced Information Systems Division.

Cheney, F.N. (1971). *Fundamental reference sources.* Chicago, IL: American Library Association.

Coates, E.J. (1960). *Subject catalogues: Headings and structure.* London: Library Association.

Emery, R. (1970). Steps in reference theory. *Library Association Record, 72*(3), 88-90; 96.

Foskett, A.C. (1969). *The subject approach to information.* London: Clive Bingley.

Hodnett, E. (1955). *The art of problem solving.* New York: Harper.

Holler, F. (1975). Toward a reference theory. *RQ, 14*(4), 301-309.

Hutchins, M. (1944). *Introduction to reference work*. Chicago, IL: American Library Association.

Jahoda, G. (1974). Reference question analysis and search strategy development by man and machine. *Journal of the American Society for Information Science, 25*(3), 139–144.

Jahoda, G., & Olson, P.E. (1972). Models of reference: Analyzing the reference process. *RQ, 12*(2), 148–156.

Josel, N.A. (1971). Ten reference commandments. *RQ, 11*(2), 146–147.

Katz, W.A. (1974). *Introduction to reference work* (Vol. 2, 2nd ed.). New York: McGraw-Hill.

Katz, W.A. (1978). *Introduction to reference work* (Vol. 2, 3rd ed.). New York: McGraw-Hill.

Lancaster, F.W. (1968). *Information retrieval systems: Characteristics, testing, and evaluation.* New York: Wiley.

Lynch, M.J. (1978). Reference interviews in public libraries. *The Library Quarterly, 48*(2), 119–142.

Meadow, C.T. (1973). *The analysis of information systems* (2nd ed. ). Los Angeles: Melville.

Meredith, J.C. (1971). Machine-assisted approach to general reference materials. *Journal of the American Society for Information Science, 22*(3), 176–186.

Needham, C.D. (1971). *Organizing knowledge in libraries* (2nd Rev. ed.). Seminar Press.

Neill, S.D. (1975). Problem solving and the reference process. *RQ, 14*(4), 310–315.

Paisley, W., & Butler, M. (1977). *Computer assistance in information work*. A report to the Division of Science Information, National Science Foundation. [Contract #C76-05489]. Palo Alto, CA: Applied Communication Research.

Rugh, A.G. (1975). Toward a science of reference work: Basic concepts. *RQ, 14*(4), 293–299.

Shores, L. (1954). *Basic reference sources: An introduction to materials and methods.* Chicago, IL: American Library Association.

Stevens, M.E. (1974). Strategies for organizing and searching. In C. Fenichel (Ed.), *Changing patterns in information retrieval* (pp. 47–79). Washington, DC: American Society for Information Science.

Vavrek, B.F. (1968). A theory of reference service. *College & Research Libraries, 29*(6), 508–510.

*Webster's New Collegiate Dictionary.* (1956). Springfield, MA: G & C Merriam.

Whittaker, K. (1977). Towards a theory for reference and information service. *Journal of Librarianship, 9*(1), 49–63.

Wyer, J.I. (1930). *Reference work: A textbook for students of library work and librarians.* Chicago, IL: American Library Association.

Wynar, B.S. (1967). Reference theory: Situation hopeless but not impossible. *College & Research Libraries, 28*(5), 337–342.

**2**

# Search techniques

## Introduction

### Scope

Search techniques are methods, heuristics, tactics, strategies, or plans that can be used by people in searching in manual or automated information systems. This chapter examines search techniques from a psychological point of view. It is the subjective experience of the human being who is doing the searching that is of interest—how a person thinks about and carries out information searching.

Because this is the first *ARIST (Annual Review of Information Science and Technology)* chapter solely on this topic, coverage goes back indefinitely, with emphasis on the period 1976-1980. Coverage is international and includes non-English materials.

Ironically, this topic is difficult to research because "searching" often covers all aspects of bibliographic searching, not just techniques, and narrower terms such as "search techniques" or "search theory" are not well established and generally used. Further, large areas of information science research that are not directly concerned with searching may nonetheless have implications for search techniques. The design of an information retrieval system, for example, determines in many respects what searching methods are possible on that system. This author chose to cover items that: 1) were retrieved by the literature search on "searching," "search techniques," and related terms, 2) were comparatively less likely to

*First published as* Bates, M. J. (1981). Search techniques. *Annual Review of Information Science and Technology, 16*, 139-169.

be covered in other chapters of this volume, and 3) proved to be strongly concerned with search techniques per se.

This chapter does not cover the following topics because they would extend coverage too much or because this reviewer is not qualified to evaluate them or both:

- Searching procedures in internal computer file organization. Search optimization by people at the online interface is considered at length but not the internal programming design necessary to produce the system with which the user interacts.

- Chemical searching. For a start in this area, see Antony (1979), Maizell (1979), and Rush (1978).

- Searching techniques for specific databases or specific online search systems. While often ephemeral, the information provided in articles on these topics is nonetheless of considerable practical use. It is excluded because "search techniques," as a research area of information science, should be generated from principles and research results of general applicability. The excellent bibliographies by Hall & Dewe (1980) and Hawkins (1980) include many references to articles on databases and online search systems.

- The reference (or pre-search) interview. Two extensive annotated bibliographies appeared in 1979 on this topic (Crouch, 1979; Norman, 1979).

## Domain

This section is included to illustrate a technique in the presentation of reviews and bibliographies that may be of great value to the searcher who subsequently uses that review or bibliography. The "scope" of a review (previous section) is the conceptual territory covered, whereas the "domain" is the bibliographical territory—i.e., the bibliographic sources searched to identify materials to review. Traditionally, the scope is well defined, while the domain is not mentioned at all.

However, a person who is doing a thorough search on a topic generally uses several bibliographic sources. A reader of this review, for example, who is researching "search techniques," may plan to look up the topic in other sources as well, such as *Information Science Abstracts* and *Library Literature.* If that reader is informed, through a domain statement, of the sources searched by this reviewer, then he or she will not have to duplicate the searching already done for this chapter. The reader who sees below that the past four years of *Information Science Abstracts* have been searched under the heading "Searching, search strategy, retrieval" then knows that it would be a waste of time in most instances to search those volumes under that topic again. Only when the scope of the person's interest is significantly different from that defined above—e.g., internal computer searching rather than human searching—is it worthwhile to go to sources that have already been covered. Thus, the searcher who is given both the scope and domain of a review or bibliography can design an efficient search strategy. This approach is elaborated by Bates (1976).

Described below is the domain—i.e., the sources, terms, and dates of coverage of the search—for this chapter:

- *Library Literature*, 1970-1980. Bibliography—Teaching; Computer-stored bibliographic data (1976-1980 only); Information storage and retrieval; Instruction in library use (1976-1980 only); Reference librarians; Reference services; Research and the library; Research techniques; Searching, Bibliographical; Searching, Computer; Use studies (1976-1980 only).

- *Information Science Abstracts*, 1976-1979. (1980 issues not published at time of search.) Sec. 1.1: Conferences, publications, bibliographies (1977-1979 only); Sec. 5.8: Searching, search strategy, retrieval.

- *Library and Information Science Abstracts*, 1975-1980. Reference work (1978-1980 only); Searching (1978-1980 only); Strategies.

- *Resources in Education*, 1976-Jan. 1981, and *Current Index to Journals in Education*, 1976-Feb. 1981. [Both sources are online in the ERIC (Educational Resources Information Center) database.] Information retrieval; Information seeking; Library reference services (through July 1980); Reference services (Aug. 1980+); Search strategies.

- *Government Reports Announcements & Index*, 1970-Nov. 21, 1980 (Issue 24 of 1980). [The online form of this resource is the NTIS (National Technical Information Service) database.] All terms beginning with "Search" or "Searching."

- *Dissertation Abstracts International*, 1861-Jan. 1981. Searched in subject indexes through 1978 under terms: Information (1973-1978 only); Reference; Retrieval (1973-1978 only); Search;

Searching; Seeking; Strategy. For 1979–Jan. 1981 scanned all dissertations under "Information Science" and "Library Science."

- *Business Periodicals Index,* July 1969–July 1980. Search theory.

- *Books in Print 1979–1980,* and *Books in Print Supplement 1979–1980.* Information science; Information services; Information storage and retrieval systems; Library science; Library science—Data processing; Reference services (Libraries); Searching, Bibliographical.

In addition, the extensive bibliographies by Hall and Dewe (1980), Hawkins (1980), and Murfin and Wynar (1977) were also searched and found helpful. The University of Washington shelf list catalog was searched; the useful Library of Congress (LC) classification numbers for this topic are Z699, Z699.3, Z711, and Z711.2. *Engineering Index* (COMPENDEX online) and *Computer and Control Abstracts* (INSPEC online, i.e., Information Services in Physics, Electrotechnology, Computers and Control) covered some information science literature on this topic but did not add to what was picked up in other sources. *Psychological Abstracts, Communication Abstracts,* and *Ergonomics Abstracts,* which might be expected to be helpful, were unproductive. Due to the time lag in the coverage of abstracting and indexing services, major information science journals that cover search techniques were scanned for relevant articles through 1980.

## Definitions

Because of its rapid development, the area of search techniques is plagued by vague terminology. The term "search strategy," in particular, is used with several meanings. Some definitions are proposed below.

Search mechanics  The methods or operations by which a database or service is accessed and a search is performed—i.e., the "how-to." This term includes the means of logging on and off a database, explanation of commands, and the mechanics of Boolean logic. For example, an article that explains the meaning of *OR, AND,* and *NOT* in a search statement and shows how to use them in searching would call this material "search mechanics" not "search strategy."

Search formulation  A search statement or series of statements expressing the search topic of a request. Working out an effective series of search statements for a particular topic can be difficult, and some searchers have consequently published their "search strategy" for a particular topic. It is suggested here that the term "search formulation" be used instead and that the term "search strategy" be reserved for the meaning below.

Search strategy  An approach to or plan for a whole search. A search strategy is used to inform or to determine specific search formulation decisions; it operates at a level above term choice and command use. For example, the "building-block" approach of Charles Bourne (Markey & Atherton, 1978) is a strategy. First, one combines with a Boolean OR the variant terms for each conceptual element of the request and enters each "building block" as a separate search statement. Then one combines all the resulting sets, using the AND operator, into a single master search statement. This strategy contrasts with Bourne's "citation pearl-growing" strategy, in which one combines and searches on a few specific terms immediately to retrieve citations that are then examined for candidate search terms to be added to the subsequent search formulation. These strategies can be understood and used independently of particular search topics.

Search formulation and search profile  The general meaning of profile is an outline or a biographical sketch of a person. This usage has been adapted in selective dissemination of information (SDI) systems to refer to a set of terms (or search statements) that describe the subject interests of a person who subscribes to an SDI service. The profile is run against records of newly arrived documents, and citations that match the user's interests are sent to him or her.

"Search profile" is also sometimes used in the sense of "search formulation"—i.e., a search statement or series of statements expressing a search topic. It is suggested here that these two phrases retain their distinct meanings—i.e., use "search profile" only to describe a person's interests, and use "search formulation" to describe those statements that express a search topic. Not only does this distinction keep the meaning of profile closer to its original English use, it also makes it possible to discuss any differences in techniques involved in the development of search profiles (of people) as distinct from search formulations (for specific search queries).

## Prologue: Is there any need to improve search techniques?

In a study published by Thomas Childers in 1971 (Crowley & Childers), 25 New Jersey public libraries were each asked 26 reference questions over a period of three months. The questions were posed unobtrusively by anonymous callers. The librarians' responses indicated that even when they thought that something was unusual, they did not suspect that a study was being conducted. The questions were not difficult—e.g., "What does the phrase 'gnomes of Zurich' refer to?"

Of all questions asked, just 55% were answered correctly. Excluding those times when a librarian did not attempt to answer a question, 64% of the responses were correct. In other words, more than one out of every three answers was wrong. Similarly poor results were obtained in a large study for the Chicago Public Library by Martin (1969), and in a recent small study by House (1974).

Childers (1980) repeated this approach recently in an even larger study for the Long Island public libraries. When answers were provided, 84% (compared with 64% above) were correct. However, these librarians frequently either failed to find an answer or referred the patron to another library or agency. An actual answer to the question was provided only 56% of the time (1980, p. 926). Since 84% of these were correct, the probability of the patron's receiving a direct (not referred) and correct answer to a question was just 47% (reviewer's computation).

The situation is similar with online searching. Since most online searching is done for bibliographic work, the objective is usually not a correct answer but an adequate set of citations. Fenichel (1980c), in summarizing the results of several studies of online searching, concluded that 1) there is considerable room for improvement in the searching of many experienced searchers; 2) for both experienced and inexperienced searchers the major problems were with search strategy, not search mechanics (in these conclusions Fenichel does not distinguish between search formulation and search strategy); and 3) a "substantial group" of experienced searchers performs simple searches and makes little use of the interactive capabilities of online systems (p. 123).

In addition, in her own study, Fenichel (1980b) found that the experienced online searchers were generally quite satisfied with their performance despite the fact that their own average recall score was 51% (1980, p. 60). There seems to be a strong need to improve training in search techniques for librarians and information specialists.

## Machine enhancement of human searching

In 1974 Jahoda concluded that it would be very difficult, if not impossible, to automate the processes involved in question analysis and search strategy development by reference librarians. His conclusion still holds in that most of the work reported in this section does not try to replace the central cognitive processes involved in information searching—i.e., the analysis of the question, the design of overall strategy, and the choice of information source(s) and acceptable search term(s). Most of the systems described here aid or augment the searcher's effort or simplify the searcher's work by masking multisystem complexities with an apparently simple, single system. However, some of these systems are beginning to move in on those cognitive processes. Jahoda's prediction may yet be disproved, and sooner than might have been thought.

Every automated information retrieval system can be seen as a machine enhancement of human searching. The discussion here is limited to systems that emphasize the "front end," that is, those systems that put new capabilities or search aids into the hands of the searcher.

One type of automated aid helps the searcher select a database or a manual information source. In 1968 Weil described an automated system that would suggest the titles of biographical reference books to those who were seeking biographical information. Shortly thereafter, Meredith (1971) described a system for the instruction of library school students called REFSEARCH. A student would enter a reference query, and the system would produce a list of sources that would be likely to contain the answer. Both systems worked by categorizing reference sources according to various aspects of their coverage and matching those aspects with corresponding elements in the query.

More recently, Bivins and Palmer (1979, 1980) described a prototype system called REFLES (Reference Librarian Enhancement System), which stores two types of information: 1) ephemeral information that cannot be found in reference sources, and 2) information about new and/or particularly useful reference sources. Librarians provide the information for the files and then access it using index terms that they develop and alter themselves.

Automated systems to help searchers select databases have been developed by Williams and Preece (1977) and by Marcus (1980). The system of Williams and Preece, called Data Base Selector (DBS), ranks databases by the number of postings they have to a requester's search terms, applies various weighting factors (time, breadth of indexing, relative frequency of terms etc.), and then produces a ranked list of the databases with values to distinguish distance between ranks. The system by Marcus, part of CONIT (Connector for Networked Information Transfer), takes the natural language phrasing of the requester and does a keyword/stem search on the phrase in a multidisciplinary database. Classification codes found in the retrieved documents are then matched with a classification of databases to produce a ranked list of relevant databases.

Several systems have been developed to ease vocabulary selection and use in searching. Robert Niehoff and his colleagues (Niehoff, 1980; Niehoff &

Kwasny, 1979; Niehoff et al., 1979) have developed VSS (Vocabulary Switching System), in which the user enters a term and receives a list of corresponding and related terms in several databases. Several different types of switching can be used. Examples are exact matching and stem phrase switching (stem each word in the candidate term, then use the stemmed phrase to access the stem phrase file). VSS is fully operational but still experimental. Switching can be done among six vocabularies (Niehoff, 1980).

Doszkocs (1978) has developed a system that uses statistical association to identify and to display terms related to those in the searcher's query. The system, known as AID (Associative Interactive Dictionary), has been implemented in the TOXLINE database of NLM. It is fully operational and requires less computer processing space than earlier experimental systems using statistical association.

Drabek et al. (1978) have developed and pilot tested an online interactive system, called Query Analysis System, to aid sociology students in identifying search terms and bibliographic resources for their research. The student enters a term and gets back lists of other terms that are hierarchically above or below the entered term, as well as a list of relevant bibliographic sources. Drabek et al. developed a hierarchical list of sociology terms to create the system.

These systems provide assistance in one or two aspects of the search process. The systems described next simplify the searcher's task in broader ways. The database selection capability of CONIT described above is just one part of this system. Marcus and Reintjes (1979) and Marcus (1980) describe CONIT and its recent additions, respectively. CONIT is a computer interface, a "virtual" system, designed so that the searcher uses a single, simple command language although he or she is actually searching on three heterogeneous vendor systems, ORBIT, DIALOG, and MEDLINE. It also has a keyword/stem searching capability so that the naive user can enter a natural language term and have the system do more sophisticated searching than the user realizes, even on a controlled vocabulary if the stem matches. Author searches can also be made in a common format, thus eliminating concern about different punctuation rules on different databases. End users without professional training have achieved accept-able—but not yet optimal—results on CONIT.

Williams and Preece (1980; 1981), and Preece and Williams (1980) describe their design for a Total Transparent Information Retrieval System (TTIRS). They designed a generalized model of what such a system should look like and then implemented a "minitransparent" system on a microcom-puter. The full system would contain "transparency aids" of various sorts, including automatic selectors for databases, communications network, and vendor. The minitransparent system, known as The Searcher's Workbench (TSW), can access Williams's and Preece's own DBS as well as VSS. TSW also enables the searcher to search several systems without knowing the specifics of any one system. Most entry is accomplished by touching points on the display, so the user seldom has to look away from the screen.

The Individualized Instruction for Data Access (IIDA) system has been developed by Charles Meadow and his colleagues (Drexel University & Franklin Institute, 1980; Landsberg et al., 1980; Meadow, 1979; Meadow & Epstein, 1977; Meadow et al., 1977; Meadow et al., 1978) to perform two functions: 1) to train new searchers and 2) to aid trained searchers as they go along in a search. The second function, the assistance mode, is of greater interest here. The program monitors searcher behavior and sends error messages and advice as needed. For example, the searcher may get a message if commands are repeated too often or if "thrashing" is observed. Thrashing occurs when the user shifts search objectives so rapidly that a particular line of reasoning cannot be completed (Meadow, 1979). The searcher can also call up a menu of "help" options, which provide various kinds of useful information. (See the chapter by Elaine Caruso in this volume for further discussion.)

Search aids similar to those described above are also being developed commercially. These systems are not described here, but organizations developing them are the Franklin Institute (Philadelphia, PA), Computer Corporation of America (Cambridge, MA), and Williams and Nevin, Ltd. (Manchester, England).

Finally, efforts are proceeding to develop information retrieval systems of such sophistication that the user can enter a query in natural language without concern for search term selection or Boolean combination. Examples of this effort are the CITE (Current Information Transfer in English) system by Doszkocs and Rapp (1979), and the THOMAS program by Oddy (1977a; 1977b). In conventional online systems the searcher manipulates the search formulation through several iterations, but in these systems the user provides relevance feedback only, and the system manipulates the formulation, in effect, for the user. By various means the search is expanded automatically to synonymous or related terms—i.e., the searcher does not have to provide the related terms. A prototype of CITE has been implemented on NLM's MEDLINE database. The THOMAS program is still experimental.

Oddy and N. Belkin are planning to develop THOMAS further, drawing on Belkin's concept of an information need as an anomalous state of knowledge, or "ASK" (Belkin & Oddy, 1979). They argue that, in general, the user is unable to specify precisely what is needed to resolve that anomalous state and, therefore, for information retrieval, the user should be asked to describe the ASK, rather than to specify the information need in a conventional query. (See also Belkin, 1980, and Belkin et al., 1979.)

## Physical search

However one may think of an information search strategically, it is also a physical act, particularly in manual systems. One moves along shelves, and through files; one searches for a single item among many, which are physically arranged according to some principle. How can this effort be minimized for the desired results?

Physical search has long been of interest to the armed forces, especially the Navy, because of the need to find downed flyers or enemy vessels. There is a long tradition of mathematical work on search and reconnaissance theory, both in the military and in operations research. Here, only introductory and bibliographic sources are discussed for the work outside of information science.

Early military and operations research materials on search and reconnaissance theory are covered in a 1966 bibliography with abstracts compiled by Enslow (1966). The 239-page bibliography published in 1979 with abstracts by Kenton (1979) updates coverage on maritime and aviation search and rescue. An old but excellent survey of the literature on physical search is provided by Moore (1970). The review begins with a chart of the various searching categories. For example, in one-sided searches the "distribution of the target is known to the searcher" (p. 11), and the target can be stationary or moving. In two-sided searches there is a conscious evader. Presumably, one-sided stationary-target searches are of most interest to us. Moore (1970) reviews the literature category by category. Morse (1974) provides a somewhat briefer but more recent and less mathematical review of the search literature for public safety experts. The review includes visual scanning of an area.

One would expect this literature to provide a rich resource for the development of physical search theory in information science. Unfortunately, except for the now-aging work by Morse and Leimkuhler (1972; discussed below) and a couple of tangential articles by Donald Kraft (1979), a student of Leimkuhler's, this leap does not seem to have been made. Since this reviewer's knowledge of mathematics is not sufficient to enable a critical evaluation of their work, material found is simply mentioned.

Both Leimkuhler (1968) and Morse (1972) deal with the optimal ordering of items in a file to facilitate efficient search. Morse is also concerned with the application of search theory to the browsing of files (Morse, 1970a; 1970b; 1973). Kraft continues an operations research approach to searching, but the interest is only marginally in physical search (Deutsch & Kraft, 1974; Kraft & Lee, 1979).

Aside from Morse's work, studies on browsing appear to be almost nonexistent. The intriguing proposal made by Licklider in the 1965 INTREX (Information Transfer Experiments) conference to compare several "browseries" was never carried out as far as can be determined. Each browsery was to be organized along different lines, and the study was to determine which mode of organization led to greatest browsing satisfaction and the most serendipitous discoveries of useful information.

Browsing *capabilities* have been built into automated systems, but the problem of how to *optimize* productive browsing in automated and manual systems apparently remains untested. It might be argued that as manual systems are replaced by automated ones and the physical location of an item becomes less important, the study of browsing becomes unnecessary. Nevertheless, the human being who interacts with the system remains the same, whether the system is manual or automated. Many years ago Miller (1968) noted that physical location is a very important mental organizing principle for human beings. He argued that information scientists should take advantage of this in designing information systems, especially computer systems where a sense of spatiality is easily lost. A recent effort to use this human characteristic is a "spatial data management system" described by Bolt (1978). It creates a "virtual spatial world . . . over which the user helicopters via joystick control" (abstract). Since it is expensive to develop browsing capabilities in automated systems, it seems worthwhile to divert some of those expenditures to determining the browsing needs and preferences of the human beings who will use the systems.

In related work, Greene (1977) found that fewer references located through browsing were as useful as those found in other ways. He concludes that browsing is not as valuable as usually claimed and suggests that the tradition of open-stack access in American libraries be reevaluated. However, browsing is usually a supplementary technique, not a primary one. The question is not whether it works as well as other techniques but whether it locates references that would not be retrieved in other ways. The issue of open and closed stacks has also been studied by Goldhor (1972), Hyman (1971; 1972), and Shill (1980).

A final topic in physical search is sign systems. A coherent system of signs in libraries is being recognized as an essential ingredient in facilitating end user searches. Pollet and Haskell (1979) edited what may be the definitive work on library sign systems. Psychological and human factors research is presented, as well as extensive information on the planning and design of library sign systems (see also Pollet, 1976). An extensive review by Spencer and Reynolds (1977) evaluates research, theory, and practice on every aspect of sign use in libraries and museums.

## The psychology of searching

Psychological aspects of searching deal with how people do think and should think in the process of searching. Drawing on *The Inner Game of Tennis* by Gallwey (1974), Wagers (1980) deals with, as it were, the Zen of information work. He suggests ways in which reference librarians can establish a state of mind that will enable them to get past psychological blocks to creative problem solving and to perform better as searchers.

Similarly, Bates (1979a) deals with the searcher who is stumped and unsure of how to proceed. She suggests "idea tactics," that is, mental devices to generate new ideas or solutions to problems in searching. For example, the tactic BREACH is "To breach the boundaries of one's region of search, to revise one's concept of the limits of the intellectual or physical territory in which one searches to respond to a query" (1979a, p. 282). This tactic deals with the situation in which a person cannot think of any more sources to search because of assumptions about limits to the search domain. Confronted initially with thousands of possible resources, one usually narrows a search to certain types of sources or locations. If the sources in that domain have been exhausted and the answer still is not found, the searcher who uses BREACH will remind himself or herself that there may be productive resources outside the initially defined domain.

Blair (1980) sets forth an intriguing analysis of searcher biases in online searching. He defines a "futility point criterion" (FPC)—i.e., the maximum size of retrieved set that the searcher is willing to examine to find a desired item—and a "prediction criterion" (PC)—i.e., a criterion that the term(s) searched under actually index the document of interest. The search has to meet both criteria for the searcher to be satisfied. However, online search formulations frequently yield postings sets that exceed the FPC, so the searcher must often satisfy the FPC first before the retrieved set can be examined to determine if the PC is satisfied. Blair is interested in what the searcher does and should do to meet the FPC and to optimize the chances of then meeting the PC.

He draws on the research of two psychologists, A. Tversky and D. Kahneman, to suggest that searchers may show systematic biases in search modification. Specifically, they may "anchor" to initial search terms and to the initial ordering of terms in the search formulation; that is, they may be reluctant to drop initial terms or to try them in the various combinatorial subsets that are possible. For example, there are 15 combinations—not permutations—of one or more terms in a set of four terms. Thus, when they revise their searches to meet the FPC, they may drop or replace only the terms added last and may not exploit all the possible combinatorial subsets of the terms that they have entered. He suggests that these subsets, with associated postings, be generated automatically by the system to make it easier for the searcher to evaluate all the possible results in the search term set. Blair's paper is a valuable contribution to the study of psychological factors in online searching. The next step is empirical testing to determine whether people do behave in this way and whether the combinatorial approach is helpful.

Although old, the study by Carlson (1964), which observed three librarians doing bibliographic searching, remains one of the most productive on the psychological factors involved in searching. He noticed, for example, that the librarians would say they would return and check out a discrepancy, but they never did unless they wrote it down (1964, p. 30).

Thorough and intriguing observations of manual searching are being done in Denmark by several researchers. Pejtersen (1979) studied 134 user-librarian conversations to determine the strategies used to help patrons find fiction materials. She identified five characteristic patterns of search. The most intriguing is what she calls an "empirical search strategy." In this pattern the librarian mentally stereotypes users and suggests similar materials to everyone in a given category. For example, "middle-aged women are repeatedly offered the same set of authors" (1979, p. 115). Contrast this approach to an "analytical search strategy," in which the librarian analyzes and tailors the assistance to the need stated by the user.

Ingwersen and Kaae (1979) present the most sophisticated model this reviewer has seen of what they call "the public library communication system from a cognitive viewpoint" (1979, p. 75). This model includes not only document generator, librarian, user, and document but also the document representation and the mental "images" or representations of the information and information need that the various players have in their minds. Ingwersen and Kaae then illustrate and discuss their detailed transcription and analysis of "thinking-aloud" protocols taken from 20 librarians and non-librarians. (In other words, the searchers said out loud what they were thinking while they were searching, and the researchers recorded and analyzed these data.) Independent searches by librarians and by users as well as user-librarian negotiation were studied. [See also Ingwersen et al. (1977; 1980). The most recent data appear in Ingwersen &

Kaae, 1979.] Other studies of manual searching have been done by Keen (1977) and by Johnson (1978).

The psychology of online searching was investigated by Standera (1978). After questioning experienced searchers, he identified 17 phases of the online search and the pressure points along it. The points of highest pressure, interestingly, were strategy design and modification. Other studies of online searcher thinking and behavior have been done by Mallen (1977) and Smetana (1974).

## Research with implications for search techniques

### Searching in general

An outstanding review of "The Process of Searching Online Bibliographic Databases" was published by Fenichel (1980c). She covers all types of research on online bibliographic searching: theory, case studies, experiments, and questionnaire and interview surveys. She discusses individual studies and summarizes major results across several studies. Some of these results are discussed above.

Buckland (1979) suggests that the dominant patterns of search in academic, special, and public libraries can be characterized, respectively, as high document specificity, high information specificity, and low document and information specificity. According to Buckland, these different patterns suggest different emphases in each type of library in collection development and access devices such as catalogs.

### Online strategies

The heart of a chapter on search techniques should be the section that describes research done to compare different strategies for their cost and productivity under different circumstances. Not a single study doing just that was found. Those discussed here deal with aspects of online search techniques but not with strategy comparison.

In a study published in 1977 by Oldroyd and Citroen, 20 searchers from eight European countries searched the same two queries on ESA (European Space Agency) RECON (similar to Lockheed's DIALOG—this system is now known as ESA-IRS). The authors then examined the records of the searches to identify search patterns. Two results are striking: 1) searchers used two strategies predominantly; these resemble Bourne's citation pearl-growing and building-block strategies (described in the Definitions section of this chapter); 2) searchers showed various poor searching techniques, such as a "tendency to lose sight of the basic logic" (1977, p. 308), and inadequate attention to vocabulary and other differences among databases.

Fenichel (1980a; 1980b; 1981) looked at the relationship between experience and performance of online searchers. Novices did surprisingly well, but experienced searchers often searched very simply—in half of their searches they did not modify their initial strategy.

## Controlled vocabulary vs. free text

In online searching studies much attention has been given to when and whether to search on controlled vocabulary or free text. In free-text searching one searches on terms or phrases that appear in the text of the record, as in the title and the abstract. In controlled vocabulary searching, one searches on the descriptors and identifiers that are assigned to each record by the database compilers.

Atherton and Markey (1979) review several studies on this question (1979, p. 62–71), and Rosson and Atherton (1979) provide an annotated bibliography. In the review by Atherton and Markey, specific combinations of elements searched on (e.g., controlled vocabulary, titles, abstracts, etc.) vary from study to study, and so comparison is difficult. All in all, the results are so mixed that simple conclusions cannot be drawn. The reader is referred to the above review and bibliography for details of studies as well as to the subsequently published articles by Markey et al. (1980) and Calkins (1980).

## Manual vs. online searching

Another choice in searching strategy is whether to search manually or online. The comparison is usually viewed in terms of cost-effectiveness—i.e., which technique is cheaper for which types of searches. However, for search strategy it is more important to determine which type of search yields optimal retrieval.

Two recent studies provide excellent discussions of this question. Johnston (1978) and Johnston and Gray (1977) report one study in which 75 searches on agricultural topics were processed both manually and online on several databases (and their corresponding manual sources), including CAIN (Cataloging and Indexing system of the U.S. National Agricultural Library, now called AGRICOLA), BIOSIS Previews (BioSciences Information Service of Biological Abstracts), Chemical Abstracts Condensates, and MEDLINE. Johnston lists 12 questions one should ask in determining which way to search. Generally, the coordination capability of online searching is its strong point, while the strength of manual searching is the ability of the searcher to interpret the applicability of candidate references to the query, particularly in cases of ambiguous terminology. In a similar study of 40 parallel searches on seven databases and their manual equivalents, Elchesen (1978) concludes that manual searches are better for extremely broad or extremely specific topics. Finally, Dolan (1979b), in a helpful-hints article, describes types of online searches to avoid.

## Bibliographic and citation index searching

Both Ayres et al. (1968) and Tagliacozzo et al. (1970) found that users who approach a catalog have fully correct title information more often than fully correct author information. In the former study the figure is 90% to 75%; in the latter, it is 70% to 42%. Further, Ortiz and Connole (1973) found that searching on the "main entry" (a cataloging term for principal, or master record, usually author) is about 90% slower than searching by title.

These studies strongly suggest that a basic technique of bibliographic (vs. subject) searching should be to search on title first, at least in manual catalogs. However, the cataloging rules in effect until 1967 called for title (added) entries only some of the time; it is only since 1967 that virtually all books are cataloged under both author and title (see also Hinkley, 1968). But, the preferability of title searching on post-1967 books seems clearly indicated, against the conventional author bias.

Some of the above research was done in connection with efforts to speed up technical processes (i.e., acquisitions and cataloging) in libraries, including the search and verification process associated with book purchasing. In a related study, McCormick et al. (1979) wanted to see if online databases could be used to verify the accuracy (for publication purposes) of the citations provided by authors of scientific manuscripts. After looking up a sample of citations from the published fisheries literature, they concluded that online databases could be used to supplement (but not supplant) manual sources and were accurate enough to be used for verification. However, the 67 differences found (some quite minor) between initial citation and database citation in 112 matches calls into question the appropriateness of online databases for at least some kinds of verification.

Cummings and Fox (1973) compared two methods of citation searching in a mathematical analysis of a "pseudo-random case." The first strategy is to generate additional citations by searching a citation index to determine who cites the items in the starting document's bibliography. The second strategy is to generate references by looking in the bibliographies of documents that cite the starting document. For reasonably sized bibliographies (greater than seven items) the latter strategy generates more citations.

## Reference work

Gerald Jahoda has studied the reference/searching process extensively and has developed instructional packages on this topic for library and information science students. In Jahoda (1977) and Jahoda et al. (1977) he presents six modules for instruction that correspond to six major decision points in the process of answering reference questions. He identified and refined those stages by having 23 scientific and technical reference librarians check them out during 20 searches (Jahoda, 1977). The steps are: 1) message selection; 2) selection of types of answer-providing tools; 3) selection of specific answer-providing tools; 4) selection of access points in titles; 5) selection of answer; and 6) query negotiation/renegotiation.

De Figueiredo (1975), a student of Jahoda, developed a typology of errors that can be made at each of Jahoda's stages in the search process. She suggests actions to prevent these errors by individual librarians, library administrators, and library schools.

Powell (1978) found a direct correlation between the percent of correct answers given to test questions by each of a group of 51 librarians and the size of their public library reference collections. Other analyses of his data showed other variables that are strongly related to reference performance—viz., number of reference questions received by each librarian in an average week and number of reference and bibliography courses completed by each. Thus, it appears that available resources, experience, and training all contribute to successful performance by searchers.

## Search heuristics

This section focuses on the literature that gives aids or "tips" to help the information specialist, i.e., intermediary, search more effectively or efficiently. All textbook materials are discussed in the next section, and instructional or heuristic articles are covered here.

Several articles recommend a series of steps in conducting a search. The oldest item mentioned in this chapter is "Technique of Library Searching," published in 1936 by Alexander. It is surprisingly, one might even say dismayingly, similar to a number of articles on the search process published in the ensuing 45 years. Although newer models vary in details, one would be hard put to say that Alexander's model is inferior or less developed than those published since his. His six steps (which include substeps by type of question) are: 1) identify the question precisely; 2) decide what type of material is most likely to have the answer; 3) array sources within that type in the order of likelihood of containing the answer; 4) locate the chosen items; 5) search the items in their order of likelihood; 6) if the answer is not found, retrace the previous steps.

The most notable innovation in modeling the search process since Alexander seems to be flowcharting, which received a burst of interest in the late 1960s and early 1970s. Eight flowchart models are reproduced by Katz (1974, Vol. II). He collected several models from the literature and reproduced other models that were gathered by Jahoda and Olson (1972). Some are eight- or ten-step models of the whole reference process (including, for example, the reference interview); others, such as those of Bunge (1967) and Stych (1966), go into more detail on the search itself. Bunge's three-page flowchart contains more than 50 decision boxes and operation boxes. The decision boxes include such questions as "Should I consult catalog?" and "Is answer likely to be in magazines?" Stych's model is similarly detailed and sometimes mentions specific titles for the searcher to consider. In addition, a descriptive flowchart model appears in Carlson (1964), and prescriptive models appear in Burkhardt (1971) and Martinson (1970; 1972).

More recently, flowchart models have appeared for online searching. Dolan (1979a) flowcharts the formulation of the search before going online; Morrow (1976) models the online phase of the search. Morrow's model is intended for searching on ORBIT but is also useful as a prototype for bibliographic searching on other systems. The suggested sequences for narrowing and broadening searches are particularly useful.

To say that the most notable innovation in 45 years of modeling the search process is flowcharting is to say little. On the whole, these models are disappointing. Modeling certainly seems to be a logical and necessary first step in understanding the search process, but now that this has been done, what has been gained? Do we really understand how top-flight searchers get their results, how best to teach fledgling information specialists, or how to design a machine to search for us? Cumulatively, the work so far constitutes a bare beginning.

The nature and usefulness of these models may be analyzed more easily by considering the four types of searching models categorized by Bates (1979b): 1) models for idealizing searching (ideal search patterns based on mathematical, system analytic, or other formal criteria of optimality);

2) models for representing searching (descriptions of actual human search behavior); 3) models for teaching searching; and 4) models for facilitating searching (helping the searcher during the process).

Benson and Maloney (1975) provide a model in which the principle of matching between the query and the system is paramount. One analyzes the query and then builds a "bibliographic bridge" to the information system by identifying the sources to be searched and translating the query into the language of the system.

Bates (1979b) takes a different tack in "Information Search Tactics." Instead of prescribing a sequence of actions, she proposes 29 different "tactics." A tactic is a move made to further a search. It can be used at any point in a manual or online search that seems appropriate. Each tactic has a mnemonically brief and striking name. The tactics are intended primarily to be facilitative and secondarily for teaching. For example, the tactic TRACE means to use information already found to derive additional search terms. One might use TRACE by looking for terms in the tracings on a catalog card or in the descriptor lists appended to citations printed out in an online search.

Kennington (1977) deals with the need for government and industry librarians to scan their environments for the information that they will need to support the decision-making of their organizations. He suggests four "modes of scanning": 1) undirected viewing, 2) conditioned viewing, 3) informal search, and 4) formal search (1977, pp. 266–267). Robbin (1977) addresses the situation in which a client of a special library wishes to locate data for research purposes. Assuming that the library does not own the data, she describes, in a six-page list of steps, the "pre-acquisition process" to use in locating the data. Other articles that give advice or hints for searching in general or manually are those by Beltran (1971), Josel (1971), Machurina (1970), Stych (1967, 1972), and Voress (1963).

Turning now to articles that deal solely with online searching, advice appears regularly in four journal columns: 1) "Offlines" by Donna Dolan, (n.d.) in *Database;* 2) "Computer Ease" by Mary Ellen Padin (n.d.) in *Online;* 3) "I Learned about Searching from That. . ." (n.d.) also in *Online;* and 4) "Search Corner" (n.d.) in *Online Review.*

Along with the explosive growth in the use of online systems, there has been a burst of articles providing heuristics for online searching. Adams (1979), Donati (1978), Knox and Hlava (1979), and Marshall (1980) give advice (with some overlap in content) for optimizing online searching. Their advice is essential to effective use of current systems; in any but the simplest cases, a searcher who does not know these techniques will do a poor job. As in-depth online training becomes more standardized and universal, such articles will increasingly be supplanted by textbooks and courses in online searching (see next section).

Although many articles present sample searches, the examples of Adams (1979) illustrate the preparation and revision of search formulations particularly well. His discussion of techniques for broadening and narrowing searches points to an area that needs research. For example, if a search statement returns too many postings, what is the best way to narrow the search with minimal loss of relevant citations? The techniques that Adams mentions need to be tested and compared in a controlled study.

Smith (1976) suggests Venn diagramming (that is, the use of intersecting circles or rectangles to provide a physical representation of Boolean combinations) to help both searcher and patron understand and formulate the search. Martinez and Zarember (1978) propose the use of the ordinarily disregarded Boolean operator *OR NOT* in certain specified cases. This counterintuitive proposal does seem to be appropriate and useful in certain narrowly defined situations, but it is not for the neophyte searcher.

Considerable interest has been shown in the searching of multiple databases. Wanger (1977) discusses how to select databases for searching, Conger (1980) notes some of the differences among nine vendor systems, and Hawkins (1978) gives an introduction to techniques of multiple database searching, with emphasis on the natural sciences. Epstein and Angier (1980) and Angier and Epstein (1980) concentrate on the behavioral sciences in two of the most thorough articles encountered on online searching. They go into great detail on the character of various behavioral science databases and provide examples of multiple database searches.

In contrast to this enthusiasm for multiple database searches, J. E. Evans (1980) argues that in most cases only one database is needed. Searchers in his academic library switched from doing only 10% of their searches in a single database to 94%. User satisfaction, based on a "crude sampling," remained high. Hawkins (1978), on the other hand, reports high use of and high user satisfaction with multiple database searches in special libraries. Different payment procedures and library type may be responsible for these different views.

Finally, Stibic (1980) discusses the practical consequences for search strategy of another searching capability that may be widespread before too long: unlimited ranking (i.e., the output of document citations in ranked order of relevance to the patron's query). Once the citations that are most likely to be relevant appear at the beginning of a large postings set, the searcher can simply have printed out the first $N$ citations, confident that subsequent citations will be less relevant. In such a case, it will not be so essential to try to reduce the number of postings returned on one's search formulation.


## Texts and search questions

Online searching as a textbook topic is coming of age. Two recent texts supersede earlier ones not only in currency but also with regard to search strategy instruction. Henry et al. (1980) have extracted the common searching features available on various online systems (truncation, saving searches, etc.) and discuss them in a general way, so that the student has a sense of the variety of searching tools that are available. A five-page appendix provides "A Checklist for Search Preparation and Search Strategy." Lancaster (1979) deals with information retrieval systems (IRSs) in general and with online search systems as a subset of IRSs. His chapter "Selecting a Data Base and Searching It" is outstanding for its detailed consideration of hierarchical level, specificity, and exhaustivity in formulating a search. These elements can have considerable impact on the effectiveness of retrieval and are often neglected or misunderstood.

This chapter has excluded materials on individual databases, but an exception is made here to discuss *ONTAP*, the Online Training and Practice manual for searching the ERIC database. Charles Bourne originally developed this material, but it remained unpublished until Markey and Atherton (1978) made it available, with full credit to Bourne. It is an excellent manual and is valuable for searchers on essentially any database. It contains full descriptions of Bourne's five searching strategies: 1) building-block, 2) citation pearl-growing, 3) successive fractions, 4) most specific facet first, and 5) lowest postings facet first. (The first two strategies are defined in the Definitions section of this chapter.)

Texts on reference work generally emphasize manual searching, concentrating on reference sources and/or policies of a reference service, and give short shrift to search techniques. However, three recent texts do an excellent job of providing instruction on the search process itself (Grogan, 1979; Jahoda & Braunagel, 1980; Katz, 1978). Katz's book, now in its third edition, is a two-volume basic reference text covering both reference sources and services, including searching. Grogan's text is rich with examples and practical advice while retaining the broad picture. Jahoda and Braunagel concentrate on query negotiation and searching and provide exercises for every major step of these processes. For example, the student reader practices identifying appropriate subject terms for searching a query.

Finally, Garfield (1979) explains how to do various types of searches in one kind of resource: citation indexes.

In research on and training for searching it is sometimes useful to have access to real questions. A collection of several thousand real queries and online searches has been developed for research purposes by Alina Vickery and her colleagues at the University of London (Central Information Service, Senate House, Malet Street, London, WC1E 7HU). They are hoping to put this collection into machine-readable form so that it will be more readily usable. Two books by Grogan (1967; 1972) describe case studies in reference—i.e., real reference questions and how they were solved by a librarian.

Finally, Slavens (1978) reports a series of real reference interviews and lists several hundred practice questions, some real and some invented.

## Conclusions

This chapter is the first in *ARIST* that is devoted wholly to search techniques. It is not entirely surprising, therefore, to find that this topic is at a relatively primitive stage of development. Sophisticated automated information retrieval systems are being developed that will give the searcher powerful capabilities, but we have only an elementary understanding of how the human searcher who will operate such systems does and should search.

Research is needed to compare and to test search strategies in both the manual and online environments. In online searching, testing is needed on techniques for narrowing and broadening searches and on the strategies of Bourne and others. There is apparently nothing comparable to Bourne's strategies for manual searching, and even his are for searching on a database that one has already selected. How should one select a database or manual source from among the many possible sources in the first place? Research is also needed on browsing and on the psychological processes involved in searching. Finally, and above all, we need to develop theory on the nature of the search process.

## REFERENCES

Adams, A.L. (1979). Planning search strategies for maximum retrieval from bibliographic databases. *Online Review, 3*(4), 373–379.
Alexander, C. (1936). Technique of library searching. *Special Libraries, 27*(7), 230–238.
Angier, J.J., & Epstein, B.A. (1980). Multi-database searching in the behavioral sciences. Part 2: Special applications. *Database, 3*(4), 34–40.

Antony, A. (1979). *Guide to basic information sources in chemistry*. New York, NY: Wiley.

Atherton, P., & Markey, K. (1979). Part IV: The redesign of the ERIC data base for online searching. In P. Atherton, *Online searching of ERIC: Impact of free text or controlled vocabulary searching on the design of the ERIC data base* (pp. 1–71). [Technical report]. Syracuse, NY: ERIC Clearinghouse on Information Resources.

Aubry, J.W. (1972). A timing study of the manual searching of catalogs. *The Library Quarterly, 42*(4), 399–415.

Ayres, F.H., German, J., Loukes, N., & Searle, R.H. (1968). Author versus title: A comparative survey of the accuracy of the information which the user brings to the library catalogue. *Journal of Documentation, 24*(4), 266–272.

Bates, M.J. (1976). Rigorous systematic bibliography. *RQ, 16*(1), 7–26.

Bates, M.J. (1979a). Idea tactics. *Journal of the American Society for Information Science, 30*(5), 280–289.

Bates, M.J. (1979b). Information search tactics. *Journal of the American Society for Information Science, 30*(4), 205–214.

Belkin, N.J. (1980). The problem of "matching" in information retrieval. In O. Harbo & L. Kajberg (Eds.), *Theory and application of information research: Proceedings of the 2nd International Research Forum on Information Science, Copenhagen, Denmark* (pp. 187–197). London: Mansell.

Belkin, N.J., & Oddy, R.N. (1979). *Design study for an anomalous state of knowledge based information retrieval system* (British library research and development report no. 5547). Birmingham, England: University of Aston, Computer Centre.

Belkin, N.J., Brooks, H.M., & Oddy, R.N. (1979). Representation and classification of anomalous states of knowledge and information for use in interactive information retrieval. In T. Henriksen (Ed.), *IRFIS 3: Proceedings of the 3rd International Research Forum in Information Science, Oslo, Norway* (Vol. 2, pp. 146–183). Oslo, Norway: Statens Bibliotekskole.

Beltran, A.A. (1971). The craft of literature searching. *Sci-Tech News, 25*(4), 113–116.

Benson, J., & Maloney, R.K. (1975). Principles of searching. *RQ, 14*(4), 316–320.

Bivins, K.T., & Palmer, R.C. (1979). REFLES (Reference Librarian Enhancement System). *Proceedings of the American Society for Information Science 42nd Annual Meeting, 16*, 58–65.

Bivins, K.T., & Palmer, R.C. (1980). REFLES: An individual micro-computer system for fact retrieval. *Online Review, 4*(4), 357–365.

Blair, D.C. (1980). Searching biases in large interactive document retrieval systems. *Journal of the American Society for Information Science, 31*(4), 271–277.

Bolt, R.A. (1978). *Spatial data management system*. Marine Architecture Group (NTIS: AD A070 243/1GA). Cambridge, MA: MIT Press.

Braga, M.J.F. (1974). *An introduction to search theory*. (Master's thesis). (NTIS: AD-777 878/0GA). Monterey, CA: Naval Postgraduate School.

Buckland, M.K. (1979). On types of search and the allocation of library resources. *Journal of the American Society for Information Science, 30*(3), 143–147.

Bunge, C.A. (1967). *Professional education and reference efficiency*. Springfield, IL: Illinois State Library.

Burkhardt, M. (1971). *Anwendung der systematischen heuristik bei recherchen* [Application of systematic searching techniques]. Germany: Bibliothekar.

Calkins, M.L. (1980). Free text or controlled vocabulary? A case history step-by-step analysis . . . plus other aspects of search strategy. *Database, 3*(2), 53–67.

Carlson, G. (1964). *Search strategy by reference librarians: Part 3 of the final report on the organization of large files*. Sherman Oaks, CA: Hughes Dynamics, Advanced Information Systems Division.

Childers, T. (1980). The test of reference. *Library Journal, 105*(8), 924-928.

Conger, L.D. (1980). Multiple system searching: A searcher's guide to making use of the real differences between systems. *Online, 4*(2), 10-21.

Crouch, W.W. (1979). *The information interview: A comprehensive bibliography and an analysis of the literature.* Syracuse, NY: ERIC Clearinghouse on Information Resources.

Crowley, T., & Childers, T. (1971). *Information service in public libraries: Two studies.* Metuchen, NJ: Scarecrow Press.

Cummings, L.J., & Fox, D.A. (1973). Some mathematical properties of cycling strategies using citation indexes. *Information Storage and Retrieval, 9*(12), 713-719.

De Figueiredo, N.M. (1975). *A conceptual methodology for error prevention in reference work.* (Doctoral dissertation). Florida State University, Tallahassee.

Deutsch, D.R., & Kraft, D.H. (1974). *A study of an information retrieval performance measure: Expected search length as a function of file size and organization.* Paper presented at the Annual Meeting of the Operations Society of America, Boston, MA.

Dolan, D.R. (1979a). Before you touch the terminal: Flowchart of the search formulation process. *Database, 2*(4), 86-88.

Dolan, D.R. (1979b). What databases cannot do. *Database, 2*(3), 85-87.

Dolan, D.R. (Ed.). (n.d.). Offline. *Database.* (Regular column).

Donati, R. (1978). Spanning the social sciences: Searching techniques when online. *Online, 2*(1), 41-52.

Doszkocs, T.E. (1978). AID, an associative interactive dictionary for online searching. *Online Review, 2*(2), 163-173.

Doszkocs, T.E., & Rapp, B.A. (1979). Searching Medline in English: A prototype user interface with natural language query, ranked output and relevance feedback. *Proceedings of the American Society for Information Science 42nd Annual Meeting, 16,* 131-139. White Plains, NY: Knowledge Industry Publications.

Doyle, J.M., & Grimes, G.H. (1976). *Reference resources: A systematic approach.* Metuchen, NJ: Scarecrow Press.

Drabek, T.E., Shaw, W., & Culkin, P.B. (1978). The query analysis system: A new tool for increasing the effectiveness of library utilization by sociology students. *Teaching Sociology, 6*(1), 47-68.

Drexel University School of Library and Information Science; Franklin Institute Research Laboratories. (1980). *Individualized instruction for data access (IIDA).* Philadelphia, PA: Drexel University School of Library and Information Science.

Elchesen, D.R. (1978). Cost-effectiveness comparison of manual and on-line retrospective bibliographic searching. *Journal of the American Society for Information Science, 29*(2), 56-66.

Emerson, S.V. (1975). *Problem-oriented literature searching.* (Doctoral dissertation). Case Western Reserve University, Cleveland, OH.

Enslow, P.H., Jr. (1966). A bibliography of search theory and reconnaissance theory literature. *Naval Research Logistics Quarterly, 13*(2), 177-202.

Epstein, B.A., & Angier, J.J. (1980). Multi-database searching in the behavioral sciences. Part 1: Basic techniques and core databases. *Database, 3*(3), 9-15.

Evans, J.E. (1980). Database selection in an academic library: Are those big multi-file searches really necessary? *Online, 4*(2), 35-43.

Evans, L. (1975). *Search strategy variations in SDI profiles.* London: Institution of Electrical Engineers.

Fenichel, C.H. (1980a). An examination of the relationship between searching behavior and searcher background. *Online Review, 4*(4), 341-347.

Fenichel, C.H. (1980b). Intermediary searchers' satisfaction with the results of their searches. *Proceedings of the American Society for Information Science 43rd Annual Meeting, 17,* 58-60.

Fenichel, C.H. (1980c). The process of searching online bibliographic databases: A review of research. *Library Research, 2*(2), 107–127.

Fenichel, C.H. (1981). Online searching: Measures that discriminate among users with different types of experiences. *Journal of the American Society for Information Science, 32*(1), 23–32.

Gallwey, W.T. (1974). *The inner game of tennis.* New York: Random House.

Garfield, E. (1979). *Citation indexing: Its theory and application in science, technology, and humanities.* New York: Wiley.

Giering, R.H. (1975). Search strategies and user interface. *Journal of Chemical Information and Computer Sciences, 15*(1), 6–11.

Goldhor, H. (1972). The effect of prime display location on public library circulation of selected adult titles. *The Library Quarterly, 42*(4), 371–389.

Greene, R.J. (1977). The effectiveness of browsing. *College & Research Libraries, 38*(4), 313–316.

Grogan, D.J. (1967). *Case studies in reference work.* Hamden, CT: Archon Books.

Grogan, D.J. (1972). *More case studies in reference work.* Hamden, CT: Linnet Books.

Grogan, D.J. (1979). *Practical reference work.* London: C. Bingley.

Hall, J.L, & Dewe, A. (1980). Online information retrieval, 1976–1979: An international bibliography. London: Aslib.

Hawkins, D.T. (1978). Multiple database searching: Techniques and pitfalls. *Online, 2*(2), 9–15.

Hawkins, D.T. (1980). Online information retrieval bibliography, 1964–1979. Marlton, NJ: Learned Information.

Henry, W.M., Leigh, J.A., Tedd, L.A., & Williams, P.W. (1980). Online searching: An introduction. London: Butterworth.

Hinkley, W. (1968). On searching catalogs and indexes with inexact title information. (Master's thesis). Chicago, IL: University of Chicago Graduate Library School.

House, D.E. (1974). Reference efficiency or reference deficiency. *Library Association Record, 76*(11), 222–223. (Also in: B. Katz, A. Tarr. [1978]. Reference and information services: A reader, [pp. 140–144]. Metuchen, NJ: Scarecrow Press.

Hyman, R.J. (1971). Access to library collections: Summary of a documentary and opinion survey on the direct shelf approach and browsing. *Library Resources & Technical Services, 15*(4), 479–491.

Hyman, R.J. (1972). *Access to library collections: An inquiry into the validity of the direct shelf approach, with special reference to browsing.* Metuchen, NJ: Scarecrow Press.

Ingwersen, P., & Kaae, S. (1979). User-librarian negotiations and information search procedures in public libraries: Analysis of verbal protocols. In T. Henriksen (Ed.), IRFIS 3: *Proceedings of the 3rd International Research Forum in Information Science, Oslo, Norway* (Vol. 1, 71–106). Oslo, Norway: Statens Bibliotekskole.

Ingwersen, P., Johansen, T., & Timmerman, P. (1977). A study of the user-librarian negotiation process. In W.E. Batten (Ed.), *EURIM II: A European conference on the application of research in information services and libraries, Amsterdam, The Netherlands* (pp. 203–207). London: Aslib.

Ingwersen, P., Johansen, T., & Timmerman, P. (1980). User-librarian negotiations and search procedures: A progress report. In O. Harbo & L. Kajberg (Eds.), *Theory and application of information research: Proceedings of the 2nd International Research Forum on Information Science, Copenhagen, Denmark* (pp. 160–171). London: Mansell.

Jahoda, G. (1974). Reference question analysis and search strategy development by man and machine. *Journal of the American Society for Information Science, 25*(3), 139–144.

Jahoda, G. (1977). The process of answering reference questions. A test of a descriptive model. Tallahassee, FL: School of Library Science, Florida State University. (For related document see ED 111 421).

Jahoda, G., & Braunagel, J.S. (1980). *The librarian and reference queries: A systematic approach.* New York: Academic Press.

Jahoda, G., & Olson, P.E. (1972). Models of reference: Analyzing the reference process. *RQ, 12*(2), 148–156.

Jahoda, G., Braunagel, J.S., & Nath, H. (1977). The reference process: Modules for instruction. *RQ, 17*(1), 7–12.

Johnson, A.R. (1978). Problem solving and the reference search. (Master's thesis). Chicago, IL: Graduate Library School, University of Chicago.

Johnston, S.M. (1978). Choosing between manual and on-line searching—Practical experience in the Ministry of Agriculture, Fisheries and Food. *Aslib Proceedings, 30*(10-11), 383–393.

Johnston, S.M., & Gray, D.E. (1977). Comparison of manual and online retrospective searching for agricultural subjects. *Aslib Proceedings, 29*(7), 253–258.

Josel, N.A. (1971). Ten reference commandments. *RQ, 11*(2), 146–147.

Katz, W.A. (1974). *Introduction to reference work* (2 Vol., 2nd ed.). New York: McGraw-Hill.

Katz, W.A. (1978). *Introduction to reference work* (2 Vol., 3rd ed.). New York: McGraw-Hill.

Keen, E.M. (1968). Search strategy evaluation in manual and automated systems. *Aslib Proceedings (UK), 20*(1), 65–81.

Keen, E.M. (1977). On the processing of printed subject index entries during searching. *Journal of Documentation, 33*(4), 266–276.

Kennington, D. (1977). Scanning the operational environment: The librarian's role. *Journal of Librarianship, 9*(4), 261–269.

Kenton, E. (1979). *Search and rescue methods and equipment* (A bibliography with abstracts). Springfield, VA: National Technical Information Service.

Knox, D.R., & Hlava, M.M.K. (1979). Effective search strategies. *Online Review, 3*(2), 148–152.

Kraft, D.H., & Lee, T. (1979). Stopping rules and their effect on expected search length. *Information Processing & Management, 15*(1), 47–58.

Lancaster, F.W. (1979). *Information retrieval systems: Characteristics, testing and evaluation* (2nd ed.). New York: Wiley.

Landsberg, M.K., Lawrence, B., Lorenz, P.A., Meadow, C.T., & Hewett, T.T. (1980). A joint industrial-academic experiment: An evaluation of the IIDA system. *Proceedings of the American Society for Information Science 43rd Annual Meeting, 17,* 406–408. White Plains, NY: Knowledge Industry Publications.

Leimkuhler, F.F. (1968). A literature search and file organization model. *American Documentation, 19*(2), 131–136.

Licklider, J.C.R. (1965). Appendix I: Proposed experiments in browsing. In C.F.J. Overhage & R.J. Harmon, *INTREX: Report of a Planning Conference on Information Transfer Experiments* (pp. 187–197). Cambridge, MA: MIT Press.

Machurina, A.T. (1970). Ob intuitsii bibliografa i logike bibliograficheskogo razyskaniia: Iz opyta raboty s chitatel'skimi trebovaniiami [Bibliographer's intuition and the logic of bibliographic searching: Experience based on readers' requests], (in Russian). *Sovetskaia Bibliografiia (U.S.S.R.),* (2), 16–24.

Maizell, R.E. (1979). *How to find chemical information.* New York: Wiley.

Mallen, M.-C. (1977). On-line information retrieval: Operators' behaviour and opinions. *On-Line Information: Proceedings of the 1st International On-Line Information Meeting, London, England* (pp. 95–102). Oxford, England: Learned Information.

Marcus, R.S. (1980). Search aids in a retrieval network. *Proceedings of the American Society for Information Science 43rd Annual Meeting, 17,* 394–396.

Marcus, R.S., & Reintjes, J.F. (1979). *Experiments and analysis on a computer interface to an information-retrieval network.* Cambridge, MA: Laboratory for Information and Decision Systems, Massachusetts Institute of Technology.

Markey, K., & Atherton, P. (1978). *ONTAP: Online training and practice manual for ERIC data base searchers.* Syracuse, NY: ERIC Clearinghouse on Information Resources.

Markey, K., Atherton, P., & Newton, C. (1980). An analysis of controlled vocabulary and free text search statements in online searches. *Online Review, 4*(3), 225–236.

Marshall, D.B. (1980). To improve searching, check search results. *Online, 4*(3), 32–47.

Martin, L.A. (1969). *Library response to urban change: A study of the Chicago Public Library.* Chicago, IL: American Library Association.

Martinez, C., & Zarember, I. (1978). OR NOT: The unused operator. *Journal of the American Society for Information Science, 29*(4), 207–208.

Martinson, T.L. (1970). A simple stratified flow chart for compiling subject bibliographies in geography. *Special Libraries Association Geography and Map Division Bulletin* (82), 32–41.

Martinson, T.L. (1972). Library of Congress author catalogs: A "micro-series" in the stratified flow chart. *Special Libraries Association Geography and Map Division Bulletin,* (87), 12–16, 50.

McCormick, J.M., Terry, R.B., & Kollgaard, J.R. (1979). Verification of citations by searching computer data bases. *Proceedings of the American Society for Information Science 42$^{nd}$ Annual Meeting, 16,* 219–228.

Meadow, C.T. (1979). The computer as a search intermediary. *Online, 3*(3), 54–59.

Meadow, C.T., & Epstein, B.E. (1977). Individualized instruction for data access. In *On-line information: Proceedings of the 1$^{st}$ international on-line information meeting, London, England* (pp. 179–194). Oxford, England: Learned Information.

Meadow, C.T., Toliver, D.E., & Edelmann, J.V. (1978). A technique for machine assistance to online searchers. *Proceedings of the American Society for Information Science 41$^{st}$ Annual Meeting, 15,* 222–225.

Meadow, C.T., Hewett, T.T., Rafsnider, D.J., Toliver, D.E., Epstein, B., Edelmann, J.V., & Maher, A. (1977). *Individualized instruction for data access (IIDA) final design report.* [ERIC: ED 145 826]. Philadelphia, PA: Drexel University Graduate School of Library Science.

Meredith, J.C. (1971). Machine-assisted approach to general reference materials. *Journal of the American Society for Information Science, 22*(3), 176–186.

Miller, G.A. (1968). Psychology and information. *American Documentation, 19*(3), 286–289.

Moore, M.L. (1970). *A review of search and reconnaissance theory literature.* Ann Arbor, MI: University of Michigan Systems Research Lab.

Morris, J.M., & Elkins, E.A. (1978). *Library searching: Resources and strategies.* New York: Jeffrey Norton.

Morrow, D.I. (1976). A generalized flowchart for the use of ORBIT and other on-line interactive bibliographic search systems. *Journal of the American Society for Information Science, 27*(1), 57–62.

Morse, P.M. (1970a). *On browsing: The use of search theory in the search for information.* Cambridge, MA: Massachusetts Institute of Technology Operations Research Center.

Morse, P.M. (1970b). Search theory and browsing. *The Library Quarterly, 40*(4), 391–408.

Morse, P.M. (1972). Optimal linear ordering of information items. *Operations Research, 20*(4), 741–751.

Morse, P.M. (1974). *Search theory.* Cambridge, MA: Massachusetts Institute of Technology Operations Research Center.

Murfin, M.E., & Wynar, L.R. (1977). *Reference service: An annotated bibliographic guide.* Littleton, CO: Libraries Unlimited.

Neill, S.D. (1975). Problem solving and the reference process. *RQ, 14*(4), 310–315.

Niehoff, R.T. (1980). The optimization and use of automated subject switching for better retrieval. *Proceedings of the American Society for Information Science 43$^{rd}$ Annual Meeting, 17,* 397–400.

Niehoff, R.T., & Kwasny, S. (1979). The role of automated subject switching in a distributed information network. *Online Review, 3*(2), 181-194.

Niehoff, R.T., Kwasny, S., & Wessells, M. (1979). Overcoming the database vocabulary barrier—a solution. *Online, 3*(4), 43-54.

Norman, O.G. (1979). The reference interview: An annotated bibliography. *RSR: Reference Services Review, 7*(1), 71-77.

Oddy, R.N. (1977a). Information retrieval through man-machine dialogue. *Journal of Documentation, 33*(1), 1-14.

Oddy, R.N. (1977b). Retrieving references by dialogue rather than by query formulation. *Journal of Informatics, 1*(1), 37-53.

Oldroyd, B.K., & Citroen, C.L. (1977). Study of strategies used in online searching. *Online Review, 1*(4), 295-310.

*Online.* (n.d.). I learned about searching from... (Regular column).

*Online Review.* (n.d.). *Search corner.* Online Review. (Regular column).

Ortiz, R.J., & Connole, T.P. (1973). *Bibliographic searching: Main entry vs. title access, a comparative time study* (Research paper presented to the faculty of the University of Denver Graduate School of Librarianship).

Padin, M.E. (Ed.). (n.d.) *Computer Ease.* Online. (Regular column).

Pejtersen, A.M. (1979). Investigation of search strategies in fiction based on an analysis of 134 user-librarian conversations. In T. Henriksen (Ed.), *IRFIS 3: Proceedings of the 3rd International Research Forum in Information Science, Oslo, Norway* (Vol. 1, pp. 107-131). Oslo, Norway: Statens Bibliotekskole.

Pollet, D. (1976). New directions in library signage: You can get there from here. *Wilson Library Bulletin, 50*(6), 456-462.

Pollet, D., & Haskell, P.C. (Eds.). (1979). *Sign systems for libraries: Solving the wayfinding problem.* New York: R.R. Bowker.

Pollock, J.J. (1977). Search properties of printed and machine-readable files. *Proceedings of the American Society for Information Science 40th Annual Meeting, 14.* White Plains, NY: Knowledge Industry Publications.

Powell, R.R. (1978). An investigation of the relationships between quantifiable reference service variables and reference performance in public libraries. *The Library Quarterly, 48*(1), 1-19.

Preece, S.E., & Williams, M.E. (1980). Software for the searcher's workbench. *Proceedings of the American Society for Information Science 43rd Annual Meeting, 17,* 403-405. White Plains, NY: Knowledge Industry Publications.

Robbin, A. (1977). The pre-acquisition process: A strategy for locating and acquiring machine-readable data. *Drexel Library Quarterly, 13*(1), 21-42.

Rosson, M.L., & Atherton, P. (1979). Part V: Online searching using free text or controlled vocabulary; 1970-1978: An analyzed and annotated bibliography. In P. Atherton, *Online searching of ERIC: Impact of free text or controlled vocabulary searching on the design of the ERIC data base* (pp. 1-39). Syracuse, NY: ERIC (ED 180 431).

Rush, J.E. (1978). Handling chemical structure information. *Annual Review of Information Science and Technology, 13,* 209-262.

Shill, H.B. (1980). Open stacks and library performance. *College & Research Libraries, 41*(3), 220-226.

Slavens, T.P., ed. (1978). *Informational interviews and questions.* Metuchen, NJ: Scarecrow Press.

Smetana, F.O. (1974). *Mapping individual logical processes in information searching.* Research Triangle Park, NC: North Carolina Science and Technology Research Center.

Smith, S.W. (1976). Venn diagramming for on-line searching. *Special Libraries, 67*(11), 510-517.

Spencer, H., & Reynolds, L. (1977). *Directional signing and labelling in libraries and museums: A review of current theory and practice.* London: Royal College of Art Readability of Print Research Unit.

Standera, O.R. (1978). Some thoughts on online systems: The searcher's part and plight. In *The Information Age in Perspective,* Proceedings of the American Society for Information Science 41$^{st}$ Annual Meeting (Vol. 15, pp. 322–325).

Stevens, M.E. (1974). Strategies for organizing and searching. In C. Fenichel (Ed.), *Changing patterns in information retrieval* (pp. 47–79). Washington, DC: American Society for Information Science.

Stibic, V. (1980). Influence of unlimited ranking on practical online search strategy. *Online Review, 4*(3), 273–279.

Stych, F.S. (1966). The flow chart method. *RQ, 5*(4), 14–17.

Stych, F.S. (1967). The flow chart method and heraldic enquiries. *RQ, 6*(4), 169–174.

Stych, F.S. (1972). Decision factors in search strategy. *RQ, 12*(2), 143–147.

Swenson, S. (1965). Flow chart on library searching techniques. *Special Libraries, 56*(4), 239–242.

Tagliacozzo, R., Rosenberg, L., & Kochen, M. (1970). Access and recognition: From users' data to catalogue entries. *Journal of Documentation, 26*(3), 230–249.

van Camp, A. (1979). Effective search analysts. *Online, 3*(2), 18–20.

Voress, H.E. (1963). Searching techniques in the literature of the sciences. *College & Research Libraries, 24*(3), 209–212.

Wagers, R. (1980). Reference and information service: The inner game. *Wilson Library Bulletin, 54*(9), 561–567.

Wanger, J. (1977). Multiple database use: The challenge of the database selection process. *Online, 1*(4), 35–41.

Wanger, J. (1979). *Evaluation of the online search process: A preliminary report: [Proceedings of the] 3$^{rd}$ international online information meeting, London, England* (pp. 1–11). Oxford, England: Learned Information.

Wanger, J. (1980). *Evaluation of the online search process.* Paper presented at the National Online Information meeting, New York, NY.

Weil, C.B. (1968). Automatic retrieval of biographical reference books. *Journal of Library Automation, 1*(4), 239–249.

Williams, M.E., & Preece, S.E. (1977). Data base selector for network use: A feasibility study. *Proceedings of the American Society for Information Science 40$^{th}$ Annual Meeting, Chicago, IL* (Vol. 14). White Plains, NY: Knowledge Industry Publications.

Williams, M.E., & Preece, S.E. (1980). Elements of a distributed transparent information retrieval system. *Proceedings of the American Society for Information Science 43$^{rd}$ Annual Meeting, 17,* 401–402.

Williams, M.E., & Preece, S.E. (1981). A mini-transparent system using an alpha micro-processor. In M.E. Williams & T.H. Hogan (Comps.), *Proceedings of the National Online Meeting, New York, NY* (pp. 499–502). Medford, NJ: Learned Information.

# 3

# Locating elusive science information: Some search techniques

ABSTRACT

Contrary to widely held assumptions, a given body of scientific research results may be published in several places, not just one. The searcher who is unable to locate one source for the information may thus find the data in another. To do so, it is necessary to be familiar with the stages of the scientific publication cycle and the various parallel and sequential points at which the information may appear. That cycle and search techniques for locating such elusive science information are described.

## Introduction

Whether searching for oneself or as a librarian for another, it can be frustrating when an urgently needed reference is unavailable in a library. After the stacks, circulation files and other sources fail to produce the item locally, the usual assumption is that the searcher must either give up or pursue the item in another library. But if it is the information contained in the article or report, and not the specific item that one wants so badly, then there are more ways to get that information than may at first appear.

The common understanding of science holds that each publication is unique, that each journal article, particularly, reports novel, original results. But in fact, individual publications in science are not so unique as might

*First published as* Bates, M. J. (1984). Locating elusive science information: Some search techniques. *Special Libraries, 75*(2), 114–120.

be assumed. It is in the nature of the scientific enterprise that a given set of results or ideas may be published in a number of slightly varied forms (Garvey, 1979; Grogan, 1976). Therefore, if the information cannot be found in one form, it may be possible to find it in another. These different forms of the information tend to appear at recognizable stages in a publication cycle that is characteristic, with slight variations, throughout all of the social, biological and physical sciences (Garvey, 1979, fig. 3).

The techniques described herein are general principles which the searcher may choose to apply in the process of using either online or manual bibliographic sources. Despite the longstanding importance of effective search techniques for the provision of quality reference service, relatively little is written on general search techniques, apart from searching on specific online systems or databases (see issues of *Online, Online Review,* and *Database*). The author's contributions to the literature include a discussion of suggested search tactics (Bates, 1979), and also a review of the literature on general search techniques through 1980 (Bates, 1981). Lynch, in her review, updated research on reference, including the question-answering process, to 1983 (Lynch, 1983).

## The publication cycle

A central fact of a scientist's life is that if he or she is to get credit for research done, the results must appear in print and must appear before anyone else's results are published. The esteem of one's peers, the promotion at work, or the Nobel Prize all come to the man or woman who is first in print with the new theorem, theory or results. One does not receive a Nobel Prize for being second to come up with the results—even if one misses being first by only a few weeks (Meadows, 1974).

Whereas a scholar in the humanities might first publish the results of ten years of research in a book summing up the work, the scientist is more likely to publish as soon as each substudy of the research is complete. It is for this reason that journals are much more important in the sciences than in the humanities. In contrast to the lengthy processes involved in book publication, journal articles represent small chunks of information and journal issues are published frequently, thus accommodating the not infrequent cases when a few weeks do make the difference in determining who gets credit for being first (Meadows, 1974, pp. 35–65; Grogan, 1976, pp. 126–168). Some scientific publishing may be in preliminary form in order to lay claim to a research topic as one's own and to discourage competitors.

(These pressures to complete work quickly and publish explain the urgency with which requests for information are often made of science librarians.)

The following discussion examines the several points in the cycle of scientific publishing at which a given body of research results may appear. Figure 1 summarizes the publishing sequence. Note that the steps in the sequence are approximate; some variation may occur in the order of appearance of various forms of the same research results.

## Informal presentations

The first discussion of the work on a research project may be in letters and phone calls between colleagues in the so-called "invisible college," i.e., that subgroup of scientists within a particular discipline who are working on the same problems (Price de Solla, 1963, p. 85). There may be a handful or a hundred or more worldwide in such a group. There is a good deal of useful information communicated this way, but at this stage the information is private and known only to a few.

Next, the work may be presented in a weekly seminar at the laboratory or academic department where the researcher is working. Presenting work to colleagues enables the scientist to get informed criticism and to detect any flaws in the reasoning or in the experimental design. Such presentations extend knowledge of the work to disciplinary colleagues outside the researcher's sub-specialty and also to other students, particularly graduate students, besides the ones directly involved in the project.

At this point, the results are still known only to a small circle. It is good to keep in mind, however, that someone who has heard of the work may ask a librarian for information on it, not realizing that it has not yet reached publication. Once this confusion has been cleared up, the solution is to put the client in touch with the researchers involved.

## Conference presentations

The work may first appear in print when it is still in preliminary form. Early results are often presented at conferences and symposia and published in the proceedings of these meetings. To take full advantage of the proceedings literature, several points should be kept in mind:

1. Proceedings may be published at the time of the conference or several years later. Therefore, when searching for the published proceedings,

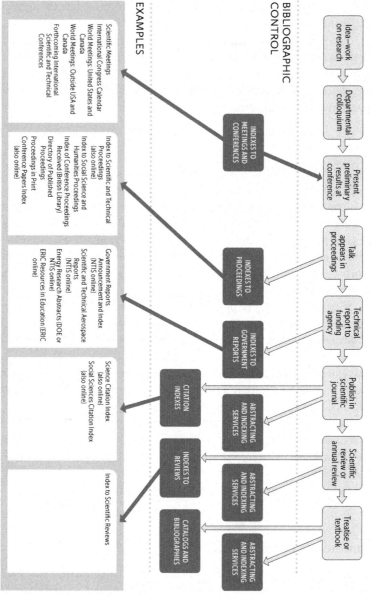

**FIG. 1.** *The scientific publication cycle.*

*NOTE: Examples of abstracting and indexing services, catalogs, and bibliographies are not provided since these classes of resources are well known and very numerous.*

it may be necessary to search anywhere from the year of the conference to three years after.

2. Often, not everything presented at a conference appears in the proceedings. Every professional society which sponsors a conference has its own rules, but it is commonly considered that some presentations are sufficiently substantial or important to warrant publication, while the less substantial ones do not. The searcher should keep in mind that even when a paper is known to have been given at a certain conference, it may not appear in the proceedings for that conference.

3. Sometimes, the substance of a paper presented at a conference is different from the version which appears in the proceedings. If the proceedings are published at the time of the conference, the articles had to be finished months beforehand in order to make publication deadlines. By the time the conference takes place, more results may be in and these may be included in the verbal presentation. On the other hand, if the proceedings are published after the conference, they may contain more results than were presented at the conference.

Because of the long lead times on journal publication (up to two years), it is even possible that results which appear in a 1984 journal article may predate the results which appear in a 1983 conference proceedings published in 1983. As noted earlier, time lag between the conference and the appearance of the proceedings may be long or short. Similarly, depending on the time of publication of the proceedings, technical reports may appear before or after the proceedings.

Presentation at conferences is a flexible way for scientists to disseminate results to their colleagues. The work does not have to be in polished form, and it may be presented in more or less formal environments at the conference. Note that not all conference presentations are of preliminary results; a researcher may also summarize several years' work, parts of which have already been published as journal articles.

This flexibility in conference presentations produces the variability in the published proceedings. But once one understands these vagaries, it is possible to use proceedings effectively as a parallel or alternate way to find the desired information if a journal article on the research is unavailable.

Major sources that provide access to meetings and their proceedings are listed in Figure 1. The *Index to Scientific and Technical Proceedings,* the *Index to Social Sciences and Humanities Proceedings,* and *Conference Papers Index* index individual articles in each proceedings volume; the other sources index only whole conference volumes.

Be prepared to look for proceedings under various entry terms. The same proceedings may be referred to by a variety of names, e.g., the name of the individual conference, the conference year in the series, and so on. Some of the proceedings index by all the significant words in the proceedings titles and/or sponsoring society names. Note also the indexes to meetings and conferences, which may help to pinpoint when and where a conference was scheduled to take place.

## Technical report literature

A legal requirement associated with U.S. federal research grants is that a report of the research be submitted to the granting agency at the end of the period of the grant. These technical reports are generally thorough and detailed descriptions of the research conducted and its results. Once submitted, the reports, if unclassified, are made publicly available for purchase in hard copy and microfiche. Report citations and abstracts appear in the Indexes to Government Reports listed in Figure 1.

Frequently, the scientist does not have time to convert the report into a (usually briefer) journal article before the end of the project. The information contained in the original report is generally more detailed and appears in the literature earlier than the same information condensed into a journal article.

Since most scientific research, especially in the physical and biological sciences, is done with federal support, one can reliably expect to find a federal technical report on it somewhere. Thus, in addition to published proceedings, technical reports are an important source for information that may otherwise only be known to exist in an unavailable journal article. Because of the thoroughness in reporting required by the federal government and, by contrast, the characteristic brevity of articles published in proceedings, one might do well to search for a technical report of a project first before going to the proceedings literature.

The best news of all is that many university and research libraries buy a large percentage of the microfiche versions of these reports. The low cost of fiche makes blanket ordering within certain subject fields economically feasible. Since fiche is generally non-circulating, technical reports are more certain to be immediately available than other sources. Additionally, copies of these reports can be ordered quickly from the National Technical Information Service. (See the sources listed in Figure 1 for ordering information.)

## Journal articles

The scientific journal article is the principal and best-known form of scientific publishing. Technical reports and proceedings volumes occupy a gray area in scientific publishing; appearance in these sources helps to lay claim to research results and to discourage competitors, but a researcher does not have an indisputable claim on a given body of results until that work appears in a refereed journal.

To guard against false claims by overeager researchers and to insure the quality of work reported, editors of scientific journals use a system of referees wherein two or more experts in the same subspecialty as the author anonymously review the paper and determine whether it is good enough to publish. If the referees disagree, an additional referee may be brought in. Since this process may take many months, some scientific journals employ a two-tiered system of publishing. Brief reports may be published quickly on only the editor's say-so, or perhaps one reviewer's, while fuller final articles go through the full refereeing process.

Keep this in mind when trying to find a given, urgently needed journal article. If the article was published in a journal to which the library does not subscribe, it may have appeared in the "Brief Reports" section of the journal, while the full refereed study results may have appeared later in another journal—one, perhaps, that is owned by the library. Check abstracting and indexing services in the field for other articles by the same author; one of these articles may report the same results as those in the desired article. An article with a related title may, in fact, be the same study described in greater or less detail. It pays to know the editorial policy of journals in the field; knowing the kinds of articles various journals publish makes it easier to spot suitable articles in the abstracting and indexing services.

The need to publish to get professional credit often induces scientists to publish their work on a particular research project in piecemeal fashion, producing several or even dozens of articles out of one project. Frequently, in order to give everyone credit, authorship is assigned almost arbitrarily to the various project team members. For example, all five project team members may appear as authors on every published item, with the authors' names rotated into the initial authorship position. Succeeding articles may refer to and summarize the results of earlier articles. Therefore, if the library does not have the one article needed, try to find other articles, especially later ones, coming out of the same project. If the desired article is at least two or three years old, the *Science Citation Index* or the *Social Sciences Citation Index* are good places to search for succeeding articles—especially since the authorship may change.

One final point about journal publication. Research work may be described in popularized form at the same time or a short time after the publication of the original, highly abstruse scientific article. Though one's first response might be to think that a technical user would not want the simplified form of the material that would appear in a popular article, it should be kept in mind that popularizations exist as many levels of sophistication. Some articles are written for the practitioner who is not interested in all the details but who still can understand the work at a very sophisticated level. Other articles are written for the sophisticated reader outside the field.

A few years ago the French mathematician René Thom developed something called "Catastrophe Theory," which generated a great deal of interest in several fields, not just in mathematics. Relevant material quickly appeared in a range of journals, some obscure; the articles were written from a variety of perspectives and required a wide range of background knowledge. Locating these materials and digesting their content would be difficult for someone outside the field of mathematics who wanted to understand the theory. Because of the strong interest in the theory, *Scientific American* quickly published a survey article on the topic, giving a basic but sophisticated explanation of the theory and reviewing the work done in the various fields (Zeeman, 1976).

## Abstracts

After reports and articles are published, abstracts of them appear in abstracting services. Under certain circumstances these abstracts can function as another source for the desired information. If the full article or report is unavailable, the requester may be able to decide whether it is really needed by reading the abstract. Frequently, the reference with a tempting title turns out to be irrelevant or redundant, and one can drop pursuit of it. Thus, the information need is, in effect, satisfied without having to see the item that was originally sought.

## Scientific reviews, treatises, textbooks

There exist other sources besides abstracts where at least some brief mention of the results of a project may be found. If a journal article is at least one year old, the information it contains may also be found in sources that appear later in the publication cycle.

The first place the material is likely to appear is in a scientific review or state-of-the-art paper. The scientific "review" is not identical to the kind of discussion and evaluation of a single item, usually a book, commonly associated with the term. Instead, the purpose of a scientific review (often used synonymously with "state-of-the-art") is to survey a segment or sub-specialty of a field and to identify, evaluate, and synthesize the principal recent research results from many published sources in that subfield. Reviews are generally written by recognized experts in the given subfield.

Scientific reviews appear in series entitled "Annual Review of . . .," "Advances in . . .," and the like, as well as in some journals, particularly in those which have "reviews" as part of the title. Reviews may also appear in federal technical reports (sometimes the entire purpose of a grant is to produce a state-of-the-art report on some topic) and in festschriften, which are volumes containing articles written in honor of a famous person in a field. The *Index to Scientific Reviews,* listed in Figure 1, provides access to reviews throughout science. Reviews are indexed in most other abstracting and indexing services as well, but they are intermingled with articles and reports which are not reviews.

As still more time passes, the research may be written up in a comprehensive monograph known as a "treatise" and, ultimately, in textbooks. Scientific abstracting and indexing services vary in their coverage of books but many do index them.

## Summary and search strategy recommendations

The results from a research project may appear in many different forms: proceedings, technical reports, variant forms of journal articles, scientific reviews, treatises and textbooks. Each of these forms is under good bibliographic control and available through abstracting and indexing services. A search strategy for locating a needed reference in a library is as follows:

1.  First, look for the item as originally requested.

2.  If that item is not available, look for an abstract of it in an abstracting and indexing service. Examine the abstract (or show it to the requester) to see if the item is still wanted.

3.  If the item is still wanted, or if you cannot find an abstract, look for the same material as presented in another form at another stage of the publication cycle. The fullest forms are going to be found in: a) a federal technical report; b) a

proceedings article; c) a journal article, or variant journal articles on the same or related work.

4. Look for other brief mentions of the work at later stages of the publication cycle, especially in: a) scientific reviews and state-of-the-art reports; b) monographs, treatises and textbooks.

## REFERENCES

Bates, M.J. (1979). Information search tactics. *Journal of the American Society for Information Science, 30*(4) 205–214.

Bates, M.J. (1981). Search techniques. *Annual Review of Information Science and Technology, 16*, 139–169.

Garvey, W.D. (1979). *Communication: The essence of science: Facilitating information exchange among librarians, scientists, engineers, and students.* New York: Pergamon Press.

Grogan, D. (1976). *Science and technology: An introduction to the literature* (3rd ed.). Hamden, CT: Linnet Books.

Lynch, M.J. (1983). Research in library reference-information service. *Library Trends, 31*(3) 401–420.

Meadows, A.J. (1974). *Communication in science.* London: Butterworths.

Price, D.J. de Solla. (1963). *Little science, big science.* New York: Columbia University Press.

Zeeman, E.C. (1976). Catastrophe theory. *Scientific American, 234*(4) 65–83.

**4**

# The fallacy of the perfect thirty-item online search

ABSTRACT

Problems in determining output size are sometimes associated with the performance of online bibliographic searches for clients in academic and other libraries. These problems are examined through discussion of a fallacy in thinking that arises when searchers try to produce the "perfect thirty-item" online search. Origins of the fallacy are explored by considering sources of misunderstandings between client and searcher and by identifying differences between manual and online searching. Several types of online searches are distinguished, and search techniques that avoid the fallacy are recommended for each search type.

## Introduction

Imagine the following situation: Sitting at an online terminal, a searcher inputs a carefully worked out search formulation for a client's query, then sits back and awaits the results. There are 1,282 postings. What happens now? Most likely, the searcher groans and says, "I've got to cut that down—1,282 is far too many." Where does this response come from? What, in fact, constitutes "too many"?

One source of that response is the client's limitation of the search either to a certain maximum number of references or to a maximum price.

*First published as* Bates, M. J. (1984). The fallacy of the perfect thirty-item online search. *RQ, 24*(1), 43–50.

The latter restriction is common in academic libraries where the client pays for the search. Even where the client does not impose restrictions, the searcher is likely to try to reduce the search output to a "manageable" number. As a teacher of online searchers, I have noticed what is apparently a spontaneous tendency on the part of students, in the absence of any stated maximum, to consider search output "too large" if it is much in excess of seventy-five or one hundred items. Conversations with more experienced searchers suggest that they feel more flexibility than this; they key search size to a combination of factors, but often still find the need to alter initial search output sizes, particularly in the direction of reducing the output.

There is more to the question of what constitutes a good output size than first meets the eye. This matter will be explored here by means of examining a fallacy in thinking about searching and search modification. Taking a figure comfortably under the seventy-five to one-hundred item limit mentioned earlier, we shall call it the fallacy of the perfect thirty-item online search. Beginning searchers may find this discussion particularly instructive, and experienced searchers may also find it useful to consider the various nuances of determining good output size.

"Search formulation" is defined as a search statement or series of statements expressing the search topic of a request. A "search strategy," on the other hand, is a plan or approach for the whole search and operates at a level above specific term choice and command use. (See also discussion in Bates [1981]).

In the next section the fallacy is described, in the succeeding section the ways in which the fallacy may arise are discussed, and in the final section solutions are proposed.


## What is the fallacy?

The fallacy lies in assuming that somewhere in the database one is searching there exists a high-quality thirty-item (or $n$-item, whatever $n$ is for the searcher) set and that if one is just clever enough, one can produce a response set of the desired size for the client. To put it differently, the fallacy lies in gearing the search to the size of the output desired instead of to the topic to be searched. It may simply be that the relevant documents available in a database on a given topic are not the same number as the searcher or client would like.

The fallacy can occur in two ways. First, the output of a search may be the "wrong" size, and the searcher goes to great and clever lengths to modify the search formulation until the output is the "right" size. Most commonly, the output is "too large," so this form of the fallacy will be called the "overcutting" version.

In this case, cutting down the output drastically for a query may yield a final set that is an unrepresentative and atypical subset of the whole set of documents relevant to the query. Its prime virtue may be that it contains only thirty items, not that it is a good or complete response. Thus, in trying to get an output of a certain size, the searcher may violate the topic itself.

But, it may be argued, clients frequently limit the output to a certain number, either by preference or because they do not want to pay for any more. The search *has* to be limited. I am not suggesting that clients be swamped with citations they do not want. But first it is important that we be clear on just what the thinking is on the part of client and searcher. It may be possible to come to a solution that produces searches of a higher quality than is likely when the fallacy is operating in their thinking. The latter part of this article will suggest ways of producing such higher quality sets.

An output set of the "wrong" size can also be too small. It is possible, figuratively, to "scrape the bottom of the barrel" to try to increase a small set up to a desired size. The dangers of producing a poor output set are less here. Because the searcher tries many variant search formulations to identify relevant citations, this approach is not likely to overlook valuable citations, and searchers are unlikely to give clients a response set full of irrelevant items. (The one real danger here is that the searcher may use up too much of the client's money searching for nonexistent citations. There comes a time when the searcher must have the confidence to declare that there is nothing on the topic in the database.) Consequently, efforts to increase the output set up to thirty will be disregarded in the following discussion of the fallacy.

The second way that the fallacy may occur is that the initial search output is the "right" size, and the searcher stops immediately, without determining whether the initial search formulation is indeed the best one for the query. It may be that in such a case, to do a thorough, careful search on the query, the searcher should OR in related terms and try variant terms either in addition to or instead of the terms used the first time. Searchers often cannot be certain to have found the best search formulation for a given query without such experimentation. But that experimentation may produce larger response sets. So the searcher operating under the fallacy stops after the first response that lists the desired output size. This form is called the "quick and dirty" version of the fallacy.

Fenichel noted a tendency on the part of many searchers to make little use of the feedback and search modification capabilities of online systems (Fenichel, 1981). Such searchers go in with just the terms asked for by the client in simple, brief search formulations. There are times when such quick searches are just what the client needs, but other times they constitute an expression of the quick and dirty form of the fallacy. This tendency to "anchor" on the initial search formulation is reminiscent of the anchoring problem discussed in Blair, in which online searchers are reluctant to alter the initial terms of their search formulations (Blair, 1980).

The above is not to suggest that every effort to modify the search is overcutting, or that failure to modify a search always means the searcher has not developed the best search formulation for a query. Clearly, judgment and experience are involved here. But if the searcher falls into one or the other forms of the fallacy, there is danger that the quality of the search output will be less than it might be.

## How does the fallacy arise?

There are a number of possible causes for the development of this fallacy in the thinking of searcher and client. It is worth going into these causes in detail because they point to ways of avoiding the fallacy.

### What the client (and sometimes the searcher) does not know

There are a lot of things about information retrieval that the typical client does not know and probably has not even thought about. The simplistic assumptions brought to the presearch interview may be presumed to have a strong influence on the demands and expectations placed on the searcher. The searcher, on the other hand, in trying to be helpful, may attempt to meet inappropriate demands that arise out of the client's limited knowledge of the system.

There are three points in particular where misunderstandings are likely to arise:

- Complexity of indexing

- Limits of Boolean logic

- The trade-off between recall and precision.

Let us take them one at a time. There is both research and anecdotal evidence that most people do not realize that any given topic may appear in an information system under many different descriptors (Bates, 1977). They have little awareness of the complex problems involved in subject indexing and the variety of ways in which any given topic is likely to be described. In its simplest form, their mental model is likely to be that a topic that interests them is to be found under a single term; all documents found under that term will be relevant to their query, and no documents relevant to the query will be found elsewhere in the system. Thus, they expect that in principle it should be possible to get a response set with 100 percent precision (percentage of relevant documents retrieved out of all documents retrieved) and 100 percent recall (percentage of relevant documents retrieved out of all relevant documents in the collection).

When clients demand high precision for their search output, as they often do, they may be basing this demand on such a naive model of online systems. They may assume that any request on their topic—especially in an automated system, which is usually thought to be much more sophisticated than manual information retrieval systems—will automatically produce a set of documents, all of which are relevant to their query.

In fact, not only is subject indexing much more problematic than most clients realize, but the online systems themselves are not as sophisticated as clients may assume. Boolean logic is simpler than natural-language syntax—and also rides roughshod over many grammatical distinctions that make a difference in the relevance of a document to a request. Consequently, false drops are endemic in online searching.

Furthermore, it has long been argued that Boolean logic is not ideally suited to be the basis of term combination in information retrieval. The OR is too weak and brings in too many documents and the AND is too stringent and cuts down output sets too severely. My purpose here is not to argue the value of using Boolean logic—only to point out that the actual conceptual system embedded in the fancy-looking technology may not be as sophisticated as the client assumes.

Above all, clients are not likely to understand the trade-off between recall and precision. Searchers are generally aware of it, but may not recognize its full practical implications for online searching.

Let us therefore look at the trade-off more closely. It is one of the best-established results of information science research that, in general, high precision is gained at the price of low recall and vice versa. Consequently, the tricks one uses in search modification to improve precision tend to lower recall and vice versa. Lancaster has an excellent discussion of this in chapters eleven and twelve of his *Information Retrieval Systems* (Lancaster, 1979).

Let us use one of Lancaster's examples to demonstrate this pattern. Suppose an aeronautical engineer wants a search on "slender delta wings." This is exactly what interests the engineer, not other types of wings. The chances are that a search on this term will produce a high precision output set.

But it may be that for all sorts of reasons there are documents of relevance to this request under other terms as well. Mention of slender delta wings may appear in documents on delta wings in general (and indexed under "delta wings") or even in documents on wings in general. Good material may also be found under synonymous terms such as "narrow delta wings," or even under closely related terms. These other terms may reflect a necessary variety in the information retrieval system or may be used because of sloppy vocabulary control, changes in terminology over time, or other reasons.

In order to improve recall and retrieve relevant documents indexed under these other terms, it is necessary to search under them as well. But in doing so, it is likely that a higher proportion of the documents indexed under these more distant terms will be irrelevant to the request than is the case with the initial highly precise term. In other words, in casting a wider net to improve recall, one also pulls in *disproportionately* more junk. Consequently, when recall goes up, precision goes down. The same thing happens, of course, in reverse: if one reduces the search formulation to only the most precise terms, precision will be improved, but recall will fall.

The practical, and virtually unavoidable, result of the recall-precision trade-off for online searching is that where recall is important to the client, there will usually be a substantial proportion of irrelevant citations retrieved in even the best-designed search. Where cost is an important factor, it may be particularly puzzling and irksome to the client to get an output set with dozens of irrelevant citations. In response to the client's dissatisfaction, the searcher may retreat to the overcutting version of the fallacy—producing high-precision searches for clients who really want high recall.

## Differences between manual and online searching

Habits and expectations formed with manual searching may carry over inappropriately to online searching. Let us compare these two forms of searching and note two important respects in which they differ.

First, the number-of-postings output from an online system in response to any query is likely to be far larger—often by an order of magnitude or more—than the output of a manual search on the same topic. This comes about for two reasons:

First, the typical manual search segments the output into yearly or biannual chunks, corresponding to the published volumes of the abstracting and indexing (A & I) service, whereas the typical online database covers many years and produces postings for all the years covered at once. The total base number of citations is the same, of course, but, psychologically, getting them all at once makes the searcher feel that the output of the online search is larger.

Second, the number of postings reported to a searcher in an online search is the number of citations indexed by a term before the searcher has had a chance to select out the potentially relevant items. In a manual search we record only the most promising citations, not all the citations listed under the term. In an online search, on the other hand, a well-stated, carefully worked-out search formulation still produces the set from which the client or searcher selects the desired items, not the final selected set.

The client, however, still wants the same low number of citations gotten previously from manual searches, and/or wants the online output especially low in number because of the cost. The poor searcher is thus squeezed between two contrary pressures: the output from any given online search is going to be quite large on the average, and the client has as much or more desire for small output sets as ever.

Now to the second point of difference between manual and online searches: In an online search, because of high print costs (on- or off-line), the searcher usually must find a way to select out the most promising subset of the database, while looking at no more than a tiny sample of the citations matching any given search formulation. In other words, the searcher must select the final output set virtually sight unseen.

Probably because the online search thus involves a lot of decision making without full knowledge, Standera found the development and the modification of the search formulation (what he calls "strategy") to be the two points of greatest stress out of seventeen identifiable phases of online searching (Standera, 1978).

It may be argued, however, that it is much easier with online systems than I have made out, because they have many capabilities not available in manual sources. These capabilities can be used to design initially precise search formulations, or to cut down (or increase) the size of the response set and get the thirty-item output the client wants and expects. Let us note some of the more common devices available in online search systems:

- Search terms may be combined according to Boolean logic.

- Search terms may be truncated, so that all variations on a root are automatically searched.

- Searching can be done on terms or strings other than assigned descriptors, often throughout the record, including the abstract.

- Searching can be done conjointly on descriptors, free-text words, classification codes, and other subject elements.

The above devices all deal with subject or topic access. In addition:

- The search can be limited by date or accession number.

- Depending on the database, the search can be limited by other characteristics, such as language, country of origin, document type, presence of literature reviews, etc.

Let us call the first set of devices "searching by subject characteristics," and, for lack of a better name, the second set of devices "searching by secondary characteristics." We will use these terms in the next section.

These are powerful capabilities; they allow many options for clever search design and modification. Use of them may indeed lead to drastic modification of the size of output sets. But the fact remains that in practice they are mostly carried out "blind." Through design and modification of the search formulation, the searcher selects the potentially relevant citations and rejects the probably irrelevant ones for the client without seeing the overwhelming majority of those citations.

The nature of searching and search modification is thus quite different for online and manual searching. In both cases the client may set a comparatively low limit on the number of citations wanted, but the danger of unwittingly rejecting large numbers of highly relevant documents is much higher in online searching. Since the client asks for a small set, and may have to pay for the output on a per citation basis in an online search, the searcher may determinedly find ways to reduce the output—and thus slip into the fallacy. We will consider ways to deal with this problem in the next section.

## What strategies can the searcher use to deal with the fallacy?

In order to identify strategies it will be helpful first to distinguish common types of search. Based on ideas developed originally by Charles Bourne, Markey and Cochrane describe three types of search: high recall search, high precision search, and brief search (Markey & Cochrane, 1981). The first two types emphasize those retrieval values, while a brief search "is done in response to the need for retrieving a few items either to lessen expenses or to perform a rapid survey of the file before a more comprehensive and lengthy strategy" (1981, p. 8).

The purpose of a recall search is very clear; the client needs everything that can be found on the topic for, say, a dissertation or review paper. With respect to precision searches, many researchers take a casual attitude toward the literature searches they do for articles they are writing. Those of us with a library background may assume recall is important; people in other fields often do not. They see the background survey that they must write at the beginning of articles as a tiresome, if necessary, task. They feel the purpose of the survey is to mention some typical articles on the topic of their research, not all the articles. They show where their work fits into the stream of research; they do not attempt to show everything that has been done. If this is the attitude taken by the client, then a precision search is indeed called for. In this case, the client's insistence that the size of the output be limited and irrelevant documents be minimized makes sense.

But there is another possibility here—that the client who is apparently asking for a precision search really wants a recall search. This can come about for reasons discussed in the previous section. Ignorant of the recall-precision trade-off, the client may think that, of course, irrelevant documents are not wanted; the output should be limited to relevant items only. It is assumed that the fancy automated system can easily produce such a result. The client may even assume—this is common—that when the search is limited to thirty items the system will produce the thirty most relevant items, i.e., a ranked output. Thus why waste money on more citations?

Furthermore, the client may make the same carryover from manual to online searches that was discussed above for searchers. Manual searches done as a student may have produced only a few items—after scanning and selecting. The output of those earlier searches may have been especially low if the client was ignorant of the complexity of indexing and the variety of bibliographic sources available in most fields. This client, in other words, may actually want high recall and assumes that the most references there could possibly be on the subject is thirty. So if a limit is set there, the search output will contain all the relevant items that exist anyway.

How can one tell whether the client really wants a precision search or recall search? What is really at issue here is how important recall is. We may presume that everyone would like to minimize irrelevant citations retrieved. So the crucial question of the client is, "Do you want everything we can find on this topic or just some examples, some typical references?"

Now, assuming that the searcher is able to identify true recall and true precision searches in the interview with the client, what strategies should be used to avoid the fallacy?

I suggest that different strategies should be used for recall and precision searches. In both cases, modification by subject characteristics (described in the previous section) is often necessary initially in order to home in on a search formulation that is both a good representation of the query and a good match with available terms in the database. But after these initial changes, emphasis should be on modification by secondary characteristics (limitation by date, bibliographic form, etc.) for recall searches and by subject characteristics for precision searches.

Why suggest these different approaches for the two types of search? As noted earlier, a good recall search will often have an extensive search formulation with many marginal terms included. It will generally produce a large output with a comparatively large number of irrelevant documents. It is thus particularly tempting to use modification by subject characteristics to reduce both the output size of a recall search and the percentage of irrelevant documents. For example, one might drop marginal subject terms, drop truncation if already used, drop broader terms, and so on. Once one is confident, however, that the search formulation is a good one for the query and for that database, the use of extensive subject modification later in the search, solely to reduce output size, simply introduces covert precision searching when a recall search is wanted. A good recall search requires those marginal terms, broader terms, etc. To drop them is to convert the recall search into a precision search.

But how then is one to deal with the client who insists on limiting the size of the output for a recall search? There are two main options: (1) Work out a fallback narrower topic with the client in the presearch interview, and/or (2) arrange as a fallback option to cut down the postings by using modification by secondary characteristics; i.e., limit by date, bibliographic form, language, etc.

Either of these approaches is preferable on recall searches to running the risk of overcutting through subject modification and missing many relevant citations. When a recall search is restricted by date or other secondary characteristic, the client knows that nothing will be retrieved prior to the stated date or outside the limit. Most importantly, the client knows that the searcher has gotten the highest recall possible within the stated limits. On the contrary, when extensive subject modification is used to cut down the output of a recall search, especially considering that the modification is mostly done blind, there is no way to know just what sort of relevant documents have been cut out as well. Thus, in such a case, what is ostensibly a recall search may, in fact, have poor recall.

In a precision search, on the other hand, by the trade-off rule of precision and recall, we expect to lose some relevant documents in order to maximize precision. (If the client cannot bear to lose those relevant items, then a recall search is what is really wanted.) With a precision search, there is less danger of overcutting, so the searcher can pull out all the stops to modify the search formulation by subject characteristics. As noted earlier, the possibilities for modification by subject are many and various, and the clever searcher can reduce the output set size considerably through ingenious exercise of these options. By using subject modification the searcher gives the client a set of references on the precise topic desired, and across all years, languages, bibliographic forms, etc. Of course, if the client wants the search limited by date or other secondary characteristic, the limit should be used.

When there is heavy subject modification, there is still some possibility of overcutting with precision searches, however, and care should be exercised. Consider the case where a searcher gets an initial output in the high hundreds or thousands of postings. In modifying this down to a small requested set, such as thirty, the modification may be so drastic that it cuts out whole subareas or branches within the stated topic. Thus, the searcher may want to arrange a fallback narrower topic in such cases as well.

Adams (1979) takes a different view on the question of how to narrow searches. He says:

> Restricting a search to several recent years—or printing just the first fifty or so items retrieved in a search—are two other frequently used techniques. It is strongly recommended that they not be used. It is very likely that useful material will be eliminated if they are. Knowledge of the other search refinement methods makes these techniques unnecessary (Adams, 1979, p. 376).

He highlights four other search refinement techniques for narrowing searches:

- Restricting to English
- Using NOT
- Restricting a term to fields such as title or descriptor
- Using AND (Adams, 1979, p. 376).

In the terminology of the present article, the first of Adams' techniques is a form of modification by secondary characteristics, and the remaining three techniques are forms of modification by subject characteristics. Adams' recommendations are well taken if the searcher habitually makes no modification whatever of the initial search formulation. As noted earlier, some initial subject modification is frequently needed on all types of searches to home in on terms used in a given database. But beyond that first step, I would split out Adams' four techniques, and recommend that the first generally be used on recall searches and the others on precision searches.

So far in this section the emphasis has been on avoiding the over-cutting version of the fallacy. What about the quick and dirty version? Here the problem is one of accepting as final the output of a simple, off-the-top-of-the-head search formulation because it produces the desired small number of citations. In cases where the client actually wants a very quick search, i.e., a "brief search," and the searcher is confident that good terms are being used, this approach is adequate. Otherwise, some initial experimentation with subject modification is always advisable to be sure the best term combination has been found.

Here are summary recommendations for avoiding the fallacy of the perfect thirty-item online search:

Presearch interview Probe carefully to determine what kind of search the client really wants. In the case of recall searches explain that it is in principle a contradiction in terms to limit in advance the number of items desired in a recall search. If practical exigencies still require limiting the search, then arrange a fallback narrower topic, and/or limitation by secondary characteristics.

In the case of precision or brief searches it is less essential to arrange fallback options, since, by definition, these types of searches allow for dropping (or failing to pick up) some relevant documents. With topics that are very broad, however, because of the difficulty of narrowing them enough to get small output sizes, it is a good idea to arrange one or both of the fallback options mentioned in the previous paragraph.

The search itself For searches of all types, use modification by subject characteristics (listed in section titled "How Does the Fallacy Arise?") to home in on the proper description of the topic. If the initial search formulation proves to be off center and retrieves large numbers of false drops or irrelevant citations, revise the formulation by these various subject techniques until one is confident that the topic is well described in the terms used by the database. This first step prevents the quick and dirty version of the fallacy. An exception may be made to this rule in the case of brief searches where the experienced searcher is confident that the initial search formulation will lead to a good match with the terms used in the database.

For brief and true precision searches, after the initial homing in on a good description of the topic in the terms used in the database, subject modification techniques may continue to be used in order to get the output set down to the desired size. (Note that these techniques may also be used in the other direction to increase output size; for reasons discussed earlier, that case is not being covered here.) Some loss of relevant documents is to be expected with these types of searches, so subject modification techniques (which often drop relevant documents) may be used extensively in order to maximize precision. The searcher is cautioned, however, to be careful about reducing initial postings sets too drastically—say, to one-tenth or less of the initial postings size—for fear of losing whole areas or classes of documents within the topic. In order to avoid the overcutting version of the fallacy, the searcher should consider using prearranged fallback options instead.

For recall searches, modification by subject characteristics should generally only be used to home in on a good description of the query, not to cut postings down to a desirable size, for fear of losing relevant documents. If the size of the output set must be limited, then to avoid the overcutting version of the fallacy, the search formulation should be modified by secondary characteristics, or a narrower topic should be used, as arranged in the presearch interview. If the client is present during the search, final selection of fallback options can be made during the search.

Use of these techniques should enable the searcher to satisfy the needs of clients without falling into the fallacy of the perfect thirty-item online search.

## REFERENCES

Adams, A.L. (1979). Planning search strategies for maximum retrieval from bibliographic databases. *Online Review, 3*(4), 373–379.

Bates, M.J. (1977). Factors affecting subject catalog search success. *Journal of the American Society for Information Science, 28*(3), 161–169.

Bates, M.J. (1981). Search techniques. *Annual Review of Information Science and Technology, 16*, 139–169.

Blair, D.C. (1980). Searching biases in large interactive document retrieval systems. *Journal of the American Society for Information Science, 31*(4), 271–277.

Fenichel, C.H. (1981). Online searching: Measures that discriminate among users with different types of experiences. *Journal of the American Society for Information Science, 32*(1), 23–32.

Lancaster, F.W. (1979). *Information retrieval systems: Characteristics, testing and evaluation* (2nd ed.). New York: Wiley.

Markey, K., & Cochrane, P.A. (1981). *ONTAP: Online training and practice manual for ERIC data base searchers* (2nd ed., pp. 7–8). Syracuse, NY: ERIC Clearinghouse on Information Resources.

Standera, O.R. (1978). Some thoughts on online systems: The searcher's part and plight. In *The Information Age in Perspective,* Proceedings of the American Society for Information Science 41st Annual Meeting (Vol. 15, pp. 322–325).

## 5
# A profile of end-user searching behavior by humanities scholars: The Getty Online Searching Project report no. 2

### ABSTRACT

The Getty Art History Information Program carried out a two-year project to study how advanced humanities scholars operate as end users of online databases. Visiting Scholars at the Getty Center for the History of Art and the Humanities in Santa Monica, California, were offered the opportunity to do unlimited subsidized searching of DIALOG® databases. This second report from the project analyzes how much searching the scholars did, the kinds of search techniques and DIALOG features they used, and their learning curves. Search features studied included commands, Boolean logic, types of vocabulary, and proximity operators. Error rates were calculated, as well as how often the scholars used elementary search formulations and introduced new search features and capabilities into their searches. The amount of searching done ranged from none at all to dozens of hours. A typical search tended to be simple, using one-word search terms and little or

*First published as* Siegfried,[1] S., Bates,[2] M. J., Wilde,[1] D. N. (1993). A profile of end-user searching behavior by humanities scholars: The Getty Online Searching Project report no. 2. *Journal of the American Society for Information Science, 44*(5), 273–291.

1   The Getty Art History Information Program.
2   Graduate School of Library and Information Science, University of California, Los Angeles.

no Boolean logic. Starting with a full day of DIALOG training, the scholars began their search experience at a reasonably high level of competence; in general, they maintained a stable level of competence throughout the early hours of their search experience.

## Introduction

Prompted by scholars' increased access to online databases, such as those offered by Dialog Information Services, the Getty Art History Information Program launched a two-year program in early 1989 to study how humanities scholars, engaging in their characteristic modes of research, use online databases when they are given the chance to do unlimited searching, unconstrained by cost. The study was intended to probe a number of aspects of the scholars' experiences with online searching, including their reactions to the use of the online databases, the role the searching had in their research work, their search techniques and learning curve, their queries, and the search terms they used. The results of the study are to be reported in a series of articles, of which this is the second.

The first report (Bates, Wilde, & Siegfried, 1993) analyzed the vocabulary used by the scholars in their searches, and the third report is to analyze the results of the interviews with the scholars about the role of the searching in their research. The purpose of this article is to analyze and profile the online searching record itself, drawing on complete transaction log data captured for the study. In particular, at the request of the Getty collaborators, Bates analyzed how much searching the scholars did, the kinds of search techniques and DIALOG features they used, and their learning curves.

Marilyn Schmitt conceived the Getty Online Searching Project; she designed the study together with Susan Siegfried and Deborah Wilde. Siegfried and Wilde carried out the collaborative project plan and oversaw the gathering of data throughout the project. Marcia Bates analyzed the data, formulated conclusions, and contributed insights from the discipline of information science. Brian Sullivan wrote and maintained the software that accessed DIALOG and captured complete transaction logs of the searches. Research Assistant Vanessa Birdsey coded the data into categories developed by Bates. Jeanette Clough and Katherine Smith transcribed the DIALOG search statements for subsequent analysis.

The next section of this article reviews the relevant literature, the section after describes the methodology used in the analyses; then the results are presented, and, finally, the last section contains discussion and conclusions.

## Background

Empirical research into information-seeking behavior among members of various academic and research communities focused almost exclusively on engineering and the sciences during the 1960s, and on the social sciences in the 1970s. Although Stone reviews a number of studies done before 1980, she points to the "relative neglect" of the humanities until the late 1970s. Her review (1982) and the work begun in the late 1970s by the Centre for Research on User Studies (e.g., Corkill & Mann, 1978) mark the beginning of a modern era in which researchers in library and information science evinced greater interest in the nature of humanities scholars' information seeking.

During these decades, reviews, research projects, and commentaries drew attention to the unique characteristics of the information-seeking behavior of humanities scholars (Broadbent, 1986; Case, 1991; Corkill & Mann, 1978; Gould, 1988; Guest, 1987; Lowry & Stuveras, 1987; Morton & Price, 1986; Rahtz, 1987; Schmitt, 1988, 1990; Stam, 1984; Stam & Giral, 1988; Stielow & Tibbo, 1988; Stone,1982; Wiberley, 1991; Wiberley & Jones, 1989). While many of these studies dealt with the research behavior of scholars in general, few paid attention to these scholars' use of online databases. However, during the last few years, this lack has begun to be remedied. Serious attention is now being paid to online searching in the humanities: its particular requirements, problems with databases and their vendors, and specific search techniques (Boyles, 1987, 1988; Crawford, 1986; Everett & Pilachowski, 1986; Katzen, 1986; Lehmann & Renfro, 1991; Loughridge, 1989; Mackesy, 1982; Ross, 1987; Ruiz & Meyer, 1990; Stern, 1988; Tibbo, 1989; Walker, 1988, 1990; Walker & Atkinson, 1991).

A few empirical studies have examined actual uses of online databases by or for scholars in the humanities. Woo (1988) studied how three graduate students at Columbia University made online use of the *Avery Index to Architectural Periodicals*. Krausse and Etchingham (1986) elicited the reactions of scholars to database searching when a grant subsidized the cost of their searches. Horner and Thirlwall (1988) tested several hypotheses regarding uses of online searching by social science and humanities scholars, and Hurych (1986) analyzed formal online search requests to compare the use of online search services across disciplines (sciences, social sciences, and humanities). In a recent major review, Tibbo (1991) described the explosive growth in information systems and technology for humanities scholars in recent years.

Research on end users of information systems has also grown rapidly in recent years, as more and more systems have come to be used by the ultimate consumer, rather than by librarians acting as intermediaries. Major reviews of this literature prepared by Mischo and Lee (1987) and Sullivan, Borgman, and Wippern (1990) indicate that end users do moderately well. For the most part, they perform "adequate" searches (Sullivan et al., 1990, p. 30), but "make more errors, prepare less well than intermediaries, and have less complete results" (p. 28). End users generally find these searches satisfactory (Mischo & Lee, 1987, p. 242; Sullivan et al., 1990, p. 28). "Analysis of the results of numerous studies on searcher behavior indicates that experienced searchers perform more complicated and better searches but that poor searches occur at every level of experience . . . It appears that search-strategy formulation is a problem at all levels of searching" (Mischo & Lee, 1987, p. 244). Mischo and Lee also mention the difficulties that end users have with Boolean logic (p. 243).

This study's purpose was not to evaluate the performance of humanities end users—although a simple error count is included—but rather to observe what happens when advanced humanities scholars are given the opportunity to do their own online searching. All reports in this series describe, each in a different way, that encounter.

## Methodology

### The study population

During 1988–89 and 1989–90 all participating Visiting Scholars at the Getty Center for the History of Art and the Humanities[3] in Santa Monica, California, were allowed to do unlimited online searching of databases through DIALOG at a workstation in the Getty Center Library. Participants were given one day's training by DIALOG staff, then had 24-hour-a-day access to the workstation to do fully subsidized searching on their own for the rest of their year at the Center. Altogether, 27 scholars participated in the two years.

All Visiting Scholars at the Getty Center during the two years were invited to participate in the project, but not all chose to do so. Eleven of the 15 scholars visiting the Center during 1988–89 (henceforth known as the 1989 group) agreed to participate in the project, and two spouses (scholars in their own right) also participated, for a total of 13 individuals. Twelve of the 18 scholars during 1989–90 (henceforth known as the 1990 group) agreed to participate, and three spouses also joined, for a total of 15.

---

3   The J. Paul Getty Trust is a private operating foundation. Two of its programs are the Getty Art History Information Program and the Getty Center for the History of Art and the Humanities. These two entities collaborated on this project.

"Participation" is defined operationally as taking the DIALOG training. As will be discussed later, some who trained did no searching subsequently.

Although the numbers of participants for the two years add to 28, one individual in the 1989 group stayed for the second year, for a total of 27 different people. Data from both years for the scholar who stayed over the second year are included in the analyses of use of commands, types of vocabulary terms, etc. discussed later. However, where initial experiences with searching are analyzed, only the record of the first year is included (also discussed later).

There were eight men and five women in the 1989 group and nine men and six women in the 1990 group. The participants came from France, Germany, Great Britain, Hungary, Italy, The Netherlands, and the United States. In 1989, five of the 13 were native English speakers, and six of the 15 in 1990. The non-native speakers' command of English ranged from adequate to excellent. (Note: Because more of the scholars produced data relevant to the factors analyzed in this report than in Report No. 1, the populations analyzed in the two reports are slightly different. Hence, the descriptions of the populations differ slightly between the reports as well.)

The scholars' research interests included the history of art and architecture, film history, social history, philosophy, comparative literature, classics, history of music, social and cultural anthropology, and psychology. The groups comprised university professors, independent scholars, curators, an architect, postdoctoral scholars, and doctoral candidates.

### Training, setting, and other arrangements

The 1989 group was trained in late January and early February 1989, and did all their searching between then and June 1989. The 1990 group was trained at the end of November 1989 and did their searching between then and July 1990. One scholar in the first year arrived late and was trained by Jeanette Clough of the Getty rather than by the DIALOG trainer, Amy Greenwood.

As noted earlier, after taking the training the scholars had 24-hour-a-day access to the workstation for DIALOG searching in the Getty Center Library near their offices until they left in the summer. Next to the workstation were placed documentation for DIALOG as well as thesauri and word lists for several arts and humanities databases. The latter included *RILA* (*International Repertory of the Literature of Art*) *Subject Headings*, *Architectural Keywords*, and *Historical Abstracts Index*.

In preparation for this project, a program was written to capture a complete transaction log of the DIALOG searches done by the scholars at the workstation. These data were captured for the study with the permission of both Dialog Information Services and the study participants. Scholars were instructed to print out all desired search results at the terminal, rather than having them sent from DIALOG. Consequently, we have a complete record of their entire searches—both search statements and results.

The Getty Trust arranged for a limited DIALOG account, which gave the scholars access to a large subset of about 60 of the DIALOG databases. Databases in the package, drawn from the social sciences, arts, and humanities, included all those thought to be of interest to arts and humanities scholars, such as *Art Literature International (RILA), The Architecture Database (RIBA),* and *Historical Abstracts.* Although RILA has since been superseded by the bilingual *Bibliography of the History of Art (BHA),* the database is still accessed through DIALOG as *Art Literature International.* Bibliographic databases covered journal articles, books, and dissertations. Some directories, e.g., *Marquis Who's Who,* and some full-text databases, e.g., *Academic American Encyclopedia* (no longer available on DIALOG), were also included. DIALINDEX®, the database of DIALOG databases, was included, as were citation databases, e.g., *Arts & Humanities Search.*

Participants were encouraged to make an appointment for an "assisted search" at some time during the months after the training. In these searches, an experienced online searcher would answer questions and help in any way desired while the scholar searched. During the first year, six scholars requested an assisted search during the spring of 1989, and one of these had a second one as well. In 1990 one scholar had three assisted searches, three had two, five had one, and six had none.

In the first year, scholars were also offered the opportunity to have an experienced searcher do a "comparative search." Essentially, the expert searcher redid one of the searches the scholar had already done. The scholar first submitted a written search request to the expert, who then conducted the search without knowing how the scholar had searched it. The results of the comparative searches were then discussed in an interview with the scholar. In 1989, seven scholars requested comparative searches (performed by Kathleen Salomon of the Getty Center Library). These comparative searches took place after the scholars had done most of their searching for the year; none occurred earlier than May 4, 1989. They were discontinued in the second year. Two group review sessions were offered during the second year. Three people attended the first one in January 1990, and five people (including one who also attended the first session) attended the second one in March. (In both years, help with assisted searches was provided by Jeanette Clough of the Getty Center Library, who also conducted the two group review sessions.) Overall, the project was designed to encourage scholars to do their own searching; generally, assistance was available only through the DIALOG help line, not locally.

## Coding and data analysis

For this study, a search statement was defined as beginning with a system prompt and ending with a carriage return. Every online search statement input by the scholars was extracted from the printouts of searches and recorded on separate coding sheets. Each statement input by each searcher for the entire year was then numbered serially from the first through the last search the individual did. Because assisted searches might be influenced to some degree by interaction with the experienced searcher, only unassisted searches were analyzed. Thus, numbers of total search statements, total search terms, etc., are all based on unassisted searches only.

As will be described in more detail later, most of the scholars did only a few hours of searching each for the entire period. One person in the second year, however, spent more than five times as many hours searching as any of the other scholars did—in fact, more time than all the others put together. Since the majority of participants did relatively little searching, we based our analyses of error rates, search techniques used, learning curve, etc., on the early hours of the scholars' experience as searchers. We decided to end the analysis of the prolific scholar's searching at a point beyond the amount done by everyone else but well before the end of his total searching time—on the grounds that analyzing later stages of searching with a sample of one would be of little use.

In that light, we decided to cut off analysis of the prolific scholar's searching at about 1,000 statements. The actual number of statements coded for that individual corresponded to the end of the first search session after the figure of 1,000 statements was recorded, i.e., 1,035 statements. (Incidentally, the scholar who stayed over a second year totaled fewer than 400 statements for both years added together, so even two years' experience did not equal that of several more active searchers. There is no evidence from the interviews that the presence of a more experienced searcher had any impact on the 1990 group.)

A list of over 70 codes was developed, each standing for a DIALOG system feature or search capability. Codes were not developed for those advanced DIALOG capabilities that were not taught to or used by the scholars. However, numbers left in the code series from 01 to 99 allowed the analyst to add codes when an additional feature was used. All search statements by all searchers were then coded in all applicable categories.

The Appendix contains coding rules and a complete list of codes. All statements both years were coded by the same individual.

Coding was done at two levels: statement and term. At the statement level, a code was marked as present or absent if what it represented appeared or did not appear anywhere in the statement. For example, if the searcher used "Select" in the statement, the code for "Select" was marked as present for that statement. Codes 1–49 (except 35–36) and 91–99 are statement-level codes. Here is a sample search statement:

S america? and weimar?

Each search term was individually coded for features that are specific to terms—e.g., suffix specification, as in "/DE," to indicate that the term should be searched only in the descriptor field. Term-specific codes were numbered 35–36 and 50–89. Also coded at the term level were substitutions for terms in search statements—i.e., use of search statement numbers (e.g., "S1") or term numbers in online indexes (e.g., "e1") and thesauri (e.g., "r1"). The number of search terms and term substitutes and their frequency of use were then tallied and analyzed.

A search term was defined as the string of characters bounded by the beginning or end of the search statement and by Boolean operators. Thus, the sample search statement above contains two search terms; "america?" and "weimar?" A search term could also contain more than one word, as many descriptors are multiword and contain no Boolean operators. A search term, as defined, could also contain proximity operators, truncation, and prefix and suffix codes. For example, the entire phrase "urban(w)experience?/ de" was considered a single term. Such proximity phrases were considered single terms, rather than combinations of terms, because searchers ordinarily combine words into a proximity phrase because the entire phrase is seen as a linguistic unit, or unitary concept, that needs to be searched as one. Terms combined with Boolean operators, on the other hand, are ordinarily seen as distinct linguistic units; consequently, search terms are counted as distinct when separated by Boolean operators.

Boolean operators *within* a proximity phrase or suffix-coded phrase were considered a part of the phrase and did not mark a separate term. For example, "urban(w)(experience OR milieu)" was treated as a single proximity phrase, and ("film? OR cinema? OR kino?)/ti" was treated as a single suffix-coded phrase. "Urban AND (experience OR milieu)," on the other hand, contains three distinct search terms. The reasoning here, again, was that whatever a searcher combines into a proximity phrase is intended to represent a single linguistic unit.

We could have attempted to break out the Boolean logic from the more complex phrases in order to count the constituent terms. For example, we could have converted urban(w)(experience OR milieu) into the two proximity phrases implicit in this complex phrase as follows:

urban(w)experience OR urban(w)milieu

However, we choose not to do so because: (1) the searchers had in fact not entered the terms this way and the count would be distorted, and (2) the searchers often confused some of the more complex DIALOG capabilities. Thus, *we* may have interpreted a phrase as being one of a certain type, but a searcher may not have intended it as such. We chose therefore to keep such complex phrases undifferentiated and to count them as they were formulated.

Both percentages of search statements and percentages of search terms are given in this study, where applicable. In the next sections, a description of the number and characteristics of the scholars' searches is presented, followed by an analysis of the features the searchers used in their search statements. Finally, the search statements are analyzed sequentially to identify changes in the sophistication of the searches.

## Results

### How much searching did the scholars do?

Table 1 presents the amount of searching done by the study participants in each year. For anonymity, individuals were given code numbers ranking them from most to least total search statements each year. These assigned numbers are used to designate the scholars throughout this report.

The scholar assigned number 10 in 1989, who returned in 1990 for a second year, ranked as number 17 in the second year. Thus, numbers 10 and 17 represent the same individual. Consequently, although 28 numbers were assigned, only 27 different individuals searched in the two years. While #10/17's data for 1990 are included for completeness in Table 1, only data from her first year, as #10, are included in the discussion of results in this section, in order to make her data comparable to that of other individuals in their first year.

In 1989, of the 13 scholars who received training, one (#13) subsequently did no searching at all, and another (#12) did only one assisted search. In 1990, of the 15 people trained, two (#27, #28) did no searching and one (#26)

TABLE 1. *Total search statements and time online of the scholars.*

| SEARCHER | TOTAL STATEMENTS | UNASSISTED SESSIONS | TIME ONLINE | NO. OF ASSISTED SEARCHES |
|---|---|---|---|---|
| 1 | 703 | 33 | 7.7 hr | 1 |
| 2 | 436 | 19 | 7.1 hr | 0 |
| 3 | 164 | 5 | 1.8 hr | 1 |
| 4 | 127 | 10 | 1.0 hr | 1 |
| 5 | 91 | 3 | 1.9 hr | 0 |
| 6 | 87 | 10 | 1.5 hr | 0 |
| 7 | 66 | 5 | 1.4 hr | 0 |
| 8 | 57 | 3 | 0.8 hr | 0 |
| 9 | 53 | 1 | 1.5 hr | 1 |
| 10 | 51 | 1 | 1.2 hr | 0 |
| 11 | 7 | 1 | 0.3 hr | 2 |
| 12 | 0 | 0 | 0.0 hr | 1 |
| 13 | 0 | 0 | 0.0 hr | 0 |
| 1989 TOTALS | 1,842 | 91 | 26.2 hr | 7 |
| 14 | 1,035[a] | 134 | 71.1 hr | 2 |
| 15 | 882 | 22 | 13.4 hr | 1 |
| 16 | 331 | 9 | 7.5 hr | 1 |
| 17 | 327 | 24 | 5.2 hr | 1 |
| 18 | 210 | 11 | 5.7 hr | 3 |
| 19 | 179 | 7 | 1.9 hr | 0 |
| 20 | 140 | 5 | 2.8 hr | 0 |
| 21 | 109 | 4 | 1.7 hr | 2 |
| 22 | 103 | 3 | 1.2 hr | 2 |
| 23 | 36 | 1 | 0.7 hr | 0 |
| 24 | 25 | 3 | 0.4 hr | 1 |
| 25 | 10 | 1 | 0.2 hr | 0 |
| 26 | 0 | 0 | 0.0 hr | 1 |
| 27 | 0 | 0 | 0.0 hr | 0 |
| 28 | 0 | 0 | 0.0 hr | 0 |
| 1990 TOTALS | 3,387 | 224 | 111.8 hr | 14 |
| GRAND TOTALS | 5,229 | 315 | 138.0 hr | 21 |

[a]*Only the first 1,035 statements of this scholar (equal to 28.7 hours) were analyzed; total number of statements for all sessions for this individual was not calculated.*

did only one assisted search. For whatever reasons, these five individuals did not make use of the opportunity the program offered.

An additional three people (#9–11) in 1989 and two (#23, #25) in 1990 had one unassisted search session each following training. This one session may have met all their needs; in any case, they did not come back a second time. (A session begins with a logon and ends with a logoff. A researcher may search one or more distinct queries during a session.) Four in each year came for three to five sessions, with four in 1989 and five (excluding #17) in 1990 conducting more than five search sessions—up to a high number of 33 sessions in 1989 and 134 in 1990.

In terms of time spent rather than number of sessions, five people, or 19%, spent no time doing unassisted searching; 15 people, or 56%, did at least some unassisted searching, but for less than two hours total. Ten of this latter group conducted more than one session, and five conducted five or more sessions.

Note also that scholar #10/17, who stayed the second year, had 1.2 hours of searching in 1989 and was counted in the group that searched less than two hours. In the second year, after a second training session, this individual did 5.2 more hours of searching—a very positive response. The remaining seven individuals (excluding #17) did extensive searching—all but one doing over five hours of searching.

Overall, about one fifth of the scholars did not take to online searching. The rest responded by doing unassisted searches, nearly all of them for at least several sessions, which showed they had developed some ease in using online searching. Over half of the scholars made moderate use of the capability; the remainder—over a quarter—made substantial use. But considering that they had come to do full-time research, and had unlimited access to the DIALOG service, they took less advantage of the opportunity than might have been expected. Some scholars may have had little need—they came planning to write, having done most of the research earlier. Others may have found only limited use for the service. The attitudes behind their response are explored in a third report on the project. The remainder of this report examines what the scholars did while online.

### What kinds of DIALOG features or search capabilities did they use?

This section presents figures for the use each year of the various features coded in the scholars' searching. Full code explanations are provided in the Appendix. In the following sections, code numbers are provided in parentheses to facilitate understanding of the source of data for each feature discussed.

As noted previously, data for both years of searching by the scholar who stayed for a second year (#10/17), are included throughout this section. This scholar's searching was minimal in 1989; consequently, use of search commands and other features analyzed in this section were deemed comparable to the searching behavior of the other scholars, and hence, appropriate for inclusion. This scholar is also included, for both years, in numbers of individuals who used given features throughout this section as well.

*Database selection* Single bibliographic databases (codes 01, 11) overwhelmingly predominated in the scholars' selections. No one used full text or other nonbibliographic databases (codes 12, 13), as they had been told in DIALOG training that few nonbibliographic databases of use to humanities scholars were available in DIALOG. They were also told about DIALINDEX, DIALOG's database to help searchers identify suitable databases, but they were not taught OneSearch, the DIALOG feature that allows searching of more than one database at a time with a given search formulation. However, OneSearch was described in the training manual all scholars received at the time of training, and was also mentioned in one of the 1990 group review sessions. In 1989, four people used DIALINDEX (code 15) at one time or another; none used OneSearch (code 17). In 1990, eight people used DIALINDEX and nine used OneSearch.

*Search commands* In the first year's study period the scholars entered 1,842 search statements; in the second year, they entered 3,387, for a total of 5,229. (Recall that only the first 1,035 statements entered by the prolific scholar in the second year were analyzed.) In Table 2, the distribution of search commands used in the statements is presented as percentages of total search statements and arrayed from highest to lowest combined frequency. Relevant codes and raw numbers are shown in parentheses. In some cases, scholars failed to include a search command in their statement or else entered commands that do not exist in DIALOG. These are listed in Table 2 under "No or non-existent command."

For every 20 commands entered, roughly nine were "Select" commands, five were "Type" commands, three were associated with database selection, and the remaining three covered everything else, including "Expand," paging, and "Display sets." Virtually all of the commands in the first category were for "Select" (code 23) rather than "Select steps" (code 24). In DIALOG, "Select" signals the system to search succeeding terms in the statement. The system then creates a single set reflecting postings of the entire statement. With "Select steps" the system creates separate sets for each component term in the statement, as well as for the final statement.

TABLE 2. *Distribution of commands across scholars' search statements.*

| COMMANDS (CODES) | 1989 PERCENTAGES (RAW NUMBERS) | | 1990 PERCENTAGES (RAW NUMBERS) | | 1989/1990 COMBINED PERCENTAGES (RAW NUMBERS) | |
|---|---|---|---|---|---|---|
| "Select" or "Select steps" (codes 23, 24) | 43.6 | (803) | 46.7 | (1,583) | 45.6 | (2,386) |
| "Type" (codes 91–98) | 28.3 | (522) | 24.8 | (840) | 26.0 | (1,362) |
| Database selection (codes 1, 11, 15–17) | 11.3 | (208) | 17.3 | (586) | 15.2 | (794) |
| "Expand" (codes 21, 22) | 10.0 | (185) | 5.7 | (194) | 7.2 | (379) |
| "Page" (code 32) | 2.4 | (45) | 3.0 | (103) | 2.8 | (148) |
| "Display sets" (code 28) | 3.4 | (63) | 0.4 | (15) | 1.5 | (78) |
| "Reduce duplicates" (code 19) | 0.0 | (0) | 0.5 | (18) | 0.3 | (18) |
| "Help" (code 27) | 0.1 | (1) | 0.0 | (0) | 0.0 | (1) |
| Search saving or executing (codes 33, 34) | 0.0 | (0) | 0.0 | (0) | 0.0 | (0) |
| No or nonexisting command | 0.8 | (15) | 1.4 | (48) | 1.2 | (63) |
| TOTAL SEARCH STATEMENTS | 99.9 | (1,842) | 99.8 | (3,387) | 99.8 | (5,229) |

NOTE: *Commands are arranged from most to least frequent in combined total. Percentages add to less than 100% due to rounding error. Raw numbers are in parentheses.*

Although available in the system, the command "Select steps" was not taught in the training. No one used this command during 1989, and three people used it just once each during 1990.

To print out information from the databases, the scholars needed the "Type" command only, not the "Print" command. "Type" prints out the information immediately at the terminal; "Print" commands the information to be typed out at DIALOG headquarters and sent to the searcher. For this project, scholars could print out everything they wanted locally with a "Type" command (codes 91–98).

Database selection was overwhelmingly for single databases (codes 1, 11). In 1989 only 20 out of 208 database-related commands (9.6%) were for DIALINDEX, and none was for OneSearch. In 1990, 5.0% of database-related commands were for DIALINDEX, and 1.7% were for OneSearch. All "Expand" commands for both years were for the general "Expand" (code 21), which presents an alphabetical list of terms in the selected index. The more sophisticated "Expand" (code 22) enables a searcher to look at the online thesaurus associated with a database. "Display sets" (code 28) displays all sets created thus far in the search in the current database. Page commands (code 32) enable the searcher to see the next entries in an index. Although search saving was taught in the training, no commands for search saving or executing (codes 33, 34) were used in either year. Given the difficulties that searchers experienced using the DIALOG command language, it is surprising that the "Help" command was used just once in two years.

In addition to the search commands described in Table 2, two other coded search capabilities can coexist in a search statement with some of the above commands: range searching and limiting. Range searching involves specifying a range of dates or codes to search on, e.g., "Select film and PY = 1982: 1989." It can be done with stated search terms, as in the preceding example (code 26), or by reference to "e" or "r" numbers in "Expand" printouts (code 25), e.g., Select e3: e6. Use of range searching was minimal. Uses of stated terms (code 26) were as follows: 1989: 1.2%; 1990: 0.2%; combined: 0.6%. Uses of "e" and "r" number ranges were 1989: 0.2%; 1990: 0.1%; combined: 0.1%.

"Limits" (code 29) were used in 1989 in 1.9% of search statements, but not at all in 1990, for a combined figure of 0.7%. (A "limit" can be a separate command in its own search statement, equivalent to a "Select" in its own statement, or it can come at the end of terms in conjunction with a "Select." The latter option accomplishes two things at once—selects terms and limits the range of dates or subfiles in which those terms will be searched. All limits used in this study were on the latter sort.)

***Boolean logic*** Both "Expand" and "Select" statements were coded for Boolean logic: that is, for codes 41–44, which include nonuse of Boolean logic (code 41) and use of it (codes 42–44). There is no need to use Boolean logic in "Expand" statements, but it was thought that such use might be common, nonetheless, because of the resemblance of "Select" statements to "Expand" statements; hence, its use was coded. In the event, no one used Boolean logic operators (codes 42–44) in 1989 in "Expand" statements, and only one individual used them a total of 11 times in 1990. Thus, use of Boolean logic in "Expand" commands will not be discussed further.

The four categories of codes 41–44 are, by definition, mutually exclusive and jointly exhaustive (41: no Boolean operators in statement; 42: ANDs and only ANDs, including AND NOT in statement; 43: ORs and only ORs in statement; 44: mixed ANDs and ORs in statement). The sum of these four categories (less Boolean-related coding for "Expand") should equal the sum of all "Select" commands. However, there is a discrepancy of about one-half of 1% between these two sums due to searcher error—for example, entering a "Select" without search terms, or a search term without a command—and possibly due to coding error.

The following statistics for the four Boolean categories of codes 41–44 are based on 790 "Select" statements in 1989, and 1,582 in 1990:

- *Code 41:* No Boolean operators in "Select" statement: 1989, 56.8%; 1990, 66.4%; combined, 63.2%

- *Code 42:* One or more ANDs and only ANDs in "Select" statement: 1989, 30.0%; 1990, 23.8%; combined, 25.9%

- *Code 43:* One or more ORs and only ORs in "Select" statement: 1989, 11.4%; 1990, 8.7%; combined, 9.6%

- *Code 44:* Mixed ANDs and ORs in "Select" statement: 1989, 1.8%; 1990, 1.1%; combined, 1.3%

Thus, overall, searchers avoided Boolean logic altogether more often than not, entering single terms nearly two-thirds of the time in "Select" statements. About one-quarter of the time they used the Boolean AND, and less than 10% of the time they used the Boolean OR.

In addition, statements were coded for the presence of NOTs (code 47), which are a form of AND, as implemented in DIALOG (OR NOT is not permitted), and so fall within the AND category. Only one "Select" statement in the whole set used a NOT in 1989; none was used in 1990. This is not surprising, as the training contained the usual cautions about the dangers of using NOT. Use of parentheses (code 45) was also coded: In 1989, 1.3% of "Select" statements used parentheses; in 1990, 4.0% used them, for a combined figure of 3.1%.

Although at first glance this pattern apparently indicates an elementary, unsophisticated use of Boolean logic, the pattern may look simpler than it actually is. The training had emphasized use of the "building block" approach to search formulation, Charles Bourne's concept (see Markey & Cochrane, 1981). In the building block strategy, the searcher breaks the query down into its distinct conceptual elements, or building blocks. Each building block is entered in a separate statement, then all blocks are combined in a single final "AND" statement. Concepts can be stated in many different ways, however. When the searcher knows more than one way to state a building block element, these variant terms are to be entered as an OR "hedge," that is, as a string of terms combined with ORs only, e.g., Term A OR Term B OR Term C. Thus, the searcher never needs to combine ANDs and ORs in a single statement. This approach helps the searcher keep the distinct concepts clearly in mind and reduces confusion about the use of Boolean logic.

The following example from the scholars' searches can be seen as a two-concept, or two-building-block, query:

S art(w)criticism

S Greece

S S1 AND S2 [S1 and S2 represent the first two search statements.]

Had the searcher wanted to search on variants of one of the terms in this case, the search could have been entered as follows:

S art(w)criticism

S Greece OR Greek OR Grecian

S S1 AND S2

Putting aside the question of whether the best vocabulary has been chosen, in terms of Boolean logic, this is a search query of excellent design. Yet it produces one statement with no Boolean logic, one with only ORs, and one with only an AND. So the apparently simple logic these scholars used may actually be quite good and be all that is needed to produce a good search.

One way to tell whether searchers are showing sophistication in their search formulations is to look at how often they employ set numbers instead of actual search terms. Set numbers, by definition, refer to earlier statements. When they are used in a search statement, therefore, they are necessarily incorporating earlier term(s) in a later statement. This would be consonant with use of the building block strategy (though other techniques could produce these results too).

Searchers used set numbers (code 35) a total of 414 times in 1,842 statements in 1989, and 556 times in 3,387 statements in 1990. We cannot convert these figures into percentages of statements in which set numbers were used, however, because they represent total uses of set numbers— sometimes two or three in a statement—rather than total statements in which they were used. We can, however, compare these figures to those for search terms: that is, the actual terms themselves (e.g., "Greece"). In 1989, 836 search terms were entered; in 1990, 1,902. Thus, in 1989 there were approximately half as many references to terms (414) as there were uses of terms themselves (836) and, in 1990, the ratio was about 30% (556 to 1,902). This high use of statement numbers suggests that some scholars made reasonably sophisticated use of the Boolean features available.

There may, however, have been some variation in sophistication from one searcher to another. Table 3 shows how many individuals ever input

TABLE 3. *Number of scholars ever employing various Boolean operators.*

| | 1989 | 1990 | COMBINED |
|---|---|---|---|
| 1. Never used Boolean logic | 2 | 1 | 3 |
| 2. No logic or ANDs (codes 41 and 42 only) | 4 | 1 | 5 |
| 3. No logic or ORs (codes 41 and 43 only) | 0 | 1 | 1 |
| 4. No logic or ANDs or ORs (codes 41 and 42 and 43 only) | 2 | 6 | 8 |
| 5. All combinations (codes 41 and 42 and 43 and 44) | 3 | 3 | 6 |
| TOTAL SCHOLARS | 11 | 12 | 23 |

NOTE: *Each row represents types of Boolean operators ever used by scholars in their entire search histories. For example, scholars falling in the fourth row input some search statements with no Boolean operators (code 41), some that used ANDs (code 42), some that used ORs (code 43), but none that combined ANDs and ORs in the same search statement (code 44). Scholar #10/17, who stayed for a second year, is counted in both years in row 2.*

search statements employing the various Boolean operators or operator combinations covered in codes 41–44. For example, the fourth row of Table 3 includes scholars who input some search statements with no Boolean operators (code 41), some with ANDs (code 42), some with ORs (code 43), but none that combined ANDs and ORs in the same search statement (code 44).

The three individuals in the first row of Table 3 who never used Boolean operators did little searching overall. Those in the second row who used either no Boolean logic or statements that contained only ANDs (codes 41 and 42) may have been using the building block strategy, but if so, it was a simplified form.

Only three scholars in each year (row 5 in Table 3) ever attempted to combine ANDs and ORs in a single search statement; the others entered search statements each of which used no Boolean logic, only ANDs, or only ORs throughout their search histories. As noted earlier, however, the building block strategy is a good one. By employing it the searcher does not need to use parentheses or remember the processing sequence for different Boolean operators (which would determine the order of entering search terms in the search statement). Incidentally, only two people in 1989 and four in 1990 ever used parentheses (code 45).

More troubling is the fact that six people in 1989 and two in 1990 (rows 1 and 2 combined) never used even a single OR. That suggests that they may not have appreciated the importance of entering a variety of terms for a single concept. In that case, they may have been entering single concepts one at a time and ANDing the final result. Alternatively, if they did understand, and wanted to enter term variants, they would have had

TABLE 4. *Use of search terms and search term substitutes.*

| | 1989 PERCENTAGES (RAW NUMBERS) | | 1990 PERCENTAGES (RAW NUMBERS) | | 1989/1990 COMBINED PERCENTAGES (RAW NUMBERS) | |
|---|---|---|---|---|---|---|
| Search terms (codes 51, 52) | 57.3 | (836) | 72.0 | (1,902) | 66.8 | (2,738) |
| Search statement numbers (code 35) | 28.4 | (414) | 21.0 | (556) | 23.7 | (970) |
| Index or thesaurus term number (code 36) | 14.3 | (209) | 7.0 | (184) | 9.6 | (393) |
| TOTAL SEARCH TERMS AND SUBSTITUTES | 100.0 | (1,459) | 100.0 | (2,642) | 100.1 | (4,101) |

NOTE: *Sum totals no more than 100% due to rounding error. Raw numbers are in parentheses.*

to use a cumbersome method of separately entering distinct searches for each possible term variant—for example, "Art(w)criticism AND Greece," then "Art(w)criticism AND Greek," then "Art(w)criticism AND Grecian." Either way, they failed to utilize the full potential of the search system.

*Vocabulary features. Total use of terms and substitutes for terms* A searcher could enter the term itself or a substitute for the term if some previous reference to it had been made. Because codes 51 for a single-word and 52 for a multiword term jointly exhaust the total possible search terms, the two codes combined should equal the total number of search terms (as distinct from substitutes) entered by the scholars. Substitutes include references to previous search statements (e.g., "S2") or index or thesaurus entries (e.g., "e1" or "r1"), and were counted with codes 35 and 36, respectively. Table 4 provides figures for all types of terms and substitutes. We see that about two-thirds of the time the scholars entered the term itself and the rest of the time they entered a substitute for it.

Because figures for total search terms in Table 4 include prefix-coded terms, they differ from those in Report no. 1 of this series (Bates et al., 1993), which excludes prefix-coded terms, for reasons explained there. Also, Report No. 1 distinguishes between search term "types," referring to distinct terms, and "tokens," referring to total uses of terms, including repetitions of the same term. All references to terms in this report are to tokens.

Drawing on data in the above tables, we find that the average number of terms or term substitutes used per "Select" statement is 1.6. (This figure is approximate, as a smattering of terms or term substitutes appear in erroneous statements that have no commands, and in "Reduce duplicates" commands. Also, we assume the "Expand" commands contain only one term; the few erroneous "Expands" with more than one term would change the figure slightly.)

*Types of search terms: proper/common, subject/author.* For many years it has been said that the vocabulary used by humanities scholars is less precise than that used by scientists, and that this imprecision makes it more difficult to search topics in the humanities. Wiberley argues that the truth of the matter is more complicated, and that many terms humanities scholars use are very precise, others less so. In two studies he has developed categories of precision of vocabulary to describe terms used in encyclopedias and dictionaries (1983) and in bibliographic services (1988). Wiberley described the kinds of terms used by information producers; we looked at those used by scholars in searching. We were less interested in identifying precision of vocabulary *per se* than in discovering broad categories of terms that characterized the search terms humanities scholars used. The distinction between common and proper terms is important to Wiberley; he argues that humanists use a large number of proper terms.

For this study, we designated four categories of terms covering proper and common terms. (Search terms were given more detailed analysis in Bates et al., 1993.) The searchers entered 836 terms in 1989 and 1,902 terms in 1990. Here are the categories, with their percentages:

- *Code 53:* Proper term—personal name—includes fictional and mythic characters: 1989, 47.1%; 1990, 40.6%; combined, 42.6% of all terms.

- *Code 54:* Proper term—geographical name: 1989, 7.2%; 1990, 10.1%; combined, 9.3% of all terms.

- *Code 55:* Proper term—other: 1989, 7.1%; 1990, 6.8%; combined, 6.9% of all terms.

- *Code 56:* Common (lower-case) term: 1989, 40.0%; 1990, 46.2%; combined, 44.3% of all terms.

Totals add to slightly more than 100% because some terms, as defined, were compound. When a searcher input the phrase, "Renaissance(w) miniature," for example, two different codes were applied to the single term (codes 55 and 56). Although the majority of search terms, proper and common, are nouns, some are not—e.g., "Renaissance" is an adjective here—hence, the use of "term" rather than "noun" in the above definitions.

Note that the above figures include *all* search terms entered, including terms with prefixes for indexes not in DIALOG's "Basic Index," a merged file of all subject related fields in a database. Therefore, the categories above include codes for journal titles, document types, and other prefixed terms. All prefixed terms added together constitute 20.9% of all search terms in 1989 and 5.0% in 1990, for a combined figure of 9.9% of all search terms (codes 81–89). Some of these prefixed terms are for subject classification codes or other types of subject terms, but most are not. The remaining 90.1% of search terms were used in subject searches.

Unlike most figures compared for the two years, the discrepancy in percentages of prefixed terms between 1989 and 1990 (20.9% and 5.0%) is strikingly large. This difference appears due to the fact that the use of prefixes varied markedly from one scholar to another: Fully 123 of the 175 prefix uses in 1989 came from a single searcher, while 56 of the 96 uses in 1990 were from a single searcher. Otherwise, no one used prefixes more than 16 times. Five people in 1989 and six in 1990 never used prefixes, three in 1989 and two in 1990 used prefixes only for authors' names.

Of the total terms, 5.4%, or just over half of the 9.9% that were prefixed terms, were "AU=," that is, author search terms (code 81). The rest represented a sprinkling of various prefixes, some qualifying for the proper term categories, some for the common term category. So the high percentages of proper noun terms found above are still largely reflective of their proportion in *subject* rather than *author* searches.

Looking again at the figures for types of vocabulary as a whole, rather than just within prefixed terms, we see that more than two out of five of all terms searched contained personal names, and nearly three out of five terms contained proper terms of one sort or another. The sciences show a dramatically different pattern of search terms. A more detailed discussion appears in Bates et al. (1993).

Finally, it is notable that only 5.4% of search terms were for author searches. Searches on names were for those names as subjects of research for the most part, not as authors. Research on library catalog use, on the other hand, shows a higher proportion of author searches. Markey reviews eight studies of online catalog use which found a combined average of 19% author searches (reported in Markey, 1984, p. 77); figures for card catalogs were even higher (p. 76). Furthermore, the more advanced the researcher, the higher the percentage of author searches in card catalogs (Montague, 1967). These findings suggest that the researchers in our study saw the databases as useful primarily for subject searching. Interviews confirmed that the scholars tended to use their access to the "ORION" online catalog for known-item searching in the Getty's collection and that of the nearby University of California at Los Angeles.

*One-word and multiword terms.* Because the scholars showed a strong tendency to use single-word terms in their search statements, we decided to create categories for single and multiword terms to see just how common this pattern was. Of all search terms, 71.1% in 1989, 58.7% in 1990, and 62.5% combined were single-word (code 51), and the remainder multiword (code 52). These figures for single-word terms seem intuitively quite high in comparison to searches done by professional searchers.

The between-years discrepancy in percentages of single-word terms is striking here as well, and seems to be associated with individual differences. In 1989 just two people used more multiword terms than single words, with many among the remaining using far more single- than multiword terms. In 1990, five people, or nearly half, used more multiword than single-word terms.

The contrasts were sometimes quite marked. In 1990, for example, one person (#15) used 493 single-word terms to 130 multiword terms; another (#16) showed the opposite pattern in using 175 multiword terms to 40 single-word. Examination of their data sheets suggests that this difference can be attributed more to personal searching style than to the content of the searches. Distribution of search terms among the four term-type categories (codes 53–56) is quite similar for these two individuals despite the difference in single-word versus multiword term use.

The caution shown by this persistent use of single word terms is understandable for beginners. The researchers were taught the distinction between word- and phrase-indexed fields during training, but understanding its implications for retrieval effectiveness is a subtle matter. Failure to understand this distinction can make for jumbled and inconsistent search formulations.

Having taught online searching for many years, Bates has found that students often do not fully grasp the implications of these concepts for several weeks—even when the initial explanation is quite elaborate. One way to avoid having to deal with the word indexing/phrase indexing distinction is to use single-word terms. A better way, however, is to use proximity operators.

*Use of controlled vocabulary and proximity operators.* In most cases, we had no way of knowing whether searchers themselves knew—or cared—if a search term they used was a controlled vocabulary term or a natural language term. Yet, in some cases, we found clues to searcher intent. We can assume that searchers expected to make a match with controlled terms in those cases where they used controlled term suffixes, specifically, DE (descriptor), DF (single-word descriptor), ID (identifier), and IF (single-word identifier) in DIALOG. Proximity operators, on the other hand, serve to make phrases searchable in word-indexed fields. In the Basic Index, phrase-indexed fields are usually descriptors, and fields that are word-indexed only are not.

We found that the scholars used little suffix specification of any type. In 1989, 2.4% of search terms had suffixes for controlled terms (code 57, which equals the sum of codes 71–74); the same figure for 1990 was 0.4%, for a combined figure of 1.0%. For search terms with other suffixes in the Basic Index (code 58, which equals the sum of codes 75–79), the 1989 percentage is 1.4, the 1990 percentage is 0.7, and the combined figure is 0.9. Overall, just 2.0% of all terms both years had some sort of suffix specification.

Scholars used proximity operators more frequently: Of all search terms, 15.7% in 1989, 20.9% in 1990, and 19.3% combined contained one or more proximity operators (codes 61–65). The operators (w), i.e., two words adjacent in exact order (code 61), and (n), i.e., two words adjacent in any order (code 63), were both prevalent in both years, (w) being used more than (n). These were the only proximity operators the scholars used in 1989; in 1990 they used a few (f) operators, i.e., words in same field (code 62). About a quarter of the time, searchers also specified the number of intervening words (code 67). But from contextual clues we suspect that some searchers thought they had to use the number 1, as in (1w), even for adjacent words with no intervening words, when (w) would have sufficed. Such an error has minimal consequences, however.

We can now put these results together to see how search patterns influence search success. Multiword terms constituted 37.5% of all search terms for both years, and yet only 19.3% of search terms used proximity operators. That leaves 18.2% of terms that were entered as multiword search phrases without proximity operators. *No multiword phrases without proximity operators will match in any field that is not phrase-indexed.* In the Basic Index it is usually only controlled vocabulary fields that are phrase-indexed. Thus, 18.2% of the time the searchers were vulnerable to zero results if their phrase did not happen to be a controlled vocabulary term, or if the query was run against a prefixed field that was not phrase-indexed. Thus, to do knowledgeable searching with multiword terms, the end user has to understand the nuances of word- versus phrase-indexing when entering a multiword phrase without proximity operators.

As a way around this problem, end users may simply be instructed to use proximity operators whenever they enter a term containing more than one word. Although users may retrieve too much, they will avoid the mysterious zero results sets that appear randomly for presumably popular topics when they enter a phrase instead of a single word for a search topic.

*Truncation.* Truncation (code 68) was moderately prevalent, being used in 16.4% (1989), 36.2% (1990), and 30.1% (combined) of search terms. No one specified the number of characters to be truncated (code 69).

*Proportions of searchers who used vocabulary features.* All or almost all searchers used the vocabulary types described above: single- and multiword phrases, proper nouns, and common terms. Nine 1989 and 11 1990 searchers used proximity operators at one time or another, and nine 1989 and 11 1990 searchers used truncation. Finally, in 1989, three people used both suffix and prefix specification, while one used suffix specification only and three others used prefix specification only, for a total of seven who used some form of affix. In 1990, two people used prefix and suffix specification both, while four used prefix only and three used suffix only, for a total of nine who used some form of affix.

**Type formats** Most searchers used several different "Type" formats. All formats were used at least a little. Everyone used format 5 (code 95), the most popular, during the first year and 11 out of 12 searchers used it in the second year. In fact, 14.0% of all search statements *of any type* were "Type" statements in format 5. Format 3 (code 93), the second most common type of format, was used by eight people in 1989 and ten in 1990. (As noted earlier, because the study's computer program printed all searches locally, the searchers did not need to use the "Print" command for remote printing.)

**Errors** Each statement was coded as follows to indicate whether a probable error or a certain error occurred anywhere within it:

- *Probable error (code 08):* Very poor strategy or grossly inefficient approach—there are common superior ways of doing this, but a searcher could conceivably have some reason for doing this. Code conservatively.

- *Certain error (code 09):* Nonexistent or incorrectly formatted or spelled command or other component of statement; something about this statement has to fail, no matter what the searcher's intentions might have been.

Of all statements, 4.0% (1989), 10.3% (1990), and 8.1% (combined) contained one or more probable errors as defined above; 6.2% (1989), 10.3% (1990), 8.9% (combined) contained certain errors. In principle, any given statement can be coded either 08 or 09 or both. In other words, adding the rates of 08 and 09 together may not give an accurate percentage of all statements, because in some cases both codes apply to the same statement.

In practice, however, both 08 and 09 were coded in only four statements out of the total 5,229, all in 1990.

Thus for all intents and purposes, percentages for 08 and 09 codes may be added together to get the complete error rates for groups or individuals. These are the grand totals for probable plus certain errors:

- 1989: 10.2% of search statements;
- 1990: 20.6% of search statements;
- Combined: 17.0% of search statements.

We can also use these data to compute the mean of the searchers' error percentages. The above figures are strongly influenced by the scores of the searchers who did a great deal of searching. Averaging gives each searcher an equal weight and results in these mean error rate percentages for combined probable and certain errors:

- 1989 mean of 11 searchers' rates: 11.4%;
- 1990 mean of 12 searchers' rates: 19.0%.

These figures are strongly influenced by the searchers who did little searching and scored high error rates for the short time they searched. If we recompute the mean without those who searched 50 or fewer statements, we get the following lower rates, which nonetheless exhibit the same general pattern—much higher error rates in 1990 than in 1989:

- 1989 mean of 10 searchers' rates: 9.7%;
- 1990 mean of 9 searchers' rates: 17.3%.

The first year's error rate is quite good, all things considered. Effective online database searching requires more knowledge than effective online catalog searching in many cases, as catalogs are designed for end users and are comparatively easy to use. Despite this fact, research on online catalog transcripts has sometimes produced higher error rates (Borgman, 1986). Error rates at this level can be easily overcome by experimentally reentering statements in a different form, which searchers frequently did.

The finding that error rates doubled in the second year, however, is one of the most puzzling produced by this study. Is this result simply due to sample variation—something inherently different about the searching styles of the 1990 group? There is no way to know this for certain in inductive research, but several alternative explanations were considered:

(1)  *Was there a change in coding pattern?* Did the coder gradually shift in error assignments, perhaps gaining greater skill in recognizing errors as time went on? This explanation is theoretically possible as all 1989 coding was done before 1990 coding began. However, we may presume that certain errors (code 09) were always easier to recognize than probable errors (code 08) and more unambiguous for a coder to assign. Presumably coding for certain errors would not change as much as coding for probable errors under such a hypothesis. Codes for certain errors rose from 6.2% to 10.3%, while probable errors went from 4.0% to 10.2%. The jump is indeed larger for probable errors than certain errors, but the jump is so great for certain errors, too, that change in coder patterns is unlikely to carry us very far as an explanation for the change between years.

(2)  *Were a few individuals with extra-high error rates influencing the results?* Combined error rate percentages of all who searched unassisted were arrayed to produce the median error rate for each year. (The median is an average that shows the midpoint in a set of figures uninfluenced by extremes. It is determined by arraying a set of figures from largest to smallest, then selecting the value which represents the midpoint in the array.) The median combined error rate in 1989 was 9.7%; in 1990, it was 16.75%. These figures close the gap a little, suggesting that extra-high error rates of some individuals in 1990 did influence the results disproportionately. A substantial difference between the two years remains, however, and can be seen in another statistic: The range of error rate percentages of individuals with over 50 statements was 4.6–12.3% in 1989, and 7.7–32.8% in 1990.

(3)  *Was the training in 1989 different enough from that in 1990 to produce different error rates?* Techniques taught and information given in both years were generally the same. The training was based on the standard DIALOG training, with some modifications—principally in the examples chosen—to meet the needs of humanities scholars. The same person conducted the training both years. Therefore, it seems unlikely that differences in initial training are responsible for error differences. However, it is always possible that an explanation of some frequently used feature just happened to be clearer one year than the other. We cannot know whether such a thing happened, because error rates were analyzed only at the global level of "probable" and "certain." Also, the use of comparative searches the first year and group review sessions the second could have had some impact. The added fact that there were twice as many assisted searches—which the searchers liked

and felt they benefited from—during 1990 than in 1989 only adds to the puzzle of higher error rates the second year.

(4) *Did the searchers during the second year try more features and therefore make more mistakes along the way?* Apparently this was not the case. Searchers in 1990 made more use of DIALINDEX and OneSearch, as well as proximity searching and truncation, but they used proportionately fewer complex Boolean statements and made less frequent use of prefixes and suffixes.

In summary, there appears to be no single, certain explanation for the large jump in error rates from 1989 to 1990. The difference between the years may be caused by a combination of several things, but we hypothesize that the largest single cause remains sample variation, that is, differences in the searching styles among individuals in the two groups.

## Was there a learning curve?
## Did the scholars' searching change with experience?

*Learning curve analysis* Although the project's purpose was not to produce better searchers, we wanted to get some sense of whether there was a learning curve through the history of each searcher's experience. Several possibilities came to mind:

- Search skills could steadily grow, with the searcher using more and more features and capabilities during the course of the project.

- Search skills could steadily decline, as the searcher used the system only rarely and more and more time passed after the date of training.

- Search skill could appear in bursts, with the searcher forgetting techniques during the long periods between searches, then remembering these techniques during the course of a session.

In this study, the learning curve was probably also influenced by the three forms of assistance the scholars received during the project: assisted searches (1989 and 1990), comparative searches (1989), and group review sessions (1990). As they were scheduled to meet the scholars' needs, these forms of assistance—particularly the assisted searches—came at different stages in each scholar's search history and with different gaps in time between the assistance and subsequent independent searching.

Further, the amount and type of assistance used varied from one individual to the next. To break a study group of this size into all the possible treatment groups generated by the above combinations would have produced cells with only a few individuals in each. We chose, therefore, to ignore these differences in individual experience and look at the group as a whole to see if any overall patterns emerged.

Next came the question of how to measure the learning curve—a tricky business for several reasons. First, skill operates at many levels, and some subtle kinds of skills would not show up in statistics on the use of specific search features. Second, a searcher could, in principle, master every feature taught in the training but not need to use a particular feature until several hours of searching had passed, which use would not reflect new learning but only a latency in need. Finally, the amount of searching done by the searchers in this study varied greatly. As a practical matter, how could we survey their searching development at comparable points?

We decided nonetheless to examine the use of features as at least a partial indicator of development of skill. Even if new uses of DIALOG features did not reflect all the subtler gains in skill and knowledge, we saw them as reflecting some kind of development. As for the possibility that searchers mastered skills during training which they did not need until later, we considered the fact that real mastery probably occurs only when there is a need to use a capability in association with a real search. Thus, the scholars' later use of techniques learned earlier in fact represented important learning. In other cases, their new use of a feature arose because, *for the first time,* they considered how to achieve a certain result and looked up the means to accomplish it.

Even overcoming these concerns, measuring the use of features remains difficult. What is the relevant unit to use to measure learning through time? Many are possible: the passage of time during sessions, passage of time overall, number of statements, number of searches, number of search sessions. But passage of time during a session, though seemingly the most direct and literal measure, has flaws. Strategic behavior is really manifested in the search statements people enter. Yet sometimes searchers sat viewing many screens of records for long periods of time without entering any search statements. In the end we decided to use the search statement as the unit of measure. Each statement entered (beginning with system prompt and ending with "enter") was numbered from the beginning to the end of an individual's search career during the project.

The next question was how to compare searches for scholars with dissimilar amounts of searching. Comparing, for example, the first 20 statements with the last 20 executed by each scholar would produce a comparison at wildly dissimilar points in the history of a scholar's experience, since some searched only a few minutes and others hours. We decided instead to sample searching patterns at comparable points in each scholar's search career, as long as that career lasted.

First, searchers with fewer than 50 statements in their search histories were eliminated because their search histories were seen as too short to demonstrate progress or the lack of it. As noted earlier, scholar #10 returned for a second year—her search history for 1990 was given the number 17. As she was not a beginner in 1990, her 1990 data were eliminated from consideration for Tables 5-7. After these deletions, ten 1989 scholars and eight 1990 scholars remained for learning curve analysis.

All these scholars had searches totaling at least 50 statements. We compared the first ten statements (numbers 1-10) with the ten close to the end of the shorter searching histories, namely statements 41-50, establishing a gap of 30 statements. We continued this pattern with subsequent 30 statement jumps for all the searchers, so that ten sequential statements were examined in every 40. Thus, figures in the tests below were tallied and compared for search statements 1-10, 41-50, 81-90, 121-130, 161-170, and 201-210 in each searcher's history until the search statements ran out. Only full sets of ten statements were used; if an individual's search history ended part way through one of the ten-statement benchmark sets, that set was not included for that individual. We looked at these statement sets to determine when searchers first used a feature, how many elementary statements they used, and how many errors they made.

*First use of features* We tallied the point of first use by each scholar of each feature coded in this study. Presumably, if the scholars continually introduced new features into their search statements, then they were learning and growing in their capabilities. On the other hand, if new features failed to appear, then in terms of technique, they were carrying out the same search again and again.

A nonredundant set of codes was selected for this analysis; specifically, where two codes represented two different ways of analyzing the same data, one of the codes was eliminated. Codes tallied in Table 5 were 11-56 and 61-99.

Table 5 shows how many new search features were introduced in each ten-statement set for each of 18 searchers who entered at least 50 statements. It also shows the total number of features ever used by each scholar (based on the entire search history of the individual, not just the test sets).

TABLE 5. *Number of features first used in each benchmark ten-statement set.*

| SCHOLAR CODE NO. | TOTAL STATE-MENTS | FEATURES EVER USED | 1–10 | 41–50 | 81–90 | 121–130 | 161–170 | 201–210 |
|---|---|---|---|---|---|---|---|---|
| **1989** | | | | | | | | |
| 1 | 703 | 40 | 12 | 0 | 2 | 0 | 1 | 0 |
| 2 | 436 | 37 | 15 | 1 | 0 | 0 | 1 | 0 |
| 3 | 164 | 26 | 10 | 0 | 3 | 1 | — | — |
| 4 | 127 | 21 | 10 | 2 | 0 | — | — | — |
| 5 | 91 | 25 | 14 | 0 | 0 | — | — | — |
| 6 | 87 | 17 | 9 | 0 | — | — | — | — |
| 7 | 66 | 26 | 10 | 3 | — | — | — | — |
| 8 | 57 | 16 | 9 | 1 | — | — | — | — |
| 9 | 53 | 18 | 9 | 0 | — | — | — | — |
| 10 | 51 | 17 | 13 | 0 | — | — | — | — |
| **1990** | | | | | | | | |
| 14 | 1,035 | 27 | 13 | 0 | 1 | 0 | 3 | 0 |
| 15 | 882 | 30 | 8 | 3 | 4 | 1 | 0 | 1 |
| 16 | 331 | 29 | 8 | 2 | 0 | 1 | 0 | 0 |
| 18 | 210 | 25 | 12 | 0 | 0 | 0 | 2 | 0 |
| 19 | 179 | 24 | 15 | 0 | 1 | 0 | 1 | — |
| 20 | 140 | 28 | 14 | 2 | 0 | 0 | — | — |
| 21 | 109 | 32 | 11 | 3 | 4 | — | — | — |
| 22 | 103 | 23 | 13 | 6 | 0 | — | — | — |

NOTE: *Regarding missing scholar code numbers, see the subsection Learning Curve Analysis for inclusion criteria for this table.*

After the first ten statements, which of course contain first uses of many features, new uses fall off, but features do continue to be introduced. The large difference between the number of features introduced in the first ten statements and the total ever used by the scholars indicates that many features were introduced later in their search histories. Incidence of new features appears to be scattered randomly over the search histories beyond the first set. The two most active searchers in 1989 used noticeably more total features than the other members of their cohort. However, the total number of features ever used is fairly evenly distributed among the 1990 cohort, regardless of the amount of searching.

*Use of elementary search statements* Six codes identified search behaviors that were seen as the most elementary search statements possible. For example, a command to select a single one-word term with no truncation or suffix modification constituted the most elementary search statement one could make and still be conducting a search. Scholars' search statements were coded for these "vanilla" traits as a measure of the sophistication of the search behavior of the scholars. If the scholars' searching consisted mostly of these six elementary statement types, then we could say that they had mastered the basics but little beyond. Further, if they started with many elementary statements and then used fewer and fewer of them as they gained more searching experience, then it would appear that they were moving beyond the basics. These were the six elementary statements:

- Enter single bibliographic database at start of a session (code 01) (switching databases later during the session represents a step beyond and is not included in this code).

- Expand a single one-word term without prefix (code 02).

- Search (select) a single one-word term, unmodified (code 03).

- Expand a single "AU=" prefixed name (code 04).

- Search (select) a single "AU=" prefixed name (code 05).

- One single (3-part) "Type" statement constitutes entire statement (code 06).

These basic codes provided all the categories necessary to do a complete, if elementary, search: database selection, expands, select statements, and "Types." In the final tally, however, we ignored codes for "Types" because printing out was a skill area in which searchers did not advance. They all used only the basic approach they had been taught. They did not have the opportunity to learn to sort output or create reports, for example.

Table 6 lists the number of basic statements (codes 01–05 only) each searcher used during each of the ten-statement benchmark periods.

These elementary codes were applicable to more than half of the first ten statements for only one searcher, and most had considerably fewer. So it appears that, even at the beginning, the one-day training the scholars received enabled them to move beyond the most elementary searching.

TABLE 6. *Rate of use of elementary search statements in benchmark ten-statement sets.*

| SCHOLAR CODE NO. | TOTAL STATE-MENTS | 1–10 | 41–50 | 81–90 | 121–130 | 161–170 | 201–210 |
|---|---|---|---|---|---|---|---|
| **1989** | | | | | | | |
| 1 | 703 | 1 | 1 | 0 | 1 | 5 | 1 |
| 2 | 436 | 1 | 0 | 1 | 2 | 3 | 4 |
| 3 | 164 | 1 | 0 | 2 | 4 | — | — |
| 4 | 127 | 6 | 7 | 4 | — | — | — |
| 5 | 91 | 1 | 4 | 0 | — | — | — |
| 6 | 87 | 2 | 1 | — | — | — | — |
| 7 | 66 | 3 | 0 | — | — | — | — |
| 8 | 57 | 4 | 2 | — | — | — | — |
| 9 | 53 | 5 | 3 | — | — | — | — |
| 10 | 51 | 3 | 0 | — | — | — | — |
| **1990** | | | | | | | |
| 14 | 1,035 | 1 | 0 | 1 | 1 | 4 | 1 |
| 15 | 882 | 0 | 0 | 2 | 1 | 3 | 0 |
| 16 | 331 | 1 | 0 | 0 | 0 | 0 | 0 |
| 18 | 210 | 1 | 0 | 0 | 0 | 2 | 2 |
| 19 | 179 | 2 | 6 | 3 | 4 | 2 | — |
| 20 | 140 | 0 | 0 | 1 | 3 | — | — |
| 21 | 109 | 3 | 1 | 0 | — | — | — |
| 22 | 103 | 0 | 1 | 0 | — | — | — |

NOTE: *Regarding missing scholar code numbers, see the subsection Learning Curve Analysis for inclusion criteria for this table.*

On the other hand, basic statements continue to appear later in the search histories. Although experienced searchers often need to enter simple search statements, too, we might have expected somewhat fewer than were used here. This continued use may be due to the practice of using a simplified form of the building block strategy, as discussed in the previous section titled Boolean Logic, or it may also indicate that scholars forgot techniques over time and consequently resorted to the basics. Finally, searching styles may have played a part. For example, searchers #4 and #19

TABLE 7. *Error rates in benchmark ten-statement sets.*

| SCHOLAR CODE NO. | TOTAL STATE-MENTS | 1–10 | 41–50 | 81–90 | 121–130 | 161–170 | 201–210 |
|---|---|---|---|---|---|---|---|
| **1989** | | | | | | | |
| 1 | 703 | 2 | 2 | 2 | 0 | 2 | 1 |
| 2 | 436 | 0 | 0 | 1 | 1 | 2 | 0 |
| 3 | 164 | 3 | 1 | 2 | 0 | — | — |
| 4 | 127 | 0 | 4 | 0 | — | — | — |
| 5 | 91 | 1 | 1 | 2 | — | — | — |
| 6 | 87 | 1 | 0 | — | — | — | — |
| 7 | 66 | 0 | 3 | — | — | — | — |
| 8 | 57 | 2 | 0 | — | — | — | — |
| 9 | 53 | 0 | 3 | — | — | — | — |
| 10 | 51 | 2 | 1 | — | — | — | — |
| **1990** | | | | | | | |
| 14 | 1,035 | 1 | 6 | 6 | 8 | 7 | 5 |
| 15 | 882 | 1 | 2 | 1 | 2 | 0 | 1 |
| 16 | 331 | 1 | 0 | 2 | 1 | 2 | 4 |
| 18 | 210 | 1 | 4 | 1 | 1 | 0 | 1 |
| 19 | 179 | 5 | 2 | 1 | 0 | 1 | — |
| 20 | 140 | 4 | 0 | 1 | 0 | — | — |
| 21 | 109 | 5 | 6 | 3 | — | — | — |
| 22 | 103 | 1 | 0 | 0 | — | — | — |

NOTE: *Regarding missing scholar code numbers, see the subsection Learning Curve Analysis for inclusion criteria for this table.*

consistently made substantial use of these types of statements throughout their histories.

***Error rate*** We also looked at error rates (codes 08, 09) as another test of learning. If searchers were learning through time, then we might expect their error rates to go down from an initial high rate. Table 7 displays the combined number of probable and certain errors identified in each of the six benchmark statement sets.

The training appears to have stood the scholars in good stead because most started their search histories with a low error rate. On the other hand, the errors do not fall off much, which suggests that they forgot from one session to another. Scholar #14, however, had a consistently high error rate, making 33 errors in the 60 statements represented by the six test sets. Furthermore, summary figures for his search history show a combined rate of more than 30%: that is, nearly one-third of all search statements he entered contained certain or probable errors. His error rate did decline somewhat beyond statement #210. Scholar #21's high error rate in Table 7 was also confirmed by a high overall combined error rate of over 20%.

In summary, although most scholars did well with the one day's training and other assistance, a few searchers may have needed more help.

*Learning curve summary* In sum, the scholars continued to introduce new features into their searching through time, and so were apparently learning. This may be due in part to the other forms of assistance available to the scholars after the initial training, namely, the assisted searches (1989 and 1990), comparative searches (1989), and group reviews (1990). At the same time, their use of elementary forms of search statements, and their error rates, started fairly low, but did not decrease appreciably over time.

These results suggest that two things may have happened simultaneously. On the one hand, the scholars were learning and were open to development during their search experience. On the other hand, the one-day training started them out with a bang, so to speak. They retained enough from the experience initially to start with relatively sophisticated search statements and a low error rate. But, we surmise, as time passed, and the training became more distant, forgetting competed with new learning, so that commission of errors and a pattern of resorting to elementary techniques continued side by side with the acquisition of new learning. The small sample size, both in terms of number of people and number of search statements, limits the assurance with which these suppositions can be stated.

## Discussion and conclusions

We analyzed the search histories of 27 humanities scholars who visited at the Getty Center for the History of Art and the Humanities over a two-year period and who searched as end users on the DIALOG search service. Five did no unassisted searching at all, 21 searched between a few minutes and just over 13 hours, and one searched over 71 hours. The majority of the participants used the search service for their own searching for less than two hours.

Since these scholars were doing full-time research during a visit to the Getty Center and had unlimited *subsidized* access to the search service, we might expect that they would have done more searching. To participate, they had to commit a full day to training—yet only five ultimately got a day's worth of searching or more out of that training. (They may continue to benefit from their training, however, when they return to their home institutions.) These results suggest that the design of database search services—either in their databases or in their search capabilities—is still far from optimal for meeting the needs of humanities scholars. If the library or archive is the laboratory of these scholars, the database search service appears to be a fairly minor tool in that laboratory. Therefore, one of the most exciting challenges in the development of future information systems is to identify what resources and search features are needed to provide an automated information resource that the humanities scholar will come to feel is an indispensable part of his or her laboratory.

The characteristics of the searching done by the scholars were analyzed in several ways. Scholars were found to make heavy use of proper terms in subject searching, thus confirming the work of Wiberley (1983, 1988) on the importance of these terms for humanities scholars. Scholars did few author searches, that is, searches for works by authors rather than about authors. Just over 5% of their search terms were for author searches, a figure considerably lower than is common with catalogs.

The training appears to have been useful to the scholars in their searching: They were able to use more sophisticated techniques such as proximity searching, truncation, and prefix specification. Their error rate started fairly low but did not decline noticeably. Average error rates for the 1990 group were substantially higher than those for the 1989 group.

A higher proportion of the search statements were more elementary in structure than is typical for professional searchers. Sixty-three percent of their search terms were single-word terms, and, coincidentally, 63% of all "Select" statements had no Boolean operators. In fact, more than one-quarter of the scholars never used a Boolean OR at any time in their searching. Thus, these searchers can be seen as beginners in their search patterns. This search pattern may be due in part to the fact that they were taught the "building block" search strategy in training. Consequently, they may have entered many terms one at a time, and then combined them with an AND at the end. Such an approach—helpful for a searcher at any stage of experience—is especially helpful for beginners because it reduces confusion and eliminates the necessity for correct application of parentheses in statements using both ANDs and ORs. Their failure to use many term variants by ORing them in the building block components may have reduced the effectiveness of the building block strategy for them, however. In sum, Boolean logic remains the problem that it has ever been for searchers. All things considered, the scholars coped fairly well with it.

Overall, the results of this study agree well with those from other studies on end-user online searchers (e.g., Mischo & Lee, 1987; Sullivan et al., 1990). The scholars succeeded reasonably well in constructing searches and getting results, but there are indications that their one day's training and their relatively few hours of search experience were not enough to make them into sophisticated searchers.

Evidence for a learning curve in their development as searchers was sought through three types of analysis: (1) points in the search histories of the scholars where the first use of various features appeared; (2) use of elementary search statements over time; and (3) error rates. The small sample size in both numbers of people and length of search histories limits the firmness of our conclusions, but the following trends seemed to be operating:

- Searchers started off well, with relatively low error rates and use of elementary structures in their search statements.

- Searchers continued to learn throughout the time of their searching, continually adding new features as they went along.

- Error rates and use of elementary structures, while fairly low, did not decline significantly through time, which suggests that forgetting after the training and between search sessions may have played a role. It should be noted that the period covered was only the first 210 search statements—still early in the life history of a searcher.

Altogether, according to our sample, humanities scholars searching as end users managed to do well, learning enough in a one-day training session to do effective searching with a tolerable error rate. They were not so frustrated that they threw up their hands; rather, most returned for repeated sessions. As judged by the amount of use, however, most did not take to searching with the enthusiasm of a teenager in a video arcade—or of a scholar who has just discovered a rich new resource. To make automated information systems more appealing and easier to use for humanities scholars constitutes an exciting challenge for information researchers in the coming years.

*Coding scheme for Getty Scholars'*
*online search statements and terms*

All coding is at the level of the search statement or the individual term within a statement, that is, look to see if the statement or term, as the case may be, possesses a given feature. If so, then record it as present. Categories 35–36 and 50–89 are coded at the term level, and all other categories at the statement level.

Operational definition of "search statement": Starts in response to system prompt, ends with carriage return (enter).

Operational definition of "term": Terms are bounded by the beginning and ending of the search statement, and by Boolean operators.

### OO ELEMENTARY OR BASELINE SEARCHING

The 00 set of categories are deliberately duplicative of the categories in the list—though only partly. Code all categories that apply.

01 Initiates search session by requesting a single bibliographic database—excludes DIALINDEX, blue sheets database, or any other database in which bibliographic citations cannot be searched directly.

02 A command to *expand* a single one-word term, unmodified, constitutes entire statement. Not restricted to first statement in session. May be common or proper noun. Presence or absence of truncation irrelevant.

03 A command to *search* one single one-word term, unmodified, constitutes entire search statement. Not restricted to first statement in session. May be common or proper noun. Uses "s" or "ss," not "expand." No truncation.

04 A command to *expand* one single "AU=" type statement constitutes entire search statement. May have more than one word in author's name. Not restricted to first statement in session. May include truncation.

05 A command to search one single "AU=" type statement constitutes entire search statement. May have more than one word in author's name. Not restricted to first statement in session. Uses "s" or "ss," not "expand." May include truncation.

06 One single (3-part) "type" statement constitutes entire statement.

Code in normal 0 column, and also write lower case "e" next to the number in other columns with which the error is associated.

08 Probable error—very poor strategy or grossly inefficient approach—there are common superior ways of doing this, but a searcher could conceivably have some reason for doing this. Code conservatively.

09 Certain error—nonexistent or incorrectly formatted or spelled command or other component of statement; something about this has to fail, no matter what the searcher's intentions might have been.

## 10 DATABASE SEARCHING

11 Single bibliographic database request, other than initial one in session. Excludes same things as in 01.

12 Single full text database request.

13 Other single non-bibliographic database request—blue sheets database, directory, other.

15 DIALINDEX.

16 SF or individual database requests within DIALINDEX.

17 OneSearch.

19 Remove duplicates.

## 20–39 SEARCH COMMANDS, ASSISTANCE

Database selection commands coded in the 10's.

21 Basic expand (with or without prefix or suffix).

22 Expand term in parentheses to get thesaurus.

23 Select.

24 Select steps.

25 Range searching of "e" or "r" numbers in an expand.

26 Other range searching.

27 Help—*specify*.

28 Display sets.

29 Limit—*specify*.

31 Stacking of commands.

32 Page.

33 Search save.

34 Execute saved search.

35 Employ set number in lieu of term(s).

36 Employ "e" or "r" numbers in lieu of terms.

## 40 BOOLEAN LOGIC

Presence of Boolean operators in a given whole search statement.

41  No Boolean operators present.
42  One or more ANDs, and only ANDs.
43  One or more ORs, and only ORs.
44  Mixed ANDs/ORs.
45  Parentheses.
47  NOT used.

## 50–89 VOCABULARY TYPES/VARIATIONS

Coding in 50–89 is specific to the *term* within an expand, select, select step, or limit statement. Start from the left of the statement and take a new line for each term within the search statement. If there are three terms in statement 6, then label them 6a, 6b, and 6c, respectively, devoting one whole row on the coding sheet to each. Terms are bounded by the beginning and ending of the search statement, and by Boolean operators. Check all categories that apply to a given term. For example, the single name-as-subject, "Marigny," would receive categories 51 and 53. Code all terms in section 50–59. In addition, code suffix-coded terms in more detail in the 70's and prefix coded terms in more detail in the 80's.

## 50 VOCABULARY TYPES

51  Single word.
52  Multiple words.
53  Proper term—personal name—includes fictional and mythic characters.
54  Proper term—geographical name.
55  Proper term—other.
56  Lower-case term.
57  Suffix specification, controlled vocabulary (DE, DF, ID, IF).
58  Suffix specification, other than controlled vocabulary (Tl, AB, etc.).
59  Proximity operator(s) used.

## 60 PROXIMITY SEARCHING

61  w
62  f
63  n
64  s
65  l
66  Specification of number of intervening words.

### 68–69 TRUNCATION

68 ?

69 Specification of number of characters.

### 70–89 INDEX SPECIFICATION

70 *Suffix Specification.* Add others as encountered. Note: Do not include here suffix specifications that are actually simplified "Limit" or subfile commands, such as /ej in ERIC for the journal subfile. Code such cases in 20–39.

71 DE

72 DF

73 ID

74 IF

75 TI

76 AB

77

78

79

### 80 PREFIX SPECIFICATION *Add others as encountered.*

81 AU

82 JN

83 DT

84 SF (except DIALINDEX)

85

86

87 Other prefixes—explain (85–89).

88

89

### 90 TYPE FORMATS

91 Type in Format 1.

92 Type in Format 2.

93 Type in Format 3.

94 Type in Format 4.

95 Type in Format 5.

96 Type in Format 6.

97 Type in Format 7.

98 Type in Format 8.

99 Other—*explain.*

# REFERENCES

Bates, M.J., Wilde, D.N., & Siegfried, S. (1993). An analysis of search terminology used by humanities scholars: The Getty Online Searching Project Report No. 1. *Library Quarterly, 63*(1), 1–39.

Borgman, C.L. (1986). Why are online catalogs hard to use? Lessons learned from information retrieval studies. *Journal of the American Society for Information Science, 37*(6), 387–400.

Boyles, J.C. (1987). Bibliographic databases for the art researcher: Developments, problems and proposals. *Art Documentation, 6*(1), 9–12.

Boyles, J.C. (1988). The end user and the art librarian. *Art Libraries Journal, 13,* 27–31.

Broadbent, E.A. (1986). Study of humanities faculty library information seeking behavior. *Cataloging & Classification Quarterly, 6*(3), 23–36.

Case, D.O. (1991). The collection and use of information by some American historians: A study of motives and methods. *Library Quarterly, 61*(1), 61–82.

Corkill, C., & Mann, M. (1978). *Information needs in the humanities: Two postal surveys,* CRUS occasional paper #2, Sheffield, England: Centre for Research on User Studies. BLR & DD Report No. 5455.

Crawford, D. (1986). Meeting scholarly information needs in an automated environment: A humanist's perspective. *College & Research Libraries, 47*(6), 569–574.

Everett, D., & Pilachowski, D.M. (1986). What's in a name? Looking for people online— humanities. *Database, 9,* 26–34.

Gould, C.C. (1988). *Information needs in the humanities: An assessment.* Stanford, CA: Research Libraries Group.

Guest, S.S. (1987). The use of bibliographical tools by humanities faculty at the State University of New York at Albany. *The Reference Librarian, 7*(18): 157–172.

Horner, J., & Thirlwall, D. (1988). Online searching and the university researcher. *Journal of Academic Librarianship, 14*(4), 225–230.

Hurych, J. (1986). After Bath: Scientists, social scientists, and humanists in the context of online searching. *Journal of Academic Librarianship, 12*(3), 158–165.

Katzen, M. (1986). The application of computers in the humanities: A view from Britain. *Information Processing & Management, 22*(3), 259–267.

Krausse, S.C., & Etchingham, Jr., J.B. (1986). The humanist and computer-assisted library research. *Computers and the Humanities, 20*(2), 87–96.

Lehmann, S., & Renfro, P. (1991). Humanists and electronic information services: Acceptance and resistance. *College & Research Libraries, 52*(5), 409–413.

Loughridge, B. (1989). Information technology, the humanities and the library. *Journal of Information Science, 15*(4/5), 277–286.

Lowry, A., & Stuveras, J. (1987). *Scholarship in the electronic age: A selected bibliography on research and communication in the humanities and social sciences.* Washington, DC.: Council on Library Resources.

Mackesy, E.M. (1982). A perspective on secondary access services in the humanities. *Journal of the American Society for Information Science, 33*(3), 146–151.

Markey, K. (1984). *Subject searching in library catalogs: Before and after the introduction of online catalogs.* Dublin, OH: Online Computer Library Center (OCLC).

Markey, K., & Cochrane, P.A. (1981). *ONTAP: Online training and practice manual for ERIC database searchers* (2nd ed). Syracuse, NY: ERIC Clearinghouse on Information Resources.

Mischo, W.H., & Lee, J. (1987). End-user searching of bibliographic databases. *Annual Review of Information Science and Technology, 22,* 227–263.

Montague, E.A. (1967). *Card catalog use studies: 1949–1965.* M.A. thesis, University of Chicago.

Morton, H.C., & Price, A.J. (1986). The ACLS survey: Views on publications, computers, libraries. *Scholarly Communication, 5*, 1–16.

Rahtz, S. (ed.) (1987). *Information technology in the humanities: Tools, techniques and applications.* Chichester, UK: Ellis Horwood/John Wiley.

Ross, J.E. (1987). Artists and poets online: Issues in cataloging and retrieval. *Cataloging & Classification Quarterly, 7*(3), 91–104.

Ruiz, D., & Meyer, D.E. (1990). End-user selection of databases—Part III: Social science/ arts & humanities. *Database, 13*(5), 59–64.

Schmitt, M. (1990). Alas, the failure to communicate: Thoughts on the symbiosis of scholars, information managers and systems experts. *Art Documentation, 9*(3), 137–138.

Schmitt, M. (Ed.) (1988). *Object, image, and inquiry: The art historian at work.* Santa Monica, CA: The Getty Art History Information Program.

Sewell, W., & Teitelbaum, S. (1986). Observations of end-user online searching behavior over eleven years. *Journal of the American Society for Information Science, 37*(4), 234–245.

Stam, D.C. (1984). How art historians look for information. *Art Documentation, 3*(4), 117–119.

Stam, D.C., & Giral, A. (issue eds.) (1988). Linking art objects and art information. *Library Trends, 37*(2), 117–264.

Stern, P. (1988). Online in the humanities: Problems and possibilities. *Journal of Academic Librarianship, 14*(3), 161–164.

Stielow, F., & Tibbo, H. (1988). The negative search, online reference and the humanities: A critical essay in library literature. *RQ, 27*(3), 358–365.

Stone, S. (1982). Humanities scholars: Information needs and uses. *Journal of Documentation, 38*(4), 292–312.

Sullivan, M.V., Borgman, C.L., & Wippern, D. (1990). End-users, mediated searches, and front-end assistance programs on Dialog: A comparison of learning, performance, and satisfaction. *Journal of the American Society for Information Science, 41*(1), 27–42.

Tibbo, H.R. (1989). *Abstracts, online searching, and the humanities: An analysis of the structure and content of abstracts of historical discourse.* Ph.D. dissertation, University of Maryland.

Tibbo, H.R. (1991). Information systems, services, and technology for the humanities. *Annual Review of Information Science and Technology, 26*, 287–346.

Walker, G. (1988). Online searching in the humanities: Implications for end-users and intermediaries. In *Proceedings of the 12th International Online Information Meeting, London, 6–8 December 1988.* (pp. 401–412). Oxford, UK: Learned Information.

Walker, G. (1990). Searching the humanities: Subject overlap and search vocabulary. *Database, 13*(5), 35–46.

Walker, G., & Atkinson, S.D. (1991). Information access in the humanities: Perils and pitfalls. *Library Hi Tech, 9*(1), 23–34.

Wiberley, Jr., S.E. (1983). Subject access in the humanities and the precision of the humanist's vocabulary. *Library Quarterly, 53*(4), 420–433.

Wiberley, Jr., S.E. (1988). Names in space and time: The indexing vocabulary of the humanities. *Library Quarterly, 58*(1), 1–28.

Wiberley, Jr., S.E. (1991). Habits of humanists: Scholarly behavior and new information technologies. *Library Hi Tech, 9*(1), 17–21.

Wiberley, Jr., S.E., & Jones, W.G. (1989). Patterns of information seeking in the humanities. *College & Research Libraries, 50*(6), 638–645.

Woo, J. (1988). The Online Avery Index End-User Pilot Project: Final Report. *Information Technology and Libraries, 7*, 223–229.

# 6

# The design of browsing and berrypicking techniques for the online search interface

ABSTRACT

First, a new model of searching in online and other information systems, called "berrypicking," is discussed. This model, it is argued, is much closer to the real behavior of information searchers than the traditional model of information retrieval is, and, consequently, will guide our thinking better in the design of effective interfaces. Second, the research literature of manual information seeking behavior is drawn on for suggestions of capabilities that users might like to have in online systems. Third, based on the new model and the research on information seeking, suggestions are made for how new search capabilities could be incorporated into the design of search interfaces. Particular attention is given to the nature and types of browsing that can be facilitated.

## Introduction

As more and more different types of databases are brought online, the universe of information available to search online is beginning to resemble the vast array of sources available in manual print environments. From an original emphasis on bibliographic databases, which are the online

*First published as* Bates, M. J. (1989). The design of browsing and berrypicking techniques for the online search interface. *Online Review, 13*(5), 407–424.

equivalent of abstracting and indexing (A & I) services, databanks have expanded to the full text of journals and other documents, as well as directories, encyclopedias, and other reference sources traditionally available in libraries. Soon there really will be something approaching whole libraries accessible by computer.

As more types of resource are brought online, however, the searcher has a more complex search environment to consider, both in terms of types of sources to use and search techniques to employ with these sources (Williams, 1986; Hawkins, Levy, & Montgomery, 1988). We need to expand our understanding of these resources and the search techniques to use in them, and at the same time, expand our view of how the search interface should be designed to assist searchers with their new, complex tasks.

In this article the following is done:

- A new model of searching in online and other information systems, called "berrypicking," is discussed. This model, it is argued, is much closer to the real behavior of information searchers than the traditional model of information retrieval is, and, consequently, will guide our thinking better in the design of effective interfaces.

- The research literature of manual information seeking behavior is drawn on for suggestions of capabilities that users might like to have in online systems.

- Based on the new model and the research on information seeking, suggestions are made for how these capabilities could be incorporated into the design of search interfaces. Particular attention is given to the nature and types of browsing that can be facilitated.

## A "berrypicking" model of information retrieval

The classic model of information retrieval (IR) used in information science research for over 25 years can be characterized as follows (compare Robertson [1977], especially p. 129):

This model has been very productive and has promoted our understanding of information retrieval in many ways. However, as Kuhn (1970) noted, major models that are as central to a field as this one is, eventually begin to show inadequacies as testing leads to greater and greater understanding of the processes being studied. The limitations of the original

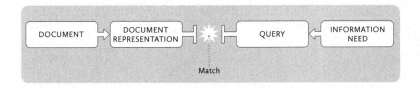

FIG. 1. *The classic information retrieval model*

model's representation of the phenomenon of interest become more and more evident.

It is only fitting, then, that in recent years the above classic model has come under attack in various ways (Ellis, 1984a; 1984b; Bates, 1985, 1986). Oddy (1977) and Belkin et al (1982) have asked why it is necessary for the searcher to find a way to represent the information need in a query understandable by the system. Why cannot the system make it possible for the searcher to express the need directly as they would ordinarily, instead of in an artificial query representation for the system's consumption?

At the other end of the model, that of document representation, powerful developments in computing make possible free text and full text searching so that the traditional document representation (controlled vocabulary) takes on a different role and, for some purposes, is less important in much information retrieval practice.

Here I want to challenge the model as a whole—to the effect that it represents some searches, but not all, perhaps not even the majority, and that with respect to those it does represent, it frequently does so inadequately. As a formal model for testing, it has taught us much; as a realistic representation of actual searches, it has many limitations. As a consequence, as long as this model dominates information science thinking, it will limit our creativity in developing IR systems that really meet user needs and preferences.

The model I am about to propose differs from the traditional one in four areas:

1. Nature of the query.

2. Nature of the overall search process.

3. Range of search techniques used.

4. Information "domain" or territory where the search is conducted.

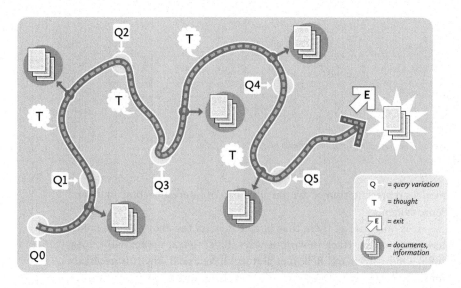

FIG. 2. *A berrypicking, evolving search*

The first two areas will be dealt with in this section and the second two in the next section.

Let us return for a closer look at the classic model. Fundamental to it is the idea of a single query presented by the user, matched to the database contents, yielding a single output set. One of Gerard Salton's (1968) contributions to research in this area was the idea of iterative feedback to improve output. He developed a system that would modify the query formulation based on user feedback to the first preliminary output set. The formulation would be successively improved through the use of feedback on user document preferences until recall and precision were optimized.

But Salton's iterative feedback is still well within the original classic model as presented in Figure 1—because the presumption is that the information need leading to the query is the same, unchanged, throughout, no matter what the user might learn from the documents in the preliminary retrieved set. In fact, if a user in a Salton experiment were to change the query after seeing some documents, it would be "unfair," a violation of the basic design of the experiment. The point of the feedback is to improve the representation of a static need, not to provide information that enables a change in the need itself.

So throughout the process of information retrieval evaluation under the classic model, the query is treated as a single unitary, one-time conception of the problem. Though this assumption is useful for simplifying IR system research, real-life searches frequently do not work this way.

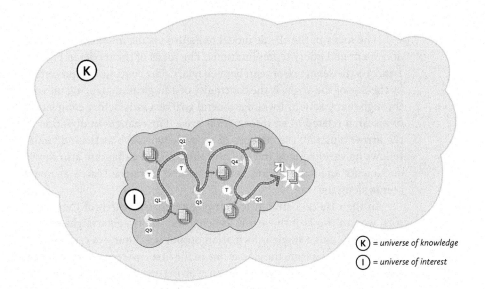

FIG. 3. *Context of berrypicking search*

In real-life searches in manual sources, end users may begin with just one feature of a broader topic, or just one relevant reference, and move through a variety of sources. Each new piece of information they encounter gives them new ideas and directions to follow and, consequently, a new conception of the query. At each stage they are not just modifying the search terms used in order to get a better match for a single query. Rather the query itself (as well as the search terms used) is continually shifting, in part or whole. This type of search is here called an evolving search.

Furthermore, at each stage, with each different conception of the query, the user may identify useful information and references. In other words, the query is satisfied not by a single final retrieved set, but by a series of selections of individual references and bits of information at each stage of the ever-modifying search. A bit-at-a-time retrieval of this sort is here called *berrypicking*. This term is used by analogy to picking huckleberries or blueberries in the forest. The berries are scattered on the bushes; they do not come in bunches. One must pick them one at a time. One could do berrypicking of information without the search need itself changing (evolving), but in this article the attention is given to searches that combine both of these features.

Figure 2 represents a berrypicking, evolving search. In Figure 3 we see the size of the picture shrunk in order to show the context within which the search takes place.

The focus of the classic model in Figure 1 is the match between the document and query representations. The focus of the model in Figures 2 and 3 is the sequence of searcher behaviors. The continuity represented by the line of the arrow is the continuity of a single human being moving through many actions toward a general goal of a satisfactory completion of research related to an information need. The changes in direction of the arrow illustrate the changes of an evolving search as the individual follows up various leads and shifts in thinking. The diagram also shows documents and information being produced from the search at many points along the way.

In the case of a straightforward single-match search of the classic sort, we can think of the arrow as being very short and straight, with a single query and a single information output set. Thus, we can see that this model differs from the classic one in the first two respects mentioned above: (1) The nature of the query is an evolving one, rather than single and unchanging, and (2) the nature of the search process is such that it follows a berrypicking pattern, instead of leading to a single best retrieved set.

There is ample evidence of the popularity of searches of the evolving/berrypicking sort. Reviews of research by Line (1974), Hogeweg-de-Haart (1984), Stone (1982), and Stoan (1984) attest to the popularity of this approach in a variety of environments, particularly in the social sciences and humanities. A recent landmark study by Ellis (1989) on social scientists supports and amplifies the results of earlier studies. Kuhlthau's work (1988) with high school students suggests that there is a great deal of exploratory searching that goes on, both before and after a topic for a paper is selected. While the research reviewed here refers largely to the academic environment, 1 would suggest that many searches by people in many contexts other than academic can also be better characterized by the berrypicking/evolving model than by the classic IR model. The sources consulted may differ, but the process is similar.

## How and where users search for information now

It was argued in the previous section that information seekers in manual environments use a berrypicking/evolving search mode. In this section we will examine in more detail some of the search techniques used and information sources consulted by users in manual environments.

We might be tempted to say that the path taken in Figures 2 and 3 is simply a series of mini-matches of the classic sort. That is, that at each point where searchers identify documents of interest, they are making a match as represented in Figure 1, and that Figure 2 is simply a representation of searching at a higher level of generality. To make that assumption, however, would be to misrepresent what is being proposed here. Figure 2 is different in essential character, not just in level of generality. Specifically, in a real search there are many different ways people encounter information of interest to them. We will discuss several of them below. Only one of those ways is the kind represented by the classic model.

Users employ a number of strategies. With the help particularly of Stoan (1984) and Ellis (1989) I will describe just six of them, which are widely used:

1. *Footnote chasing* (or "backward chaining" [Ellis, 1989]). This technique involves following up footnotes found in books and articles of interest, and therefore moving backward in successive leaps through reference lists. Note that with this technique, as with other citation methods, the searcher avoids the problem of subject description altogether. This method is extremely popular with researchers in the social sciences and humanities. See, for example, Stenstrom and McBride (1979).

2. *Citation searching* (or "forward chaining" [Ellis, 1989]). One begins with a citation, finds out who cites it by looking it up in a citation index, and thus leaps forward.

3. *Journal run* Once, by whatever means, one identifies a central journal in an area, one then locates the run of volumes of the journal and searches straight through relevant volume years. Such a technique, by definition, guarantees complete recall within that journal, and, if the journal is central enough to the searcher's interests, this technique also has tolerably good precision. In effect, this approach exploits Bradford's Law: the core journals in a subject area are going to have very high rates of relevant materials in that area.

4. *Area scanning* Browsing the materials that are physically collocated with materials located earlier in a search is a widely used and effective technique. Studies dating all the way back to the 1940s confirm the popularity of the technique in catalog use. Frarey (1953), in reviewing three of those early studies, found that use of the subject catalog is divided

about equally between selecting books on a subject on the one hand, and finding the shelf location of a category in the classification in order to make book selections in the stacks on the other hand. The latter is, of course, the sort of area scanning described here. Recent work by Hancock (1987) again confirms the importance of this approach.

5. *Subject searches in bibliographies and abstracting and indexing (A & I) services* Many bibliographies and most A & I services are arranged by subject. Both classified arrangements and subject indexes are popular. These forms of subject description (classifications and indexing languages) constitute the most common forms of "document representation" that are familiar from the classic model of information retrieval discussed earlier.

6. *Author searching* We customarily think of searching by author as an approach that contrasts with searching by subject. In the literature of catalog use research, "known-item" searches are frequently contrasted with "subject" searches, for example. But author searching can be an effective part of subject searching as well, when a searcher uses an author name to see if the author has done any other work on the same topic (Ellis, 1989).

Until now most of the emphasis in online databanks and other automated IR systems—theoretical, experimental, and operational—has been on use of just one of the above techniques, namely, searching abstracting and indexing services. It is assumed that to do an automated information search one is searching on a bibliographic database, a list of references with or without abstracts, that is just like an abstracting and indexing service, except that it is online. In experiments, the "document representations" in the classic IR model may involve very sophisticated methods, but most come down to some form of representation of the contents of documents that is usually much shorter, and different from, the documents themselves. In short, most IR research, until a recent flurry of interest in full text databases, has been research on databases of document surrogates.

Real searches, by contrast, use all the above techniques and more, in endless variation. It is part of the nature of berrypicking that people adapt the strategy to the particular need at the moment; as the need shifts in part or whole, the strategy often shifts as well—at least for effective searchers. So, to return to an earlier point, the berrypicking model does not represent a number of mini-matches of the classic sort, i.e., between search term and A & I service (database) term. Rather, the evolving/berrypicking search also involves the third and fourth features mentioned earlier: (3) the search techniques change throughout, and (4) the sources searched change in both form and content.

We have generally assumed in library/information science that the fifth technique in the list above, the A & I search, is clearly superior to the others. That is an important reason for the primacy given to the bibliographic search in our research and practice. However, Stenstrom and McBride found, when they asked the social science faculty where they got the references for journal articles they used, that over 87% of them said they got the references from abstracting journals only occasionally, rarely, or never (Stenstrom & McBride, 1979, p. 429). They relied far more heavily on footnote chasing: 69% (p. 429). Both Stoan (1984) and Ellis (1989) provide evidence and are very persuasive on the power and effectiveness of these other techniques for academic researchers and students at the very least.

Some of the other search techniques described above are possible on some systems—see, for example, Palay and Fox (1981), Croft and Thompson (1987), Cove and Walsh (1988), Noerr and Noerr (1985). See also Hildreth's masterly review of intelligent interfaces for bibliographic retrieval systems (Hildreth, 1989). Nowhere, to my knowledge, however, are all of these techniques easily applied by a searcher within a single system.

A model containing a unified perspective, incorporating the full range of searcher behaviors in the information seeking process, may make it easier to design many more such features for information retrieval systems. Ellis (1989) has presented the results of his own research on social scientists and, on that basis, argues for the implementation of most of the above techniques, as well as others not discussed here. The particular mix of different capabilities that should ultimately be made available is a question deserving much more attention in the future.

Citation searching is also available, of course, in online systems in the Institute for Scientific Information databases. This searching method is now widely accepted in library/information science as another valuable database approach. Not all readers may be aware, however, of how hard Eugene Garfield had to work in the 1960s and 1970s to persuade librarians of the value of citation searching. I vividly recall observing an otherwise very capable reference instructor telling a class in the late 1960s that a citation index was a waste of money, that it was just a vanity publication for professors—its only value being for them to look up and see who was citing their own work. My point here is that we have yet to fully accept all six of these techniques as valid, effective approaches to information. Even citation indexing, now widely used, was not received easily into the thinking of library/information science.

From the standpoint of general effectiveness in searching, it is clear, on reflection, however, that, other things being equal, the searcher with the widest range of search strategies available is the searcher with the greatest retrieval power. We in information science feel that information searchers should take more advantage of A & I services in online or manual form. We, in our turn, should recognize that these other techniques used so commonly by researchers must have some real value for them, and that there may be times when they are preferable (see Stoan, 1984). With each of the six retrieval techniques described above, it is possible to think of instances when that technique is clearly superior to the others as a route to the desired information.

I would argue on two grounds that these techniques should all be available in at least some future automated IR systems, and that our model of information retrieval should include berrypicking through use of these and other techniques:

1. The more different strategies searchers can use an information store, the more retrieval effectiveness and efficiency is possible.

2. There are many experienced searchers who use these techniques already—in a berrypicking mode—with great satisfaction. These approaches represent well established patterns that are handed down from scholars to their students and which work well for them in many cases. If we want to meet users' needs, we should enable them to search in familiar ways that are effective for them.

To summarize the argument to this point, this model of searching differs from the traditional one not only in that it reflects evolving, berry-picking searches, but also searches in a much wider variety of sources, and using a much wider variety of search techniques than has been typically represented in information retrieval models to date. With this broader picture of information retrieval in mind, many new design possibilities open up. In the next section, some of those possibilities will be examined, with particular attention to the role of browsing in the broader search process.

# Search capabilities for a berrypicking search interface

*Browsing.*

The view of searching as frequently being an evolving/berrypicking process, and one which uses a variety of types of information sources and search techniques, changes our sense of what browsing capabilities should be like in online systems, and how the database and the search interface should be designed. Concepts of browsing in IR systems are becoming more and more sophisticated. See Noerr and Noerr (1985), Wade and Willett (1988), Cove and Walsh (1988), Hildreth (1982), Bawden (1986), Ingwersen and Wormell (1987). But there is still a lingering tendency in information science to see browsing *in contrast* to directed searching, to see it as a casual, don't-know-what-I-want behavior that one engages in separately from "regular" searching.

However, as Ellis notes (1989), browsing is an important part of standard information searching; he calls it "semi-directed or semi-structured searching" when used this way. He recommends that browsing of a variety of types of information, e.g., contents pages, lists of cited works, subject terms, should be made available in automated systems. He further argues that since the user is doing the browsing, and we therefore do not have to design a cognitive model of user browsing into the system, that providing browsing features should be relatively simple.

Relatively simpler perhaps, but making effective provision for browsing capabilities involves its own complexities. The techniques above combine browsing and conventional use of the information access apparatus in a variety of specific configurations. With all of the six techniques above, as well as with other features that might be designed for browsing, it will be desirable to set up combinations of features that incorporate browsing in different ways in each case.

The nature of browsing associated with each of the techniques listed above is examined in more detail below. Key design features recommended for automated IR systems will be stated for each technique.

So that there is no confusion, however, I want to emphasize that browsing and berrypicking are not the same behavior. There will be a great deal of discussion of browsing in the remainder of this article, but only because browsing has received less attention in our field than other kinds of searching. Berrypicking involves the use of a wide variety of techniques, some of which are very standard and others which involve a considerable amount of browsing. One of the points emphasized in this model is precisely that people use a wide variety of techniques.

Each of the six techniques is discussed below, followed by some general points about database and interface design for berrypicking and browsing.

## Footnote chasing

In footnote chasing one might want both to be able to browse through the article or book that generates the references as well as through the list of references—in fact, to move back and forth easily between the two parts of the document. The body of information browsed in footnote chasing has a coherence and meaning that clusters around the idiosyncratic purposes of the author of the article or book. Browsing in the footnotes or endnotes will be minimal if the searcher only looks up individual references found in the text, and sticks to them. Browsing of the references can be more extensive if the searcher scans the list, independently of an originating textual reference.

KEY DESIGN FEATURES Users can get the following easily, preferably by direct manipulation, e.g., with mouse and pull-down menus:

1. Overview of document contents a chapter or section headings.

2. Full text of documents and references.

3. Ability to jump back and forth between text and references.

## Citation searching

In citation searching, one might want either to browse the set of references that cite a given starter reference, or read any of the citing articles. No single human has created this grouping of citations; rather they come together because they all happen to cite the originating reference. They may otherwise be quite unrelated. Such a collection of references is likely to be stimulating to creativity, as the citing articles may not be on the "same" topic in the conventional sense, yet nonetheless create a grouping that has at least one key thread of similarity that may go along unconventional lines. (See also Bawden [1986].) Because of this unconventional grouping, the user might well want to expand the search indefinitely in any direction, that is, upon finding a citing article, learn which articles cite it, and so on.

KEY DESIGN FEATURES Users should have the ability to:

1. Scan lists of citing references.

2. Make simple single step jumps to (a) full text of citing articles, (b) full list of references in citing article.

3. Make jumps in any direction ad infinitum, i.e., the user should not have to "return to go" and re-enter a starting article for each jump in any direction.

## Journal run

Looking through journals manually, the searcher flips through issues, scanning large chunks of the text of the articles, as well as the contents lists and abstracts. Here the grouping of articles is the subject area represented by the coverage of the journal. When the journal has a very broad subject coverage, such as that of *Science* or *American Psychologist,* it is unlikely to meet a searcher's need for information on a topic of the normal degree of specificity associated with a research project. To put if differently, browsing such general journals is probably useful more for general monitoring of the environment, rather than contributing to a well defined need.

In cases where the journal coverage is a more specific subject area, however, reviewing the contents lists or articles in that journal may be an excellent way to see quickly a large number of articles exactly in the heart of an area that interests one. The grouping of articles that results from their joint publication in a journal can be expected to be coherent and well thought out, since the focus of journals is generally well defined by editors for prospective authors.

### KEY DESIGN FEATURES

1. Easy specification of journal title and starting date in journal run search.

2. Easy jumps between contents lists and articles and back again.

3. Capability of requesting, if wanted, standard section headings in scholarly articles, such as "Methodology," or "Conclusions," so the searcher is shown these sections directly.

## Area scanning

This technique is most commonly used with books arranged by a library classification scheme on the shelves of a library. With area scanning, one may either follow the exact arrangement of the classification scheme by reading linearly along the shelves, or alternatively, and, I suspect, more commonly, deliberately not follow that order. In practice, one of the most useful aspects of area scanning is that one can visually scan in a random manner over the shelves in a subject area of interest.

The effect of this latter method is to "jump the rails" of the classification scheme, to skip to other parts of the scheme that are near the starting point, without having to look at every single intervening book and category. This technique represents a deliberate breaking up of the conventional classified order, while enabling the searcher to remain in the same general initial subject area. Thus the search domain may consist of a variety of specific areas within one larger area.

Area scanning is the quintessential form of browsing in manual environments. As noted earlier, the research shows that it has remained very popular over many years among users. It is reasonable to presume that it meets some real needs. More research into why this approach is popular is desirable. However, here are a couple of guesses:

(1) The searcher is exposed to a variety of related areas, some of which, because of the jumping around, may be related in unexpected ways—thus producing serendipitous discoveries.

(2) The searcher can look directly at the full text of the materials. By flipping through the pages and reading a passage here and there, the searcher gets a quick gestalt sense of the "feel" or character of the author and his or her approach. Whatever that feel is, it is almost never accessible through any classification or subject description.

KEY DESIGN FEATURES

1.  A library's listing of its books on the shelves arranged by the order of the classification scheme is called a shelf list. Thus, for area scanning linearly along the shelves, a capability of browsing the shelf list can be provided.

2.  For "jumping the rails" of the classification scheme, browsing at several levels of generality within the classification scheme itself can be provided, i.e., giving the searcher the option of browsing a list of the most general categories in the scheme, or a list of the general categories plus their subdivisions, and so on, down to the full detail of the scheme.

3.  At any point, with either of the first two capabilities listed in this section, the searcher should be able to ask for "snapshots" of full text of books (more discussion later).

## Subject searching in bibliographies and A & I services

In discussions of "browsing" in online databases, the term usually refers to reading short lists of alphabetically arranged subject terms or reading citations and their associated abstracts. In fact in such activities there is little sense of the random visual movement usually associated with browsing. Indeed, the lists of terms printed out are short, and the printing of citations is costly, so searchers often keep it to a minimum. When the cost of printing out abstracts falls, and/or CD-ROM database use becomes more widespread, true browsing may be easier to do.

It may help the discussion here if we compare the manual form of A & I services, and consider how they are used for browsing. We may be able to do more, of course, with the online form, but let us first see if the text lends itself to browsing in principle. A very common pattern in manual forms of A & I services is to arrange the abstracts by a classified order, and attach a subject index using more specific subject terms. When an online searcher searches by controlled vocabulary, or by free text on the titles and abstracts, all the entries associated with the more specific subject terms are brought together in one location, so they become easy to examine. In the manual form, usually only the abstract numbers are brought together in the index. So grouping entries by these specific terms is a useful function of online services, though the browsing potential is limited for the reasons given above.

Since the A & I services generally arrange the abstracts by a classified order, it is possible in the manual form to browse through the abstracts in a classified section. This is generally impractical in online databases unless the search is also limited to certain dates or issues of the service, because the online database usually combines many years of the service in one, and each classification category therefore contains very large numbers of items (see Bates, 1984). However, in a database in which cost per reference is not a factor, then some sort of browsing in the classified sections might be possible, particularly if brief forms of the reference were printed out, so many could be seen on the screen at once.

KEY DESIGN FEATURES The user should have the capability of:

1. Rapid browsing of many references without cost, and/or ability to ask to see every nth reference in a large set (see further discussion in Bates, 1976, p. 21ff).

2. Browsing the classification used in an A & I service, as well as abstracts within each classification, either all or every nth one.

*Author searching*

Author searching makes sense as a form of *subject* searching in that authors tend to write on similar things from one article or book to another. Thus, if one item pays off, maybe another by the same person will too. While bibliographies and catalogs have brought together in one place the references to an author's work since time immemorial, it would be a novel contribution of online systems if they made it possible to see grouped in one place the full text of an author's works. Library stacks do it for books, but there is currently no way to bring together other forms of publication, or to combine book texts with those other forms. When the day comes that full text online becomes very cheap, this grouping of an author's work in one place will be possible. The question in the meantime is, can we design the interface to make it easy to "flip through" the pages of the author's work?

KEY DESIGN FEATURES When author searching, the user should have the capability of calling up:

1.  Bibliographies of authors' work,

2.  "Snapshots" of the text of works (see discussion later), and

3.  Features that enable footnote chasing and citation searching.

Each of these approaches can be seen as a different way to identify and exploit particular regions in the total information store that are more likely than other regions to contain information of interest for the search at hand. To put it differently, these are different ways of identifying berry patches in the forest, and then going berrypicking within them.

## Database and interface design

Suggestions for implementing specific design features have been made above. In this section some across-the-board proposals are made for the design of databases and interfaces for browsing and berrypicking:

- To reproduce the above search capabilities, databases will need to contain very large bodies of full text, as well as different types of text (narrative, statistical, bibliographic references, etc.). At the same time the structure of the databases will need to be such that the searcher can move quickly from one form of information to another, in other words, not have to follow a complicated routine to withdraw from one database and enter another.

- Several authors have pointed out the value of helping the user of a system develop a mental model or "metaphor" of the system to guide them (Norman, 1988; Carroll & Thomas, 1982; Elkerton & Williges, 1984). Various models have been used in the design of interfaces for information systems, for example, Weyer (1982) used the book, which approach was also supported by Elkerton & Williges (1984) in their research, and Borgman (1986) used the card catalog. In teaching students general information searching, Huston (1989) has suggested using the model of community-based information networks as a basis for explaining the online literature reviewing process. Hannabuss (1989), on the other hand, has argued for a view of information seeking as a form of conversation, especially with reference to the pattern of turn taking in conversation, and those parts of conversation that involve question asking and answering.

Now that so many different types of information are going online, including much full text, a good place to start as a model of information searching for a berrypicking interface might be the physical library itself. It is the actual physical layout of a library that people are most familiar with, rather than the complex intellectual relationships we develop among catalog entries, books, periodical indexes, journals, etc. Creating a virtual physical layout on the screen may make it easier for the searcher to think of moving among familiar categories of resources in an information retrieval system, in the same manner in which they move among resources in the actual library. This may be particularly useful at the beginning of a search, when the user could see a physical representation of an imaginary library on the screen. The searcher might then be reminded of whole classes of resource which they might otherwise forget.

Many years ago, the psychologist George Miller (1968) pointed out how very physical our memories are, and how easily we remember things by their physical location. Jones and Dumais (1986) challenge the idea that spatial metaphors help information system users recall where something was filed. However, I am suggesting the idea primarily as an orientation device, a way to give users a familiar basis from which to move forward. (See also Bennett, 1971; Bolt, 1978; Woods, 1984; Michel, 1986; and Hildreth's discussion of the General Research Corporation's "Laserguide" CD-ROM online catalog, [1989, pp. 90–94].)

There are many complex issues involved in adapting such a model in an interface, which cannot be dealt with here. Suffice to say that the transfer will not be simple, and may ultimately be modified somewhat away from the more literal image of the library as testing proceeds and as users gain greater familiarity with computer interfaces generally.

Browsing in a manual environment is a physical activity, involving body or eye movements of a fairly random character. Thus to be effective in an online environment, a browsing capability should also allow for random movement, at least of the eyes. An aspect of browsing that has been commented upon is the juxtaposition, in time or space, of different ideas or documents that stimulate the thinking of the information searcher (Foskett, 1983, p. 53). To reproduce this in an online environment, it will be necessary to make rapid movement across large amounts of text possible.

The physical metaphor of the library that was suggested above may facilitate such searching particularly well. For example, if the interface can produce a picture on the screen that looks like the books on a shelf, the searcher can transfer a familiar experience to the automated system. So that if a mouse or similar device makes it possible to, in effect, move among the books, a familiar physical experience is reproduced and the searcher can take advantage of well-developed browsing skills. Until the full texts of books are online, the searcher may examine extensive subject information about the book, such as contents lists, index entries, and the like (Atherton, 1978).

Once such a form of movement is possible online, it should be transferable to other kinds of information environments where such movement was more difficult in manual situations. For example, the searcher might move among categories of a classification scheme used in an A & I service, or follow up leads of related terms in a high-powered online thesaurus. (See also Bates, 1986.)

As noted earlier, the value of flipping through the pages of a book may be due, at least in part, to being able to read passages of a writer's work to get a feel for his or her approach and determine whether it appeals. In large full text databases it will be desirable to be able to do this as well. It would be easy to program a command that would produce a series of randomly selected passages, or "snapshots," each two or three paragraphs in length. Such passages should be truly randomly selected—just as happens when we flip through an article or book—because it is precisely what is not indexed that we want to sample.

Incidentally, in a recent study, based on a random sample drawn from three different types of libraries, I learned that both reference books and "regular" books use a surprisingly limited and robust set of patterns of organization within the book. These patterns have endured in very stable form over hundreds of years and in many Western cultures (1986). The overwhelming majority of contents lists, for example, are two pages or less in length. Plans to use snapshots of text for browsing purposes, therefore, should not produce nasty surprises in terms of displaying segments of complex or unusual file structures. (I am speaking of the structure of the book as a whole, not of what may appear internally to a diagram or illustration.)

The searcher should be able, with a single command, to call for a search mode and screen that is set up for one of the six techniques above (or others). That is, it should not be necessary to issue a string of commands to get the information needed on screen to begin. Each whole technique should be built in as a package that the searcher can call upon when desired. Movement through screens should resemble movement through a real-life source using a given strategy (again the physical metaphor). For example, for the searcher doing a journal run, it should be possible to type in a journal title and year, preceded by some phrase such as "journal scan." The contents page of the first issue of that year then appears on the screen. The searcher can then by, say, highlighting a title, easily ask to see the article full text. Another command or highlight sends parts or all of the article to be printed. And so on.

Hypertext approaches appear tailor-made for berrypicking searching (Conklin, 1987). Being able to jump instantly to full bibliographic citations from references in the text, for example, is a technique that hypertext handles well.

Berrypicking frequently requires the capability of seeing substantial qualities of information on the screen at once. Screens used should be high definition for easy reading and scanning.

The interface design should make it easy to highlight or otherwise flag information and references to be sent to a temporary store. Such a store can then be printed out when the searcher is ready to leave off searching. The necessity otherwise of either writing information down by hand or printing out information in bits and pieces interspersed between search commands would be tiresome and would reduce search effectiveness.


## Conclusions

As the sizes and variety of databases grow and the power of search interfaces increases, users will more and more expect to be able to search automated information stores in ways that are comfortable and familiar to them. We need first to have a realistic model of how people go about looking for information now, and second, to find ways to devise databases and search interfaces that enable searchers to operate in ways that feel natural.

A model of searching called "berrypicking" has been proposed here, which, in contrast to the classic model of information retrieval, says that:

- Typical search queries are not static, but rather evolve.

- Searchers commonly gather information in bits and pieces instead of in one grand best retrieved set.

- Searchers use a wide variety of search techniques, which extend beyond those commonly associated with bibliographic databases.

- Searchers use a wide variety of sources other than bibliographic databases.

Drawing on the research of Ellis (1989), Stoan (1984), and others, a half dozen typical search techniques used in manual sources have been described (footnote chasing, citation searching, journal run, area scanning, A & I searches, author searches). The specific behaviors associated with these techniques, in particular, browsing behaviors, have been analyzed. Methods have been proposed for the implementation of these techniques in database design and search interface design in online systems.

In conclusion, as Rouse and Rouse note, after an extensive survey of the literature of information seeking behavior:

Because information needs change in time and depend on the particular information seeker, systems should be sufficiently flexible to allow the user to adapt the information seeking process to his own current needs. Examples of such flexibility include the design of interactive dialogues and aiding techniques that do not reflect rigid assumptions about the user's goals and style (Rouse & Rouse, 1984, p. 135).

## REFERENCES

Atherton, P. (1978). *Books are for use: Final report of the Subject Access Project to the Council on Library Resources,* (ED 156 131). NY: Syracuse University School of Information Studies.

Bates, M.J. (1976). Rigorous systematic bibliography. *RQ, 16*(1) 7–26.

Bates, M.J. (1984). The fallacy of the perfect thirty-item online search. *RQ, 24*(1), 43–50.

Bates, M.J. (1986). An exploratory paradigm for online information retrieval. In B.C. Brookes (Ed.), *Intelligent information systems for the information society. Proceedings of the Sixth International Research Forum in Information Science (IRFIS 6), Frascati, Italy* (pp. 91–99). Netherlands: North-Holland.

Bates, M.J. (1986). Subject access in online catalogs: A design model, *Journal of the American Society for Information Science, 37*(6) 357–376.

Bates, M.J. (1986). What is a reference book? A theoretical and empirical analysis. *RQ, 26*(1) 37–57.

Bawden, D. (1986). Information systems and the stimulation of creativity. *Journal of Information Science, 12*(5) 203–216.

Belkin, N.J., Oddy, R.N., & Brooks, H.M. (1982). ASK for information retrieval: Part 1: Background and theory. *Journal of Documentation, 38*(2) 61–71.

Bennett, J.L. (1971). Spatial concepts as an organizing principle for interactive bibliographic search. In D.E. Walker (Ed.), *Interactive Bibliographic Search: The User/Computer Interface* (pp. 67–82). Montvale, NJ: AFIPS Press.

Bolt, R.A. (1978). *Spatial data management system.* Marine Architecture Group (NTIS #AD-777 878/OGA). Cambridge, MA: MIT Press.

Borgman, C.L. (1986). The user's mental model of an information retrieval system: An experiment on a prototype online catalog. *International Journal of Man-Machine Studies, 24*(1) 47–64.

Carroll, J.M., & Thomas, J.C. (1982). Metaphor and the cognitive representation of computer systems. *IEEE Transactions on Systems, Man, and Cybernetics, 12*(2), 107–116.

Conklin, J. (1987). *A survey of hypertext.* Microelectronics and Computer Technology Corporation. (MCC Technical Report #STP-356-86, Rev. 2). Austin, TX.

Cove, J.F., & Walsh, B.C. (1988). Online text retrieval via browsing. *Information Processing & Management, 24*(1) 31–37.

Croft, W.B., & Thompson, R.H. (1987). I³R: A new approach to the design of document retrieval systems. *Journal of the American Society for Information Science, 38*(6) 389–404.

Elkerton, J., & Williges, R.C. (1984). Information retrieval strategies in a file-search environment. *Human Factors, 26*(2) 171–184.

Ellis, D. (1984a). The effectiveness of information retrieval systems: The need for improved explanatory frameworks. *Social Science Information Studies, 4*(4) 261–272.

Ellis, D. (1984b). Theory and explanation in information retrieval research. *Journal of Information Science, 8*(1) 25–38.

Ellis, D. (1989). A behavioural approach to information retrieval system design. *Journal of Documentation, 45*(3) 171–212.

Foskett, D.J. (1983). *Pathways for communication.* London: Bingley.

Frarey, C.J. (1953). Studies of use of the subject catalog: Summary and evaluation, In M.F. Tauber (Ed.), *The Subject Analysis of Library Materials* (pp. 147–166). New York: Columbia University, School of Library Service.

Hancock, M. (1987). Subject searching behavior at the library catalogue and at the shelves: Implications for online interactive catalogues. *Journal of Documentation, 43*(4) 303–321.

Hannabuss, S. (1989). Dialogue and the search for information. *ASLIB Proceedings, 41*(3) 85–98.

Hawkins, D.T., Levy, L.R., & Montgomery, K.L. (1988). Knowledge gateways: The building blocks. *Information Processing & Management, 24*(4) 459–468.

Hildreth, C.R. (1982). Online browsing support capabilities. *Proceedings of the ASIS Annual Meeting, 19*, 127–132.

Hildreth, C.R. (1989). *Intelligent interfaces and retrieval methods for subject searching in bibliographic retrieval systems.* Washington, DC: Library of Congress Cataloging Distribution Service.

Hogeweg-de-Haart, H.P. (1984). Characteristics of social science information: A selective review of the literature. Part II. *Social Science Information Studies, 4*(1), 15–30.

Huston, M.M. (1989). Search theory and instruction for end users of online bibliographic information retrieval systems: A literature review. *Research Strategies, 7*(1) 14–32.

Ingwersen, P., & Wormell, I. (1986). Improved subject access. Browsing and scanning mechanisms in modern online IR. *Proceedings of the 9th annual International Conference on Research and Development in Information Retrieval,* Pisa, Italy (pp. 68–75). New York: Association for Computing Machinery.

Jones, W.P., & Dumais, S.T. (1986). The spatial metaphor for user interfaces: Experimental tests of reference by location versus name. *ACM Transactions on Office Information Systems, 4*(1) 42–63.

Kuhlthau, C.C. (1988). Developing a model of the library search process: Cognitive and affective aspects. *RQ, 28*(2) 232–242.

Kuhn, T.S. (1970). *The structure of scientific revolutions* (2nd ed.). Chicago, IL: University of Chicago Press.

Line, M.B. (1974). Information requirements in the social sciences, In *Access to the Literature of the Social Sciences and Humanities,* proceedings of the Conference on Access of Knowledge and Information in the Social Sciences and Humanities, Queens College, City University of New York (pp. 146–158). New York: Queens College Press.

Michel, D. (1986). *When does it make sense to use graphic representations in interactive bibliographic retrieval systems?* (Manuscript). Los Angeles: University of California Graduate School of Library and Information Science.

Miller, G.A. (1968). Psychology and information. *American Documentation, 19*(3) 286–289.

Noerr, P.L., & Bivins Noerr, K.T. (1985). Browse and navigate: An advance in database access methods. *Information Processing & Management, 21*(3) 205–213.

Norman, D.A. (1988). *The psychology of everyday things.* New York: Basic Books.

Oddy, R.N. (1977). Information retrieval through man-machine-dialogue. *Journal of Documentation, 33*(1) 1–14.

Palay, A.J., & Fox, M.S. (1981). Browsing through databases. In R.N. Oddy et al. (Eds.), *Information Retrieval Research* (pp. 310–324). London: Butterworths.

Robertson, S.E. (1977). Theories and models in information retrieval. *Journal of Documentation, 33*(2) 126–148.

Rouse, W.B., & Rouse, S.H. (1984). Human information seeking and design of information systems. *Information Processing & Management, 20*(1–2) 129–138.

Salton, G. (1968). *Automatic information organization and retrieval.* New York: McGraw-Hill.

Stenstrom, P., & McBride, R.B. (1979). Serial use by social science faculty: A survey. *College & Research Libraries, 40*(5) 426–431.

Stoan, S.K. (1984). Research and library skills: An analysis and interpretation. *College & Research Libraries, 45*(2) 99–109.

Stone, S. (1982). Humanities scholars: Information needs and uses. *Journal of Documentation, 38*(4) 292–312.

Wade, S.J., & Willett, P. (1988). INSTRUCT: A teaching package for experimental methods in information retrieval. Part III. Browsing, clustering and query expansion. *Program, 22*(1) 44–61.

Weyer, S.A. (1982). The design of a dynamic book for information search. *International Journal of Man-Machine Studies, 17*(1) 87–107.

Williams, M.E. (1986). Transparent information systems through gateways. Front ends, intermediaries, and interfaces. *Journal of the American Society for Information Science, 37*(4) 204–214.

Woods, D.D. (1984). Visual momentum: A concept to improve the cognitive coupling of person and computer. *International Journal of Man-Machine Studies, 21*(3) 229–24Z4.

# 7

# Speculations on browsing, directed searching, and linking in relation to the Bradford Distribution

## ABSTRACT

Extensive literatures exist on information searching theory and techniques, as well as on the Bradford Distribution. This distribution, also known as "Bradford's Law of Scattering," tells us that information on a subject is dispersed in a characteristic and robust pattern that appears consistently across many different environments. This pattern may be expected to have important implications for information searching theory and techniques. Yet these two research literatures are rarely considered in relation to each other. It is the purpose of this article to distinguish three Bradford regions and speculate on the optimum searching techniques for each region. In the process, browsing, directed searching in databases, and the pursuit of various forms of links will all be considered. Implications of growth in size of a literature for optimal information organization and searching will also be addressed.

## Introduction

Extensive research literatures exist on information search techniques and on the Bradford Distribution—but rarely are the two considered in relation to each other. (A search produced a handful of references linking

*First published as* Bates, M. J. (2002). Speculations on browsing, directed searching, and linking in relation to the Bradford Distribution. In H. Bruce, R. Fidel, P. Ingwersen, & P. Vakkari (Eds.), *Emerging frameworks and methods: Proceedings of the fourth international conference on conceptions of library and information science (CoLIS4)* (pp. 137–150). Greenwood Village, CO: Libraries Unlimited.

the two—Lancaster et al., 1991; Leimkuhler, 1977; White, 1981—but none of these items address the questions being considered in this paper.) The Bradford Distribution, or, Bradford's Law of Scattering, describes how information on a subject is distributed among the resources where such information may be expected to be found. The distribution will be described in more detail shortly, but the key point is that the distribution tells us that information is neither randomly scattered, nor handily concentrated in a single location. Instead, information scatters in a characteristic pattern, a pattern that should have obvious implications for how that information can most successfully and efficiently be sought.

It is the object of this paper to link the Bradford Distribution with searching techniques, and to consider what techniques might work the best for which regions of the Bradford distribution. In the process, I will also speculate on a variety of other possible implications of the connections between Bradford's Law and searching.

## The Bradford Distribution

Samuel Bradford originally developed his data on the basis of studying the distribution of articles in journals in two areas, applied geophysics and lubrication. He studied the rates at which articles relevant to each subject area appeared in journals in those areas. He identified all journals that published more than a certain number of articles in the test areas per year, as well as in other ranges of descending frequency. He wrote:

> [I]f scientific journals are arranged in order of decreas-
> ing productivity of articles on a given subject, they may
> be divided into a nucleus of periodicals more particularly
> devoted to the subject and several groups or zones con-
> taining the same number of articles as the nucleus, when
> the numbers of periodicals in the nucleus and succeed-
> ing zones will be as $1:n:n^2$ ... (Bradford, 1948, p. 116).

In principle, there could be any number of zones, with the number of articles in each zone being the total number of articles divided by the number of zones. In his empirical data, however, Bradford identified just three zones, and three will be used here for simplicity's sake. Bradford found in his empirical data that the value of "n" was roughly 5. Suppose, then, that someone doing an in-depth search on a topic finds that four journals constitute the core, and contain fully one-third of all the relevant articles

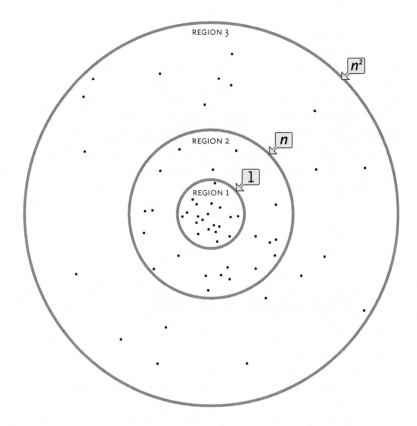

FIG. 1. *The Bradford regions. Each search region contains one-third of the articles on the subject. Each ring is five times the area of the next smaller one.*

found. ("Relevant" is used here strictly in the sense of topical relevance.) If the value for n is 5, then 4 x 5 = 20 journals will, among them, contain another third of all the relevant articles found. Finally, the last third will be the most scattered of all, being spread out over $4 \times 5^2 = 100$ journals. See Figure 1.

The distribution indicates that one could find a great many relevant articles on a topic nicely concentrated in a few core journals. But finding the rest of the relevant articles involves an increasingly more extensive search, as the average yield of articles per additional journal examined becomes smaller and smaller the farther out, i.e., the more remotely from the core journals, one goes. The Bradford data thus tell us that desired material is neither perfectly concentrated in one place, as we might hope, nor is it completely randomly distributed either, as we might fear.

There has been considerable debate about the exact formulation of the distribution. However, for our purposes, the general formulation given by Bradford himself (above) is sufficient. Many types of recorded information have been found to follow the Bradford Distribution. See reviews in Chen and Leimkuhler (1986), Fedorowicz (1982), and Wilson (1999). Recently, Hood and Wilson (2001) found the same pattern operating regarding the number of databases to search to find the literature on 14 test queries. (For simplicity's sake, the discussion in this paper is restricted to materials on a subject, though other kinds of searches, such as for materials by authors, materials coming out of research institutes or government agencies, etc., probably also follow a Bradfordian pattern.) In sum, it seems reasonable to assume, in the absence of any contrary information, that recorded information of all types on a subject, and in many different physical forms, is distributed in this same Bradfordian manner.

## Searching the Bradford regions

Assuming then that information on a subject is distributed in the Bradfordian pattern, what are the implications for search strategy? The proposed relationship between the Bradford Distribution and searching techniques will first be described below in a general way, then more specific details will be developed.

From the searcher's perspective, the innermost core of the distribution—let us call it Region 1—is the richest in materials on one's subject of interest. One might therefore expect it to be the easiest to search, because there is so much wheat, so little chaff. Perhaps one might even be able to find items in Region 1 without any conventional formal search techniques at all—one may simply browse.

In the next ring, Region 2, there are still a good number of items on one's subject to be found, but they are now scattered more widely, and many non-relevant items (that is, many items not on the desired subject) are interspersed among the (topically) relevant items. In this region, it is no longer adequately efficient to search by browsing, though one can, of course, always browse if one wants. But for any reasonably efficient search effort, some kind of formal information organization of the material is needed, coupled with search techniques specifically designed to take advantage of that organization. Region 2 is where indexing and database searching come into their own. This approach is here called "directed searching." More precisely, directed searching is done in situations where some form(s) of information organization, description, and/or indexing of the information exists, thus enabling explicit query development and search of that query.

In Region 3, the outermost area, a substantial number of relevant items are still to be found, but they are so widely dispersed that finding the occasional relevant item is rather like the proverbial problem of "finding a needle in a haystack." Here, following citation or other links from articles closer to the core may prove to be the most efficient sort of searching. Of course, links may lead to articles in any part of the distribution, from the core out to the periphery.

However, in the far edges of the distribution linking may be especially useful as a search technique. In conventional database searching terms, as one moves outward from the center, the precision gets worse and worse— one must review more and more irrelevant items to find any one relevant item, and the recall climbs more and more slowly. Here, conventional indexing/retrieval may be seen to break down. Searching through vast resources becomes inefficient, and the number of "false drops" is so high that it becomes ever harder to detect the occasional desired item. Here, in Region 3, the best solution may be to create links, or to take advantage of pre-existing links, such as article notes/citations or Web links.

*Thus, at the most generalized level, we may see the core region of the Bradford distribution as the ideal location for browsing, the middle region as the ideal location for searching in the mode of indexing/retrieval, and the outer region as the ideal location for pursuing links.*

Having conjectured this pattern for ideal searching, however, it will be demonstrated shortly that all three generic search techniques are currently used throughout the Bradford regions. Should they be?

## Generic search techniques

We will want to examine the Bradford regions in more detail shortly, but in the meantime, it will reward us to examine these three general search techniques in more detail—browsing, directed searching, and linking.

### Browsing

The first generic search technique is *browsing,* which involves successive acts of glimpsing, fixing on a target to examine visually or manually more closely, examining, then moving on to start the cycle over again. This definition is strongly based on Kwasnik's (1992) conceptualization of browsing. (See also discussion in Chang and Rice, 1993.)

We can see browsing as having several functions in information searching. First, with respect to the Bradfordian distribution of literature, *one purpose of browsing is to find the core.* Browsing, in its nature, ignores the file structure or other formal organization of information. For example, when we browse in library stacks or in a bookstore, our glimpsing of the materials on the shelves does not follow the call number or alphabetical order of the materials. In other words, we generally do not scan in a strict left to right order along the shelf. Our glance is not systematic—though we do take advantage, in a larger sense, of any relatedness in the arrangement of the materials on the shelves. Browsing is therefore a quick technique, but also a chancy one. When one does not know where the heart of a subject area is to be found, however, this rapid technique may enable one to zoom in quickly on the richest area to be searched.

*A second purpose of browsing is to search the core.* As the core is densely populated with relevant material, it is generally not necessary to create or negotiate one's way through additional formal information organization structures. The population of relevant items is large enough that one can simply browse the area and reliably locate a good number of desirable materials in a short time.

Two techniques described in Bates (1989) represent specific forms of this generic browsing technique. *Journal run* consists of reviewing contents pages of core journals in an area.

> [This] technique, by definition, guarantees complete
> recall within that journal, and, if the journal is cen-
> tral enough to the searcher's interests, this technique
> also has tolerably good precision (1989, p. 412).

Journal run is a clear case of browsing in the Bradford core (Region 1) of a subject. The materials are collocated in the journal because editorial decisions have brought them together, not because anyone indexed them and collocated them in an information system.

The second specific browsing technique described in Bates (1989) is *area scanning*. This technique consists of browsing the materials that are physically collocated with materials located earlier in a search. The classic example of area scanning is browsing through the classified arrangement of books on library shelves. So, in effect, area scanning is a kind of browsing that is used in the second Bradford region, where directed searching normally takes place.

Another common type of browsing is *Web-browsing*, that is, moving around via links between and within documents on the World Wide

Web. Materials from all three Bradford regions may be found on the Web. However, finding Region 3 items may be particularly successful, given the nature and structure of the Web.

Thus, some form of browsing has been used in all three regions of the Bradford Distribution. In general, the strengths of browsing are its intuitiveness (building on age-old foraging behavior of our hunter-gatherer forbears—Sandstrom, 1994) and its directness—what you see is what you get. The downside of browsing is that it is limited; we can do it only for so long and in a relatively narrow area, before we are overcome by our modern need to move on to the next task.

## Directed searching

The second generic searching technique is what is here being called *directed searching,* to distinguish it from "searching" in general. Directed searching is done (and can only be done) where some sort of previous indexing, cataloging, or classification has been done on the materials being searched. To put it differently, the information is deliberately structured in order that subsets of the information can be selectively targeted for retrieval. The deliberate structuring may be as simple as the automatic coding of all individual words in a database so that they can be individually searched ("free-text" searching), or as intellectually complex as deep and detailed human indexing and cataloging.

In either case, a descriptive or metadata structure is created by human beings in front of or in addition to the original target information. The searcher then may utilize whatever searching capabilities are provided to exploit this representational structure, in order to find desired information from among a much larger set of resources.

In Bates' 1989 article, two of the techniques described there are classic directed searching techniques: *subject searches in bibliographies and abstracting and indexing (A & I) services,* and *author searching* (p. 412). Directed searching has been a primary focus of information science research and discussion over the last thirty years. Most of the 29 searching tactics described by Bates (1979) are moves that the searcher can make to promote an effective search in the context of these elaborate indexing structures and retrieval capabilities.

Directed searching has been used on all three Bradford regions. The browsable core generally is automatically included in any good search formulation, so that items located in both Regions 1 and 2 are retrieved. Region 3 items have long been found in online searching through use of extensive search formulations containing many OR'd terms ("hedges"), as well as by searching several databases representing peripheral subject areas. The strength of directed searching is its thoroughness and extensive reach. Its weaknesses are that it lacks the directness of browsing and the targeted precision of the citation link.

The advent of the more-effective Google search engine, which is based on linkage patterns as well as conventional search engine retrieval mechanisms, suggests that heavy utilization of links in *really* large information environments, especially in the outer limits of Region 3, may be the best way to go when the Bradford territory has grown very large. On the other hand, because of the recency of the Internet, we may simply have not yet found the best forms of directed searching for it.

Incidentally, Jaime Pontigo-Martinez' dissertation work (1984) tested whether scientific experts, unaware of which Bradford ring specialist articles in their field came from, would judge the articles from all rings as being of equal value. The null hypothesis, that there would be no difference in assessed value between the rings, was supported. This result suggests that, despite the difficulties in searching for articles in outer rings, it is still valuable to locate them, if possible.

## Linking

Linking long pre-dates the Internet, but has come into its own in recent years with the advent of sophisticated networking technology (Kleinberg, 1999; Lempel and Moran, 2001). *Links* are deliberate connections created by people or automatically by software between parts of a document or between documents. Linking has been utilized to connect texts with relevant related references (footnotes) for centuries. Linking may include the references from index entries to page numbers in books, the "see" and "see also" references between catalog entries, the links within and between documents on the World Wide Web, and the citation links in citation indexes, among other things.

Strictly speaking, we should distinguish between the *creation* of links by authors or Web-page designers, and the *pursuit or following* of links by searchers. It is the latter sense that is being used in association with the discussion of searching techniques in this paper.

In their nature, links may be made between records in any Bradford ring to any other ring. Thus, in principle, searching via links may move anywhere in the Bradford space. Links, while very targeted and precise, may also be capricious and incomplete. Following links, the searcher may range widely, but incompletely, across the relevant materials.

Two of these kinds of links are mentioned among the search techniques described in Bates' 1989 article, *footnote chasing*, and *citation searching* (p. 412). Footnote chasing, also called "backward chaining" (Ellis, 1989), "involves following up footnotes found in books and articles of interest, and therefore moving backward in successive leaps through reference lists" (Bates, 1989, p. 412). Each such leap, of course, takes one farther back in time.

To utilize citation searching, or "forward chaining," there must be in existence citation indexes that have already located in a single index the relationships of a large number of citing and cited works. Major citation indexes are the three produced by the Institute for Scientific Information, the *Science Citation Index,* the *Social Sciences Citation Index,* and the *Arts & Humanities Citation Index.* One searches in a citation index by looking up an earlier article or book of interest and discovering who has cited it since its publication, thus coming forward in time.

Linking has exploded with the advent of the World Wide Web; indeed the Web, even in its name, can be seen as the primary and best place to manifest links between every imaginable form of information, so long as it can be resident in a computer.

## Impact of domain size

We have been skirting an important issue, which now needs to be addressed. If we think about real-world searching, the size of the domain has a very important impact on searching; specifically, different search techniques are appropriate for differently-sized bodies of information, regardless of ring. It turns out that there is a nice illustrative analogy that can be used here. It has been long recognized in the field of geography (Wilson and Bennett, 1985, p. 84) that towns and cities grow in patterns that look very much like our circular model of the Bradford Distribution. Indeed, such distributions are universal statistical phenomena. Bradford did not so much as invent his distribution, but rather applied this general phenomenon to information science.

When communities grow, they follow a certain characteristic pattern. This pattern was well illustrated in the settling of the American West. A new area opening up would draw farmers, ranchers, or miners. Then a merchant would set up a general store to serve the needs of these groups. As the community grew, the filling in of the community would follow the pattern of Figure 1, with denser settlement in the heart of town, and characteristic scattering toward the edges of town. Thus the distributional pattern remains the same throughout the time of growth, from village to metropolis.

Nonetheless, cities do not look like villages. With the growth in size and increased density at that core, more and more kinds of activities became sustainable. Saloons, livery stables, and assay offices appeared next, followed later by the sheriff, schools, and churches. Continued growth eventually supported concert halls, libraries, operas, and many other less common institutions.

A town of regional importance can sustain more rarefied types of institutions than smaller towns in the area. So in the growth of towns, we can see that size matters a lot. Though the Bradford-style distribution characterizes the scattering of settlement from the time of the tiny beginning outpost to the large city, the kinds of institutions that these settlements will support varies tremendously with size.

The same pattern can be seen with information resources. That is, the Bradford pattern operates throughout, from the time of a tiny beginning literature known to only a handful of people to the development of a vast literature of interest to millions of people. On the other hand, the kinds of searching, the kinds of access that make sense for selecting information from this literature will vary with the size of the total domain.

Derek de Solla Price illustrated this pattern in his discussion of the early days of science. He noted that in the seventeenth century, scientists initially developed journals in order to lighten the load of reading books, personal correspondence, and other sources of information on the ever-growing scientific enterprise. Initially, the journals "had the stated function of digesting the books and doings of the learned all over Europe" (Price, 1963, p. 63). After a while, the journals themselves became important publication venues for new discoveries. Eventually, however, it became difficult to follow all the journals being published, and abstracting indexes were developed (Price, 1961, pp. 96ff). Indeed, it may well be that every major technological and intellectual development in information access in succeeding centuries has arisen out of the pressures of literature growth.

Let us now look more closely at what a Bradford-distributed literature would look like as it grows in size. When a small group of originators begins producing small numbers of documents, the absolute size of the domain is so small that while Bradford regions might be present in an incipient form, they are not yet very evident. One individual or one paper may be more important than others, and form the Region 1 focus of social and documentary networks. However, the total number of resources and connections among them are few, and interested individuals can generally find all they want by browsing and following citations. In very small towns one does not need a map, because everything is visible on one street; likewise, one needs little or no assistance once one has come upon the "small town" of a starter literature on a subject.

With the growth in the literature, however, just as with the growth of the town, auxiliary devices are necessary to enable one to find desired locations—maps and directories for geographical locations, classifications and indexing for bibliographical regions. As the literature grows, one access method after another is shed, as more sophisticated techniques and technologies must be developed to maintain effective access to the literature.

With very small literatures, one may need only one or two distinct types of search method to do effective searching over the whole subject matter domain. In a very mature, highly developed literature, there may be half a dozen discernible Bradford regions, each, perhaps, requiring different search techniques to maximize search effectiveness.

Until the late nineteenth century, library collections, and topical literatures on given subjects were still comparatively small. As Price, Senders, and others have demonstrated, the numbers of book and journal titles have been growing exponentially since the scientific journal (seventeenth century) and the modern printed book (fifteenth century) began. In practical terms, exponential growth means that the number of titles doubles every so many years—for journals, every fifteen years (Price, 1961, p. 100), and books every 22 years (Senders, 1963, p. 1068). Such growth does not make much difference in the early days—1,000 book titles doubling to 2,000 book titles in 22 years is not particularly conspicuous—but book titles doubling from 20 million to 40 million in 22 years is *very* conspicuous! Thus the publishing and library collecting of documentary forms of various types was quite stable for centuries, with relatively glacial change. The need for innovation became particularly acute in the nineteenth century, however, as the absolute numbers of new titles quickly outdistanced every new innovation introduced.

It is probably not accidental that the modern profession of librarianship emerged at that same time. The days of the interested amateur librarian ended when the need for attention to ever-newer techniques and ever-larger buildings made library work a full-time focus of whoever took the job.

It may even be the case that the growth of collections and of materials within any given subject area reached the point in the nineteenth century that sophisticated Region 2 devices had to be introduced for the first time. Before then, catalogs were barely more than inventories of collections. With growth, however, anyone who was not a dedicated scholar in a narrow subject field needed the selectivity offered by more advanced techniques of cataloging, indexing, and classification, in order to maneuver among the growing collections.

In the speculative spirit of this paper, I would suggest that as literatures grew over the last century and a half, each major new intellectual and physical technology for information access represented another "institution," in the geographical analogy, in the growing turf that was information. Just as larger cities can sustain orchestras and concert halls, so also can larger literatures sustain databases, bibliographies, and sophisticated indexing and online system design.

In the meantime, more sophisticated forms of browsing and linking have been introduced recently as well. Online browsing is becoming better supported through subtler and more user-centered system design. The introduction of the citation indexes in the 1960s and 1970s enabled forward chaining as a linking method, and, of course, the Internet created an explosion of linking possibilities for the searcher.

## Final speculations: Best searching techniques?

We have seen in the prior discussion that on the one hand, browsing, directed searching, and linking, respectively, might best be matched with Bradfordian Regions 1, 2, and 3. On the other hand, we have seen that all three generic techniques have been used with all three regions, indeed, have generally been used in the absence of thinking about the Bradford Distribution altogether. A profusion of technologies continues to develop, which supports improvements in all three generic searching techniques. How should we move forward on the question of the relationship between the Bradford Distribution and searching techniques?

In teaching undergraduates, I have observed that it is common for them to expect to find resources or websites that provide all the relevant information for their paper in a single location, exactly matching the topic of their paper. In other words, the naive assumption is that chunks of information are perfectly self-contained and complete. At the same time, I have found that beginners often have no idea how to start finding information, and, appear to believe that their one perfect chunk of information may be literally anywhere, that there is no rational way to find it.

Both of these assumptions are inaccurate. Having a generalized understanding of the Bradfordian distribution of all information may provide the basic grounding for a realistic search. As librarians rarely understand this distribution either, we are not always in the best position to help.

What has long been an article of faith among librarians is that all information is findable through the mechanisms of indexing, cataloging, and classification, and that the good searcher invariably utilizes these carefully developed intermediary bibliographic resources. Information literacy instruction for non-librarians is almost always centered around bringing the user into fluency with these sorts of resources.

The experienced humanities scholar constitutes an interesting contrast to the college student and the librarian. The scholar does not have librarian training, but is nonetheless familiar with a number of library research techniques, learned in the course of acquiring the Ph.D. The information seeking research indicates that these scholars rely heavily on browsing and on following citation links (footnote chasing). They rarely, if ever use periodical index databases, and tend to use catalogs only for searches for known items (Stone, 1982; Watson-Boone, 1994; Wiberley, 1989).

The naive user, say, the beginning college student, thus has two models to follow: the librarians, who encourage use of every intermediary access device, from catalogs to online databases, and their professors, who rely most heavily on browsing and footnote chasing.

Another historical metaphor may be suitable at this point. We may view the primary use of browsing and citation linking as an "artisan" approach to searching, that is, a method that dates from the age of skilled craftsmanship. Scholarly research methods have been passed down from mentors to protégés for centuries. By keeping their scholarly focus narrow and deep, humanities researchers have been able to continue that artisan tradition. By searching in a narrow area, the scope of the intellectual territory is kept small enough to allow the continuation of such individualized techniques.

The nineteenth century explosion of new methods of access through classifications, subject indexes, and card catalogs, constituted the beginning of the "industrialization" of searching. With the aid of such devices, one may search vastly more resources in a given period of time (the advantage of "mass production"), but without the personalization made possible by the countless individual search move decisions made in a browsing/footnote-chasing searching technique.

Librarians professionalized in the nineteenth century, at a time when new (Region 2) cataloging and classification techniques were flourishing. Perhaps for that reason, the field created a fused identity with Region 2 devices. Librarians have thus operated on the assumption that all regions of the Bradford distribution of a subject area are best accessed by Region 2 devices, such as catalogs and indexes. In the meantime, scholars and general users tended to muddle along with browsing and footnote chasing as their primary retrieval mechanisms.

Finally, in the late twentieth century, we arrived at the beginning of the Networked Age. When the Web came along, scholars expanded their searching to following Web links, because this technique had a lot of similarities with the footnote chasing they were already familiar with. There have been impressive developments in the potential of networked retrieval to date, but we are still very early in the development of information searching design through networking.

In the end, I believe we should have all three broad types of searching available to us. Work by craftsmen was not abandoned with the advent of the Industrial Revolution, and mass production has not been given up in the Networked Age. We will use them all, with ever more powerful technologies, and ever greater flexibility and effectiveness in our searching. Further, by designing systems to facilitate all three information access methods, effective searching can be supported for all literature sizes and regions.

At the same time, having an understanding of the dynamics of literature distributions may enable us as searchers to make better and more sophisticated decisions about how we want to search and where. It may also prove valuable to test the general conjecture made here, that areas with high numbers of topically relevant materials (relative to all materials in the area) are best searched by browsing, areas with middling numbers of topically relevant items are best searched by directed searching on information-organizational structures, and areas with very sparse ("needle in a haystack") numbers of relevant items are best searched by using links.

## REFERENCES

Bates, M.J. (1979). Information search tactics. *Journal of the American Society for Information Science, 30*(4) 205-214.

Bates, M.J. (1989). The design of browsing and berrypicking techniques for the online search interface. *Online Review, 13*(5), 407-424.

Bradford, S.C. (1948). *Documentation.* London: Crosby Lockwood.

Chang, S.-J., & Rice, R.E. (1993). Browsing: A multidimensional framework. In M.E. Williams (Ed.), *Annual review of information science and technology, 28,* 231-276. Medford, NJ: Learned Information.

Chen, Y.S. & Leimkuhler, F.F. (1986). A relationship between Lotka's Law, Bradford's Law, and Zipf's Law. *Journal of the American Society for Information Science, 37*(5), 304-314.

Ellis, D. (1989). A behavioural approach to information retrieval system design. *Journal of Documentation, 45*(3), 171-212.

Fedorowicz, J. (1982). The theoretical foundation of Zipf's Law and its application to the bibliographic database environment. *Journal of the American Society for Information Science, 33*(5), 285-293.

Hood, W.W., & Wilson, C.S. (2001). The scatter of documents over databases in different subject domains: How many databases are needed? *Journal of the American Society for Information Science and Technology, 52*(14), 1242–1254.

Kleinberg, J.M. (1999). Hubs, authorities, and communities. *ACM Computing Surveys, 31* (supp. 4), U21–U23.

Kwasnik, B.H. (1992). *Descriptive study of the functional components of browsing.* Paper presented at the Proceedings of the IFIP TC2\WG2.7 working conference on engineering for human-computer interaction, Elivuoi, Finland, August 10–14, 1992.

Lancaster, F.W., Gondek, V., McCowan, S., & Reese, C. (1991). The relationship between literature scatter and journal accessibility in an academic special library. *Collection Building, 11*(1), 19–22.

Leimkuhler, F.F. (1977). Operational analysis of library systems. *Information Processing & Management, 13*(2), 79–93.

Lempel, R., & Moran, S. (2001). SALSA: The stochastic approach for link-structure analysis. *ACM Transactions on Information Systems, 19*(2), 131–160.

Pontigo-Martinez, J. (1984). Qualitative attributes and the Bradford Distribution. (Unpublished doctoral Dissertation). Champaign-Urbana: University of Illinois.

Price, D.J. de Solla. (1961). *Science since Babylon.* New Haven, CT: Yale University Press.

Price, D.J. de Solla. (1963). *Little science, big science.* New York: Columbia University Press.

Sandstrom, P.E. (1994). An optimal foraging approach to information seeking and use. *The Library Quarterly, 64*(4), 414–449.

Senders, J.W. (1963). Information storage requirements for the contents of the world's libraries. *Science, 141,* 1067–1068.

Stone, S. (1982). Progress in documentation: Humanities scholars: Information needs and uses. *Journal of Documentation, 38*(4), 292–312.

Watson-Boone, R. (1994). The information needs and habits of humanities scholars. *RQ, 34*(2), 203–216.

White, H.D. (1981). 'Bradfordizing' search output: How it would help online users. *Online Review, 5,* 47–54.

Wiberley, S.E. Jr., & Jones, W.G. (1989). Patterns of information seeking in the humanities. *College & Research Libraries, 50*(6), 638–645.

Wilson, A.G., & Bennett, R.J. (1985). *Mathematical methods in human geography and planning.* New York: Wiley.

Wilson, C.S. (1999). Informetrics. *Annual review of information science and technology, 34,* 107–247. Medford, NJ: Information Today.

# 8

# What is browsing—really? A model drawing from behavioral science research

ABSTRACT

Introduction It is argued that the actual elements of typical browsing episodes have not been well captured by common approaches to the concept to date.

Method Empirical research results reported by previous researchers are presented and closely analyzed.

Analysis Based on the issues raised by the above research review, the components of browsing are closely analyzed and developed. Browsing is seen to consist of a series of four steps, iterated indefinitely until the end of a browsing episode: 1) glimpsing a field of vision, 2) selecting or sampling a physical or informational object within the field of vision, 3) examining the object, 4) acquiring the object (conceptually and/or physically) or abandoning it. Not all of these elements need be present in every browsing episode, though multiple glimpses are seen to be the minimum to constitute the act.

Results This concept of browsing is then shown to have persuasive support in the psychological and anthropological literature, where research on visual search, curiosity and exploratory behavior all find harmony with this perspective.

*First published as* Bates, M. J. (2007). What is browsing—really? A model drawing from behavioral science research. *Information Research, 12*(4), paper 330. *http://www.informationr.net/ir.*

Conclusions It is argued that this conception of browsing is closer to real human behavior than other approaches. Implications for better information system design are developed.

## Introduction

Though often seen as a casual, incidental behavior in the general society, browsing, in the information world, is widely recognized as an important information seeking technique. In an academic context, scholars have argued that frequent browsing is often the only way to locate information and resources that cannot be readily described by index terms. Further, some kinds of information are recognized as relevant only upon discovery. In short, there are the things you know you do not know and the things you do not know you do not know. Browsing provides an alternative strategy for locating information of the first kind and may provide one of the crucial ways for information of the second kind to be encountered.

Information seeking is, after all, about finding out things that one does not know before the search begins. Therefore, uncertainty always accompanies the process to a greater or lesser degree. Sometimes it is possible to specify the information need very closely—"What was the population of Turkey in 1960?"— but other times specification in advance is impossible, as when the ugly duckling was surprised to discover serendipitously that he was actually a swan.

Much has been written about browsing in the library and information science literature, but it has generally been found difficult to specify browsing too closely, because 1) the conditions under which browsing is used vary widely, 2) it seems to be rather unpredictable in its very nature and 3) it seems to be employed in both more and less directed, intentional ways. In *Accessing and Browsing Information and Communication,* by Rice et al. (2001) the source in which browsing appears to have been most comprehensively reviewed and discussed, the authors find definitions of the following sort to be common: "Herner (1970) derived three . . . categories: 1) directed browsing, 2) semidirected or predictive browsing and 3) undirected browsing" (1970, p. 177).

After reviewing several of these sorts of definitions, the authors conclude that four dimensions have been most prominent in discussion of the subject (Rice et al., 2001):

1. "The act of scanning. Browsing embodies an act of scanning, which has been variously described as looking, examining,

or sampling where the person's body or eyes move smoothly at will" (2001, p. 178).

2. "Presence or absence of a purpose. . . . Although a purposeful act can be goal-directed or non-goal-directed, the presence of an intention suggests that the concept of browsing cannot be adequately described by behavioral characteristics alone" (2001, p. 178).

3. Search criteria may be extensively, minimally, or not at all specified. "At one end of this continuum, the objective of browsing is well defined; at the other end, the objective of browsing is not defined" (2001, p. 178).

4. The browser's knowledge of the resource browsed—either search paths in or contents of—can affect the quality of the interaction with the resource substantially (2001, pp. 178–9).

The above conclusions were based on a review of the literature of library user studies. The authors then continued by reviewing six other fields that have some reason to be interested in this general sort of behavior: 1) End-user computing and information science; 2) consumer research, 3) audience research, 4) organizational research—environmental scanning, 5) organizational research—informal communication and 6) environmental planning and architectural design (Rice et al., 2001, 182–210). The key insight for our purposes from this extensive review is that the authors found that the core cognitive and behavioral activity involved in browsing in these several literatures was largely the same as found in library user studies. In five of the six fields, the authors identify "scanning" as a part of the definitions of browsing applicable in that field. Scanning was missing only in their review of the literature of "organizational research—informal communication." There, Rice et al. define browsing thus: ". . . the notion of browsing in this context refers to casual access to social links and unpredictable exposure to many possible social interactions and to the implied knowledge available through these interactions" (Rice et al., 2001, p. 203).

We generally know intuitively what browsing is, because we have engaged in it ourselves and observed it in others. However, if we did not have that intuitive knowledge, we might have to conclude, based on the four points above (Rice et al., 2001), that browsing, at a minimum, consists of intentional visual scanning, with or without a well-defined objective and with or without fore-knowledge of the resource(s) browsed.

In this article, I would like to consider browsing more deeply. First, does browsing, at its core, only consist of *intentional visual scanning*, "where the person's body or eyes move smoothly at will" (Rice et al., 2001, p. 178)? Is there more to it?

Second, why do we browse at all? After all, there are many kinds of searching, known to trained information personnel, that the average untrained person does not engage in—but browsing seems to be widespread. Where does this impulse come from? How do people even know to do it?

## Browsing in information studies

Our principal objective here is to understand browsing in the context of information behavior and for the purposes of information science. However, it is valuable for us to know, based on the Rice et al. review (2001) that something like browsing appears in the research of other disciplines, such as consumer research and organizational theory. Such a result suggests that browsing is a more general behavior, something human beings do under a variety of impulses, not only in moments of information need. We will come back to this more general perspective in a later section.

Here, however, I wish first to challenge the common perspective, shared by Rice et al. (2001), that browsing is a matter of visual scanning, "where the person's body or eyes move smoothly at will" (p. 178). If we imagine literally doing what this clause says, then we visualize the proverbial fur-trapper or scout in the woods or on the edge of a meadow, shading his eyes with a flattened hand held perpendicularly out from the forehead and rotating the head from one side to the other in a smooth scan of the environment.

The term "to scan" itself requires elaboration. The first three and most relevant, definitions of the verb in the *American Heritage Dictionary* are these:

1. To examine closely. 2. To look over quickly and systematically: *scanning the horizon for signs of land.* 3. To look over or leaf through hastily: *scanned the newspaper while eating breakfast* ("Scan." *American Heritage Dictionary*, 2000).

The dictionary's usage note explains that the verb *to scan* has historically had two "opposite senses"—one "to examine closely" and the other "to look over quickly." It explains that the latter meaning is more recent and is now fully established. Rice et al. (2001) take advantage of this dual—and, arguably contradictory—set of meanings to claim that browsing includes both quick looks, "glancing around" (p. 218), as well as lengthier examination of resources: "scanning within a potential resource for assessment tends to be more thorough . . ." (p. 219). The authors base their understanding of the cognitive and behavioral process of browsing on this central idea of scanning.

They elaborate as follows:

> ... [T]he notion of browsing has been construed as a shopping activity, a viewing pattern and a screening technique in addition to a search strategy. In the most fundamental sense, these various interpretations of browsing share a central characteristic: they are *scanning* processes (Rice et al.,2001, p. 218).

In the final, refined framework for browsing (Rice et al., 2001, p. 295), which is a slightly modified version of the original tentative model presented on page 234, the *process* of browsing is seen to consist of 1) a behavior: scanning; 2) motivation: a goal; 3) cognition: an object; and 4) resource: form. Rice et al.'s summary of these components of the model goes as follows:

> Thus, in the new model for describing the browsing process, scanning is the salient component of the behavioral dimension. Goal is the central element of motivational dimension. Object is the major cognitive process. And form appears to be characteristic of the resource dimension. (Rice et al., 2001, 291–292).

Their perspective could be re-worded as follows: browsing consists of the behavior of scanning, driven by the motivation of having a goal directed toward an object. When the object is an information resource, the influential variable about that object is its form.

Is browsing really like this? How could we characterize the act of browsing to distinguish it from all the other types of acts human beings commit? Is browsing really only the intentional scanning of an object?

Instead, I would argue, browsing consists of a series of glimpses, some glimpses leading to further, closer exploration of the thing(s) glimpsed and some not. In this view, browsing consists of numerous stops and starts, with some reading, or surveying, alternating with other actions, such as sampling and selecting. Rice et al. (2001) are clearly well aware of this pattern to browsing, as indicated by their discussion of identification of units for analysis on page 242. The empirical observations made of people browsing were analyzed into a hierarchy of case, movement and episode. Each case was an observation of an individual's activities in a library, each movement reflected movement from one part of the library to another and each episode represented a distinct goal or object within a movement (pp. 238–242). "A new episode within a movement begins when either the goal or the object under consideration changes and it is distinguishable by a question similar to movement: 'I observed you do . . . what was your intent with that activity?'" (p. 242). Rice et al. (2001) are thus clearly aware of the segmented, or step-wise, nature of the act of browsing, but this awareness is not evident in the final model.

Further, they produce a taxonomy, which consists of nine types of browsing and one type of non-browsing (p. 286). (These types are distinguished largely by the intent or context of browsing, not by differences in the act of browsing itself.) Both the browsing and non-browsing members of the taxonomy involve scanning; thus the one distinctive behavioral characteristic of browsing that the authors identify—scanning—is not, after all, truly defining for browsing, because scanning can occur in non-browsing situations as well. What, then, uniquely defines the act of browsing?

Elsewhere, the authors come much closer to dissecting the distinctive characteristics of browsing. They note "The four distinct acts of browsing were derived from the observation of scanning as a non-verbal behavior" (p. 290). These four acts are defined as *looking, identifying, selecting,* and *examining* (p. 291). After their brief mention, these intriguing activities are not incorporated in the final model of browsing, however, and are not addressed again in the book. Nor did a literature review on the concept of browsing for the years subsequent to their book produce any further developments on these elements.

These intriguing components of browsing, which indicate that browsing is a more complex and interesting behavior than just scanning, are addressed insightfully; however, in a short paper by Kwasnik (1992) (cited, but apparently not drawn upon substantively, by Rice et al., 2001). Her results are based on just four people and were intended to precede a larger study. Two of the individuals were observed in a farmer's market and the other two used a mail-order catalog of gifts, so browsing both among physical objects and among informational representations was included. Kwasnik notes:

> In our analysis we focused on the movement of people's attention from item to item or from representation to representation. Movement was signaled by physical movement (walking, page-turning, finger pointing and so forth) and by verbalizations that showed evidence of a shift in focus. The definition of unit of analysis proved to be a thorny problem. If browsing is a kind of movement among a set of well-connected nodes, then what is a 'node'?

and

> We then developed the notion of a view. A view is what
> a person articulates as seeing at one time, that is, a
> span of attention. We have some good clues for oper-
> ationally identifying views because the participants
> almost always labeled them (Kwasnik, 1992, p. 194).

Kwasnik's definition of browsing, which follows below, is, in my view,
less than ideal—more on a definition shortly—but her characterization of
the activities of browsers is entirely accurate:

> We defined browsing as movement in a connected space.
> In order to achieve this movement, people undertake cer-
> tain actions: they shift their gaze, they alter their position,
> they skip over things, they glance at things briefly, from
> afar, or close up, they back up, they pause or stop and they
> respond to interesting phenomena (Kwasnik, 1992, p. 195).

Kwasnik then goes on to identify six activities that play a role in browsing:

1.  *Orienting* to the environment—a persistent activity, not only
    one at the beginning.

2.  *Place marking* "Marking a view for potential second con-
    sideration" (p. 195).

3.  *Identification* "or recognition of potentially interesting or
    definitely not interesting items" (p. 195).

4.  *Resolution of anomalies* "Consistent with the notion that
    browsers create structure and orient themselves as they go
    along is their pronounced effort to resolve anomalies, even,
    it seems, when the item being 'resolved' does not seem to be
    of great interest otherwise" (p. 195).

5.  *Comparison* "These comparisons serve to orient, identify
    and solidify purposes and aims" (p. 195).

6.  *Transitions* "The movement from one view to another is a
    transition" (p. 195). Transitions may be movement toward
    an object of interest, or away from one, when the browser
    has identified something and rejected it or exhausted its
    information potential.

## The proposed definition

Here the activities described by Kwasnik are interpreted to be a part of a combined cognitive, motivational and behavioral pattern that can be presented as follows (my definition):

> *Browsing is the activity of engaging in a series of glimpses, each of which may or may not lead to closer examination of a (physical or represented) object, which examination may or may not lead to (physical and/or conceptual) acquisition of the object.*

Though the above may work as a definition, that definition needs to be analyzed even more closely to express fully what the act of browsing is about. Human beings rely very strongly on vision; it is our predominating sense. In browsing, both visual movement and physical movement, to a greater or lesser extent, typically come into play. We may examine something only visually, or with touch or other senses, such as smell or hearing. If we want to acquire the thing examined, we may do so by reading, listening, smelling, or other activities that allow us to take in some experience about the thing examined. That *taking in* may include actual physical acquisition of the object, or be limited to informationally absorbing the object in some way.

Let us apply this definition to a prototypical browsing situation, looking at magazines at an airport news stand. Based on experience, you know that the news stand could be a browsing-rich experience. You walk over and stand close enough to the shelves to read the headlines. You glimpse a section. You see a headline or picture that interests you. You pick up the magazine, i.e., you select it. You read a bit, i.e., you examine it and put it back. You glimpse something out of the corner of your eye. You turn your head and look at that magazine. No, not interesting after all. You now look in the other direction on the shelf. Ah, now that's really interesting! You pick up the magazine and read a little. You think, "I'm going to buy this one. I can read it on the plane," i.e., you acquire. You then either browse additional magazines or go to the check-out stand to buy your magazine.

You have glimpsed, selected and acquired. Not every glimpse led to selecting and not every selection led to acquiring. You could have left the news stand unable to find something you wanted to buy. You might have walked up to the news stand and discovered that all the magazines were in the language of the country you are travelling in and you do not read the language, so you would not even have selected anything. There are many combinations possible out of these elements. Further, you probably moved your body in a variety of ways during this process, often to help or support the visual or haptic examination of the magazines.

We need to examine more closely the second step in this model of browsing. The word *selecting* has been used. Indeed, in many cases, the thing that catches our eye is something that we can expect to be drawn to by our pre-existing interests. You like skiing and cooking; the magazine's headlines mention some words in one or the other of those areas, the words catch your eye and so you reach out and pick up the magazine to look at it more closely.

On occasion, however, the act of selecting should more properly be called *sampling.* For example, you walk up to a rack of blouses in a department store. The colors of the articles are not very appealing; as a consequence, you are not drawn to any one item. But in hopes that you might find something interesting after all, you sample one of the items by picking it up off the rack and looking at it more closely. Maybe there will be something cute in the design of the blouse after all. Here, you are truly sampling; one blouse, or one color, is as good as any other in order to see the styling.

So, sometimes, perhaps most of the time, we select *something in particular* to look at out of the field of vision created by the glimpse. We make this selection because a preliminary assessment of that field of vision has led us to feel the most attraction to or interest in that one particular object within the field of vision. We select that something because we prefer it to any other object in the field of vision. This second step in the browsing process is properly called *selection.* At other times, however, as discussed in the preceding paragraph, this second step is more properly called *sampling,* because we are more or less randomly reaching out to examine any one of the objects in the field of vision; it does not matter to us which one.

With these thoughts in mind, browsing can be seen to contain four elements, iterated indefinitely, until the overall episode ends:

1. glimpsing a field of vision;

2. selecting or sampling a physical or representational object from the field;

3. examining the object; and

4. physically or conceptually acquiring the examined object, or abandoning it.

At a minimum, all browsing consists in, at the least, glimpsing a field of vision, abandoning it and glimpsing again, iterated until the end of the browsing episode. Most browsing episodes, however, include repeated selecting and/or sampling and repeated instances of examining objects. Further, browsing episodes may contain one or more instances of acquiring examined objects, which acquisition may be conceptual, as with reading, or physical, as with picking up and keeping the item.

Another way to describe browsing is to say that it is multi-step: 1) glimpsing, that is, acquiring a field of vision, 2) *latching on* to an object within that field of vision, 3) examining that object, 4) keeping the object, or abandoning it. The next moment in a browsing episode begins with the first step, glimpsing.

At first, the work by O'Connor on browsing appears to come closest to the approach taken here. He, too, describes four phases, beginning with "Make Glimpses" (O'Connor, 1993, p. 223). However, his emphasis throughout is quite different. He is primarily concerned with the cognitive processes involved in processing the information seen and less so with the act of browsing per se. His four phases are "Make Glimpses" (p. 223), "Connect Attributes" (p. 224), "Evaluate Connection" (p. 226) and "Evaluate Search" (p. 227).

Even his "make glimpses" is about picking a starting point for evaluating the content of a collection or browsed area. "The individual glimpse is the instrument which enables the searcher to create the appropriate representation system" (O'Connor, 1993, p. 223). The searcher then determines the attributes (document features) that will be examined to determine if an item is of value or interest. The second phase, connecting attributes, involves matching the attributes of documents seen with the attributes wanted by the searcher, the third phase, evaluating connection, involves determining the degree of overlap between searcher and document features and the fourth phase, evaluate search, refers to assessing the value of the connections discovered.

Returning to the approach to browsing that has been presented here, when does browsing behavior stop being browsing and become something else? For one, it can be said that scanning is *not* browsing. As noted earlier, scanning involves, just as Rice et al. (2001) said, a systematic, smooth movement. But browsing, as described here, is very different from that. Browsing is a complex process, involving a series of glimpses, usually followed by actions between the glimpses. Browsing is not a smooth scan. I glimpse one section of the magazine stand, seize something interesting within it, put it back, then glimpse again. This is anything but a case "where the person's body or eyes move smoothly at will" (Rice et al., 2001, p. 178).

There are, in fact, cases where we do scan or skim. Generally, we engage in these smooth, sequential, orderly activities when we want to find something quickly but want to be sure not to miss anything (*American*

*Heritage Dictionary's* second sense of "scan"). For example, suppose we have looked up an encyclopedia article alphabetically and now are scanning the article from start to finish to locate a specific fact that we guess should be in the article. Browsing, by contrast, is more open to surprise. The glimpse may land us anywhere within a reasonably wide visual range. Scanning or skimming, on the other hand, are very focused. The reader is reviewing as fast as possible, but systematically, in order to cover everything within a chosen area and not miss anything that might be there. To return to the magazine stand, we seldom browse by starting at one end of the racks and smoothly scanning across every rack, one after the other, left to right in a systematic way, in order to be sure to see every magazine as we scan. Rather, we move around and our eyes move around, landing here and there on things that interest us. We may well miss many magazines in the process and glance at some repeatedly, in true browsing.

One final point: Browsing has been defined in terms of vision, with a series of glimpses seen as the sine qua non of the act of browsing. It seems possible in principle, however, to extend this definition to, say, browsing sound clips on one form or another of a music player. Further, people who are blind presumably also find some way to engage in this fundamental behavior, through touch or other means.

## Support for this approach from other disciplines

I cannot claim the Ph.D.'s expertise in the fields from which literature will be cited and discussed below. Consider this section speculative. However, nor is it the case that marginal authors are being sought out and emphasized from these other fields. I have some sense of the mainstream, or at least ideas widely recognized and taken seriously, as opposed to fringe approaches. Though I lack the professional qualifications to make the case fully, the ideas presented below provide strong preliminary justification for pursuing the line of attack proposed in this article.

### Psychology: visual search

Very strong support for the visual aspects of the above model come from psychology. Wolfe's model of visual search (1994), called Guided Search, has been cited over 700 times and is still considered a valid contender among visual search theories at least as recently as Logan's 2003 review article on theories of attention (Logan, 2003). Basically, Wolfe's model holds that we glimpse widely initially, then home in on points of interest within the broader visual field for more complex interpretation and understanding.

> ... the model distinguishes between a preattentive, mas-
> sively parallel stage that processes information about basic
> visual features (color, motion, various depth cues, etc.)
> across large portions of the visual field and a subsequent
> limited-capacity stage that performs other, more complex
> operations (e.g., face recognition, reading, object identi-
> fication) over a limited portion of the visual field. ... The
> heart of the guided search model is the idea that attentional
> deployment of limited resources is *guided* by the output
> of the earlier parallel processes (Wolfe, 1994, p. 202).

Thus, in visual search, we first glimpse widely, processing only the simpler, grosser characteristics of the scene in front of us. This *massively parallel* stage means just that; a wide area is viewed *all at once,* not in a smooth scan from one side to the other. The output from this initial glimpse, namely detection of possible points of interest in the visual scene, leads to a second stage where a point or points of interest is processed more intensely and with more sophisticated mental capabilities, such as the ability to recognize faces, or to read language. These latter capabilities take lots of processing space in the brain. "There is not enough room in the skull for all of the neural hardware that would be required to perform all visual functions at all locations in the visual field at the same time. ... A large set of visual functions can be performed only in a restricted part of the visual field at any one moment" (Wolfe, 1994, p. 202).

> ... there are *parallel processes* that operate over large por-
> tions of the visual field at one time and there is a second
> set of *limited-capacity* processes that are restricted in
> their operation to a smaller portion of the visual field at
> one time. In order to cover all of the visual field, these
> limited-capacity processes must be deployed *serially* from
> location to location (Wolfe 1994, p. 203; italics are Wolfe's).

Thus, we glimpse a scene all at once, then select one or more things within the scene to examine more closely. We then examine the selected objects with more sophisticated, processing-intense capabilities. These latter capabilities use so much brain capacity that they can be applied only to selected, smaller parts of the initial visual field. If we want to examine more than one element of the scene with these powerful capabilities, we must examine the elements one after the other, i.e., serially.

### Psychology and behavioral ecology: curiosity and exploratory behavior

Modern discussions of curiosity begin with Berlyne's classic, *Conflict, Arousal and Curiosity* (Berlyne, 1960). The frontispiece of the book is a photograph of a cat standing on a chair with its front paws perched on the top of a typewriter, sniffing at the typing mechanism of the machine. Curiosity and exploratory behavior seem to be found generally in animals and, of course, cats are supposedly among the most curious of all, to the point of getting themselves killed on occasion.

For browsing, especially of texts, human reliance on visual search can be almost total. However, there is a kinesthetic element, too, in much browsing. After identifying something of interest, we may examine it only visually, but in many cases, we also move in closer to the item, pick it up, or otherwise move in some way in the process of examining it. With our nerve-rich fingers and opposable thumbs, haptic examination often becomes an important part of exploratory behavior.

Interestingly, Berlyne posited three stages of exploratory behavior, which remind one of the elements of Wolfe's visual search model. Berlyne's three elements were: 1) orienting responses, 2) locomotor exploration and 3) investigatory responses (1960: xi). There is a rough parallel here to 1) the initial wide glimpse, 2) homing in on some specific object or feature of the environment and 3) examining it.

It would appear that something very fundamental to the nature of animals, including human beings, is being described here. Just as was argued by the visual-search researchers, efficiency in processing may require this approach of surveying the territory first, followed by a focus on some part of the territory. After all, other kinds of search could be carried out by animals, such as a serial examination of one thing after another in the territory, with no preliminary survey. We may guess that evolution has led to survival of the most efficient exploratory method.

So why do animals explore? What model can psychologists use to explain this behavior? In a recent review, Hughes (1997) traces the history of the various theories developed to explain exploratory behavior in psychology. Hughes defines *intrinsic exploration* as follows: "Intrinsic exploration involves exploratory acts that are not instrumental in achieving any particular goal other than performance of the acts themselves" (1997, p. 213). This is contrasted with *extrinsic* search, which is driven by some goal, such as the need for food or escape from danger.

I will jump to the bottom line by saying that Hughes concludes that there is no persuasive model at the time of his review to explain this behavior. He notes that animals seem to manage to stay between extremes of boredom on the one hand and over-stimulation, on the other. Hughes concludes, "If a motivational force has to be proposed, it is probably sufficient to go no further than accept that . . . organisms appear to have some type of behavioral 'need' for sensory change which can be satisfied by intrinsic exploratory responses" (1997, p. 219).

Loewenstein, in an extensive review of curiosity (1994), likewise found available theories wanting and only partially explanatory. He posits a sense-making theory for explaining curiosity.

> . . . the information-gap theory views curiosity as arising
> when attention becomes focused on a gap in one's knowl-
> edge. Such information gaps produce the feeling of depriva-
> tion labelled *curiosity.* The curious individual is motivated
> to obtain the missing information to reduce or eliminate
> the feeling of deprivation (Loewenstein, 1994, p. 87).

This description comes perilously close to being a circular explanation. We discern a gap and want to fill the gap. But why do we want to fill the gap? Why does having this gap make us feel deprived? Does not the word *gap* already imply a deficiency? Perhaps this is just a *space* in our knowledge. Why should this space in our knowledge lead to curiosity? As Loewenstein says on the same page: "As noted earlier, the remaining question—the cause of curiosity—is inherently unanswerable" (p. 87).

However, it seems that one can posit a straightforward evolutionary explanation for curiosity, an explanation that makes this behavior quite understandable. In motile (as opposed to sessile) animals, exposure to new environments or new stimuli or new information all bring with them the possibility of discovering new food sources, new mates, new nesting or sleeping sites, or new ways to escape predation. Thus, the ability to move, combined with the ability to sense the environment, had a positive payoff for the animal with these capabilities. Bell's massive 300-plus-page review of searching behavior of animals throughout the animal kingdom, "The behavioural ecology of finding resources," as his sub-title states, finds that exploratory behavior pays off for animals in a variety of ways (Bell, 1991, pp. 165–169). However, the brevity of his chapter on exploratory behavior (five pages) within the larger body of research on animal searching confirms his statement therein that "Exploratory behaviour is probably a more significant component of searching than is usually appreciated" (p. 165).

Let us develop this idea more. Exploratory behavior in any territory previously unknown, whether of the physical world, or, in humans, of emotional or intellectual territory, can lead both to new, valuable discoveries and *to devastating harm*. Tasting a new mushroom found in the forest, slipping off the edge of a heretofore unseen crevasse, being captivated by a charismatic but dangerous leader, or fretting in a sophomore philosophy class about the existence of free will, can all lead to damage or even death for the vulnerable individual.

There is an inherent trade-off in exploratory behavior, between the good things that can come of it and the danger that can result from it. Over the evolutionary history of this planet, this trade-off must have been played out a googolplex (more or less) of times. For each currently existing species, we can expect that a tendency to explore and a tendency to stay put or traverse only familiar territory exist in the current members of that species in a balance that is a result of natural selection. Too static a pattern and the animal may lose out to competing species that explore more and discover more things of value to their survival. Too much exploration in risky environments and members of the species may die or fail to reproduce often enough and thus harm the survival of the species. After millennia of natural selection, what remains is a balance between the impulse to explore the unknown and the impulse to stay with the familiar. This balance represents the cumulative trade-off between these risks that the species has encountered in its history.

Cats may or may not have a higher level of curiosity than do humans or other animals. But suppose, for the sake of argument, that they do explore more than many other animals. They probably have this level of exploration because, over their evolutionary history, in the environments in which they existed, that level of curiosity paid off positively for cats. Another animal, in a different environmental mix, might have been harmed by being so curious and so came to explore less.

General exploratory behavior in humans is manifested in a number of ways, with many of the activities being similar, though not necessarily identical to browsing information: shopping, Web- or channel-surfing, mingling at parties, sightseeing (sampling new experiences), dating, nibbling at a buffet table, etc. (Jenna Hartel, 2003, personal communication). All these activities may be manifesting a general exploratory impulse, with the physical and psychological constraints of the particular situation shaping the specifics of the cognition and movement.

## Berrypicking

This author has written on a related behavior labeled *berrypicking,* and the distinction between berrypicking and browsing should be made clear here. Berrypicking characterizes whole information searches, or, more precisely, whole episodes of information searching. A berrypicking search has an *evolving* query, which shifts during the course of the search. As the searcher discovers sources and learns new information, the query changes accordingly; the searcher adds and drops elements and sometimes reconceptualizes the whole query as understanding of the relevant information domain increases. The searching during the episode is in a berrypicking mode, that is, involves getting a bit of information here, another bit there, just like picking berries in a forest. In a berrypicking search, there is no assumption that the system will produce a single complete, final retrieved set. Finally, during the course of an episode, the berrypicking searcher may use many different sources and may use varying searching techniques, each suitable to the source and circumstances of the search.

Thus, berrypicking characterizes whole information searches or search episodes. When browsing is done in the course of an information search, it may play a part in many different types of search strategies and techniques. The searcher may adopt browsing and then cease browsing seconds later in the course of a complex berrypicking search.

Here is an example:

> The searcher is doing a berrypicking search on information seeking behavior among humanities scholars. She has done a directed search for the topic in article databases, searched by title keyword in library catalogs and read over the reference lists in several books and articles she has found to this point in her search. These approaches involve several different search techniques and she has collected relevant material, like picking huckleberries in a forest, here and there, bit by bit. As she goes, she gets a better sense of her topic and narrows and changes her focus (evolving search).
>
> While in the stacks finding the books she liked from the catalog search, she browses among the neighboring books to see if any look promising. She pulls out some of the books that catch her eye, randomly browsing a bit on this or that page. Something she reads in one of the books reminds her of an article she has seen recently. What was that author's name? Started with a W. She goes back to an article database, searches by topic and then scans down the list of retrievals, looking for last names starting with W. Ah hah! There it is. She prints off

*the article, then scans down the list of references in that arti-*
*cle to see if there is anything good that she has missed. . . .*

Scanning, browsing, directed searching were all involved in this berrypicking search.

## Implications for information system design

If the cognitive/behavioral act of browsing is different from what Rice et al. (2001) assume and closer to what Kwasnik (1992) identified and I have conceptualized and if, as I have argued, it arises from a fundamental animal exploratory behavior that goes back millions of years and has long rewarded animals (and also put them at risk), so what? What are the implications for information systems?

Browsing appears to be a manifestation of a fundamental animal exploratory behavior. If so, it is natural to people and can be engaged in spontaneously, without training, *provided* information system interfaces lend themselves to this behavior. Most *browsing* capabilities in Web-based and other online information systems consist of the capability of opening some text or images and scanning down a long list or a set of thumbnails. Such a capability is better than nothing, but it does not facilitate browsing very well. Put differently, such design facilitates *scanning,* but not *browsing.*

These designs appear to be based on an assumption that browsing equals scanning, rather than being based, as argued here, on a deeper understanding of the nature of browsing. Good browsable interfaces would consist of rich scenes, full of potential objects of interest, that the eye can take in at once (*massively parallel processing*), then select items within the scene to give closer attention to.

Elaine Toms's (2000) research on browsing is very revealing in this regard. She studied people browsing articles from newspapers, presented in an interface in such a way that the searcher could see article titles and go off and review different articles at will. Thus, the people browsing were not scanning so much as clicking on points of interest that caught their attention, and a click would lead to an article.

Specifically, in addition to a window in which to view the actual article text, there were three key elements to the interface: menus of broad topics, a conventional search tool requiring a term to be input and a *suggestions list* of related articles. (Items on the latter list were automatically generated by algorithms that identified similar articles.) In a typical screen shot in Toms's study, half the screen is taken up by a window displaying the text of the latest article being examined. (See Toms, 2000, pp. 430–431, Figures 1 and 2.) The other half contains two windows, one displaying menus and the other displaying either the Search Tool or the Suggestions. Toms noted the following in her discussion:

> Overall, participants were quite clear about the function of the different tools. Menus were seen as a structured approach to examining the newspaper and were widely used throughout the experiment. . . . The menu was treated as an anchor in the interaction with articles and served for route-finding and orientation. For example, not once did participants comment about being disoriented or getting lost, typical reactions to many information systems. . . . The Search Tool was acknowledged as essential for looking for information on a specific article, while the Suggestions provided the diversion and encouraged meandering which then uncovered items of interest to participants. Participants clearly understood these roles (Toms, 2000, p. 446).

I argue that the design used by Toms better supports the natural physical sense of browsing that feels most native to human beings, than do many other experimental and operational systems. In effect, the menus provided the orientation that is normally implicit in the physical environment, but which must be provided explicitly in some way in an electronic environment where screen can instantly replace screen and thus disorient the searcher, as in a typical World Wide Web browser. In the design she used, Toms implicitly demonstrated that orientation can be retained without sacrificing the sense of movement implicit in the clicking and going to another document. Because moving around from screen to screen left browsers disoriented in some past experiments, designers may have cut back on the movement and limited the options for the browsing individual mostly to scanning. Instead, in this design, Toms allows the browser to remain oriented through use of the menus, while glimpsing the Suggestions and clicking on them (*moving* to them) to examine them more closely.

This glimpsing and *moving* to another screen permits the browsing process to mimic much more closely the physical act of browsing that takes place away from the electronic world. The browser takes in a number of article titles at once (ten titles appear in a list in the upper left corner of the screen, taking up about a sixth of the whole screen area; see her Figure 1, p. 430). Clicking on one title is equivalent to moving to an item and picking it up or looking at it more closely in the physical world. The full article text appears in the screen text window while the suggestions and menus remain in other parts of the screen, thus enabling the searcher to remain oriented (cf. Kwasnik, 1992). Here the browser can acquire, i.e., read, the article, or just glance at it and move on. A return to the menu or suggestions list is equivalent to putting the item down in the physical world and continuing to browse.

Toms was not testing the model presented herein, of course. Her definition of browsing was "an activity in which one gathers information while scanning an information space without an explicit objective" (Toms, 2000, p. 424). But intentionally or not, the online system she tested supported or paralleled the physical behavior of browsing in the real world better than do many other online information systems. I suggest that in her research, she implicitly demonstrated the superiority of the model of browsing provided herein. Obviously, a more explicit and self-conscious test of this model would be needed for greater confidence that my model is a good one. One can reasonably suggest, however, that testing the model of browsing presented herein, both in physical and electronic environments, is a very promising direction to go in and may lead to a more accurate representation and understanding of the human behavior of browsing than we have had to date.

## Summary and conclusions

Based on the discussion herein, what can we say about browsing?

1.  Animals that can move (motile as opposed to sessile animals) may use their movement capability to explore in a more or less random manner. This behavior exposes them to new places and possibilities. Such exposure may lead to new food sources, mates, nesting or hiding places and escape routes from predation. Such exposure may also lead to harm or death.

2.  Presumably, the amount and extent of exploratory behavior exhibited in a given species is the result of the historical trade-off experienced by the species between explorations that led to positive results and explorations that led to deleterious results. (Another, non-conflicting, possibility is that there may be a range of exploratory behavior within the species as well, with some animals doing more or less exploration. Thus, this variation is the engine for further natural selection and,

therefore, evolution of the species' exploratory propensities in one direction or another.)

3. Based on the above, we accept that most animals have a propensity toward exploratory behavior.

4. In humans, at least, visual search is optimized for efficiency and constrained by brain capacity, in such a way as to require a particular kind of search. Specifically, we take in a scene all at once in a *massively parallel glimpse,* then select or sample a spot within the glimpsed area to examine more closely, using higher-level capabilities which require much more mental processing space. The glimpse notes basic features such as color and movement. The higher-level processing at the examination stage engages in such activities as face recognition, reading and object identification.

5. Browsing is a cognitive and behavioral expression of this exploratory behavior. The in-built motivation for this exploratory behavior can be called curiosity. Because humans are so strongly reliant on vision, bodily motion often mirrors visual search, in that the second stage of browsing often involves physical movement toward items of interest, which movement, of course, also supports closer visual inspection.

6. Browsing is here considered to have four elements. The first element is essential to our understanding of browsing, the later elements almost always occur as well: 1) glimpse a scene, 2) home in on an element of a scene visually and/or physically (if two or more elements are of interest, they are examined serially, not in parallel), 3) examine item(s) of interest, 4) physically or conceptually acquire or abandon examined item(s). This sequence is repeated indefinitely through further glimpses. Browsing is thus not a smooth scan of a scene.

7. Formally, browsing is defined thus: *Browsing is the activity of engaging in a series of glimpses, each of which exposes the browser to objects of potential interest; depending on interest, the browser may or may not examine more closely one or more of the (physical or represented) objects; this examination, depending on interest, may or may not lead the browser to (physically or conceptually) acquire the object.*

8. The design of interactive information systems needs to incorporate an awareness of human browsing characteristics. Specifically, browsing for information in such systems should not be limited to the opportunity to scan, but instead enable the searcher to manifest the instinctive tendency to engage in a browsing sequence: to glimpse, then to examine or not something glimpsed, then to keep or not the things examined.

## REFERENCES

*American Heritage Dictionary of the English Language* (4th ed.). Retrieved April 18, 2007, from http://www.bartleby.com/6/1.

Bates, M.J. (1989). The design of browsing and berrypicking techniques for the online search interface. *Online Review, 13*(5), 407–424.

Bell, W.J. (1991). *Searching behaviour: The behavioural ecology of finding resources.* London: Chapman and Hall.

Berlyne, D.E. (1960). *Conflict, arousal and curiosity.* New York: McGraw-Hill.

Herner, S. (1970). Browsing. In *Encyclopedia of library and information science* (1st ed., Vol. 3, pp. 408–415). New York: Marcel Dekker.

Hughes, R.N. (1997). Intrinsic exploration in animals: Motives and measurement. *Behavioural Processes, 41*(3), 213–226.

Kwasnik, B.H. (1992). *A descriptive study of the functional components of browsing.* Paper presented at the Proceedings of the IFIP TC2/WG2.7 working conference on engineering for human-computer interaction, Ellivuori, Finland, August 10–14, 1992.

Loewenstein, G. (1994). The psychology of curiosity: A review and reinterpretation. *Psychological Bulletin, 116*(1), 75–98.

Logan, G.D. (2003). Cumulative progress in formal theories of attention. *Annual Review of Psychology, 55,* 207–234.

O'Connor, B. (1993). Browsing: A framework for seeking functional information. *Knowledge: Creativity, Diffusion, Utilization, 15*(2), 211–232.

Rice, R.E., McCreadie, M., & Chang, S.L. (2001). *Accessing and browsing information and communication.* Cambridge, MA: MIT Press.

Toms, E.G. (2000). Understanding and facilitating the browsing of electronic text. *International Journal of Human-Computer Studies, 52*(3), 423–452.

Wolfe, J.M. (1994). Guided search 2.0: A revised model of visual search. *Psychonomic Bulletin & Review, 1*(2), 202–238.

# 9

# What is a reference book?
# A theoretical and empirical analysis

Reference books have traditionally been defined administratively (e.g., as books that are noncirculating) or functionally (e.g., as books used for reference), rather than descriptively (i.e., in terms of the essential characteristics that distinguish reference books from other books). It is argued that in order to provide a scientific basis for the study of reference, as well as to promote the study of search strategy, a descriptive definition is needed. Such a definition—based on the organizational structure of reference books—is provided and defended. An empirical study was conducted in three libraries—academic, public, and special—to identify types of book organization and to determine their frequency in reference departments and stack collections. The definition was strongly supported by the data, and the contents of books were found to fall in a surprisingly small set of forms of organization, across the three types of libraries, across national boundaries, and through time.

The answer to the question in the title would seem to be an obvious one. We all know what a reference book is, do we not? Here I will argue that the standard, accepted definitions in our field of "reference book" are useful in some respects and quite inadequate in others, particularly as a basis for scientific research or analytical thinking on topics relating

*First published as* Bates, M. J. (1986). What is a reference book? A theoretical and empirical analysis. *RQ, 26*(1), 37–57.

to reference books in reference service. When we use the term "reference book," we are relying much more on our unexpressed intuitive sense of what a reference book is than on the limited definitions to be found in print.

In this article I will review existing definitions of the term and propose an additional definition to supplement our understanding of this core concept in librarianship. The new definition will be based on an analysis of the textual and file structure of "regular" books and reference books, thus illuminating common forms of information organization to be found in books of all types. Much work has been done in computer and library/information science to develop models and theories of databases using the terminology of file, record, and field. Manual information sources share many of the characteristics of these computer databases (and some differences), but have generally not been viewed in relation to them. The use of such terminology here in the analysis of manual sources should contribute to a broader understanding of information organization and to a future where all databases, both manual and automated, are viewed within a common context and vocabulary.

After the theoretical analysis and development of the new definition, an empirical study relating to this matter is reported and analyzed. Reference and stack collections in three different libraries—academic, public, and special—were randomly sampled to identify types of book formats not anticipated by the author, and to see if the definition provided herein of "reference book" is indeed borne out by the character and placement of materials in (at least) these sample libraries. The study identified an interesting range of materials appearing in both reference and stack collections, strongly supported the definition given herein, and also produced a few exceptions. The data are analyzed in detail and conclusions drawn.

## Current definitions of reference book

The standard approach to defining *reference book* can be found in the pair of definitions provided by the *ALA Glossary:*

1. A book designed by the arrangement and treatment of its subject matter to be consulted for definite items of information rather than to be read consecutively.

2. A book whose use is restricted to the library building (Young, 1983, p. 188).

The British *Librarians' Glossary* uses a similar pair:

1. Books such as dictionaries, encyclopaedias, gazetteers, year books, directories, concordances, indexes, bibliographies and atlases, which are compiled to supply definite pieces of information of varying extent, and intended to be referred to rather than read through.

2. Books which are kept for reference only and are not allowed to be used outside the building (Prytherch, 1984, p. 647).

These pairs of definitions are used throughout the field. They, or variants of them, appear in source after source discussing reference books, specifically, in at least the following: Barton (1966, p. 7), Gates (1979, p. 66), Goggin and Seaburg (1964), Grogan (1979, p. 25), Hutchins (1944, p. 82), Roberts (1956, p. 1), Sheehy (1976, p. xiv), Shores (1976, p. 92), Shores and Krzys (1978, p. 137), and Wyer (1930, p. 62).

These two pairs of definitions each contain what Stiffler has called an "administrative" definition of a reference book, i.e., specifying a book as reference because it has been put in the reference section or because it may not be circulated (Stiffler, 1972). This type of definition has obvious practical uses in the administration of a library. A book may be put into the reference section while not really being a reference book in any intuitive sense. For example, fears that a book may be stolen or defaced may lead to designating it as "reference." But at bottom, an administrative definition essentially says that a reference book is what we call a reference book—not very illuminating when we are trying to identify the distinctive character of this type of library material.

Stiffler also identifies what he calls "functional" definitions. A functional definition of a reference book states "the anticipated use which the user can typically be expected to make of the book" (Stiffler, 1972). The other definitions in each of the two pairs above are essentially functional definitions. Both of them state that a reference book is to be referred to rather than read through.

Stiffler identifies a third type of definition, one he calls "descriptive," which defines the reference book "by virtue of the intrinsic characteristics of the book itself" (Stiffler, 1972). Such a descriptive definition—lacking in the popular sets—is what would best meet the requirements of science: a statement of the essential features or characteristics that reference books have and that other books lack.

The current functional definitions are helpful as far as they go, but they do not go far enough. It is useful to know that a reference book is one to be referred to for information and is not, say, a binder full of letters of reference that a domestic servant takes around to show prospective employers. But a functional definition does not identify the essential features of a reference book; it does not tell us what it is about reference books that leads us to *want* to use them for reference. Is our inclination merely arbitrary?

The first *ALA Glossary* definition hints at a description when it says "designed by the arrangement and treatment." Thus there is something about the arrangement of such books that leads us to want to consult them rather than to read straight through, but we are not told what the nature of that arrangement is. The first British definition enumerates some classes of books that are well suited for reference, but it, too, does not say what it is about these types that makes them well suited.

These primarily functional definitions state how a reference book is to be used, but not what it *is*, its essential character. The lack of a descriptive definition in these popular sets is puzzling when we come to think of it. If the definitions only state how a reference book is supposed to be used, then how is one to identify the book to use that way in the first place? The introductions to some books say that they are to be used for reference purposes, but many other "reference books" have no introductions at all. Certain named types of books, such as those mentioned in the first British definition, are associated with reference use, but not all books used for reference have one of these names.

One reason why we lack descriptive definitions in the field may be the conclusion on the part of some that it is impossible to provide such a definition. Davinson states,

> To say there are a class of books and other materials which can unequivocally be recognized, fundamentally and distinctively, as reference material is misleading. To library users reference material is likely to be anything which is useful to them in finding the solution to any information problems they have (Davinson, 1980, p. 12).

He further adds, "fundamentally whether items are designated for reference or home use is more a function of an administratively convenient decision rather than an obvious intrinsic difference in quality" (Davinson, 1980, p. 12).

Similarly, in his introductory reference text, Katz says, "A reference source is any source, regardless of form or location, which provides the necessary answer or answers" (Katz, 1978, p. 14). (In the later, fourth, edition of his text [1982], Katz drops all efforts to define the term.)

Along these same lines, Rugh says that reference books serve the convenience of the user, convenience is relative, and that therefore "reference book" has to be defined in relative rather than absolute terms (Rugh, 1975).

All of these arguments are valuable in that they remind us that information may be gotten from any of the resources in a library (and many outside it). Since instruction in library schools so strongly emphasizes what are conventionally called reference books, it is easy to forget the other resources. But in making this point, it is not necessary, I believe, to make the further claim that there is nothing distinctive or identifiable about reference books. There may still be something about certain books that inclines us to consider those books to be particularly well suited for reference purposes, and consequently to group them in "reference" departments and use them for referral. Having made his point about the value of ranging widely to answer questions, even Katz himself restricts the coverage of his text overwhelmingly to the materials conventionally called "reference."

A different definition is provided by the International Organization for Standardization. A "reference work" is a "Document providing rapid access to information or sources of information on a given subject" (International Organization for Standardization, 1983). This definition states a distinguishing characteristic of a reference book—that it provides rapid access. But it does not tell us how rapid is rapid enough to qualify a given book as a reference book, so this definition still does not enable one to *identify* a reference book.

Of all the writers reviewed, S.R. Ranganathan came the closest to providing a true descriptive definition. First, he describes an "ordinary book":

> It is made of continuous exposition. Sentences mount
> into a paragraph. Paragraphs mount into a chapter.
> Chapters get woven into a single swelling exposi-
> tion, in the continuous pursuit of a single idea, sim-
> ple or complex (Ranganathan, 1961, p. 257).

A reference book, on the other hand, is not like this. Rather,

> it is characterized internally by an ensemble of disjointed
> entries of short, though varying lengths. The sequence
> of the entries is not determined, strictly by intimate
> thought-sequence. It is determined by the scheme of

arrangement chosen. It is often alphabetical in the main. It is occasionally systematic. Even then, the connection between consecutive entries is not as compelling and continuous or as free from jerks as between the paragraphs in an ordinary book (Ranganathan, 1961, p. 257).

So at last we have some articulation of what distinguishes ordinary books from reference books. Ordinary books contain a continuous, developing exposition, while reference books have disjointed entries; movement from one entry to the next is in "jerks."

Because it says something about the intrinsic properties or characteristics of reference books, this definition is indeed descriptive, in Stiffler's terms. But it is also vague and would be difficult to operationalize. How could one determine whether the text was more or less free from "jerks"? In the succeeding sections an attempt will be made to develop a fully descriptive definition—unambiguous, easy to operationalize—that can be added to the administrative and functional definitions used now.

## A descriptive definition of "reference book"

### Preliminary note

Before getting into the discussion proper, some preparation is in order. I have shown preliminary versions of this paper to at least a dozen people in the field, both practitioners and library school faculty. A common reaction has run through the responses which is so paradoxical as to require comment. The same respondent in the same conversation will say on the one hand that the ideas herein are obvious and "I knew that all along," and on the other hand that the ideas are flat wrong. One individual cycled through these alternate positions fully three times in one conversation!

I do not know the full reasons behind this response, but I have some suggestions that may help the reader better analyze his or her own reactions. The ideas may seem obvious because they use terminology that is familiar—"files," "records," and the like. There is a traditional bias against the term "file" in librarianship because of its association with lower-level positions in libraries such as "file clerk." For librarians to discuss files is seen in some quarters as lowering our professional standing. A moment's reflection, however, will remind us that computer scientists use the term all the time without reducing their professional standing. There are questions of file organization and database design to be discussed here that need to be approached from a quite sophisticated level and that are well beyond the expertise of a file clerk! To analyze books in terms of their file structure is to *add another level* to the conceptual analysis of information resources and their retrieval—not to substitute for the existing levels of analysis, such as subject content, quality and reliability of information, etc. I can assure the reader that taking these terms and adapting them to the needs of manual sources in a reasonably parsimonious way was not at all obvious and took considerable thought.

Secondly, the ideas may seem obvious because we have an *intuitive* awareness of the structural and organizational characteristics of reference books even though we do not discuss them in analyses of reference work and searching techniques. We know it but we do not. Here, too, the process of bringing this subliminal awareness to conscious analysis was not as easy and straightforward as the end result may make it appear.

As to why this analysis is "wrong," a common objection goes something like this: "When I buy books I select them on the basis of all sorts of criteria. It is ridiculous to say I select a reference book on the basis of its file structure." True, we seldom *select* a book on the basis of its file structure. We indeed bring many criteria to bear on our selection of all kinds of books, both reference and stack materials. But what makes us *assign* a book to the reference or stack collection—whether at the time of selection or later—is, I will argue, primarily file structure. Whether we like a book or not, or buy it or not, what brings us to view that book as a reference book or a stack book is primarily its structure. We do this precisely because certain features in the organizational structure of a book are what makes that book a good one to use for reference or for consecutive reading.

## Some needed terminology

Since some definitions have hinted that there is something about the arrangement of certain books that makes them suitable for reference purposes, let us now see if we can find out what that something is. Some common terms are here defined in ways suitable to our needs for analyzing manual files:

- *Manual file* A set of two or more records ordered by a rule or principle and existing in directly readable printed form (not requiring computer assistance to read).

- *Record* A unitary or internally related body of information; an information "individual."

- *Field* A unit or chunk of information within a record.

A manual file is such in two senses: in the physical sense it is manual because it is neither in a computer nor does it require computer assistance to read (as off computer disks). In the conceptual sense, a "manual file" has a different definition than "file" as used in computer database design, because manual files are subject to different, and more limited, constraints than computer files. We shall explore these characteristics in more detail in the next section.

The heart of these definitions, the one upon which the others logically depend, is "record." A record is any body of information whose creators or organizers wish to treat as a unit, as an "individual." The information in a record may be descriptive of some other record or object and gain its unity by virtue of the fact that all items of information in it describe that one other record or object. For example, an entry in a catalog is a record and its unity consists in the fact that all the information relates in some way to a single book. Alternatively, the information in a record may itself constitute a body of internally related information that has a unitary character. James Herriot's book, *All Creatures Great and Small,* has a unity as a body of discourse, and so we find it convenient to treat this body as an information individual.

Fields are segments of information within a record that people want to distinguish from other parts of the record for some reason. Librarians typically label certain items of information in a book as distinct fields, with names like author, title, etc., because they have important uses for each of those elements. Other people, with different uses for a book, might divide and label the segments of information in different ways. For our purposes, *All Creatures Great and Small* may be considered to have several fields—the usual bibliographic elements, appearing mostly on the title pages—and one very large field, the unified body of discourse that constitutes the actual text of the book. Fields, in other words, are segments of information in a record that we find useful to distinguish for our purposes, whatever those purposes may be.

A manual file is a set of two or more records that have been ordered, that is, arranged, according to some principle. Let us call the latter the "ordering principle." Common ordering principles are alphabetical, numerical, and classified (e.g., arrangement according to the biological classification). By the definitions used here, a set of records, in order to be a manual file, must be arranged according to a principle or rule. Even a random collection of records has *some* order, or sequence, but chances are there is no rule by which that arrangement could be described. We will not use the very general definition of file—as simply a collection of data—that is often employed in the computer science literature, e.g., Flores (1977, p. 378). Manual files are characteristically *ordered,* and for good reason, as we shall see later.

Even when the arrangement of a file can be described by a rule, in practice, that ordering principle must be one that is readily recognizable within the cultural context where the file is to be used. The sounds of the Thai alphabet, for example, are arranged in a completely different order than that found in Western languages. Though it may truthfully be said that tens of millions of people, namely, the Thais, would recognize an alphabetizing scheme that begins with the sound *k* (the first letter of the Thai alphabet), such a scheme would not be considered "readily recognizable" for Western users of files in Western languages. Similar arguments can be made about intellectual cultures. For example, biologists may immediately recognize files arranged according to the biological classification and know where to look for a certain taxon. For the lay person, however, such a scheme would be as mysterious as one arranged by the Thai alphabet.

Note that there must be at least two records to constitute a manual file, since files are ordered. (Ordering, or sorting, implies a relationship, and there must be at least two things in a relationship.) By the above definitions, a set that contains only one record is not a file, and a set that contains more than one record but that is not ordered by a rule or principle is also not a file. (Henceforth "file" will be used here to refer to "manual file.")

The field(s) by which a record is ordered in a file is (are) the "access field(s)." For example, the simple phrase, "Alphabetical by author's name," contains both the ordering principle and the access field for a file. One finds a record in a manual file by searching on the access field(s) according to the ordering principle. If one does not have the access field information, the record is virtually inaccessible. For example, in the average manual catalog, one has almost instant access to information on a book if one has the author's name, but knowing only the publisher is worthless, even though the records contain this information, because the entries are not arranged by publisher.

The most efficient searching in manual files is accomplished when the information in the access field is a part of the record (intrinsic) rather than an arbitrary field imposed from the outside (extrinsic). For example, when we search on "author" in a file arranged by author, it is possible to go directly to the file and search it with the author's name. In contrast, when the entries are arranged by abstract number, we must first consult some other file, such as an author index, to find the arbitrary number.

## Files and reference books

With these terms in mind, let us now look at their application to reference books. The term "reference book" is used within librarianship in two senses. In the narrower sense, reference books are contrasted with bibliographic sources, with reference books being those that contain the ultimate information sought, while bibliographic sources contain pointers (citations) to other sources of information (books, articles, reports, etc.), which may be presumed to have the ultimate information sought. In the broader sense, "reference" includes both reference (narrow) and bibliographic sources. For example, the "Reference" department of a library contains both types of books, and one may refer to all the books there as reference books. In the discussion in this article, "reference book" is almost always used in the broader sense. Where it is used in the narrower sense, it will be clearly identified.

Now, how may the file terminology be applied to reference books? Armed with these terms, we see that reference books tend to be full of files. Consider first a bibliographic source, the periodical index *Readers' Guide*. It contains five sections: "Abbreviations of Periodicals Indexed," "Periodicals Indexed," "Abbreviations," "Readers' Guide to Periodical Literature," and "Book Reviews." Note that each of these sections fits the definition of "file." Each consists of records arranged by some ordering principle. The periodical abbreviations file contains records consisting of two fields, the abbreviated title and the full title of each periodical indexed, arranged alphabetically by abbreviated title. The records in the main file ("Readers' Guide") are bibliographic citations. Each citation is entered under author and subject; authors and subjects are in turn interfiled and arranged alphabetically, and so on. *Readers' Guide* as a whole can be considered a manual database, with its five files serving the common purpose of providing access to a collection of records in the general periodical literature.

When there are many citations under a given author or subject, the editors of *Readers' Guide* have, for brevity's sake, removed the repeats of the author or subject name at the beginning of each citation. For example, "Video games," the actual access field for the twenty citations that may appear in a given volume under that subject term, appears only once at the beginning of the list of twenty items. But it is the implicit access field for all twenty items. So it is each individual citation that is an independent record, not the term "Video games" plus the twenty citations that constitute a record.

A moment's reflection will suggest that organization into files is to be found throughout bibliographic sources. Bibliographies, periodical indexes, abstracting and indexing services, and catalogs invariably contain records arranged by some access field or fields into files. A wide variety of access fields are used—author, title, subject, publication date, classification categories—arranged by various ordering principles, but there are always distinguishable records and they are arranged by *some* principle. Randomly arranged sets of citations in manual sources would be worthless for most conceivable purposes.

In their nature, bibliographic sources contain readily distinguishable records, i.e., bibliographic citations, and in practice those citations are arranged in some order. There is thus a great deal of regularity in bibliographic sources, and that regularity can be recognized as a database-file-record-field structure.

Now let us look at reference books (in the narrow sense). Are they, too, organized into files? Dictionaries, biographical indexes, directories, gazetteers, encyclopedias, atlases, handbooks, and almanacs can all be seen to be organized into files. The entries may be highly structured, with specified fields in consistently the same order, as in most dictionaries, directories and gazetteers, or more flexible and variable—but still in file arrangement—as in handbooks and encyclopedias. Each word in a dictionary, each person or organization in a directory, and each location listed in a gazetteer constitutes the access field for the records in these sources. The information provided about each word, person, etc. constitutes the remainder of each record (and may be more or less highly structured into fields), and the records are in turn organized by some ordering principle.

In most encyclopedias the main file consists of entries arranged alphabetically by subject. After the access field, usually in boldface print, the other most important field of the entry, the text, may be quite variable in length and format. But these encyclopedia entries nonetheless constitute a file; there are two or more records, and access fields of these records are arranged by an identifiable ordering principle.

Similarly, atlases also contains files. An index to location may be an important subsidiary file while the maps themselves are arranged in the main file alphabetically, geographically, or chronologically (as in a historical atlas). Each record in the main file of an atlas typically consists of the title of the map (usually the name of the area covered), which constitutes the access field, plus a second field, the map itself. Thus it can be seen that while information in files is generally linguistic, it need not be. Maps, diagrams, photographs, etc., can also be fields in records. Map file plus index file constitute the manual database that is an atlas.

Handbooks and almanacs often consist of a great many files. This may not be as immediately apparent as in the examples above. A table can be viewed as a two-way, or two-dimensional file. Consider a table that lists the names of countries down the left side, and decade years (1900, 1910, etc.)

across the top. The information in each cell (i.e., the intersection of each country name with each year) consists of the population in that country that year. This same information could have been presented linearly, in one dimension. If this were done, under "1900" the file would list all the country names followed by their population that year, followed by "1910," followed in turn by the country names again and their populations in the later year—and so on through all the years. Such a file would thus be arranged chronologically by date and subarranged alphabetically by country. But the file would be very lengthy; the country names would be listed repeatedly. Instead, in a table, the data for each decade are listed parallel. The country names need not be repeated, and the information is presented in a way that is condensed and easily referred to. Tables are thus simply files in two dimensions.

Arranging information into a file structure, is, in general, a way both to organize information compactly and to make it much more quickly accessible. The two-dimensional file structure of a table is even more compact and quickly accessed than linear (one dimension) files. Handbooks and almanacs such as the *World Almanac and Book of Facts* contain a very large number of these small, compact files. Each of the small files, such as the example above, has some internal order and so meets the definition of "file." The files themselves need not be arranged relative to each other, however, (other than by page number) in the manual database that constitutes the *World Almanac,* because the user gets access to these files through another file in the almanac, viz., the alphabetical index.

Finally, let us consider catalogs. A card catalog is not a *book,* and therefore cannot be a reference book, though it may certainly serve a reference function. A book catalog, on the other hand, consists of files in a book form and is therefore a reference book. Catalogs from other libraries are frequently designated "reference"; is there any reason why one's own library's book catalog should not also be considered a reference book?

What about a parts catalog in an auto parts dealer? It may be that no library in the world contains that particular parts catalog. Is it a reference book? Yes; books do not have to appear in libraries to be reference books.

Reference books vary on an enormous range of characteristics—subject content, type of information, language, etc. In fact, this blooming, buzzing variety of reference books is, I believe, one of the things that has stopped efforts heretofore to define the term descriptively. But there is one feature reference books have in common; they are organized into files. A tentative first cut on a descriptive definition can thus be given as follows: *Reference books are books substantially or entirely composed of files.* File structure in reference books explains the "jerks" Ranganathan referred to; movement from one record to another produces the jerks that distinguish files from the continuous flow of normal printed discourse. In succeeding sections this definition will be refined and potential exceptions considered.

## Book structure related to function

If we feel that the function of reference books is their use for referral purposes, while "regular" books, i.e., books containing running discourse, are to be read through, and if, as I have argued, reference books overwhelmingly contain a characteristic file structure, then perhaps there is a causal connection: perhaps certain characteristic book organizations lend themselves to these two uses, referring and reading through, and if we understood those structures better, we could see why use so often follows structure.

First, we must look more closely at function. What does it really mean to say a book is designed for referral? The searcher can use a book for referral when it is possible to find a desired datum or segment of information in a body of information directly without having to search through the information linearly (from the beginning to the point of encountering the information) or, in desperation, randomly. With referral there is a leap from the whole body of information to the specific information desired, or at least to a significantly smaller segment of the information than the whole body. The leap from the whole to the part is crucial to the idea of referral.

What makes it possible to leap from the whole to the specific information desired? The answer for manual sources is file structure. Once records are arranged according to some identifiable ordering principle, the information seeker can make that leap. By glancing at a small portion of the file, the searcher discerns the ordering principle and access field, and is thus able to use a modified binary search approach (cf. Bates, 1979, p. 210), which is vastly more efficient than linear searching. The searcher then selects the specific value on the access field. For example, if the access field is "country," then the searcher mentally summons the specific country name. Then using the ordering principle, the searcher homes in on the desired entry, needing only a glance at the occasional record along the way to determine location in the file. Since the files are ordered, the searcher can rely on the items in the file being in a certain position relative to each other. It is no longer necessary to examine every record in the file to find the desired one. Where manual information is not ordered and structured in this way, it is not possible to make this leap. It may well, in principle, be possible to have other forms of information organization that make lookup possible, but in practice this seems not to be the case with manual sources.

We are beginning to get a very strong sense of what it is about reference books that makes them reference books. The function we want is referral, and referral in manual sources appears practical only where file structure exists. Thus it is not surprising that organization into files is such a widespread characteristic of reference books.

A question may be raised here: *must* function follow form? Ranganathan has commented that some people like to read dictionaries and encyclopedias rather than strictly use them for referral (Ranganathan, p. 256). On the other hand, every reference librarian can remember occasions when he or she was forced back on trying to find the answer to a question in a book with no contents list or files of any kind. Do structure and function then not go together?

It is possible to read through, rather than refer to, the information in file structures, but this use of information sources is exceptional and idiosyncratic—rare enough that we comment on it when it occurs. And it is possible to search for definite items of information in a body of information not organized for that purpose, but the librarians who have been forced on that difficult recourse would not recommend it. To put it differently, we can use a potato masher as a hammer, and a hammer as a potato masher, but we still know the difference between the two and which we prefer to use for what.

So, as a rule, we refer to files and read through text. But book structure is more complicated than just files versus text. Let us now look at various common book structures and relate them to book functions.

One category, already implied, is that of books containing only written discourse, i.e., text. These books contain no files whatsoever, that is, no ordered records. Such books are often fiction. No lookup access is possible; the user can find information only by browsing or reading through the text. Books in this first category are intended to be read through, not referred to. Their structure, pure running text, matches and promotes this function.

A second broad category is books composed entirely of files. These are the very opposite of the first category, and by the earlier discussion, would all be considered reference books, because they are ideal for speedy lookup access.

A third category is books that are mostly text but that also contain a contents list, a back-of-the-book index, or both. Here, both the structure and function are more complicated. A back-of-the-book index is a file, and it provides lookup access into the main text of the book through page-number access. Thus, while the main text itself does not consist of ordered records, the presence of an index nonetheless makes it possible to leap from index to a segment of text in true referral fashion. This is made possible by designating wholly artificial "records," which are numbered pages (i.e., physical rather than logical records).

A contents list, on the other hand, while superficially similar, speeds access in a way that is fundamentally different from that for the back-of-the-book index. A contents list reproduces the order of discourse found in the text of the book. That order is unique and idiosyncratic to the author's own sequence of thought in the text and therefore does not generally follow a readily recognizable ordering principle. Thus the searcher does not have referral access within a contents list; there is no way to leap from the whole list directly to a desired term or number according to an ordering principle, as one can with a back-of-the-book index. Instead, it is necessary to scan the list from the beginning to find the promising segment of text and its associated page numbers. For example, a textbook on library cataloging may devote a section to problems of retrospective conversion. The searcher can look up that term directly in an alphabetical back-of-the-book index, but would need to scan the contents list from the beginning to find the same section listed there. The contents lists speeds access only because it is much shorter than the text itself, containing, as it does, only headings rather than the full text.

These different methods of access can be clarified by comparing the process the searcher engages in during use of the various book structures discussed so far. To find a specific piece of information in a text-only book, one must scan from front to back, or else randomly riffle through the pages in hopes of finding a promising segment of text. There is no referral access.

Using a book containing text plus contents list, the searcher must scan the contents list to find the desired section, and then can do a referral leap from the list into the text by means of the page number provided in the contents list. Since sections listed in the contents are often large, the searcher, once in the text, may have to scan through several or even dozens of pages to find the specific information desired. So the search pattern here is scan (contents list), referral (from list into text), scan (text).

Using a book containing text plus a back-of-the-book index requires the searcher first to do a lookup on the desired term in the index (no front-to-back scanning needed here), then a lookup from index into text, and then a scan of the designated text page or pages to find the specific information desired. Since entries in back-of-the-book indexes are usually more specific than entries in contents lists, the searcher will probably not have to scan as many pages as was necessary in using the contents list, so the access is faster here.

Finally, there is the case of a book containing a single large file, or several files, and no text at all except that which is contained within

## BOOK STRUCTURE          SEARCH PATTERN

| BOOK STRUCTURE | SEARCH PATTERN |
|---|---|
| File(s) only | One or several referrals, or referral—brief scan |
| Text plus back-of-the-book index | Referral—referral—moderately brief scan |
| Contents list plus text | Scan—referral—moderate scan |
| Text only | Lengthy scan only |

FIG. 1. *Search patterns for common book structures.*

records as fields. In this case all the information has been converted into file structure. If using the proper file, the searcher can do a referral directly into the desired record, where the needed information will often be directly available without any scanning, or can be found by scanning a few lines, in contrast to the multipage scanning necessary with the other structures described. The searcher may do a single referral, as into a dictionary, or several referrals, as when moving around among several files in a complex bibliographical source like *Granger's Index to Poetry* or *Biological Abstracts,* but in either case the search is accomplished through one or more quick referrals. Scanning, when it does occur, is very brief.

The searcher's pattern in use of these various book structures can thus be summarized, as in Figure 1. Scanning almost always takes longer than referrals do, so this sequence of book structures can be seen to go from most to least efficient for reference purposes. The differences are even greater than this referral/scan contrast implies, however, because the typical amount of scanning also increases greatly from the first to the last structure listed above. It is now possible to begin to operationalize the ISO definition of reference book given earlier. In that definition rapidity of access was a defining characteristic of reference books. We now see that books with "rapid" access are those designed so that relatively more referral than scan access is possible in their use.

This brings us to the question of where the dividing line is between reference and nonreference books. How much referral versus scanning should be possible in making a book a reference book? Files-only books clearly serve the referral function best and are thus definitely reference books. Books containing text plus contents lists and/or back-of-the-book indexes serve both functions. Most of the length of these latter books is devoted to text, and the lists and indexes combined usually add to less than 10 percent of the books' lengths. These are the sorts of books that Davinson, Katz, and others are principally referring to when they say the whole library can serve as the reference collection. Though they are not as efficient as files-only sources, these books can be used fairly easily for referral purposes. In practice, however, we nonetheless give preference to the reading-through function of these books by storing them with the other stack books rather than with the reference books. With the overwhelming bulk of the book devoted to reading through, we seem to accept the primacy of that function. Given the supreme efficiency of files-only books for reference purposes, it makes sense not to dilute them by interfiling them with the much larger number of less efficient books serving both reading-through and referral functions. Thus it is appropriate to consider the middle categories (text plus contents list and/or index) as stack books, not reference books.

There are a few more points about book structure that need to be made. First, how shall we view books of text that have occasional tables scattered through them, embedded in the text? Since the tables are a type of file, are books containing these tables then reference books? No, they are not, because the tables *are* embedded in text. To have a table in text is rather like having a few shelves arranged by a classification scheme in the middle of a library's stacks, while books on all the other shelves are randomly arranged. The table, lost in a sea of text, like the ordered shelves among the unordered, is not easily found in lookup mode. Books of running text with occasional tables may provide contents lists of tables, but such lists have the same idiosyncratic selection of topics for tables and order of presentation of tables that the contents of the books as a whole have. Thus, books containing occasional tables embedded in text fit into the middle categories described above (text plus contents list or index).

But suppose there are *many* tables and not much text? In the empirical study that follows, the operational dividing line was the chapter level; if a book contained whole chapters that were files or tables, then segments of the book that were this large were considered sufficiently independent and substantial to stand alone and function as a sort of minireference source within the book, and the pages of such chapters were considered files and counted as such. Tables that were embedded in running text were counted simply as text. We shall see that these middle cases are less of a worry than might be expected—they are actually quite rare.

Another point of possible confusion can be expressed in two related questions as follows: suppose a book, such as a novel, has its text segmented into pages—with the pages numbered and ordered numerically. Do the page numbers constitute fields arranged by a readily recognizable ordering principle, the pages therefore records, and the novel therefore a file? In other words, do purely physical records, e.g., numbered pages, make up a file? Similarly, suppose a novel is segmented into chapters, and the chapters numbered. (Here the segments of text are logical, rather than physical.) Is the novel therefore a file?

There is more than one argument that can be made against viewing these two cases as files. The simplest and most direct is the following: in both cases, the text identified by the numbers is not a record (in any but the physical sense), because the segments of text on each page are not "information individuals." An operational test of information individuals is that they can be arranged in different orders with respect to each other without harming their meaning or use; they can stand alone. For example, records in a typical bibliography could be ordered under several different ordering principles and still be of value, no matter where they appeared in the ordering with respect to other records in the file. On the other hand, reordering the pages of a book or the chapters of text in a book would produce a jumble. Therefore, the pages or chapters of a novel are only *segments of text,* not records; thus, the novel is not a file.

This then leads to another question with respect to books that are collections. A book that is a collection of poems or short stories does contain information individuals rather than segments of text. Are all collections therefore files? A file, in addition to containing information individuals, must contain *ordered* individuals. If a collection is ordered according to a readily recognizable ordering principle then the collection is also a file; if it is not so ordered, it is not a file. For example, the poems in a book of British poetry arranged alphabetically by poet do compose a file; those in a collection of poems arranged by the poet's own idiosyncratic choice, and thus unknowable in advance to an educated user, are not arranged by a readily recognizable ordering principle and so are not a file, therefore not a reference book. This distinction makes intuitive sense. If we wanted to find a popular poem by Pope, we could use the former book in lookup mode, but not the latter.

The distinctions made in this section still leave open the question of what to do about books that fall between being files-only and text-mostly. Might we not expect a number of these? Intuitively, a book that is largely text but that has noticeably more files than the usual 10 percent or less might begin to feel more like a reference book, that is, a book in which the reference function begins to overwhelm the reading-through function. Reference books were earlier defined as books consisting substantially or entirely of files. How much is "substantially"? We have argued in this section that there is a relationship between structure and function in books. Can we provide a more precise descriptive definition of "reference book" and still preserve that relationship? We shall find that the empirical data reported in the next section will provide clues and solutions in some unexpected ways. We shall return to these questions after the empirical study is described.

## Empirical data

### Introduction

So far our analysis has shown that the function for which we use reference books, referral, is made possible by a certain organizational structure, which has been described in detail. We label books "reference" because they have the structure that facilitates exactly that use.

Are there exceptions—books with other organizations that we still call reference books? Alternatively, are books containing this structure stored in stack collections too? A sample of books in reference departments does not provide a perfect answer to these questions because, as noted earlier in the discussion of administrative definitions, books may be put in reference departments for reasons other than anticipated use for reference purposes. A librarian, when asked, would admit that the book is not a reference book in any but the administrative sense, and is kept there for other reasons, such as to protect it from theft. Similarly, some books are stored in the stacks because they are earlier issues of a reference book whose current copy is kept in the reference department. So a sample drawn from libraries cannot be expected to contain 100 percent of books that are structurally reference books in the reference department and structurally running text in the stack collection. Nonetheless we would expect most of them to fit the structures discussed here, if this article's thesis is correct. Furthermore, such a sample will enable us to see what types of books do appear in typical American libraries and uncover types not thought of by the author. Finally, we may analyze the exceptions and see if the thesis herein is supported or disconfirmed.

### Sample

I wanted to examine reference and stack books in a variety of environments, and so selected one large academic research library, one medium-sized branch public library, and one medium-to-large industrial special library in a major aeronautics firm. Careful systematic samples were drawn from the reference and stack collections at each library. The books were examined closely, bibliographic data recorded, and number of pages in files, lists, and

TABLE 1. *Libraries and samples*

| LIBRARY | NUMBER OF VOLUMES | | SAMPLES ACTUAL (INTENDED) | |
|---|---|---|---|---|
| | REF. BOOKS | GEN. STACKS | REF. BOOKS | STACK BOOKS |
| University Research Library, UCLA | 43,451 *(1983–84 statistics)* | 2,080,952 | 92 (100) | 99 (100) |
| City of Los Angeles regional public library branch | ≈ 50,000 combined (librarian's estimate) | | 53 (50) | 49 (50) |
| Special library in major aeronautics firm | ≈ 60,000 combined (librarian's estimate) | | 25(25) | 25 (25) |
| TOTAL | | | 170 (175) | 173 (175) |
| GRAND TOTAL | | | 343 (350) | |

running text were counted for each item. I expected the large university library to have more different types of books from various cultures and periods in history and so selected a larger sample there to expose the variety. Altogether, 343 books were analyzed. Table 1 describes the sample. Further details of the sampling are provided in appendix A.

## Results

The fundamental variable measured in each book is the percent of book length in pages devoted to files and lists. The distinction between files and lists was discussed earlier. Lists were overwhelmingly contents lists and lists of tables or illustrations. They were rarely longer than two pages and constituted a minor factor in the total calculations.

Overall, 82.3 percent of the books in reference departments contained 80–100 percent of their length in pages in files and lists. In fact, only 4.7 percent had percentages of files between 80 and 90; all the rest, i.e., 77.6 percent of the total, contained over 90 percent files. On the other hand, 89.6 percent of the books in the stack collection contained 0–20 percent of their length in files and lists. Of these, nearly all (82.1 percent of the total) contained less than 10 percent of their length in files/lists.

Figure 2 illustrates the differences between reference and stack samples vividly. The contrasting cumulative distributions of percent of book devoted to files and lists in the total combined reference samples and total combined stack samples demonstrate how very structurally different the materials in these two parts of the libraries are. *Either librarians do assign*

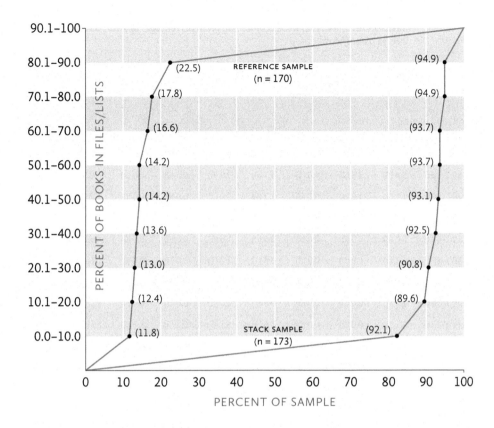

FIG. 2. *Cumulative distributions of percent of each book devoted to files/lists.*

books to the stack or reference collection based on book structure, or else they decide on the basis of some other highly correlated factor.

Very few books have intermediate percentages of files/lists. Of the entire sample of 343, only 18, or 5.2 percent, fall between 20 and 80 percent in length in files/lists. It appears that while we can imagine mixed formats in principle, few of them occur in fact. Apparently, authors' and publishers' decisions about book format (assuming librarians' selections are reasonably representative) are fairly black and white: people produce reference books or running text books and little in between.

Table 2 summarizes the data for all samples and percent ranges. While the great majority of items fall above 80 percent or below 20 percent, we may also ask which percentage level provides the best discrimination between reference and stack books, i.e., which percentage figure most

TABLE 2. *Percentages of books containing given percentages of files/lists (raw numbers in parentheses)*

| PERCENT OF FILES | REFERENCE DEPARTMENT SAMPLES | | | | STACK COLLECTION SAMPLES | | | TOTALS | |
|---|---|---|---|---|---|---|---|---|---|
| | RESEARCH LIB. REF. | PUBLIC LIB. REF. | SPECIAL LIB. REF. | TOTAL REF. BOOKS | RESEARCH LIB. STACKS | PUBLIC LIB. STACKS | SPECIAL LIB. STACKS | TOTAL STACK BOOKS | TOTAL BOOKS |
| 90.1–100 | 83.7 (77) | 66.0 (35) | 80.0 (20) | 77.6 (132) | 4.0 (4) | 10.2 (5) | 0.0 (0) | 5.2 (9) | 41.1 (141) |
| 80.1–90.0 | 5.4 (5) | 3.8 (2) | 4.0 (1) | 4.7 (8) | 0.0 (0) | 0.0 (0) | 0.0 (0) | 0.0 (0) | 2.3 (8) |
| 70.1–80.0 | 1.1 (1) | 1.9 (1) | 0.0 (0) | 1.2 (2) | 2.0 (2) | 0.0 (0) | 0.0 (0) | 1.2 (2) | 1.2 (4) |
| 60.1–70.0 | 3.3 (3) | 1.9 (1) | 0.0 (0) | 2.4 (4) | 0.0 (0) | 0.0 (0) | 0.0 (0) | 0.0 (0) | 1.2 (4) |
| 50.1–60.0 | 0.0 (0) | 0.0 (0) | 0.0 (0) | 0.0 (0) | 1.0 (1) | 0.0 (0) | 0.0 (0) | 0.6 (1) | 0.3 (1) |
| 40.1–50.0 | 1.1 (1) | 0.0 (0) | 0.0 (0) | 0.6 (1) | 1.0 (1) | 0.0 (0) | 0.0 (0) | 0.6 (1) | 0.6 (2) |
| 30.1–40.0 | 0.0 (0) | 1.9 (1) | 0.0 (0) | 0.6 (1) | 3.0 (3) | 0.0 (0) | 0.0 (0) | 1.7 (3) | 1.2 (4) |
| 20.1–30.0 | 1.1 (1) | 0.0 (0) | 0.0 (0) | 0.6 (1) | 2.0 (2) | 0.0 (0) | 0.0 (0) | 1.2 (2) | 0.9 (3) |
| 10.1–20.0 | 1.1 (1) | 0.0 (0) | 0.0 (0) | 0.6 (1) | 6.1 (6) | 10.2 (5) | 8.0 (2) | 7.5 (13) | 4.1 (14) |
| 0.0–10.0 | 3.3 (3) | 24.5 (13) | 16.0 (4) | 11.8 (20) | 80.8 (80) | 79.6 (39) | 92.0 (23) | 82.1 (142) | 47.2 (162) |
| TOTALS | 100.1 (92) | 100.0 (53) | 100.0 (25) | 100.1 (170) | 99.9 (99) | 100.0 (49) | 100.0 (25) | 100.1 (173) | 100.1 (343) |

NOTE: Variation in total percentages due to rounding error.

cleanly separates the two types, leaving the fewest books falling in the "opposite" category. That figure is 60 percent; 85.9 percent of the reference department books contain 60 percent or more in files/lists, and 93.6 percent of the stack collection books contain fewer than 60 percent files/lists. (Since there are so few items in the 20–80 percent range—and none between 51 and 62 percent—it would be necessary to take a larger sample to be confident that the best cutoff point has been identified.)

## Foreign and pre-1900 items

As noted earlier, larger samples were taken in the research library in the expectation that a large research collection might contain a greater variety of forms of organization within books. In particular, foreign items and those published before 1900 might be expected to show particularly strong deviance from the norm of modern English-language materials. So the research library samples were broken out along these lines for comparison

TABLE 3. *Percentage breakout of foreign and early items in the research library samples (raw numbers in parentheses)*

| PERCENT OF FILES | FOREIGN | EARLY | BOTH | 1ST 3 COMBINED | NEITHER | TOTAL |
|---|---|---|---|---|---|---|
| RESEARCH LIBRARY REFERENCE SAMPLE | | | | | | |
| 80.1–100 | 96.8 (30) | 66.7 (2) | 50.0 (1) | 91.7 (33) | 87.5 (49) | 89.1 (82) |
| 20.1–80.0 | 3.2 (1) | 0.0 (0) | 50.0 (1) | 5.6 (2) | 7.1 (4) | 6.5 (6) |
| 0.0–20.0 | 0.0 (1) | 33.3 (1) | 0.0 (0) | 2.8 (1) | 5.4 (3) | 4.3 (4) |
| TOTAL | 100.0 (31) | 100.0 (3) | 100.0 (2) | 100.0 (36) | 100.0 (56) | 99.9 (92) |
| RESEARCH LIBRARY STACK SAMPLE | | | | | | |
| 80.1–100.0 | 5.6 (2) | 7.7 (1) | 0.0 (0) | 5.3 (3) | 2.4 (1) | 4.0 (4) |
| 20.1–80.0 | 11.1 (4) | 0.0 (0) | 0.0 (0) | 7.0 (4) | 11.9 (5) | 9.1 (9) |
| 0.0–20.0 | 83.3 (30) | 92.3 (12) | 100.0 (8) | 87.7 (50) | 85.7 (36) | 86.9 (86) |
| TOTAL | 100.0 (36) | 100.0 (13) | 100.0 (8) | 100.0 (57) | 100.0 (42) | 100.0 (99) |

NOTE: *Variations in total percentages due to rounding error.*

purposes. (There was only one foreign item and one pre-1900 item in the public library samples and none in the special library samples, so these were not examined.) Classified as "Foreign" were those items in a foreign language that had not been published in the U.S., Canada, Great Britain, or Australia; classified as "Before 1900" were those items that did not fit the "foreign" category and that were published before 1900, while the category "Both" covered those falling in both classes.

The results are displayed in Table 3. As can be seen on inspection, particularly in comparing "First three combined" against "Neither," the pattern is essentially the same for all groups; it would take a much larger sample to discover substantial differences, if any. These results indicate a striking stability in the organization of books across cultures and through time.

As noted in the appendix, items printed in non-Roman alphabets were excluded from the samples, so a separate study would have to be done to determine if the pattern of those foreign items was the same. Perhaps even more remarkable than the similarity across cultures is the stability through time of patterns of organization. Here the samples are smaller and so may be misleading. Nonetheless, one wonders how far back it would be necessary to go before strikingly different organizational patterns would be in evidence, if at all.

*Exceptions analysis*

As discussed earlier, and visible in Table 2, the overwhelming majority of reference books fell in the range of 80-100 percent in files/lists, and stack books in the range of 0-20 percent. So for exceptions analysis, three classes of books were examined: (1) Books of discourse (0-20 percent files/lists) that are housed in reference collections (21 books); (2) reference books (80-100 percent files/lists) that are housed in the stack collections (9 books); and (3) books with middling percentages of files/lists (20-80 percent) that are housed in either collection (18 books). These groups totaled to 48 items. The third group was of interest because it is relatively rare—only 5.2 percent of all books sampled. Was there anything distinctive about these, or were they simply reference and stack books that happened to have a few more files than typical stack books or fewer than typical reference books?

After preliminary analysis of all three groups, I concluded that the third category was not unusual in any way. It was suitable, therefore, to use the dividing line discussed earlier; books containing 60 percent or more in files/lists were considered reference books, and those containing less than 60 percent in files/lists were considered stack books. Of the 18 items in the 20-80 percent range, 6 contained between 60 and 80 percent files and were stored in reference departments. An additional 7 of the 18 contained between 20 and 60 percent files and were stored in stack collections. These 13 were thus considered to be typical reference and stack books, respectively, and fell out of the set of exceptions. The remaining 5 items (of 18) were analyzed with the rest of the exceptions. So in the end, there were 35 books (48 less 13), or 10.2 percent of the total that were evaluated as exceptions.

Figure 3 summarizes my analysis of the 35 exceptions. A full analysis of why books are housed where they are would require a knowledge of librarians' thinking over many years as they made decisions, much of it undocumented. Thus, some of my evaluations are necessarily guesses and should be taken as such.

**Reference collection exceptions**  The one category that appears to be a true exception to the rule that reference books are books with file structure is a group of materials that I will call "canonical texts," that is, texts the culture considers authoritative in some way. There are 14 of these, falling into four subcategories, for a total of 8.2 percent of the reference samples. These contain texts rather than files.

Most texts are stored in the stacks—so why do these appear in the reference department? Apparently, the few that are housed in the reference collection are there because they carry some form of cultural authority. Each of the subcategories discussed below carries a different form of cultural authority.

I. REFERENCE COLLECTION EXCEPTIONS (*i.e., books with less than 60 percent of length in files/lists housed in reference collections*)
  A. Canonical texts (14 Total)
    1. Treatises  5
    2. Laws, regulations  5
    3. Standards, specifications  2
    4. Literary, religious, and other authoritative texts  2
  B. High demand stack items protected in reference collection  3
  C. Appearance  2
  D. Other  5

                                            24  TOTAL

II. STACK COLLECTION EXCEPTIONS (*i.e., books, with more than or equal to 60 percent of length in files/lists housed in stack collections*)
  A. Earlier dated editions  6
  B. Comic material in reference book form  1
  C. Other  4

                                            11  TOTAL

                                    35  GRAND TOTAL

FIG. 3. *Exceptions analysis.*

*Treatises* are texts that are intended to be authoritative expositions of what is known about a field or topic. They may be written by one person or, commonly, many people, each contributing a chapter on his or her area of particular expertise. Their coverage is so extensive and detailed that one would rarely read all the way through a treatise; rather scientists and scholars refer to them to find the accepted wisdom on a particular topic. Examples in the study are a five-volume history of technology, each chapter written by a different expert (public library) and an eight-volume "comprehensive treatise" on inorganic and theoretical chemistry (special library).

Laws and regulations are texts, often with numbered segments of discourse, that carry another kind of authority. The public library carried a comparatively large law collection, and 5 of the 53 reference collection sample items fell into this category: for example, the *United States Code, Annotated. Title 29. Labor.*

Standards and specifications may or may not have the force of law, but they describe the standardized sizes, processes, and testing methods deemed acceptable in engineering and related fields. For example, the special library contained the *ASME Boiler and Pressure Vessel Code.* Expressing a somewhat less formal set of standards was a style manual for print and proof corrections in the research library.

Finally, literary, religious, and other authoritative texts round out the categories of canonical texts. The research library sample contained a volume from a series of sacred books of the East. The other example in this category is the *Master Plan for Higher Education in California, 1960–1975*. For a campus of the University of California, this may certainly be seen as an authoritative text, though it may also have been put here because of high demand or theft rates. Compared to the other libraries, the public library had the largest number of exceptions in the reference collection. Specifically, 14, or 26.4 percent, of the 53 sample items contained less than 60 percent of their length in files/lists. Of these 14, 8 were canonical texts, most of these, in turn, laws and regulations.

While I generally see these canonical texts as exceptions to the pattern of reference books being books composed largely or entirely of files— because they do not, in fact, contain mostly files and records as defined earlier—they do nonetheless often have some file-like characteristics, and so some may be considered borderline. For example, canonical texts often have some arbitrary numbering imposed on them to make it easier to find particular segments of text, as with chapter and verse numbers in religious texts, section numbers of laws, or numbers of regulations, standards, or specifications. Sometimes these canonical texts become so widely used that the section numbers themselves become a part of the knowledge of an educated person, as in the case of famous biblical passages, legal statutes, etc., thus enabling a kind of speedier "reference" lookup.

Earlier, the argument was made that numbering such as chapter numbers did not make a book a reference book because the numbers identified segments of text instead of information individuals, i.e., records. These various canonical texts also tend to be borderline with respect to whether they contain information individuals or segments of text. Some sets of laws or regulations, for example, have text that must follow in a certain logical order; in other cases individual regulations may be quite freestanding with respect to each other.

Aside from canonical texts there are 10 items in the reference collection exceptions. These are all either not true exceptions, as will be argued, or else constitute categories so small and miscellaneous in this sample as to be undecidable.

Three are high-demand stack items protected by storage in the reference collection. Examples are a binder of photocopied magazine articles on ratings of colleges in the research library sample and copies of the *American Heritage Magazine* kept in the public library's reference department.

An interesting category among reference department exceptions was formed by two cases that had the *appearance* of reference books, but which on closer examination proved not to contain ordered files. For example, the public library contained a book on American colonial coinage that discussed, and was arranged by, the coins that had been produced by the colonies. There may have been an order to the coins known to coin fanciers, but I was unable to discern it. The special library reference collection contained *NASA Tech Briefs,* a series intended to promote technology transfer. Each chapter is devoted to a topic and within each chapter new technical products are highlighted in descriptions that are a half-page to one-and-a-half pages long. Each item's name is so highly outlined that the book has the look of a reference book, but there is no discernible order for the products within each chapter.

The final category of reference exceptions, "Other," covers 5 truly miscellaneous items. The *Congressional Quarterly* and the *Congressional Record* appeared in the reference departments of the research and public libraries respectively. These could be there due to high demand or worries about loss. The public library reference department contained a ninety-six-page book of running text entitled *Wheels: A Pictorial History.* There was no evident reason why it was stored here. The research library contained a book titled *The Illinois Fact Book and Historical Almanac,* which contained 47 percent files. It fits our intuitive sense of a reference book and appears to be simply a borderline book in length of files.

Finally, the last item in the "Other" category was particularly interesting. Titled *The California Water Atlas,* it contained only 6.5 percent in files/lists, not what would ordinarily be expected of an atlas. The authors note that "the atlas was intended in part as a demonstration" of ways in which government information "can be reconstituted in a form which is more readily accessible to the general reader" (State of California, 1979, p. 116). In other words, the authors were conscious that they were violating expectations for what a typical atlas should be and felt compelled to comment on their different approach.

**Stack collection exceptions** Whereas some high demand stack books may be housed in the reference collection to protect them, some *low*-demand reference books may be stored in the stack collection. Chief among the latter is the class of items that are earlier dated editions of reference books. Examples from the six items in this study are statistics of the European Economic Community for 1968–69, U.S. census data for 1910 and 1974, and an 1873 catalog of the University of Aberdeen library, all in the research library. (Note: These early items were *presumed* to be superseded; since statistical series change configuration, needs of the university change through time, and so on, no effort was made to find later editions of the same thing in the reference department.)

The public library stacks contained Robert Townsend's *Further Up the Organization,* a book of humor in which each topic was arranged alphabetically. Here the arrangement is part of the joke and is not intended for serious use.

Four other miscellaneous items complete the stack collection exceptions. In the public library a booklet containing alphabetical categories of information on running is stored in the stacks (too slight or fragile for reference use?), along with a dictionary of Asian philosophy and a AAA tour book of four *southeastern* states (both low-demand in a suburban public library in California?).

Finally, the research library stacks contained a New Testament commentary by John Calvin, arranged in chapter and verse order, originally published in 1553. The works of a major theologian like Calvin are timeless in one sense; on the other hand an authoritative book on the Bible selected for the reference department is likely to be a more modern commentary, benefiting from recent research. Thus Calvin's work has some of the features of the above-mentioned earlier dated editions. (Note: a commentary on the Bible, in contrast to the Bible itself, was treated as containing a file, because each commentary [on a verse or set of verses] is a freestanding individual and could be reordered if for some reason the original text were reordered. The same argument can be made for commentaries keyed to numbered sections of tax and legal codes. The user of the commentary either knows the chapter and verse numbers "by heart" for reference in the commentary, or else has already used the original text as a source book for chapter and verse number, and so gains some sort of lookup access. This is a debatable position, however, and could be argued the other way as well. In that case, if the commentary were seen as text rather than as a file, then it would simply be a regular stack book and would not be discussed here as an exception. Final resolution of the question may await analysis of *linked* manual files, which has not been done here.)

*Can we refine the definition?* Now that we have seen how few books fall in the middle ranges of percent of length in files, it becomes less important to define "substantially" in the earlier definition of a reference book as a book composed substantially or entirely of files. Only about five percent of books are likely to fall anywhere between 20 and 80 percent of their length in files anyway. Based on the study herein, if we pick a figure like 50 or 60 percent, we will get the best division between reference and running-text books. At the same time, between about 5 and 10 percent of the books in reference collections will be canonical texts, and so constitute exceptions to the purely file-structure way of defining reference books.

We may recall the earlier figures that 85.9 percent of reference collections contained more than 60 percent files and 93.6 percent of the stack collections contained under 60 percent files. Turning these figures around, if we were to instruct a clerk to note the percent of length in files of all books coming into the library, and that clerk assigned all books with over 60 percent files to the reference department and under 60 percent to the stacks, the clerk would make the correct assignment about 90 percent of the time. It would have taken a librarian, of course, evaluating the books on many criteria, to select them in the first place.

## Implications for theory and research

This effort to find a descriptive definition for "reference book" has led to extensive analysis of the organization of both reference and other books, and made it possible to see underlying structural similarities within classes of books that would not be evident otherwise. One benefit of this new view may be that we will be better able to see both manual and computerized sources in terms of the same vocabulary of file/record/field. There are, after all, many similarities in file organization in the two circumstances and it is time we used a common vocabulary to describe them. Much of our literature still deals with these two areas as though they were utterly unrelated.

It can also be seen that the organizational possibilities with manual files appear to be limited compared to those in automated files. While a great many different forms of file organization have been developed for the latter (Flores, 1977, p. 378), manual files seem to gain their lookup potential overwhelmingly through the mechanism of search on *ordered* records. Hence "file" has a definition here which is more limited than that used for computer files, but which does not conflict with those broader definitions.

I believe that another major benefit may result from this article's analysis. There is great potential in this structural approach for the study of search strategy through manual files—and most materials in libraries will remain in manual form for some time. Efforts to study search strategy to date have been limited to examination of fairly global behaviors on the part of searchers (Bates, 1981, pp. 139–169) because of the immense variety of search topics and available resources within which to search. How can one give a recommendation for how to search that is both general enough to apply to many potential searches and specific enough to help in a particular search?

Some light may be shed on that dilemma by examining the file organization of materials to be searched (also see Fairhall [1985]). Underneath all the immense variety of materials in a library lie a limited range of organizational structures, most of which have been discussed here. Searching can be seen as a series of file and text accesses, each access having certain lookup and scan characteristics. Lookup power can be measured in terms of amount of search time reduction due to organization into files, and average scan times needed for books of certain characteristics can be measured. For example, if a file has 400 pages, a certain degree of readability in the formatting on the page, and an average of 12 entries per page, the average searcher may be found to take twenty seconds to find a desired entry.

Searches involving a *series* of linked file lookups can be studied based on number of file accesses, time taken with each access, percent of lookup versus scanning needed in searching, and so on. For example, even a search as ostensibly simple as using the *Readers' Guide* involves several file lookups—first in the main *RG* file to find articles on the desired subject, then a look (if needed) at the journal title abbreviations in *RG* to find the correct full title, a file lookup in the library catalog to find the journal call number, then a lookup into the stacks (another file) to find the journal volumes, and so on. The culmination of such analyses would be to compare different search routes to find optimal ones for various classes of search.

## Conclusions and summary

Traditional definitions of "reference book" (1) have recognized the *administrative convenience* of labeling as "reference" any book that is stored in the reference department and (2) have identified the *function* of reference books, namely, for referral use. These sorts of definitions are valuable as far as they go, but they do not state what a reference book *is*, i.e., its intrinsic character, what it is about a book that makes a person want to use it for reference rather than reading through.

In this article reference books have been defined as books that contain a substantial percentage of their length—operationally defined for the time being as 60 percent or more in pages—in files and/or lists. Files are sets of records ordered according to a readily recognizable ordering principle, and lists are sets of records ordered in the same manner as the author's idiosyncratic ordering of content in a book. Reference books containing files have been contrasted with books of running text, or discourse, which contain, operationally, less than 60 percent of their length in files/lists. Consequences for searching of various book organizations have been analyzed and the power and effectiveness of the referral function of reference books has been seen to arise out of the file structure. It is no accident, in other words, that manual file structure is extremely frequently associated with books designed for referral use.

The theoretical analysis was supplemented by an empirical study of reference and stack books in three libraries: academic, public, and special. Out of a total systematic sample of 343 books, 89.8 percent fell into the expected category based on the above operational definition of more or less than 60 percent of length in files/lists (85.9 percent of the reference books and 93.6 percent of the stack books). To put it differently, if we were to take each book that came into the library and assign it to stack or reference collections *solely* on the basis of its file structure (percent of files/lists in pages), we would be correct 90 percent of the time. Further, as the average library buys far more stack books than reference books, and stack books can be placed with higher accuracy than reference books, the expected value for the library as a whole would be even higher than 90 percent.

Of the 35 exceptions (10.2 percent of all the books), i.e., stack books with 60 percent or more of length in files and reference department books with less than 60 percent files, 24 were found in the reference departments and 11 in the stacks. The chief exception noted to the identification of reference books by file structure is the case of *canonical texts*, i.e., books of discourse carrying some kind of cultural authority, whether the authority of law, religion, or expertise. Fourteen items, or 8.2 percent of the combined reference department samples, were of this type. Other exceptions, among other miscellaneous ones, were high-demand stack items stored in the reference stacks for their protection and earlier dated editions of reference works stored in the stacks.

Though 60 percent was used as the cutoff point, there were actually very few books that fell between 20 and 80 percent of lengths in files: only 18, or 5.2 percent of the entire sample. In fact, 77.6 percent of all the books in the reference department samples had over *90 percent* of their length in files, and 82.1 percent of the stack samples had 10 percent or less of their length in files/lists. It appears that these two main classes of books, those used for referral and those used for reading through, can, for the most part, be sharply and easily distinguished on the basis of their file structure alone.

The research library sample contained a number of foreign language and pre-1900 books. These classes were broken out and their file structure compared to that of the modern English books. Organizational patterns were remarkably similar across cultural/language barriers and through time.

The use of files and lists appears to be *the* prime means Western cultures have found to organize material for referral use in manual sources, thus confirming in yet another way the tight association between file structure and use of books for reference.

It has been suggested that the use of the file terminology in this analysis will contribute to a way of looking at all information resources, both manual and automated, within a common vocabulary and conceptual structure. Finally, this structural view of manual reference sources will make it possible to study human search strategy in a novel, and potentially very precise, way.

## APPENDIX A: DESCRIPTION OF SAMPLING

The sample was systematic, that is, the entire reference or stack collection in a library was measured in terms of number of ranges or shelves and divided by the desired sample size to select one book in every *n*th range or shelf. This form of sampling is considerably easier with large populations than simple random sampling, and is essentially random if done properly. Once she had identified the desired shelf, my research assistant, Cecilia Wittman, counted a certain number of books in from the left edge of the shelf. (The selected number was randomly drawn from the numbers 2–9 and turned out to be 8.)

The UCLA University Research Library contains a preponderance of humanities and social science books, while most fine arts, behavioral science, and natural science books are in other campus libraries. The public library branch, as a regional library, is larger than typical branches of the system and contains a larger variety of reference books than most branches. In fact, half the adult budget goes for reference materials. The children's collection was excluded from the sample. The special library has a strong engineering and science collection. The collection size given (and the sample) excludes the report collection and branch library collection. Journals are interfiled in the University Research Library collection and were included in that sample; they were separately filed in the public and special libraries and were excluded from those samples.

Books in any language in a Roman alphabet were included; all non-Roman alphabet books were rejected, with the next Roman alphabet book on the shelf being selected. There is a slight bias built into this sampling method since selection is by volume, not work; hence, multivolume works are more likely to have one of their volumes selected. Second selections in the same multivolume work or journal were rejected.

# REFERENCES

Barton, M.N. (1966). *Reference books,* (6th ed.). Baltimore: Enoch Pratt Free Library.

Bates, M.J. (1979). Information search tactics. *Journal of the American Society for Information Science, 30*(4), 205–214.

Bates, M.J. (1981). Search techniques. *Annual Review of Information Science and Technology, 16,* 139–169.

*The California water atlas.* (1979). Sacramento: State of California.

Davinson, D.E. (1980). *Reference service.* New York: K.G. Saur.

Fairhall, D. (1985). In search of searching skills. *Journal of Information Science, 10*(3), 111–123.

Flores, I. (1977). *Data structure and management* (2nd ed.). Englewood Cliffs, NJ: Prentice-Hall.

Gates, J.K. (1979). *Guide to the use of books and libraries* (4th ed.). New York: McGraw-Hill.

Goggin, M.K., & Seaburg, L.M. (1964). The publishing and reviewing of reference books. *Library Trends, 12*(3), 437.

Grogan, D. (1979). *Practical reference work.* New York: K.G. Saur; London: C. Bingley.

Hutchins, M. (1944). *Introduction to reference work.* Chicago, IL: American Library Association.

International Organization for Standardization. (1983). *Documentation and information—Vocabulary—Part 2: Traditional documents,* (International Standard ISO 5127/2, 1st ed.). (ISO 5127/2-1983[E/F]). Geneva: ISO.

Katz, W.A. (1978). *Introduction to reference work* (Vol. 1, 3rd ed.). New York: McGraw-Hill.

Katz, W.A. (1982). *Introduction to reference work* (4th ed.). New York: McGraw-Hill.

Prytherch, R. (1984). *Harrod's librarians' glossary of terms used in librarianship, documentation, and the book crafts* (5th Rev. ed.). Brookfield, VT: Gower.

Ranganathan, S.R. (1961). *Reference service* (2nd ed.). London: Asia Publishing House.

Roberts, A.D. (1956). *Introduction to reference books* (3rd ed.). London: Library Association.

Rugh, A.G. (1975). Toward a science of reference work: Basic concepts. *RQ, 14*(4), 293–299.

Sheehy, E.P. (1976). *Guide to reference books* (9th ed.). Chicago, IL: American Library Association.

Shores, L. (1976). *Reference as the promotion of free inquiry.* Littleton, CO: Libraries Unlimited.

Shores, L., & Krzys, R. (1978). Reference books. In A. Kent, H. Lancour, & J.E. Daily (Eds.), *Encyclopedia of Library and Information Science* (Vol. 25, p. 137). New York: Dekker.

Stiffler, S.A. (1972). A book is a book is a reference book. *RQ 11,* 342.

Wyer, J.I. (1930). *Reference work: A textbook for students of library work and librarians.* Chicago, IL: American Library Association.

Young, H. (Ed.). (1983). *The ALA glossary of library and information science.* Chicago, IL: American Library Association.

# 10

# Rigorous systematic bibliography

## Introduction

Systematic bibliography, or enumerative bibliography, as it is sometimes known, has long been viewed as a poor relation to descriptive/analytic bibliography. The practice of making bibliographies to be used in literature searches has been seen to be a much humbler activity than that of creating exquisitely detailed descriptions of the physical and textual aspects of books. Debates have raged through decades over the primacy of the two branches within bibliography, but even the champions of systematic bibliography usually concede that the prize of technical complexity goes to descriptive/ analytic: any primacy due to systematic bibliography arises out of its practical utility, not out of the subtlety or skill needed by the bibliographer.

It is the purpose of this paper to provide a first foundation for a technically subtle systematic bibliography, in which the immense practical utility of resource bibliographies is matched by the skill in information seeking, selection, and organization required of the bibliographer. The bibliographies so created will make possible a more truly rational search strategy for users, and will contribute to bibliographic control in a way current bibliographies do not. Building on current approaches, and drawing particularly on the ideas of Patrick Wilson, I will endeavor to demonstrate that systematic bibliography has earned disdain only because it has been woefully underdeveloped, not because it is intrinsically a trivial activity.

*First published as* Bates, M. J. (1976). Rigorous systematic bibliography. *RQ, 16*(1), 7–26. *This work was supported in part by a grant from the General Research Board of the University of Maryland.*

We will begin, in this introduction, by defining some basic terms and detailing the objectives of this paper. In the second section we will consider what the requirements are for a good systematic bibliography. Requirements will be examined first from the user's standpoint, then from the bibliographic control standpoint. The case is made for two basic requirements, the first of which is generally met by current resources and the second of which is not. Therefore, in succeeding sections we develop the second requirement, that bibliographies state their own specifications, in considerable detail. Six types of specification are described and explained in the third section. Selection principles (one of the specification types) to be used in creating selective bibliographies are developed in the fourth. The paper concludes with a summary and specifications model.

There is a long history of controversy in the field over the definition and purpose of bibliography. Thus, the moment we attempt even to define the terms being used here, we are troubled by variations in authority. As the purpose here is not to enter yet another set of definitions into the fray, but rather to put forth the beginnings of a framework for *doing* systematic bibliography better, these arguments will not be recapitulated. The reader who is interested is advised to consult the works of Greg (1966, pp. 75–88; 239–266), Schneider (1961), Stokes (1969), Hibberd (1965), and Robinson (1971) that are listed in this paper's references, for an understanding of at least some of the points of view in this debate.

A clear and relatively neutral consensus definition of the two main branches of bibliography is provided by Verner Clapp. Regarding systematic bibliography, he says:

> Its immediate aim is to identify and describe in a systematic arrangement the books that may be suitable for a particular purpose or that have other common characteristics (1974, p. 722).

He divides this branch into two subclasses, enumerative and subject bibliography. He says, "Enumerative bibliographies, whose primary purpose is to present an inventory, may be contrasted with subject bibliographies, where the primary purpose is content" (Clapp, 1974, p. 722). He gives national and trade bibliographies and catalogs as examples of enumerative bibliographies, and periodical indexes and abstracting services as examples of subject bibliography. The principles of bibliography preparation to be developed in this paper may, for the most part, be applied to both subclasses of systematic bibliography. Hence the distinction between "enumerative" and "subject" will not be developed and the term "systematic" will be used throughout. The phrase "bibliography on a subject or area" will be used to incorporate both types of systematic bibliography, the word "area" being used to represent all the many types of criteria that may be used for defining coverage of enumerative bibliographies. Examples of the latter are geographical area, location of collection (as with a catalog, which lists the material to be found in a particular library or book dealer's), form of materials, and "works by. . . ."

Regarding analytic bibliography (also known as descriptive bibliography), Clapp says:

> It attempts to organize information, based on or derived from the physical characteristics of books, which will provide evidence regarding their history and especially the history of the texts that they reproduce (Clapp, 1974, p. 724).

This latter sort of bibliography, in which every imaginable aspect of the history of a text and the physical manifestation of that text in book form is examined and described according to minute instructions, is not of interest in this paper—except where it draws upon systematic bibliography principles. The uses and purposes of descriptive bibliographies vary, but where such a bibliography is produced to meet the needs of some anticipated information seekers in the ways described below, then the good descriptive bibliography would also draw upon practices appropriate to systematic bibliography.

It was stated above that the purpose of this paper is to begin to develop a technically subtle systematic bibliography. There are several particularities about this purpose that need to be discussed.

First, we are starting from the place where the decision has already been made to construct a bibliography on a given topic. We are not concerning ourselves with how to decide *whether* to compile a bibliography on a topic. All good bibliographic work should be based on at least some assessment, however crude, of the likely usefulness of, or need for, the resultant product. Staff time is too precious to be wasted on the creation of bibliographies "because someone might want it sometime." But in this paper, we will look only at what the user might require of a bibliography, given that its topic, or coverage, has already been selected.

Second, this paper draws on the work of Patrick Wilson in his book *Two Kinds of Power: An Essay on Bibliographical Control* (Wilson, 1968). The book is a powerful, rigorous, detailed work on bibliographic control. In this paper, we will take just a few of Wilson's ideas, those relating most closely to systematic bibliography, add some ideas of my own, and apply them to the practice of making bibliographies for use by patrons and librarians.

Wilson's book is an important contribution to reference theory, but it is highly abstract and not linked to daily library practice. This brings me to a third point about the focus of this paper. My purpose is to translate and develop a chunk of this reference theory into a form that can be used by practicing librarians. Most librarians, like physicians, are too busy with the immediate demands of their clientele to be able to work on (1) basic research or theory, or even on (2) the *application* of theory to day-to-day practice. They must serve their clients now, today, and therefore have reason to expect from their professional literature articles in which (1) and (2) have already been done for them.

It is this latter, the development of theory and its application, which I view as one of the jobs of the library school professor. We are often criticized for having our heads in the clouds, but it is that very concern for theory that is the strong suit of professors. New theoretical approaches can ultimately advance the field greatly and help us cope with new political/social realities. The trouble lies in linking theory with practice. This is a need unique to professional fields and a very difficult one to meet. In this paper I make an attempt to build such a link.

## Requirements for a good systematic bibliography

In this section, a general definition for "a bibliography" will first be given, and then two basic requirements proposed and supported in a very general way. The ways in which the imposition of those requirements would help first, users, and then, bibliographic control, will be discussed. By the end of this section it will be considered that the case has been made for the two basic requirements. In succeeding sections of the paper the methods of preparing bibliographies meeting the stated requirements will be considered in detail.

Let us define what a bibliography is:

*Bibliography* A list or sequence of descriptions of graphic materials on a given subject or area.

Let us consider each of the words in the definition in turn. "Sequence" is a somewhat milder word than "list." It implies merely that descriptions of materials come one after the other. List, on the other hand, implies greater structuring of the descriptions. The structuring may refer to the descriptive fields within each of the entries, or citations, in the bibliography. Each citation may have to follow a prescribed format, for example. Structuring may also be present in the ordering applied to the citations in relation to one another. Citations may be grouped by subject, literary form, or other aspect, or may be fully ordered by some principle such as alphabetization of author's last name.

The term "description" points to the fact that bibliographies always *describe other things*. This is central to our concept of a bibliography, that it is a pointer, a directory to other things, which are our ultimate goal. Bibliographies are intermediaries. We will come back to this in subsequent discussion.

Bibliographies could point to many things, to people, to locations of cities, for example, but in fact they point to only one type of thing: graphic materials. We use this latter phrase to indicate all information or messages recorded by human agency in some non-ephemeral medium.

Now let us look at "given subject or area." The phrase "subject or area" was defined for use in this paper earlier. The word "given" implies that we must state some scope or limit to a bibliography. All bibliographies must have some such limit in coverage. Even if we attempted, in this age, to create a universal bibliography, we would still inevitably choose to leave some things out, hence limiting its scope. If we did not exclude high school newspapers or federal government "Request for Proposals," then we would surely draw the line at advertising circulars, personal letters, department store receipts, or grocery lists.

A bibliography has been defined. Now, what requirements should be placed on a bibliography to make it a good one? The first, minimal requirement is that it *be* a bibliography, i.e., that it meet the definition above and list or provide a sequence of descriptions of graphic materials on a given subject or area.

For the second requirement, let us turn to Wilson. He says that the user of a bibliographic instrument needs to know its "specifications," i.e., "the rules according to which it was constructed." He goes on to say:

> Even if I examine the contents of the instrument, item by item,
> I do not know what I can properly conclude about the items
> I find and, just as importantly, the items I do not find. My
> knowledge of the power given me by an instrument depends on
> the clarity of the rules according to which it was constructed,
> and on my knowledge of those rules (Wilson, 1968, p. 59).

We may make, therefore, a second requirement that a bibliography state in an introduction its own specifications. By implication, the specifications should be formulated and thought through early in the process of compiling the bibliography so that they may be honestly and intelligently stated ultimately in the bibliography itself.

Let us now consider why the two requirements may be seen to be desirable for bibliographies, first from the standpoint of users, then from the standpoint of bibliographic control.

## The user's standpoint

It has already been noted that bibliographies always point to other things. They are sometimes called "secondary sources" because they do not carry the ultimate, desired information themselves, but rather point to other, "primary" sources that do contain the information.

Let us now ask a very elementary question. Why would a user ever want a secondary source? Why would a user ever go to a pointer source instead of directly to original sources? There are a number of answers to this question that relate to problems of *physical* access. For example, a user goes to the catalog (a secondary source) to find the call number of a book in the stacks. Otherwise, finding the book is next to impossible. Or, a librarian looks in the *Union List of Serials* to find where he/she may borrow a periodical.

But putting these other uses aside, what good is a bibliography for *intellectual* access? Why do people look through subject bibliographies, periodical indexes, and catalogs when they could look at books and journals directly? When we create a bibliography we select certain pieces of information about and from each item to be described and array each item and its information in a list. That's what bibliographies come down to, just lists of other items, usually with only a very minimal bit of information about each of the items. Why do people in and out of the library field go on endlessly arranging, selecting, and rearranging these little snippets of information *about* sources of information?

We must do it out of a conviction that sheer *allocation* of (descriptions of) materials in certain ways in these lists materially aids people in their information-seeking activities. We assume, for example, that if one person selects out of the universe of graphic materials just those on air pollution and collocates them in a list, then the search and selection process for other people interested in that subject will be vastly speeded up or even eliminated.

We have said earlier what a bibliography *is*; now we can say what it *does*: to be of use to information seekers, a bibliography necessarily collocates materials related to each other by some principle. Is this obvious? It may seem so once said, but in fact, the consequences of this function of bibliographies are not, in my view, generally carried through to their logical conclusion. If we provide bibliographies so that information seekers can find materials *grouped in certain ways,* then it is crucial to the effective use of those bibliographies that the *principles of selection and collocation* used in preparation be made crystal clear to all subsequent users of the instruments. When we view bibliographies this way, the second requirement, that specifications be stated in the bibliography, flows directly from the first. Consider:

Through the creation of bibliographies we have certainly improved the user's search situation. The searcher interested in air pollution, for example, will be able to look at one or more bibliographies on the subject instead of having to search through all available graphic materials. This represents a definite improvement in intellectual access.

But have we done all we could? Most bibliographies are not prepared with a specific user in mind. Periodical indexes and subject bibliographies prepared by librarians are usually intended to be general enough to suit several or even very many anticipated possible search requests. Hence it is likely that in most situations users may have call to wonder whether references useful for their purposes have been missed, in other words, to wonder whether there is a good match between the coverage of the bibliography and the area of the user's particular search interest. Even where a bibliography is prepared with a specific user and specific need in mind, as in a special library, the user may wonder whether the bibliography that is finally produced really meets the original stated need.

If told the exact specifications of the bibliography, the user would know exactly what he/she was getting. The user might then decide, for example, that just looking at this one bibliography was entirely adequate, provided that the specifications indicated a thoroughness of coverage and a good match on subject or area. Thus, without spending any more time or energy *compiling* the bibliography, by simply making the specifications of our search available to the user, we would have greatly improved the instrument's utility and effectiveness for the user's search.

In any extensive search, furthermore, any given bibliography is likely to be just one of many resources used. The user, therefore, needs to evaluate any given resource in terms of its suitability in relation to an information need, and to fit that resource into an overall information search strategy.

Most bibliographies available today, whether published or produced in libraries for local use, do not provide the information about themselves to enable the user to make this evaluation.

Let us suppose, for example, that a searcher uncovers, one way or another, a total of five bibliographies on air pollution. If they are like most bibliographies they will be titled with the subject covered, e.g., "Research in Air Pollution" or "Smog." Then, they may or may not have an additional note describing the bibliography, perhaps specifying the subject in a little more detail, or saying where the bibliography was researched.

But there will be no more said. There is no standardized, accepted form for stating the coverage of bibliographies, and a great deal is left unsaid about the actual selection process and criteria for selection of items. (Often that selection is not really clear in the mind of the bibliographer, and has a number of haphazard elements in it that have crept in unnoticed—more on this later.) The user of the five sources may sense that, while there are differences among the coverages of the bibliographies, there are also considerable overlaps. In addition, some areas may have been missed, as well. *But there is no way for the user to tell if there are overlaps or gaps, and if so, what they are.*

This makes for at least two problems for the user. (1) One or more of the bibliographies may be largely or even entirely redundant with one or more of the others. If enough information were available to the user about the contents of the several resources, some sources could be eliminated entirely, others that were largely redundant left to the last in case they were not needed, and so on. In other words, a real search strategy could be formulated, and the speed and effectiveness of the search much improved. (2) Without adequate information about selection for the bibliographies, users cannot determine what has been left out either. Could a subject search be rounded out and a truly thorough coverage be achieved by looking up some subsubject in additional resources? The user often cannot determine this, and has the option of either ending the search or continuing to search on the *entire* topic of interest in additional resources. The principles to be proposed in this paper should enable the user not only to have materials collocated in bibliographies, but also to create a more rational search strategy in approaching graphic materials.

One more point here: if we look at how most library users search in libraries now, we note, in most cases, very little forethought and almost nothing deserving the name "strategy." Most users do not do "smart" searches now. But they *could*—if we provided the information they need on the bibliographies. It goes without saying that trained librarians, who are more conscious of the need for strategy, could make good use, in their own searching, of specification statements on bibliographies.

## Bibliographic control

Now let us turn to the requirements made of bibliographies from the standpoint of bibliographic control. "Bibliographic control" is a phrase that has many meanings. Just one particular meaning will be selected for our purposes here. We as library and information specialists are managers of the universe of bibliographic records. That universe is so huge that we recognize the impossibility of ever searching it in its entirety for any information need. Therefore, we look to bibliographies as preselection devices, making it possible for users to search only a tiny portion of that universe to meet their needs. Bibliographic control, then, is an activity we engage in to detect and record the existence of these preselection devices and to see that new ones are created as needed.

The first requirement, then, when viewed from the standpoint of bibliographic control, can be stated as follows: the bibliography should be so designed as to perform the elementary control function of collocating materials defined by a given subject or area. This is indeed what current bibliographies do. In terms of bibliographic control, we may say that once a systematic bibliography is created, we may view some part of the graphic universe as "pinned down," organized in such a way that a person armed with the bibliography may be said to have effective access to some portion of the bibliographic universe.

But let us now look beyond the first requirement. Bibliographic control should consist not only of identifying and labeling the literature that is out there, but also of creating an integrated structure for physical and intellectual access to recorded materials. Shera and Egan made this point in print in 1952 (Shera & Egan, 1965, pp. 18–33). They distinguished a *macrocosmic* and a *microcosmic* view of bibliography. The macrocosmic view is represented by those "who would view bibliography as one of the instrumentalities of communication and communication itself as an instrumentality of social organization and action" (Shera & Egan, 1965, p. 18). Representing the microcosmic view "are those who look upon each bibliography as a separate tool, . . . each separate bibliography having little or no acknowledged relationship to any other" (Shera & Egan, 1965). They go on to say:

> The hodgepodge of bibliographic services available today to scholars and research workers in various fields is the result

of 'microcosmic' thinking. It is as though each of our rail-roads had been established by a small separate group, each running around and around its own little circuit, exchanging the produce of the local inhabitants within its own area, but with no junction point to connect it with other similar circuits and with no overall plan to facilitate general exchange at national or international levels. Bibliography is, or should be, a carrier system for ideas and information analogous to a well-articulated railroad system for the transportation of physical commodities (Shera & Egan, 1965).

Shera and Egan deal with macrocosmic bibliography in the very broadest social terms, and propose a science to deal with it which they call social epistemology (see also the discussion in Brookes, 1973). The concern in *this* paper is more practical. No attempt is being made to deal with the broader social consequences of such a science, nor is a utopian universal bibliographic control, implicit in Shera and Egan's statement, being proposed. "*Universal* bibliographic control" is a phrase that has almost as many meanings as "bibliographic control." No international political structure, no central location or computer for the processing of bibliographic information is being suggested here.

Rather, it is being proposed that our second requirement, that resources should state their specifications, can, when viewed from the standpoint of bibliographic control, serve to create a kind of integrated structure under the current "hodgepodge" circumstances. Furthermore, if a politically integrated or centralized system is developed in the future, bibliographies meeting *both* requirements will contribute more to that structure than those meeting only the first requirement, under almost any conceivable structure that is actually adopted.

There is a kind of system, or structure, in the current bibliographic situation; a large part of the bibliographic universe is in fact "pinned down," sometimes very well. The trouble is, we do not know how well, and we do not know the exact extent, where the edges are of that control. It is rather as if we had a hazy, blurry picture, instead of a clear one, of what is going on out there. There *is* structure; we just do not know what it is. The set of principles being proposed here is one that should bring that structure into focus, and make possible an integrated *macrocosmic* view, even under current conditions.

Even now, it is possible to provide better control if individual bibliography makers simply always include a specifications statement that enables other bibliographers and users to place the work in its proper location in the overall control structure or system. Let us consider this point in more detail. From the system's point of view most systematic bibliographies can be placed in a very general way into the structure. Bibliography X, for example, is on such and such a subject and covers the journal literature over such and such a time range. But in these cases we cannot pinpoint with any real precision the limits of coverage of the bibliography. Our bibliographic control is still very loose and unrigorous. Did a scientific subject bibliography cover a certain subfield? We cannot tell without scanning the full bibliography. Did a literary bibliography include a certain obscure author? Or trickier, did it include the obscure works of a well-known author? Were all recorded media or only some covered? Was the bibliography exhaustive in most respects, and only selective in others? If selective, what was the basis of the selection?

In most cases, such questions simply cannot be answered. The information is forever hidden in some bibliographer's mind. It is thus impossible to state with conviction that all major aspects of a subject or area have been thoroughly covered. By the same token, aspiring bibliographers, whether publishers or individuals, cannot determine where they can best make a contribution. Hence what labor we do have available to produce bibliographic materials is misused to the extent that the same areas are covered again and again and others left untouched.

If, at a later time, a centralized structure is developed, it will be possible to view existing resources as building blocks, their role and place in the structure-to-be readily determined by a reading of their specifications. If those specifications are developed and described by a common set of principles, then, no matter how diverse the bibliographies, it will be relatively easy to fit them into a single structure.

In the meantime, while we cannot do anything about bibliographies already published, each individual bibliographer or publisher can greatly improve bibliographic control by stating specifications clearly within the instrument itself. As more of this is done, the picture will come into increasingly sharp focus, and the gaps and overlaps will be very evident. It will then be possible, at some time in the future, for individuals or organizations to survey the bibliographic universe and compile recommendations for territories yet to be mapped bibliographically. An integrated, macrocosmic view of bibliography is thus made possible within the current decentralized pattern.

Because people and publishers are sometimes lazy and want to make themselves look as good as possible, some will resist stating specifications. Who wants to limit the sweep of that magnificent title? It might therefore be appropriate for an organization such as the American Library Association to publish standards for statement of specifications in bibliographic materials. Since many published reference sources are bought almost exclusively by libraries, the American Library Association could quickly make its expectations felt with publishers. I have been dismayed, again and again, when teaching reference courses, by how little most sources say about their coverage. When you stop and think about it, is it not absurd how little information reference sources provide about themselves? What kind of search strategy can a user or librarian devise, what kind of bibliographic control do we have, when we do not have any more than the most general information about the coverage of an index or bibliography? The day will come when we will look back and marvel at the primitiveness of descriptions of bibliographic sources in the mid-twentieth century, the way we exclaim today over the fact that at one time libraries did not have "reference" librarians.

Requirements have now been discussed for systematic bibliographies from the complementary standpoints of the user and of the bibliographic control system. Simplifying, we can say that in both cases the bibliography should not only list materials, but also state information that enables the bibliography to be located *relative to the rest of the graphic universe*. In order to accomplish the latter, we must state precisely what is and is not covered in the bibliography in its introduction. This presupposes that the selection and collocation process itself was done in a way sensible and intelligent enough to permit description. The remaining sections of the paper will deal with the development and description of specifications in both comprehensive and selective bibliographies. As will be seen, there is a good deal more to this process than one might think.

## Types of specification

Wilson states that there are five sorts of specifications that need to be made about a bibliographic instrument. A sixth will be added here, which he mentions but does not distinguish.

Let us first cite Wilson directly on his five types of specifications. For convenience of later discussion, labels have been assigned to each type:

*Domain* "The first I shall call the *domain* of the instrument, the set of items from which the contents of the work, the items actually listed, are selected or drawn" (Wilson, 1968, p. 59).

*Selection principles* ". . . the second thing we must know about an instrument, to estimate the power it gives us, is the principle, or principles, according to which items represented in it have been drawn from the domain" (Wilson, 1968, p. 61).

*Bibliographic units* "Texts and works can be divided up and assembled in various ways, as can the units of the librarian's or publisher's universe, the books and pamphlets and issues of periodicals; and the third thing we must know about an instrument is how it is determined what is to count as a unit for listing and description" (Wilson, 1968, p. 61).

*Information fields* "We must, further, know what information we can expect to find about an item, given that it will be represented as a unit" (Wilson, 1968, pp. 61–62).

*Organization* "Last, we must understand the frequently extraordinarily complex system of arrangement or organization. . . ." (Wilson, 1968, p. 62).

Throughout this paper so far, catalogs have been included in the discussion as a type of systematic bibliography. What distinguishes a catalog from other types of bibliographies is that it is a listing of the contents of a particular institution or establishment, such as a library or book dealer's. As such, there are particular problems in developing and stating specifications for catalogs that are different from the requirements for other types of bibliographies. Describing catalog *organization*, for example, including classification, subject headings, and filing rules, can be an extremely complex matter, and deal with issues that seldom arise with other types of bibliographies. Therefore, because of the distinctiveness of their problems, catalogs will be eliminated from further consideration in this paper. Discussion of the specifications will center around the problems most frequently associated with non-catalog bibliographies.

The last three types of specification are more problematic on the whole with catalogs than with other bibliographies. We will deal with them first briefly, therefore, concerning ourselves only with their applications to non-catalog bibliographies.

## Bibliographic units

The purpose of this specification is *not* to say what media forms are covered by the bibliography. That will be done elsewhere. Rather, the concern here is with the *level* of unit. Discussing catalogs, Wilson notes some of the unit-level ambiguities that can arise with any bibliography:

Most modern library catalogs give no separate listing to texts which happen not to be published as the entire contents of a physical volume; many such catalogs give no separate representation to texts occupying entire volumes, or even several volumes, if the volumes are part of a series published by a learned institution (Wilson, 1968, p. 61).

In such cases the level of unit described is not consistent from one entry, or record, to another.

Any time such inconsistencies in choice of bibliographic level, or unit, exist in a bibliography, the inconsistency should be noted. For example, the compiler of a bibliography on research on the use of nonconventional media in the classroom may feel that some collections of research reports (each report by a different author but compiled in a single volume under a collective title) are sufficiently important that each report should be separately listed. In the case of other reports of the same type, considered not as important, the compiler wishes to give only the citation for the collective title, and not the individual studies. If this is done, then the different levels, or units, that do show up in the bibliography should be named in the specifications, and the basis, or principle, for selecting one level or the other should be stated as well.

When called upon to clarify the basis for the level choice in this way, a bibliographer may suddenly find that the choice is not being made very sensibly. As a result, the need to state specifications may result in a healthy exercise in regularizing and rationalizing (in the good sense of the word) the compilation process.

Wherever possible, the principles for determining the bibliographic unit(s) should be ones which the user can apply in his/her turn when searching. As an example, let us return to the instance given above of a bibliography on the use of nonconventional media in the classroom. If the compiler says, "Separate entries for articles and reports *within* volumes have been given where the items seemed important," this is so much a matter of individual judgment that the user cannot do a lot with it in search strategy. Suppose a user remembers vaguely a report on this subject that appeared as one of many in a volume but does not have a complete citation and is trying to locate it. The statement above tells the user that there is a *chance,* depending on how the compiler judges, that the desired study will be separately listed in the bibliography. Saying this is certainly better than not telling the user whether that level is covered at all.

But where possible, and useful, still more clearcut principles should be selected. For example, suppose that the Teaching Methods Institute at

University X is renowned for its research on this subject. If the compiler were able to say, "Separate entries for articles and reports *within* volumes have been given when published by the Teaching Methods Institute of University X," those users who are seeking a report out of another lab need read no further than the specifications. (Note how seldom one can make such quick search decisions with existing bibliographies.)

## Information fields

If we were going to be very thorough, we would provide, in the specifications, models of the descriptive format used for major different bibliographic forms appearing in the list. For example, we might say something like:

> Books: Author, *Title*. Place of publication: Publisher, Date of publication.

In most cases this should not be necessary, as the format is straightforward and evident in every entry.

It is important, however, that some consistent pattern be followed, preferably a pattern published in a recognized authority on bibliographic format. A recognized authority, rather than one's own system, should be preferred because there are in fact a great many different bibliographic forms. It is easy and fun to invent one's own format for, say, books and journals, but it is the rare bibliographer who is willing to go to the trouble to develop models for all possible forms. It then becomes easy for inconsistencies of description to creep in for the occasional reference representing the rarer forms.

The specification *should,* however, include the full citation for the authority followed. This assures the user that some consistent pattern is being followed. Thus, for example, when a journal citation gives a number but no volume, the user can feel assured that the journal does not use volume numbers, and need not worry about whether the bibliographer just did not happen to put it in in that case.

Finally, in any case where there is likely to be any confusion or misunderstanding, full, detailed models of the information fields should be provided and explained. In printed periodical indexes, particularly, where entries are brief and cryptic in the interests of saving space, models and explanations of format should be provided. Also, in any case where something new or unusual is included in some or all entries, an explanation should be given in the specifications.

Everything stated so far about information fields presupposes, of course, a consistent, conscientious effort on the part of the bibliographer to have every entry complete and correct. Based on my experience, I would say this is a good deal harder to achieve than it sounds. I have discovered errors in my own work even after double and triple checking, and have also found errors in highly reputable sources. For a searcher, there is nothing more frustrating than a promising reference that leads nowhere. The ultimate purpose of making bibliographies, even beyond the idea of collocating materials to help users in searching, is to *facilitate information transfer*. As bibliographers and librarians we are intermediaries, facilitators, in that transfer process. Every blind lead in a bibliography, every misfiled catalog card, is a clog in the flow of information. We have blocked information transfer, not aided it. A mistake, therefore, in handling or describing information is not just a mistake, it is a small defeat of the very purpose of our profession.

## Organization

Organization becomes a very complex matter with catalogs. But it is important, if often less troublesome, for other bibliographies too. The specifications statement at the beginning of the bibliography should include the following items: access points, ordering principles, and entry terms. Information on these items should relate to the *bibliography being compiled*, not to the organization of resources searched to create the bibliography.

Let us take each of these in turn. An access point is the type of information field by which a searcher can gain access to a file. The entries in a typical dictionary catalog are arranged (interfiled) by author, subject, title, and series, i.e., have these four access points. The individual entries contain information on publishers, for example, but one cannot get access to the entries by publisher; hence publisher is not an access point in such a catalog. Even though the information is there, the entries are not *ordered* by publisher, so the book historian wanting, say, all the books produced by a small publisher cannot look it up and find those items collocated in the catalog.

The access points in a bibliography should be stated in the specifications. Even with popular periodical indexes, one must determine access points by scanning the entries. It is not immediately evident in some of these indexes, for example, whether one can get access by title. In smaller, locally done bibliographies, there will often be only one access point, perhaps subject, subarranged by author. This should be so stated.

Ordering principle refers to the way in which items are ordered, or arranged. The most common ordering principles are alphabetical, numerical, chronological, and classified. In the example given above, of author arrangement within subject, an incorporation of ordering principles within the description would lead to something like the following: "Entries are arranged alphabetically by author under each subject term. Subject terms are themselves arranged alphabetically."

Entry terms should be listed separately by themselves (without the citations) so that the searcher can peruse them easily. Separate listing also makes the subject coverage of the bibliography clearer to the user than the discussion of domain and scope alone can do (see below for discussion of latter two terms). If the bibliography is a short one, say, of fifty items, divided into six subject categories, then the categories should be listed separately at the beginning. If the bibliography is a very long one, like a periodical index, the entry terms should still be listed separately, either at the beginning or in a separately published thesaurus.

Exception should be made only where there are nearly as many entry points as citations. For example, in a bibliography arranged by author, where there are few authors with more than one entry, it will little facilitate searchers to have all the authors listed separately. But where an extensive bibliography attempts, for example, to provide complete listings of all works of, say, a half dozen literary authors, then by all means the authors should be listed separately, without the individual item entries. This same principle holds, of course, for subject entry terms as well, even if it means publishing a thesaurus for larger bibliographies.

Why should we require this? Aside from enhancing the user's grasp of the subject coverage of the bibliography, this practice is also important for searching. The wise searcher in any bibliography, long or short, will not just look up the first term that comes to mind and start writing down references. Instead, he/she will look up several terms that might be useful, locate the ones actually used in the bibliography, and decide on the best one(s) to search under. This process is made easier by having all the terms together in a list instead of scattered with many citations interspersed. In the case of published indexes that appear at regular intervals, a term may not even appear in a given volume. Going back to Wilson's general principle again, of telling the user something about what is *not* there, the presence of a term in a thesaurus of all terms used in a periodical index will tell the user that if that term did not appear in a volume, it means that there was nothing in the literature on the subject that time; it does not mean, "We don't cover the subject area."

Now let us turn to the first two specifications, plus a third, added one, which are the most important in doing systematic bibliography.

## Domain and scope

"Scope" has been added as a sixth specification type. As we shall see, Wilson mentions it (under a different name), but does not call it a separate type.

Let us first examine the concept of "domain" in more detail, drawing upon more passages from Wilson.

> The domain, then, consists of the set of items about which the maker of the instrument is prepared to make a guarantee, the set of items from which he will guarantee to have drawn all that meet the requirements for inclusion. So a trustworthy bibliography tells us something about items not listed, as well as about the items listed: it tells us that a certain domain has been exhausted of one sort of material, and thus enlarges our power beyond the actual contents of the list. But it also indicates the limits of that power, if it tells us the extent of the domain, for it tells us what are the items, those outside the domain, about which we can draw no conclusions at all. Among the items outside the domain, in the "counter-domain," there may in fact be nothing that meets the requirements for inclusion, but no guarantee is made about that (Wilson, 1968, p. 60).

In addition, he makes the point that ". . . we need not demand that the domain be made co-extensive with the set of works actually examined, or even available for examination; for there may be ways in which one can know without inspection that some set of items all fail to meet the requirements for inclusion, and items about which one knows this to be true, however one knows it, may be added to the domain" (Wilson, 1968, pp. 59–60).

Domain, then, is the bibliographical territory searched. Stating domain would in practice mean stating the locations searched in the process of compiling the bibliography. Such a statement might take this form: "Searched catalog of Library X under headings A, B, and C, and *Reader's Guide*, 1965–1974 volumes, under terms B, D, and E." The domain in this case consists of all the items that fell under those terms in those sources.

Defining the domain this way tells the searcher some useful things about the bibliography. At the very least, it tells the user that, assuming the compiler is honest and conscientious, it is not necessary—in fact, pointless—to reexamine the domain that has already been searched by the compiler. In the example, the bibliography compiler has eliminated the necessity of looking in ten years of *Reader's Guide* on that subject. This is not a trivial service to perform for someone. The trouble with most bibliographies today is that that service is kept a secret, i.e., not stated in the introduction, so the conscientious searcher, not knowing any better, may feel constrained to search also in the very sources used to create a bibliography that he/she has already used.

As Wilson notes, it is not necessary to have examined every item in order to include it in the domain. It is possible and frequently necessary to compile bibliographies without examining personally the items considered for inclusion. A good practice, however, would be always to examine items where possible in those cases where there is doubt as to whether the items meet the "requirements for inclusion."

Additionally, it is important to state unproductive locations searched. By doing so, we enlarge the domain, telling the user, "nothing can be found there, don't bother." Now it is conceivable, but not likely, that there will be value in telling a sociologist interested in race relations that *Chemical Abstracts* has nothing on the subject. In other words, there is not much point in expanding the domain for its own sake. But it *is* of value to tell the sociologist that there was nothing on the subject in a resource where one might *expect* to find something. It is thus valuable and not braggartly to include in the domain description sources that have been found to be completely unproductive.

What Wilson calls "requirements for inclusion" are here being called "scope," and being named as a distinct specification type. Developing and stating the scope of a bibliography is a distinct process from consideration of domain, and one which is probably even more important to the effectiveness of the bibliography. We use the following definition:

> *Scope*  That subject and/or area declared to be the range of coverage, or requirements for inclusion, of a bibliography.

Scope and domain must not be confused. Domain is the bibliographical territory searched. Scope is the conceptual territory covered by the bibliography. In a search, every item in the domain is examined (or considered indirectly in the manner discussed earlier) and tested to see if it meets the scope, that is, if it falls within the range defined by the scope statement. Thus, in principle, by the end of a bibliography search, every item in the domain has been found either to match or not to match the scope statement.

To take a simple example, suppose that a school librarian has been asked to compile a bibliography on airplanes for an upcoming class project. The *domain* in this case may be only the items listed under the term "Airplanes" in the card catalog. The *scope* is the *content* "Airplanes." In this case, the librarian may list all the items in the domain in the final bibliography. In most cases there will be fewer, sometimes far fewer, items in the bibliography than in the domain.

Recall also Wilson's point that there may be items meeting the "requirements for inclusion" (scope) outside the domain. For example, there may well be other items in the library on airplanes besides those listed in the card catalog. Periodical articles, for one thing, will not be covered in the catalog. So both domain and scope are very important, each in a different way, in determining what ends up in a bibliography.

It is important to realize that scope should be determined independently of domain. Scope should not be allowed to degenerate into being identical with domain. This becomes clear with an instance more complicated than the airplane example above. Suppose we search under "Teacher skills" and "Teacher education" in one bibliography, and "Teacher education" and "Teacher training" in another. We may be tempted to let the scope definition consist of these domain terms, without further thought. But, in fact, those terms have particular meaning to the makers of those resources. "Teacher education" in one might cover quite different conceptual territory than "Teacher education" in the other. The compilers of the bibliography using "Teacher skills" may have dumped some marginally related items in there for lack of another term in their particular thesaurus. If we accept this domain as our scope, without our own independent definition of scope, then our resultant bibliography is going to collect together in one place all the inconsistencies existing in the domain. Only when we define the scope in principle before, or in the early stages of, searching the domain, and then examine each item in the domain to see if it fits the scope, will there result the coherent, consistent bibliography that is desired.

In an exhaustive, or comprehensive, bibliography, the effort is to find absolutely everything, within the domain, that fits the scope. The selection principle in this case would be "exhaustive" or "100 percent selection." A selective bibliography is one in which some selection principle is applied to those items meeting the scope, so that not all those fitting the scope end up in the final bibliography. It must be made clear that it is necessary to determine domain and scope for *all* types of bibliographies; selective bibliographies require the additional determination and description of selection principles.

Let us now consider how to determine and describe scope in more detail. Scope comprises the same types of elements normally used in descriptions of reference sources: subject, bibliographic forms, date ranges, geographical and language coverage, and so on. Current bibliographies generally state only one or a few of these elements, and then not in sufficient detail. Defining and holding to the scope would seem to be a straightforward business—but, in fact, doing a good job of it requires considerable care. The goal is to make every element in the scope explicit.

Let us take an example. Suppose we set out to prepare an exhaustive bibliography on automatic indexing for information scientists. At first, we may define the scope simply as "automatic indexing" and think we are being quite adequately thorough with that definition. But in fact there may be a number of implicit scope factors, or criteria, operating. We may fail to notice that we are also implicitly limiting our search to post-1960 materials. This may come about simply because we know that not much was written on it before then, so there may not seem much reason to state this explicitly in the bibliography. Not all users of the bibliography will know this, however. We may also, in fact, be limiting it to English-language items, or only American, and only to books, journal articles, and technical reports, without noting the fact. Even sneakier implicit criteria may come in without our noticing. We might, in this example, be actually selecting only articles that reported research, and leaving out chatty or newsy articles on the subject. Other items may be rejected because they are so obviously bad. In other words, quality is an unspoken selection criterion, too. So in fact, our bibliography's scope may be: "High-quality, research-oriented, American books, journals, and technical reports published since 1960, on the subject of automatic indexing."

Specification of the subject aspect of scope, particularly, often requires more detail than has been used in the examples so far. It is not enough to say that a bibliography is on trees if it in fact has been defined to include shrubs, or if it is meant to cover only materials on tree species and not to cover ecology of trees. Every meaningful nuance should be included in the scope specification, every aspect that makes a difference in the decision to include or exclude items.

A really hard look at one's selection behavior may turn up quite a number of these implicit criteria. Every one of them should be made explicit. Once this is done we are liable to find that some of the criteria do not bear close examination. Major chunks of literature relevant to the subject may be found to be left out for reasons of momentary convenience.

It may often be the case that one will become fully aware of all the elements of the scope only after searching has begun. In this case, ground already covered should be rechecked to see that the final product is consistent throughout. A good way to find out if there are any as yet undiscovered implicit scope elements in one's selection behavior is to notice those occasions when one wants to reject an item, but finds that there is nothing in the scope statement that the item fails to meet. If this approach is carried out consistently, it will almost always be found, especially with short bibliographies, which necessarily have a narrow topic, that the scope has many more defining criteria than was first thought.

If every single element of the scope has been made explicit in the mind of the bibliographer, then it is possible to make a well-founded, consistent decision about every item considered for inclusion in the bibliography. In the final bibliography, every item included is there because it meets the scope and every item (in the domain) not there is excluded because it does not meet the scope. A resource so prepared is quite different from the hodgepodge agglomerations that sometimes go under the name of "bibliography."

## Principles of selection

This section deals extensively with the sixth and final specification type: selection principles. We may suspect that the word "selective" in the titles of bibliographies is sometimes a code word for statements such as the following: "Some Things I Found on the Subject of . . . ," or "Major Bibliography X Wasn't Available, But Here's What I Found Elsewhere on the Subject of. . . ." In other cases the word may have a much more carefully defined meaning, but unless the user knows what that meaning is, the word "selective" does not tell him/her much except, "This bibliography does not cover everything on the stated subject."

In this section several principles of selection will be discussed, principles which can be used by the bibliographer and then explained, in more colloquial terms, to users. It will be evident that a good selective bibliography is not just a half-baked comprehensive bibliography, but rather is compiled with as much care and effort as one in which every item meeting the scope is accepted.

The phrase "selection principles," as used here, has a different meaning from that in Wilson's original definition. Wilson defined it as the principles according to which items are drawn from the domain. We have used the *scope elements* as the basis for drawing items from the domain. "Selection principles" in this paper refers to rules by which items are selected for the final bibliography out of the items meeting the scope. To put it another way, we use "selection principles" to refer to various principles of selection to be applied to items already meeting a bibliography scope statement, *not* to the selection of items from the domain.

There is an ambiguity connected with the first selection principle that needs to be explained. When we select the "best," "most," or even "favorite," it can be argued that we are not "selecting" any more than we were with a comprehensive bibliography when we listed everything that fit the scope. It can be said that "best" or "highest quality" is simply an *additional element of the scope,* so that we might be seeking, for example, *every single document* that meets the scope statement "high-quality research papers on automatic indexing."

On the other hand, we certainly have an intuitive sense connected with "best"-type judgments that we are first defining a scope, and then picking out the best ones from among those that fit that scope. For our purposes it probably does not matter how we resolve this ambiguity. "Best" or "most" selection will be listed as the first principle in this section.

The succeeding principles discussed, however, may be viewed as indisputably distinct from scope. In those instances, we find all items meeting the scope and then take a sample from that set, for reasons explained below.

Before discussing the various selection principles, let us first consider a question that has not been dealt with: Why would we want a *selective* bibliography? The value of a bibliography for users was discussed earlier; it was seen as a collocation of related materials so that the user would not have to search through many unrelated materials to find desired items. What good is it to pick out only some of the items meeting a stated scope? It is suggested here that the process of bibliographic search may be facilitated in various ways by having available "samples of the territory." At various stages of a search a user may wish to get a "feel," a sense of the "lay of the land" in an area, before homing in on a particular stage of the search. An example of this (A) will be given below under selection principle 2. Or, the user may wish to get acquainted with an area and would like a sampling of "typical" references in the area. An example of this (B) is also given under selection principle 2. Other examples are given throughout the following. In selection principles 2–4, three different approaches to sampling from items meeting the scope will be described.

Finally, a user may wish to look at just a few examples in an area, because it is felt that only one or a few references will be needed to meet the ultimate information need. This might be because the user expects to find the desired information in most any source, so thoroughness to insure that all references, or a representative sample, are found is not needed. In this case, the user requirements placed on a bibliography are less stringent than in the two previous types of need discussed above. In this situation, an exhaustive bibliography or a selective one drawn on almost any principle will do. Either sort of bibliography will be underutilized relative to its potential. For this reason, this type of need will not be further discussed and we will focus in this section on meeting needs for selective bibliographies that tax the instruments more nearly to the limit of their ability to aid users.

### Selection principle 1: Expert judgment, and "most" or "best"

Where a bibliography is selective because it is being compiled by an expert in an area (whether librarian subject expert or other) who is selecting just some items on a subject, the principle of selection should be made explicit. For example, is the person selecting items found to be the most original, the most useful for beginning students, the worst examples of research method, or what? Even where a bibliography is labeled "Most" This, or "Best" That, there is usually something more that can be said to define those terms in a way that lets the user know exactly what can be expected.

Another way of picking "most" or "best" articles, which we will just briefly mention, is to use citation counts. This "bibliometric" approach represents a huge area of research in information science. Much work has been done in using frequency counts of citations in book and article bibliographies to determine the most central journals in a given subject field. Results of such studies are used by librarians to decide which journals to purchase for their library. Now with the availability of the huge, computer-produced indexes *Science Citation Index* and *Social Sciences Citation Index* (or their associated computer files), it is possible to extend this approach to the creation of bibliographies which collocate items that are known to be "best" or important because they have all been cited by other people at least so many times.

### Selection principle 2: Random sample

"Random" has a colloquial meaning of "casual," or "unplanned," when used in reference to actions. If we pick an apple out of a bowl "at random," for example, then we do it without concerning ourselves with picking the best or juiciest one. But "random" has a technical meaning in sampling theory, and it is that meaning that is used here. In a truly random sample, the sampling is designed and carried out so that each item in the population to be sampled, whether apples, books, or people, has *a precisely equal chance of being selected.* This is a lot harder to achieve than it sounds. With the bowl of apples, our selection is not random at all. Even though we do not seek the juiciest apple, we will still be most likely to select from the top of the bowl. Hence, the ones at the bottom are not as likely to be picked, i.e., will not have an equal chance of being selected, compared with the apples at the top of the bowl. We could get closer to randomness if we put the apples in a large box, closed the box, shook it up thoroughly, and then reached in with our eyes closed and picked the first one that came to hand.

In the bibliographic realm, if we wanted to make a random selection, say, to provide someone with an accurate picture of the types of references to be found on a given subject, it would be quite difficult to do. We would first have to find everything meeting the scope, and then through some rather complicated business with random numbers tables, select the desired sample.

But there is one area where a random sample would be easy to achieve and might be very useful. With proper programming, near-random sampling can be done easily in bibliographic on-line search systems. For most purposes a sampling policy of taking every $n$th item, e.g., every fifth, or tenth, or twenty-fifth, is effectively random. (The only exception would be where the data base was itself structured in patterned numerical sequences, so that certain categories of references were consistently missed by taking every $n$th item.)

A common pattern currently with bibliographic on-line search systems is for the user first to formulate a Boolean search and then key it in. The machine then searches and states to the user how many items meet the search statement. If there are none, the user expands the search statement; if there are too many, the user reformulates the search more specifically, and does this repeatedly, if need be, until a reasonable number of items is reported out. At this point the searcher has the citations printed out. A "sample $n$" command, which would allow every $n$ items meeting a search request to be printed out, could be very useful. Here are a couple of examples:

**A. Help with search formulation**  A searcher does not know the vocabulary of the system well yet. She puts in a request and gets out a reasonably small number of items, say seventy-five, but this number is still too large to have printed out. She is afraid that narrowing the search may cut out valuable items, yet clearly the search must be narrowed somehow. She then inputs a "sample 5" command and gets out every fifth citation, or fifteen altogether. In examining the fifteen she sees two minor subjects she can "not" out of her next request, and also gets an idea for a more specific term that will still cover the desired area. She goes back and reformulates a satisfactory search.

**B. "Get acquainted" with an area**  A searcher wants to get a feel for an area he does not know well. He deliberately puts very general terms in his search formulation, because he wants to get a sense for the whole area. The response is impracticably large, say 1,225 items. But now he inputs a command "sample 30" and gets back about forty items, which collectively present a good picture of the subject area.

## Selection principle 3: Representative sample

The idea lurking behind taking a random sample in the previous selection principle was representativeness. What we were really seeking, and got effectively with a random sample, was a representative picture of an area. A representative selection is one in which we get an accurate, if simplified, picture of a subject or area through a selection of just some of the items in that subject or area. Even where we cannot take a random sample, or find it impossibly cumbersome to take one, there are ways we can achieve representativeness nonetheless. By taking a random sample we eliminate the vagaries and biases of individual judgment. This is, of course, necessary in research studies where experimenter bias may defeat the whole purpose of a study. But in bibliography preparation the good judgment of an experienced reference librarian, combined with his/her understanding of the concept of representativeness, can produce an excellent selected bibliography.[1]

If we can say to the user that a bibliography has been selected so as to present a representative picture of the much larger set of items available meeting the scope description, then the user knows that he/she can rely on the sense gotten of the subject or area from perusing the bibliography. After examining such a bibliography, the user can confidently say, for example, "Ah hah, a lot of work on concept formation recently, but nothing much on cognitive dissonance." As the "literature explosion" grows to ever more dizzying size, good selected bibliographies, whose selection principles are explained to the user so he/she knows what can be expected, will become more and more valuable.

A random sample selects from the literature on every possible characteristic simultaneously. If, among all the items meeting the scope

---

1 In fact, a humanly selected bibliography may be more representative than a randomly selected one. Random sampling is done to eliminate human biases that may unconsciously slip in where there are emotional pressures pushing one toward bias; for example, pushing one toward deliberate selection of experimental subjects who will confirm a theory. Hence, random selection in research is important. But there is usually less pressure of this sort leading a bibliographer to select items non-representatively. Furthermore, random selection makes representativeness likely, but not certain. There is a small probability that any given random sample is not representative of the population from which it is drawn.

specification, 20 percent are on subject Y, 20 percent have been published in New York, and 25 percent are on microfilm, then approximately the same distribution will show up in the final bibliography. With manual representative sampling, the bibliographer can play with these traits to meet desired requirements.

For example, the compiler may select items that are perfectly representative regarding subject. If the approximate distribution of four subsubjects among items meeting the scope specification is as follows—subject A, 20 percent; B, 30 percent; C, 45 percent; D, 5 percent—then the final bibliography will have items on each subject approximately in the above proportions, that is, there will be about one reference on subject D for every four on subject A. But at the same time, the compiler, to meet certain anticipated needs, may select for certain things on other traits and be deliberately non-representative. She/he may select for certain authors, for quality, intellectual level, ease of access, medium, etc. The important thing is that the compiler should be self-consciously aware of selection decisions being made and should include them all in the final specifications.

Let us take a simple, specific example. An academic librarian might prepare a bibliography with the following scope and selection principle statements:

*Scope* Journal research literature on motivation training from a psychological standpoint published in English since 1970.

*Selection principles* Materials selected so that the number of items in each subject section of the bibliography is approximately proportional to the number of items on each subject appearing in the literature. This is done with the purpose of providing a representative picture of research being done in the topic area of this bibliography. Within this constraint, items have been preferred which are available in this library.

The choice may of course also be made to be representative on something besides subject, to suit all sorts of particular situations. One might select to represent the productivity of authors, for example.

There is another kind of representativeness, however, that might not present a picture of the actual distribution in the literature at all. Let us take an example from our own field of a kind of bibliography that might be very useful to librarians and information scientists. There are available a great many studies and discussion articles on the information needs of scientists and technologists. A very useful bibliography for both working librarians and students might be one designed along the following lines: the first part of the bibliography is a literature-representative sample of the sort we have already discussed, presenting a selection of general articles on what is known about information needs of scientists and technologists and the methodological problems in user needs research. In addition to articles of this sort, there are many studies in the field reporting research on the information needs of scientists in particular scientific fields. Now there may be many more studies on the needs in some subject fields than in others. There has been a great deal of work done on the information needs of psychologists, for example. But we may surmise that all most library/information scientists need is one good thorough study on needs of scientists in each subject field. So, the second half of the bibliography would consist of a number of studies, selected so that the needs of scientists in each subject field is represented by just one paper. In this case, it is the range of subjects, rather than the number of items in the literature, that is represented accurately.

We may not always have an opportunity to exercise such sophistication in the development of selection principles in bibliography preparation, but as may be evident from examples already, some sophisticated approaches on our part can nonetheless be explained simply and usefully for the patron. Above all, whatever the selection principles are, explain them! Even if they are fairly haphazard, the user is entitled to know the limits, as well as the strengths, of coverage of a bibliography.

It is appropriate at this point, since we are dealing with the making of sometimes sophisticated judgments and selections, to mention the perennial issue of whether a librarian needs subject expertise to prepare a good bibliography. Some writers on this subject, including Wilson, take the flat position that subject expertise is absolutely necessary for good work (see, for example, Greg [1966, p. 81] and Wilson [1968, p. 56, footnote]). I do not agree. Certainly, in general, the more subject expertise, the better the bibliography the compiler is likely to be able to produce, but only in general. Whether a non-subject-grounded bibliographer can do a good job on a particular bibliography is a function of a lot of factors—whether crucial selection criteria revolve around detailed subject knowledge, whether the subject is diffuse and hard to describe or falls invariably under one rubric, and so on. Ideally, all bibliographers would have Ph.D. degrees in the very subject being researched, as well as a library master's degree. Short of that, and we will remain short of that for a long time, there is no sense underestimating what a good librarian can do with his/her expertise (knowledge of resources—something the subject experts are often woefully lacking in) and some ingenuity in interpreting the use of subject terms in article titles and bibliographic resources.

### Selection principle 4: Functional equivalence sets

In the previous section we discussed producing representative bibliographies, ones that gave a picture of an area. Another term we might have used for this picture is "map." Just as a map, while picking up many details of the territory mapped, is nonetheless much smaller and simpler than the real territory itself, so also our bibliographies gave the "lay of the land" only, and often left out a great deal more than they included. Implicitly, in the previous three selection principles, we were dealing with ratios of number of items in bibliography to number of items meeting the scope specifications of anywhere between 1:100 to perhaps 1:10 to 1:5. In this section, we are dealing with ratios of 1:2 or 3 or 5. Instead of giving people a sampling from which they would select some items to read, or which they would use to assess an area before exploring it further on their own, we are providing a list which is intended to be completely adequate for most conceivable circumstances. This kind of selection is much more likely, but still not necessarily, to require subject expertise. It may be particularly useful for pedagogical purposes.

The approach here is to take those items meeting the scope statement and then arrange them in small sets, or groups, of items which are considered functionally equivalent, that is, equivalent for the purposes of the bibliography. A functional equivalence set is defined here as a group of items selected such that, as best the bibliographer can anticipate, the user would find any one item in the set as good for his/her purposes as, or functionally equivalent to, any other item in the set. No two publications are identical, of course, but for the user's purposes it is anticipated that to read one of the set is to read them all. In other words, *if the user reads one item of the set he/she does not need to read any of the others.*

After grouping the items meeting the scope into functional equivalence sets (FESs),[2] the compiler then selects one item from each set to include in the final bibliography. The user armed with such a bibliography should, in most circumstances, have no need to seek additional references in the area covered by the bibliography.

We assume two major kinds of equivalence here, hierarchical and substitution. We have *hierarchical equivalence* when one item is functionally

---

2 Note that it is not the sets that are equivalent, but rather the items in any one set that are equivalent. Hence the phrase "functionally equivalent sets," which implies the former, would be inaccurate.

equivalent to several other items. A review paper may be functionally equivalent, for a reader, to a number of research papers, i.e., only the review paper need now be read; a textbook may be functionally equivalent to a number of review papers and original papers. (A distinction needs to be made here between types of review papers. They may be considered in parallel to indicative and informative abstracts. Some review articles—those in the *Annual Review of Information Science and Technology* are examples—cannot substitute for the articles themselves. They only indicate, suggest, the contents and do not fully describe and inform the user of the contents of the original articles. Other review papers, such as the Information Analysis Papers produced by the ERIC Clearinghouses, may frequently provide enough of the substance of the articles reviewed to serve as a substitute, i.e., a true hierarchical equivalent, for the original articles.)

Within the same form, or hierarchical level, there may also be functionally equivalent items; this is a case of *substitution equivalence.* For the purposes of the user, several textbooks or research papers can be considered equivalent to each other. Each research paper is different, of course, but some test the same thing, or vary the test only in some aspect of no interest to the prospective reader. So for the user's purposes, just one item in the substitution set will do.

Let us consider an example of a bibliography prepared with the concept of functional equivalence in mind. A researcher tells a special librarian that she wants to get a quick education in a certain subject field, and to please select a set of materials for her to read. By now the researcher has learned that she can rely on the librarian to make good selections in instances like this, even though he does not have as much subject background as she does. Of several review articles on the subject, he picks the one that most closely fits the researcher's stated interests. In the review articles he notices repeated references to four seminal papers and notes them down. He assures himself that the review article plus the four major articles cover early material adequately, and he now concentrates on finding materials that have appeared in the three years since the date of the review. Looking through the literature, he notes major themes and lines of research. He selects six or seven research articles which collectively cover the current research front. He copies the articles locally available and borrows others on interlibrary loan. A few days later he presents the researcher with a dozen or so items which constitute a good introduction to the field of interest, and which, in all probability, are completely adequate for her purposes. In explaining his selection to her he need say nothing about "functional equivalence sets," but the concept was implicit in all of his selection.

## Summary and specification model

After an introductory background discussion, a "bibliography" was defined in a general way, and two requirements suggested as desirable for all systematic bibliographies to meet. The first requirement was the elementary one that the "bibliography" be what it had been defined to be. The second requirement, drawn from the work of Patrick Wilson, was that the bibliography should state its own specifications.

Next we considered why the two requirements might be seen as desirable for bibliographies to meet, first from the standpoint of the user and then from the standpoint of bibliographic control. It was found that the first requirement (met today by typical bibliographic resources) provided a given level of service, and that the addition of the second requirement (generally not met by existing resources) would provide an anticipated much higher level of service. With bibliographies meeting both requirements users would be able to develop more rational, effective search strategies, and it would be possible to develop a more integrated bibliographic control structure.

Next, the types of specifications that might be included in the introductions to bibliographies were examined in detail. The six types of specifications discussed were domain, scope, selection principles, bibliographic units, information fields, and organization. Problems associated with the preparation of both comprehensive and selective bibliographies were considered. Four selection principles were discussed: expert judgment, random sample, representative sample, and functional equivalence sets.

A model format for bibliography introductions is provided below; the specification types are listed in the order of likely interest to the typical lay user.

It should be kept in mind that the terms used to label the specification types will not be familiar to lay bibliography users. There is no need to give them a lesson in bibliography making—they probably will not be interested anyway—but the information under each specification category should be *self-explanatory for their purposes*. The scope statement, for example, should not begin: "Scope: Books on sea shells . . . ," which presupposes an understanding of the meaning of "scope," but rather, something like: "Scope: This bibliography covers books on sea shells. . . ."

Since our use of the phrase bibliographic units can be confused with that aspect of the scope statement that deals with bibliographic forms, the specification category *Bibliographic Units* should not be used at all when there are no problems with unit level to be noted. When the category is used, it is easy enough to make its meaning unambiguously clear within the explanation—see example earlier in appropriate section.

Finally, like all publications, the bibliography should state its own title, compiler, place of publication, "publisher" (where meaningful), and date of compilation.

### Specifications of this bibliography

1. *Scope* (Include here *every* element that played in decisions to include or exclude any item from bibliography.)

2. *Selection principles* (If exhaustive bibliography, state that all items found in the domain, no. 4, that met the requirements stated in the scope, no. 1, have been included. If selective, state any and all principle(s) used, in readily understood, colloquial terms, but without ambiguity.)

3. *Organization* (State access point(s) and ordering principle(s) for bibliography in generally understandable terms. Entry terms or categories—except where all or most such terms lead to only one item for each term—should be grouped together here, or where necessary, reference should be made to separate thesaurus used for entry terms.)

4. *Domain* (State first something along these lines: "The following resources were searched to create this bibliography: ... " Then state major determining bounds for all sources used, e.g., title, subject terms searched under, and date bounds of periodical indexes searched. Include unproductive sources too.)

5. *Information fields* (At a minimum, citation is given of standard source used for bibliographic format. In addition, any cryptic elements in typical entries are explained, and any other unusual elements likely to show up in a citation are anticipated.)

6. *Bibliographic units* (Any unusual combinations or inconsistencies in the bibliographic units, or levels, covered in the bibliography are noted and explained.)

### REFERENCES

Brookes, B.C. (1973). Jesse Shera and the theory of bibliography. *Journal of Librarianship*, 5(4), 233–245, 258.
Clapp, V.W. (1974). Bibliography. *Encyclopedia Americana* (Vol. 3, pp. 722–724).

Greg, W.W. (1966a). Bibliography—An apologia. In J.C. Maxwell (Ed.), *Collected Papers* (pp. 239-266). Oxford, England: Clarendon Press.

Greg, W.W. (1966b). What is bibliography? In J.C. Maxwell (Ed.), *Collected Papers* (pp. 75-88). Oxford, England: Clarendon Press.

Hibberd, L. (1965). Physical and reference bibliography. *The Library: Transactions of the Bibliographical Society, 5th ser*(20), 124-134.

Lewin Robinson, A.M. (1971). *Systematic bibliography: A practical guide to the work of compilation,* (3rd Rev. ed.). Hamden, CT: Linnet Books.

Schneider, G. (1961). *Theory and history of bibliography* (R.R. Shaw, Trans.). New York: Scarecrow.

Shera, J.H., & Egan, M.E. (1965). Foundations of a theory of bibliography. In J.H. Shera (Ed.), *Libraries and the organization of knowledge* (pp. 18-33). Hamden, CT: Archon Books.

Stokes, R. (1969). *The function of bibliography.* London: André Deutsch.

Wilson, P. (1968). *Two kinds of power: An essay on bibliographical control.* Berkeley, CA: University of California Press.

# Content list of Volumes I, II, and III

# INFORMATION AND THE INFORMATION PROFESSIONS: SELECTED WORKS OF MARCIA J. BATES, VOL. I

ISBN 978-0-9817584-1-1

*All entries are by Bates unless otherwise noted.*

## INFORMATION SEARCHING THEORY AND PRACTICE: SELECTED WORKS OF MARCIA J. BATES, VOL. II

ISBN 978-0-9817584-2-8

*All entries are by Bates unless otherwise noted.*

## INFORMATION USERS AND INFORMATION SYSTEM DESIGN: SELECTED WORKS OF MARCIA J. BATES, VOL. III

ISBN 978-0-9817584-3-5

*All entries are by Bates unless otherwise noted.*

# Index

abstracting and indexing (A & I) services, subject searches in, 264, 271, 285
abstracts, 200
access, 61–69, 70f, 71. *See also* subject access
access field, 323
access vocabulary interfiled with catalog entries, 53–54
action codes, 69, 71
Adams, A. L., 183, 213–14
adjective (vs. noun) form, 107
AID (Associative Interactive Dictionary), 171
Alexander, C., 180–81
almanacs, 326
alphabetico-classed catalogs, 29–30
alphabetico-classed principles, 29
alphabetico-specific approach, problems with, 26
alphabetico-specific catalog, 29, 52, 158
alphabetizing, 363–64. *See also* ordering principles
analytic bibliography, 350
animals
    browsing in, 310, 312–13
    curiosity and exploratory behavior in, 306–8
anomalies, resolution of, 300
appearance(s), 110, 130
area scanning, 263–64, 269–70, 284
areas of study (as search terms), 108
Ashby, W. Ross, 47
anomalous state of knowledge (ASK), 55, 172–73
assisted searches, 221
ASK. *See* anomalous state of knowledge
Associative Interactive Dictionary (AID), 171
author searching, 234, 235, 264, 272, 285
author/title catalog vs subject catalog search, 5
automatic indexing, 368
auxiliaries, 155

backward chaining. *See* footnote chasing
Belkin, N. J., 55, 172–73, 259
Bell, W. J., 307–8
Berlyne, D. E., 306

berrypicking and browsing, 257–58, 267–68, 275–76
    design of databases and interfaces for, 272–76
    distinction between, 309–10
    how and where users search for information, 262–66
berrypicking/evolving search, 260, 260f, 261. *See also* berrypicking and browsing
berrypicking model of information retrieval, 258–62
berrypicking search, context of, 261, 261f
berrypicking search interface, search capabilities for a, 267–72
BIBBLE (file structure tactic), 153
bibliographic control, 149, 350–51
    meanings of the term, 356, 357
    universal, 357
bibliographic form, 107
bibliographic searching, research with implications for, 179–80
bibliographic units, 360–62, 378, 379
bibliographies
    branches of, 349–50
    compilation of, 354, 361–63, 365–67, 374
    domain of (*see* domain)
    purpose and functions of, 349, 354, 363
    scope of (*see* scope)
    structuring of, 351–52
    subject searching in, 271, 285
bibliography
    definitions of, 349, 351–52, 378
    macrocosmic and a microcosmic view of, 356–57
bibliometric approach (bibliographies), 371
binary searching, 155–56
BIOSIS Concept Codes, 86f, 87
BIOSIS "Keywords," 82
Birdsey, Vanessa, 217
Blair, D. C., 175–76, 206
BLOCK (search formulation tactic), 157
Bolt, R. A., 174
book catalogs, 326. *See also* catalogs

385

Getty Online Searching Project (report no. 2),
  *continued*
  how much searching scholars did, 224, 225t,
    226
  methodology
    coding and data analysis, 222–24
    coding scheme for online search
      statements and terms, 251–54
    study population, 219–20
    training, setting, and other arrangements,
      220–22
Google search engine, 286
Gray, D. E., 178–79
guided search, 304–5

Harris, J. L., 28
Haykin, David, 29–30
headings
  consensually preferred by experts over the
    library-assigned headings, 11–12, 12t
  *See also* subject headings
Heisenberg, Werner, 42–43
Herner, S., 295
hierarchical classification, 87, 87f
  vs. faceted classification, 85, 87, 89, 91
  labelled categories for, 87, 88f
hierarchical equivalence, 376–77
high precision search, 210–11, 214–15
high recall search, 210, 211
Hughes, R. N., 306–7
humanities scholars, search terminology used
  by. *See* Getty Online Searching Project
hunting, 62, 71–72
hypertext, 275

idea tactics, 148, 160, 175
  defined, 175
idealizing searching, 146
identification (in browsing process), 300
impatience, user, 73
index terms, 82–84
indexer thesaurus (IT), 63–65
indexes, back-of-the-book, 328, 329
indexing services. *See* abstracting and indexing
  (A & I) services
indirect entry, 29
Individualized Instruction for Data Access
  (IIDA), 172
individuals as subjects (searching), 107, 115, 116,
  118, 132, 133, 136, 137
informal search, 182
information fields, 360, 379
information-gap theory, 307
information individuals, 332, 340
information retrieval (IR), classic model of,
  258–59, 259f, 262f
information retrieval systems (IRSs), 184
  strategies in the design of, 48–49
information science
  history, xiii
  problems of, xii
  research on, 42
information searching. *See* searching
information seeking, nature of, 295

information specialists, 143
information theory, Shannon's, 49
Ingwersen, P., 176
INSPEC, 92, 98f, 99
intentional visual scanning, 296–97
Internet. *See* Web-browsing
intrinsic exploration
  defined, 306
  vs. extrinsic search, 306–7

Jahoda, Gerald, 169–70, 180
Johnston, S. M., 178–79
Jones, W. P., 273
journal articles, scientific, 199–200
journal run, 263, 269, 284
  defined, 263, 284

Kaae, S., 176
Kahneman, D., 175–76
Kantor, Paul, 115–18, 132, 133
Katz, W. A., 318–19
Kennington, D., 182
Knapp, P. B., 26
Kraft, Donald, 173–74
Kwasnik, Barbara, 283, 299–301, 310

Lawrence, G. S., 73
Leimkuhler, F. F., 173–74
Lemann, Nicholas, xii
librarian stereotype, xiii
Library of Congress (LC) subject headings, 12,
  13, 50, 53, 58–60, 65–67. *See also specific topics*
library science and information science, xii–xiii
Licklider, J. C. R., 174
linguistic units, 223
linking, 286–87
Loewenstein, G., 307

main entry, defined, 179
make glimpses (phase of browsing process), 303
manual file, defined, 321–23
Markey, K., 65, 210
massively parallel glimpse, 313
massively parallel processing, 310. *See also*
  parallel processes
Matthews, J. R., 73
McCormick, J. M., 179
Meadow, Charles, 172
Miller, George A., 174, 273
Mischo, W., 68
monitoring tactics, 150, 151t, 152
  defined, 148
Morse, P. M., 173–74
moving (to another screen), in browsing, 311

narrowing a search, 213
  refinement techniques for, 213–14
National Science Foundation (NSF) study, 115–17
  frequencies of subject categories in, 116, 117t
  Getty Online Searching Project contrasted
    with, 116, 117t, 118–19